Palgrave Debates in Business History

Series Editors
Bradley Bowden, Melbourne, VIC, Australia
Michael Heller, Brunel Business School, Brunel University, London, UK

Scholarship in business history often produced divergent opinions that seldom engage with each other. Business historians have continued their scholarly endeavors with little obvious concern to the popular discontents around them. This book series will foster debate among business historians, bring together a variety of opinions from around the globe to confront the key issues of our time with the intent of becoming a fulcrum of debate. The series will use a broad understanding of "business history" so that it brings together work that is currently operating in tandem with each other without ever engaging with each other: work from business and management history, social history, economic history, cultural history, labor history, sociology, and political history whose focus is societal rather than personal or narrowly institutional. The series will focus on the following current debates in the field: the nature of globalization; the nature of capitalism; the nature and effects of western civilization (particularly as relates to industrialization); the mediatisation of business; gender, class and identity; and business and shifts in wealth, power and inequality. Within these topics there is passionate dissension, creating an opportunity engage multiple perspectives.

Editors
Bradley Bowden, Griffith University, Australia
Michael Heller, Brunel University, UK

Associate Editors
Jeffrey Muldoon, Emporia University, USA
Gabrielle Durepos, Mount Saint Vincent University, Canada

Editorial Board
Bernardo Batiz-Lazo, University of Northumbria, UK
Arthur G Bedeian, Louisiana State University, USA
Amanda Budde-Sung, US Air Force Academy, USA
Andrew Cardow, Massey University, New Zealand
Matteo Cristofaro, University of Rome, Italy
Sébastien Damart, Paris Dauphine University, France
Carlos Davila, University of the Andes, Colombia
Nick Dyrenfurth, Curtin Research University, Australia
Anthony M. Gould, University of Laval, Canada
Scott Hargreaves, Institute for Public Affairs, Australia
Albert Mills, Saint Mary's University, Canada
Jean Helms Mills, Saint Mary's University, Canada
Elly Leung, University of Western Australia, Australia
Jan Logemann, University of Göttingen, Germany
Mairi Maclean, University of Bath, UK
Vadim Marshev, Moscow State University, Russia
Patricia McLaren, Wilfrid Laurier University, Canada
Peter Miskell, Henley Business School, University of Reading, UK
Milorad Novicevic, University of Mississippi, USA
Andrew Popp, Copenhagen Business School, Denmark
Nimruji Prasad, Indian Institute of Management Calcutta, India
Michael Rowlinson, University of Exeter, UK
Stefan Schwarzkopf, Copenhagen Business School, Denmark
Philip Scranton, Rutgers University, USA
Grietjie Verhoef, University of Johannesburg, South Africa
James Wilson, University of Glasgow, UK

More information about this series at
https://link.springer.com/bookseries/16405

Bradley Bowden

Slavery, Freedom and Business Endeavor

The Reforging of Western Civilization and the Transformation of Everyday Life

Bradley Bowden
Griffith University and Institute
for Public Affairs
Hamilton, VIC, Australia

ISSN 2662-4362   ISSN 2662-4370   (electronic)
Palgrave Debates in Business History
ISBN 978-3-030-97231-8   ISBN 978-3-030-97232-5   (eBook)
https://doi.org/10.1007/978-3-030-97232-5

© The Editor(s) (if applicable) and The Author(s), under exclusive license to Springer Nature Switzerland AG 2022
This work is subject to copyright. All rights are solely and exclusively licensed by the Publisher, whether the whole or part of the material is concerned, specifically the rights of translation, reprinting, reuse of illustrations, recitation, broadcasting, reproduction on microfilms or in any other physical way, and transmission or information storage and retrieval, electronic adaptation, computer software, or by similar or dissimilar methodology now known or hereafter developed.
The use of general descriptive names, registered names, trademarks, service marks, etc. in this publication does not imply, even in the absence of a specific statement, that such names are exempt from the relevant protective laws and regulations and therefore free for general use.
The publisher, the authors and the editors are safe to assume that the advice and information in this book are believed to be true and accurate at the date of publication. Neither the publisher nor the authors or the editors give a warranty, expressed or implied, with respect to the material contained herein or for any errors or omissions that may have been made. The publisher remains neutral with regard to jurisdictional claims in published maps and institutional affiliations.

This Palgrave Macmillan imprint is published by the registered company Springer Nature Switzerland AG
The registered company address is: Gewerbestrasse 11, 6330 Cham, Switzerland

To Fr Peter Hayes, Order of St. Augustine, friend and mentor.

Foreword

Bradley Bowden's work, *Slavery, Freedom and Business Endeavor: The Reforging of Western Civilization and the Transformation of Everyday life*, is a work of erudition, reflecting a lifetime of rigorous learning. Bowden is as masterful in writing about ancient Greece and Rome as he is about modern history; his ability to apply modern management and economics theory to explain how modern business emerged is an exemplar for scholars. As befitting a two-time winner of the Academy of Management's John F. Mee award for Outstanding Contribution to Management History, Bowden has produced a brilliant thought-provoking work.

For Bowden's epistemological supporters, this book will inspire, edify and educate. For his opponents, it will provoke, prod, and even potentially infuriate. Whether friend or foe, the reader will find this an important book, especially during these trying times, where we find ourselves questioning previously settled matters. How this orthodoxy came into being is of importance to any serious student of business. For those questioning current orthodoxies—which increasingly portray both western civilization and capitalism in a negative light—there will be an appreciation of Bowden's ability to muster primary and secondary source material in support of his arguments. Whatever one's perspective, this is a substantial work.

Before I continue, I must confess to the reader that Bowden serves with me as co-Editor-in-Chief of the *Journal of Management History*; we co-edited (with Anthony Gould and Adela McMurray) *The Palgrave*

viii FOREWORD

Handbook of Management History, we are also members of the Tacitus Forum. More than that, Bowden has been a friend, mentor, and a significant intellectual influence on my development as a scholar. I (like others) have found him uncommonly generous with his time and energy. His willingness (whether you agree with him or not) to take unpopular views that go against the norm should be an example for any scholar. As such, he has been a constant champion of the intellectual legacy of western civilization: freedom, reason and open inquiry. Once these were considered unchallenged ideals. Now, they are increasingly under fire.

Part of the reason for this attack is that these concepts have been too successful. As an example, the theme of this book should be "The Great Escape" as it is a triumphal account of how we escaped the Malthusian trap that had condemned our ancestors to lives of scarcity and want. Basically, prior to the development of the modern world, people's lives were "nasty, brutish, and short". The overwhelming majority of humans who lived prior to the nineteenth century could not even read this sentence. This is to say nothing of the technology used to compose this foreword. In fact, they would have denounced us as wizards for this technology. Both the wealthy and poor suffered, perhaps not equally, but nevertheless they all lived in squalor. Even the wealthiest potentates of the past could succumb to something as harmless (in the modern world) as a common cold. As late as the Battle of Waterloo, Napoleon and Wellington received information about their armies as quickly as Alexander or Caesar did—which was basically as fast as a horse could travel.

Around 1840, matters began to improve at a rapid pace. When Samuel Morse created the telegraph, the first message he dispatched was "What hath God wrought". No one, not even a genius like Morse, could have predicted the consequences that instantaneous communications around the world would have for the average person. Suddenly, one could inquire as to a relative in another continent and expect a reply within days, if not hours. This change is what this book is about. As such, Bowden focuses on the average person. It is, in his words, a "book that places everyday life rather than grand culture at center stage". Such a focus is rather different to his previous work, *Work, Wealth and Postmodernism*, which dealt with matters pertaining to grand theory (as exemplified by postmodernism). In shifting his focus, Bowden makes a contribution similar to the French Annales School (such as Marc Bloch, Lucien Febvre and Fernand Braudel) in that he shows how changes in theory and thought have led to improvements for the average person. Of particular note is his

FOREWORD ix

focus on the number of calories consumed by the average person prior to the Industrial Revolution. It was typically barely enough to sustain life. In itself, Bowden's evidence as to how—due to the private sector's invention and ingenuity—most of humanity came to avoid living in a condition of perpetual starvation should allay many concerns about the ethics of modern business. It is private-sector profit-seeking that has rescued us from an economic abyss, not government regulation.

Likewise, Bowden notes that, in earlier times, "What we think of as civilization—cities, literacy, the leisured comfort of Pharaohs and Caesars—was confined to a tiny minority". Of course, the Caesars had plenty of food, comfort and shelter. But even they were paupers by our standards. The houses he lived in lacked many basic amenities. In terms of music, the Caesars would have paid musicians. Now, all a person needs to do is go to Spotify. A middle-class person living in the United States, or any other advanced economy, also has access to more information than not only the Caesars, but also that enjoyed by any head of state in the 1960s. Even comforts such as cable television now seem minor in comparison to streaming, which allows viewers the ability to "binge watch" their favorite television programs.

Throughout his book, Bowden correctly points out that the transformation of modern life has been overwhelmingly liberating and democratic, rather than exploitive or destructive as modern critics of western civilization would have us believe. All of this, Bowden notes, was made possible by "mechanization [which] spread from mining and textile manufacturing to transport, communications, agriculture and even household activities". The last point is particularly important. Modern critics of capitalism constantly assert that it is exploitive of women. There is a tremendous amount of literature on this. Such commentators, however, fail to notice that it is the capitalist-induced transformation of household activities (washing, ironing, vacuuming, cooking and so on) that has freed women to pursue careers. For, as Bowden points out, citing the Frankfurt School Marxist Herbert Marcuse, one of the defining characteristics of modern capitalism is that it has allowed an "affluent society" for the first time in history.

The heroes of Bowden's book are "the entrepreneur, the engineer, and the factory worker", the people who made The Great Escape possible. Western civilization—as exemplified by Great Britain, the Netherlands, and the United States—has also placed the individual at the forefront of society in ways that allow an unprecedented level of personal autonomy.

This, in turn, has enabled risk takers to try out their new ideas without fear of prosecution. To use the example of Morse again, in a different country or century he would have burned at the stake as a heretic. Previously, scientists, such as Galileo, iconoclasts such as Luther and freethinkers such as Marlowe, all faced persecution. However, the emergence of a political ideology and popular culture that places the individual at center stage has created conditions where risk taking could occur in not only business but also in science and culture.

The irony is that the success of western civilization has, in some ways, sowed the seeds of its own destruction. For, as Bowden argues, the modern bureaucratic state "is as much a part of the current iteration of western civilization as capitalism". Even prior to the COVID-19 pandemic and its associated "stimulus packages", government spending in OECD nations was typically in the range of 40 to 50%. In the United States, a nation where the state's footprint is less than elsewhere, almost 20% of the workforce was directly employed by the state.

Constantly, Bowden argues, the liberating values of individualism and liberalism have found themselves threatened by collectivism and state control. For, as Bowden writes, "individualism, the core value and driving force of the new civilization, is the opposite of collectivism". Whatever the merits of collectivism, it denies the existence of the individual or as Bowden writes: "individual identity, as an expression of individualism, is something that can never be bestowed by a collective, be it one based on religion, race or sexual preference". Despite protests that collectivism is avant-garde or more modern, it is in truth simply a regurgitation of premodern or pre-industrial-age thinking. For example, in ancient Rome either you were a citizen or not; a patrician or a plebian; from Italy or not. Your life was determined by your social status. Even a man as accomplished as Marcus Agrippa (both as a military leader and builder) with his less-than-distinguished background needed a sponsor such as the patrician Octavian Caesar. Now, with modern meritocracy, an individual can climb.

As Bowden notes in the final section of the book's introduction, under the heading "The Winter of Western Civilization?", the ongoing tension between collectivism and individualism finds expression in what he refers to as the "milletization" of life—by which he means that "identity groups" are assuming a power over beliefs and attitudes similar to that exercised by the "millets" of Ottoman Turkey. For, under the "millet" system—which supposedly protected group diversity—no one could express an opinion that was contrary to that of the "millet" to which they belonged (for example, Armenian Christian, Greek Orthodox and so on).

This, Bowden argues, had two adverse consequences: first, individual conformism was the price of group diversity; second, it produced an ultimately deadly intergroup rivalry as every individual identified their success in life with the supremacy of their "millet". Bowden detects similar dangers in the rise and rise of "identity politics". For, Bowden concludes, "Once jobs and other means of advancement are allocated on the basis of group membership rather than merit, an unseemly rivalry between 'minorities' becomes inevitable".

Of course, the virtues of our modern western civilization (including individualism, liberalism and democracy) have often been contradicted by outcomes that betray these ideals. An example of this is slavery, most particularly American chattel slavery. This system represented the worst tendencies of the premodern world. You were born a slave, and as such, you had no rights. You were a slave based on your race. Even if your father (and this happened more frequently than we care to admit) was the plantation owner, you were still a slave. The father of the great nineteenth-century abolitionist Frederick Douglass probably owned his mother. This created a system whereby your parent or sibling could literally determine every facet of your life. Recognition of such barbarity should not, however, ignore the fact that slavery was destroyed by the liberal ideals that emerged from the European Enlightenment of the seventeenth and eighteenth centuries. The great irony, of course was that some of the proponents of these Enlightenment ideals were themselves slaveholders—as exemplified in the writings and experiences of Thomas Jefferson, James Madison and other founding fathers of the United States. This nuance is often ignored by modern critics. Such obliviousness would have confounded slavery's unambiguously greatest opponent, Abraham Lincoln, who used Jefferson's Declaration of Independence to first oppose the extension of slavery and then bring about its eventual destruction.

Whatever the case, slavery was not unique to America or the West in general. There were slaves in antiquity, in non-western lands such as Africa, China and elsewhere, and, unfortunately, there are still slaves today. What was unique in Great Britain, the United States and other western societies in the nineteenth century was a generation of politicians, activists, clerics, academics and business leaders who challenged the

xii   FOREWORD

orthodoxy that one person had the right to own another. Their justification in opposing such an ancient practice was that it denied the existence of the individual—an idea that was relatively new.

Bowden devotes roughly a quarter of his book to the vexed issue of slavery. In doing so, Bowden draws on a wealth of primary material: the Trans-Atlantic Slave Trade Database, which records both the number of slaves transported and their place of disembarkation; British customs receipts; and American cotton exports. In considering this impressive array of data, Bowden clearly demonstrates that America's slave-produced cotton was never a decisive factor in either the Industrial Revolution, nor was it a factor in the development of modern capitalism. In response to Sven Beckert's claims that American cotton was seminal to the Industrial Revolution, Bowden writes: "there were no US cotton exports prior to 1802, by which time the "Industrial Revolution" was half over. In four years—1808, 1809, 1811, 1812—US cotton exports were close to zero. In 1813 and 1814, during the War of 1812 (1812–1815), there were no US cotton exports at all". Likewise, in terms of the argument put forward by Leon Prieto and Simone Phipps (both of whom have served as editors at the *Journal of Management History*) that "slavery played a central role in the economic development of Europe", Bowden observes that if "this argument is true we … would also expect that the societies most involved in the slave trade, namely Portugal and Spain, would have enjoyed markedly higher living standards than those societies that played little or no role in the slave trade, such as Italy, Austria or Poland". For, as Bowden notes, not only were Portugal and Spain responsible for two-thirds of slave shipments, it is also the case that two-thirds of those transported ended up in Portuguese or Spanish colonies. However, Bowden notes, as *societies*, Portugal and Spain obtained little benefit from slavery—even if individual Portuguese and Spaniards grew rich. Instead, Bowden concludes, "Portugal and Spain remained poor, economically backward societies".

Likewise, Bowden is highly skeptical of arguments made by Bill Cooke and others that slavery was "intrinsic" to the development of capitalism and modern management, that the practices perfected in the slave plantation left "an ongoing imprint in management practice and thought". To ignore this reality, Cooke suggests, is to engage in a "logic of denial". In contradicting claims that slavery was a central component in the rise of modern capitalism, Bowden notes that this line of thinking was one explicitly rejected by Karl Marx in Volume 3 of *Das Kapital*. In capitalism, Marx noted, the key to success is investment in machinery and other capital goods. It is this "capital" that allows for the extraction of "surplus labor". By contrast, a slave owner invests their "capital" in labor. As such, Marx noted, "It is a deduction from the capital which he had available for actual production. It has ceased to exist for him". In other words, by investing "capital" in slaves a slave owner surrenders any possibility of "capitalist" production methods. In highlighting the central role of Quakers in the abolition movement, Bowden also exposes the fallacy of Cooke's argument that a Quaker and Congregationalist scion like Frederick Winslow Taylor would find inspiration in slavery.

In discussing slavery, its abolition and legacies, Bowden is also skeptical of the argument provided by Nikole Hannah-Jones in the *1619 Project* that abolition in the United States occurred only when African Americans "began taking up arms for his [Lincoln's] cause as well as their own". This argument has an element of truth. African American soldiers were a key reason why the North won the Civil War, because they provided the North with a large number of troops. Unfortunately, this truth is pushed beyond its breaking point. In the first instance, as James Oakes has written about, the introduction of former slaves into the Union's army required the support of important leaders such as the then-president Abraham Lincoln. Second, the primary reason that North prevailed in the Civil War reflects the fact that its embrace of capitalism provided it with an enormous advantage in productivity over the slave economy of the South. In a short period of time, the North's productive capacity allowed it to build up the world's largest army and arguably its largest navy. And, on top of that, it also built a new iron dome for the Capitol building in Washington, DC. This production was only possible due to the entrepreneurship that characterized the North's culture—a culture that prioritized individualism and, hence, innovation.

Some readers—even people presupposed to support his arguments—will find Bowden's book to be an unusual selection for a business history series. After all, tracing western civilization's impact on business practices is not a usual topic in today's academia. However, this approach stands as a corrective. Too often business professors make pronouncements about ethics without considering the incremental material and moral improvements of the past. Likewise, there is a tendency on the part of intellectuals in the West to claim that the collapse of freedom is both inevitable and probably beneficial, in that a large degree of state-enforced coercion is (supposedly) needed to "solve" problems relating to inequality, climate change and the like. What such lines of argument overlook, however, are the blessings of freedom—which, ironically, include an ability to *critique* the blessings of freedom.

In conclusion, Bowden's book stands in comparison to a previous one published in this series, Elly Leung's *The (Re-making) of the Chinese Working Class*. Like Bowden, her book is one of bravery in that she questions a modern orthodoxy, namely the belief that collectivist societies and values are superior to those that prioritize individualism. Look, for example, at the writings of authors such as Thomas Friedman, who praises China's system as technocratic, rational and inherently superior to America's divided democracy. If both Bowden and Leung place the clash of individualism and collectivism at the center of their work, Leung's study primarily concerns itself with the ill effects of collectivism. As such, her book reads like a Dickensian or Orwellian nightmare. Much like Winston Smith—the "hero" in George Orwell's *1984*—the Chinese workers that Leung interviews know that there is something wrong with their system. They lack, however, the means and vision to reject it. In consequence, the one ray of light in Leung's book is the endurance of the ordinary Chinese person in the face of awful and appalling conditions. In part, this grim perspective is a product of Leung's Foucauldian perspective. Basically, people are educated, trained and beaten into submission. My own perspective on postmodernism, like Bowden's, has been well documented. Whatever the case, Foucault, like Leung, places freedom as his apotheosis. That much of humanity remains in chains, drives such writers to despair. Bowden stands as a corrective to this approach in that a societal emphasis on the individual can lead—and has led—to great improvement in the human condition. The question remains, will this focus on the individual continue, or will we return to a new age of collectivism. Hopefully, our descendants will not ask the question that Ayn Rand's hero, Prometheus, asked in *Anthem*: why did we abandon the individual?

January 2022

Jeffrey Muldoon
Emporia University
Emporia, USA

Preface: The West and the Nature of Its Civilization

Reflecting on the nature of civilization, the French historian Fernand Braudel concluded that "at bottom, a civilization is attached to a distinct geographical area", a region that determines its "opportunities and constraints" as well as its "more or less fixed limits". Braudel also concluded that each civilization was fundamentally conservative at heart, a mechanism through which the habits and values of "the distant and far distant past" cling "to life" in the present.[1] In his estimation, the current iteration of western civilization is something that emerged from a fusion of Germanic and Roman cultures during the Carolingian period (c. 800 AD), a period that saw "the cradle" of the West shift from the Mediterranean to the North Sea.[2] Whatever changes had occurred since then—the Renaissance, the Reformation, the Industrial Revolution—mattered little. Instead, the bedrock of the civilization—rooted in language, religious values, law, social norms—remained largely intact, resistant to fundamental change.

In his *Decline of the West*, Oswald Spengler articulated a very different understanding of both the West and the nature of civilization. According

---

[1] Fernand Braudel, *The Mediterranean and the Mediterranean World in the Age of Philip II*, vol. 2 (New York, NY: Torchbooks, 1975), 770, 775; Fernand Braudel (trans. Richard Mayne), *A History of Civilizations*, (London, UK: Penguin, 1995), 11.

[2] Fernand Braudel (trans. Siân Reynolds), *The Identity of France: People and Production*, (London, UK: Fontana Press, 1991), 134–139.

xvi PREFACE: THE WEST AND THE NATURE OF ITS CIVILIZATION

to Spengler, each civilization represented the final flowering of the culture that produced it: a ripening that was destined to "decay, and never return".[3] As a civilization, the modern West is, Spengler believed, a successor to the earlier medieval or early modern civilization, but distinct from it. A product of the nineteenth and twentieth centuries, Spengler argued that what distinguished the modern iteration of western civilization from every one that came before it was a "Faustian" pact with mechanization—an arrangement that saw "the entrepreneur, the engineer, and the factory-worker" emerge as the civilization's flagbearers.[4] It was, moreover, this Faustian pact with mechanization and the attractiveness of the material bounty that it provided that gave the West its global ascendancy, creating a unique "world economy" constructed around vast megacities with "cosmopolitan" cultures and peoples.[5]

How then can we understand the nature of western civilization and its modern western iteration? Is it simply an extension of a long-established civilization, forged more than 1,200 years ago? Or is it, alternatively, something profoundly different? Is the West's pact with mechanization made in hell or heaven? Is the modern West confined within "fixed limits", or has it become a truly global civilization, embodying societal practices and values that have universal appeal?

In exploring these questions this book places everyday life rather than grand culture at center stage.

Historically, societies in every part of the globe were caught within a "Malthusian trap" in which economic expansion drove population expansion to unsustainable limits, causing an eventual crash in both living standards and population. As we explore in Part 1 of this book, this Malthusian trap was as much a characteristic feature of the societies of the New World as the Old. For societies caught within a Malthusian trap—which was every premodern civilization—the consequences for the ordinary person were catastrophic. Most were physically and intellectually stunted, perpetually undernourished and condemned to premature death. What we think of as civilization—cities, literacy, the leisured comfort of

[3] Oswald Spengler (trans. Charles Francis Atkinson), *The Decline of the West*, revised edition (New York: Alfred A. Knopf, 1927), 11.

[4] *Ibid*, 504.

[5] *Ibid*, 504.

Pharaohs and Caesars—was confined to a tiny minority. The modern iteration of western civilization, which this book argues emerged around the middle of the nineteenth century, was profoundly different. As mechanization spread from mining and textile manufacturing to transport, communications, agriculture and even household activities (for example, washing, ironing, vacuuming, and so on) a total new mode of life was created.

Like Spengler, this book argues that the modern iteration of western civilization is a successor to the earlier medieval or early modern civilization, but distinct from it. Like Spengler, this study also argues that the new expression of western civilization that emerged around 1850 was, from the outset, a "world economy"—one constructed around global interdependence and the appeal of new technologies and lifestyles. Unlike Spengler, however, this book concludes that "the entrepreneur, the engineer, and the factory-worker" were the product of a pact made in heaven rather than hell. It is to them we owe our escape from the Malthusian trap that previously doomed societies to an endless cycle of expansion and collapse, expansion and collapse.

From the outset, the new iteration of western civilization was the product of far more than machines and technology. It also owed its existence to a set of values that underpinned its economic expansion, and which were also seminal to the transformation of everyday life: individualism, democracy, economic and political liberalism. Even within Europe, these values were both novel and contested in the mid-nineteenth century. They remain contested. Individualism, the core value and driving force of the new civilization, is the opposite of collectivism. One takes one's identity from one's own opinions, behaviors, experiences and beliefs. Individual identity, as an expression of individualism, is something that can never be bestowed by a collective, be it one based on religion, race or sexual preference. Individualism and its key societal expressions— economic and political liberalism—also entail choice and, therefore, risk. Individualism is thus a friend of markets and the associated ability to freely choose one's job and to spend one's money as one likes. Conversely, it is the enemy of the state and state-directed controls. Yet, as this study explores, the modern state with its bureaucracies, taxes, benefits and restrictions is as much a feature of our modern western civilization as are markets. At times the state has proved individualism's protector, setting out a series of constitutional and legal norms that protect both democracy and the rights of the individual. At other times it has sought to strangle individualism, either by stealth or through a sudden and abrupt imposition of authoritarianism.

An historical novice, the fate of our modern iteration of western civilization has often hung by a thread. In the 1930s, much of Europe lived under totalitarian regimes of one sort of another. Today, its survival once more hangs in the balance. Everywhere, as we discuss in our final chapter, we are witnessing what this study refers to as the "milletization" of society, whereby various identity groups become homogenous enclaves in ways that resemble the *millet* system of Ottoman Turkey—a system that bestowed upon each religious and ethnic group its own distinct legal identity. The inevitable result of this system in the Ottoman Empire was not pluralism, but fragmentation; not harmony, but inter-ethnic strife and the Armenian Genocide. Whether our civilization survives is, in the final analysis, up to the choices we make. Do we value individualism, choice and thus risk? Or do we prefer the security of the collective, be it the state or a de facto millet?

Hamilton, VIC, Australia   Bradley Bowden
January 2022

Acknowledgments

The ideas and inspiration for this book were multiple, some of which related to the value of freedom and some to the dangers of tyranny. On the latter score, I would acknowledge the influence of Dan Andrews, who, at the time of writing was the Premier of the Australian State of Victoria, and who locked down the great city of Melbourne for longer than any major city in the world. In his Orwellian speech and behavior, he highlighted the precarious nature of freedom.

More positively, I would like to acknowledge the intellectual influence of my co-editor at the *Journal of Management History*, Jeffrey Muldoon, who not only read the manuscript but also constantly supplied me with a host of recommended readings.

I would also like to acknowledge the intellectual influence and support of my colleague at the Institute for Public Affairs in Melbourne, Scott Hargreaves.

At Palgrave Macmillan in New York, I owe a special debt to Marcus Ballenger, who has been a source of support for both this work and my earlier study, *Work, Wealth and Postmodernism: The Intellectual Conflict at the Heart of Business Endeavor*.

Finally, I would like to thank my wife, Peta, who has had to live through yet another major writing project with her normal fortitude and good humor. I owe her an immeasurable debt.

PRAISE FOR *SLAVERY, FREEDOM AND BUSINESS ENDEAVOR*

"For those wishing to understand how modern civilization, especially how capitalism became a dominant theme in the west, this book is invaluable. Professor Bowden explores, explains and provides credible alternatives to existing thought paradigms around the concepts of how 'we' arrived at the present. His narrative is at once thought provoking and entertaining."

—Andrew Cardow, *Past Division Chair of the Management History Division, (2021–2022) Academy of Management*

"Bowden's book provides a provocative prism through which to view western civilization and capitalism. It reveals Bowden's understanding of the freedom and courage required to defend and sustain the values upon which the survival of modern society depends: individualism, democracy, economic and political liberalism. With the growing ascendency of social movements that prioritize group-based identities over individual achievement, his powerful warning about the "milletization" of society is more urgent than ever."

—Art Bedeian. Louisiana State University and founding member of Management History Division, Academy of Management

xxii PRAISE FOR *SLAVERY, FREEDOM AND BUSINESS ENDEAVOR*

"Bowden's work on Western Civilization reveals the genesis of modern business culture. This work is built on a lifetime of erudition and is packed with insights. Bowden's work is something both critics and supporters of capitalism and modern business need to consider."

—Jeffrey Muldoon, *Emporia State University and Executive Member, Management History Division, Academy of Management*

"*Australians are ineradicably heirs to and beneficiaries of the ideas, institutions and values of western civilization, and in age of wilful misrepresentation and relentless denigration of that legacy Bradley Bowden performs a magnificent service for humanity, highlighting the force of the West's animating genius and the unprecedented prosperity it brought to the modern world from the late 18th century onwards.*"

—Scott Hargreaves, *Executive General Manager, Institute for Public Affairs, Australia*

"An electrifying work. The reader is dragged – sometimes kicking and screaming - to a confronting realisation: whatever the problems faced by the 21st century's ordinary people, the roots of such problems are not to be found in the forces that spawned and shaped Western civilisation. To suggest otherwise is the intellectual equivalent of sawing of the branch upon which one is highly perched because a tree limb provides an uncomfortable place of repose. If we are to have mandated mask-wearing for the unvaccinated, then this book should be mandated reading for the unaware."

—Anthony Gould, *Laval University (Quebec) and Editor-in-Chief, Relations Industrielle/Industrial Relations*

CONTENTS

1	**Introduction: Civilization and Lived Experience**	1
	What Is Modern Western Civilization?	6
	1850 and the Dawn of a New Civilization	12
	Not Only Economics, but Also Freedom	21
	Not Only Freedom, but Also State Power	25
	Escaping Humanity's Eternal Curse—The "Malthusian	
	Trap"	29
	The Winter of Western Civilization?	36

Part I	**The Quests that Created a New Western Civilization (and Destroyed Others): Crops, Climate, Calories**	
2	**The 3-Cs: Crops, Climate, Calories**	47
3	**Crops and the Shaping of Civilizations**	55
	Wheat	57
	Rice	63
	Corn	67
4	**Climate: The Destroyer of Civilizations, and How Early Modern Europe Rose from Catastrophe**	73
	The North Atlantic and El Niño–Southern Oscillations	79
	The Maya: A Civilization in a Terminal Malthusian Trap	82

xxiii

xxiv CONTENTS

Europe: Climate and Transformative Malthusian Traps,
AD 350–1500   87
The Rise of Early Modern Europe: Another Trap?   94

5   **The Eternal Challenge: Calorific Expenditure**
and the Emergence of an Industrialized Civilization   99
Slavery, Agriculture, Industry and Capital Intensity   109
Transport and the Suffocation of Markets   119
Energy, Iron and Escaping the Malthusian Trap   125
More Than "Modernization"   135

Part II   **Freedom, Slavery and the Rise of an Industrialized**
Western Civilization

6   **Time, Scale and Understandings of Western**
Civilization   139

7   **What Is Freedom? What Is Slavery?**   149
What Is Freedom?   149
What Is Slavery?   155

8   **Freedom, Democracy and Individualism: Cause**
of Business Success or Mere Correlation?   167
Greek and Roman Antiquity: Bounded Individualism,
Bounded Freedom   171
The Premodern West: Individualism as Agent of State
Absolutism—Scholarly and Aristocratic Individualism   176
The Premodern West: Individualism as Agent
of Innovation—Bourgeois Individualism   183
The Premodern West: Individualism as Agent
of Innovation—Peasant Individualism   189
Revolution, Freedom and the State   194

9   **Slavery and Its Legacies**   203
The Nature of Slavery   210
The Economics of Slavery   220
Slavery in the Americas: The Source of Western Wealth?   225
Abolition   230
Legacies   239

Part III Global Transformation: The Embrace and Rejection of an Industrialized Western Civilization

10 Global Transformation — 251
Political and Social Choices in a Multifaceted Civilization — 257

11 A Globalized Civilization: Ascendancy, Contradictions and Interdependence — 265
The Transformation of Everyday Life: The Rise and Decline of the Industrial Working Class — 274
The Transformation of Everyday Life: The Rise and Rise of the Salaried Professional Class — 283
Different Models — 293
Global Interdependence — 305
Sameness — 314

12 Choices and the *Milletization* of Western Society — 317
Industrialization and Societal Choices: The Experiences of Egypt, Iran and India — 325
The Milletization of the Modern World — 333
Economic and Social Choices — 343

Index — 351

ABOUT THE AUTHOR

Bradley Bowden is a Past Chair of the Management History Division of the Academy of Management and an Adjunct Fellow at the Institute of Public Affairs in Melbourne, Australia. He is also co-editor with Jeffrey Muldoon of the *Journal of Management History* and co-editor with Michael Heller (editor), Jeffrey Muldoon (associate editor) and Gabrielle Durepos (associate editor) of the Palgrave Macmillan *Debates in Business History Series*. His previous works with Palgrave Macmillan are the sole-authored *Work, Wealth and Postmodernism: The Intellectual Conflict at the Heart of Business Endeavor* and the two-volume edited collection (with co-editors Jeffrey Muldoon, Anthony Gould and Adela McMurray), *The Palgrave Handbook of Management History*.

ABBREVIATIONS

AUD	Australian Dollar
BTU	British Thermal Unit
Capesize Ship	Ship Forced to go Around Cape of Good Hope as too Large for Suez Canal
GDP	Gross Domestic Product
GNP	Gross National Product
HDI	Human Development Index
hp	Horsepower
hp·h	Horsepower Hour
IPCC	Intergovernmental Panel on Climate Change
Kg	Kilogram
Km	Kilometer
lb.	Pound
LGBTQIA+	Lesbian, Gay, Bisexual, Transgender, Queer, Intersex, Asexual, plus
OECD	Organisation for Economic Co-operation and Development
UK	United Kingdom
US	United States

LIST OF FIGURES

Fig. 1.1   Real wage of skilled building worker in southern England, 1264–1930 (1447 = 100) (*Source* Brown and Hopkins: "Seven centuries of ... builders' wage rates", Appendix B)   13

Fig. 1.2   Britain's installed horsepower, 1760–1830 (*Note* stationary machinery only. *Source* Allen, *British Industrial Revolution in Global Perspective*, Table 7.1)   14

Fig. 1.3   Shipping tonnage at United States' ports, 1790–1914 (thousands of tons) (*Source* US Department of Commerce, *Historical Statistics*, Series 506–507)   15

Fig. 1.4   Output per capita (1990 dollars), 1500–1850 (*Note* No figures for Spain and Italy for 1550.*Source* Palma and Reis, "From Convergence to Divergence", 6)   20

Fig. 1.5   Population history of Mayan Three Rivers Region, 400 BC–AD 1250 (*Source* Gill et al., "Drought and the Maya Collapse", Figure 5)   30

Fig. 1.6   Real consumption wage index for unskilled building laborers, 1500–1849 (London, 1500–1549 = 100) (*Source* Broadberry and Gupta, "The early modern great divergence", 7)   35

Fig. 1.7   Human Development Index, selected countries, 1870–2018 (*Sources* Crafts, "Human Development Index 1870–1999", 396—for years 1870–1975; United Nations Development Programme, *Human Development Report, 2019*, Table 2—for years 2000–2018)   38

xxxii   LIST OF FIGURES

Fig. 2.1	Life expectancy in pre-industrial and modern populations (*Sources* Clark, *Farewell to Alms*, Tables 5.2, 5.3; Storey, "Mortality in a Pre-Columbian Urban Population", Tables 6, 9; UN Development Programme, *Human Development Report 2020*, Table 1)	52
Fig. 3.1	Adult male height: pre-industrial societies (in centimeters) (*Sources* Clark, *Farewell to Alms*, Tables 3.8, 3.9; US Department of Health and Human Services, *Anthropometric Reference Data*, Table 11)	61
Fig. 3.2	Purchasing power of unskilled laborers, kilograms of wheat or rice equivalent (*Sources* Clark, *Farewell to Alms*, Tables 3.4, Table 3.5; UN Development Programme, *Goal No. 1*)	67
Fig. 4.1	El Niño–Southern Oscillation weather patterns (*Source* National Aeronautics and Space Administration)	80
Fig. 4.2	European population, AD 1–1600 (*Sources* Russell, "Late ancient and medieval population", Table 152; Cipolla, *Before the Industrial* Revolution, 4, Table 1.1)	89
Fig. 4.3	Real wages of skilled building workers in southern England, 1264–1597 (1447 = 100) (*Source* Brown and Hopkins, "Seven centuries of … builders' wage rates", Appendix B)	93
Fig. 5.1	Price of energy in grams of silver, 1500–1700 (*Source* Allen, *British Industrial Revolution*, Table 4.2)	106
Fig. 5.2	Agricultural productivity, percentage increases, 1841 to 1900–1901 (*Note* French figures are for period from 1841 to 1909. *Source* Trebilcock, *Industrialization of the Continental Powers*, 434, Table 7.5a)	110
Fig. 5.3	Percentage of labor-active population engaged in agriculture, 1841 and 1901 (*Note* No Indian figure for 1841. *Sources* Trebilcock, *Industrialization of the Continental Powers*, Table 7.5b; Parliament of UK, *Statistical Abstract Relating to British India*, 1894–1895 to 1903–1904, Table 18, Clark, *Conditions of Economic Progress*, 404)	117
Fig. 5.4	Average annual British output (thousands of tons), by decade (*Source* Riden, "British iron industry before 1870", 448, 455)	128

Fig. 5.5	British and United States coal production (thousands of tons), 1560–1914 (*Sources* Riden, "British iron industry before 1870", Tables 1–2; Pollard, British coal production, 1750–1850"; UK Department of Business, Energy & Industrial Strategy, *British Coal Data 1853–2018*; US Department of Commerce, *Historical Statistics*, Series M 76–92)	130
Fig. 5.6	British merchant fleet engaged in foreign trade, 1840–1900: sailing and steam-powered (millions of tons) (*Source* Parliament of the UK, Statistical Abstract 1840–1853, 20, Table 19)	135
Fig. 6.1	Immigration to the United States, 1790–1900 (*Source* US Department of Commerce, *Historical Statistics of the United States*, Series C 89–119)	140
Fig. 6.2	British wool imports, 1835–1906 (in millions of lbs.) (*Sources* Clapham, *Economic History of Modern Britain: Free Trade and Steel*, p. 6; Ville, "International market for Australian Wool", Table 3; Knibbs, *Commonwealth of Australia Yearbook*, 1908, p. 293)	142
Fig. 6.3	The United States cotton exports, 1793–1914 (millions of lbs.) (*Source* US Department of Commerce, *Historical Statistics of the United States*, Series U 274–294)	144
Fig. 6.4	Leading US manufacturing industries, 1860: value of product (*Note* Value in historic US dollars. *Source* North, "Industrialization in the United States", p. 49, Table 1)	146
Fig. 6.5	Leading US manufacturing industries, 1860: employment (*Source* North, "Industrialization in the United States", p. 49, Table 1)	147
Fig. 9.1	Transportation of African slaves, 1501–1875, by flag of carrier (*Source* Trans-Atlantic Slave Trade Database, https://www.slavevoyages.org/voyage/database#tables)	208
Fig. 9.2	Transportation of African slaves, 1501–1875, place landed (*Source* Trans-Atlantic Slave Trade Database)	225
Fig. 9.3	Transportation of African slaves, 1501–1875, by flag of carrier: Netherlands, Great Britain and Portugal / Brazil (*Source* Trans-Atlantic Slave Trade Database)	227
Fig. 9.4	Output per capita in constant US dollars, 1990 value (*Source* Palma and Reis, "From convergence to divergence", Table 4)	227

xxxiv LIST OF FIGURES

Fig. 9.5 British transportation of African slaves, 1501–1850, in thousands/real wage of skilled building workers in southern England, 1264–1597 (1447 = 100) (*Note* see footnote. *Sources* Brown and Hopkins, "Seven centuries of … builders' wage rates", Appendix B; Trans-Atlantic Slave Trade Database) 229

Fig. 9.6 Average US farm values, 1890 and 1910 (historic dollars) (*Source* US Department of Commerce, *Historical Statistics: Immigration,* Series K17–81) 240

Fig. 9.7 US South, farm ownership by race, 1910–1969, in millions (*Note* Key, W = white, AA = African American. *Source* US Department of Commerce, *Historical Statistics: Commerce,* Series K109–153) 244

Fig. 9.8 Male labor force participation, 25 years and over, by educational qualification and race, 2019 (*Source* US Bureau of Labor Statistics, *Labor force … by race and ethnicity,* 2019) 245

Fig. 9.9 Female labor force participation, 25 years and over, by educational qualification and race, 2019 (*Source* US Bureau of Labor Statistics, *Labor force … by race and ethnicity,* 2019) 245

Fig. 9.10 Labor force participation, high school education only 25 years and over, by race, 2000, 2008, 2019 (*Sources* US Census Bureau, Statistical Abstract, 2010; US Bureau of Labor Statistics, *Labor force … by race and ethnicity,* 2019) 248

Fig. 10.1 Cultivated acreage, British India—non-food and food (excluding oil seeds and sugar) (*Sources* Calculated from UK Parliament, *Statistical Abstract … British India,* 1876–1877 to 1885–1886, 1903–1904 to 1911–1912) 254

Fig. 10.2 Benchmark wheat prices: Chicago, Melbourne and London, 1871–1901 (US dollars) (*Source* Bowden, *Transformation: The First Global Economy,* 288, Figure 6) 255

Fig. 11.1 Life expectancy, 1800–1900: UK, France and Japan (*Source* Steckel and Floud, "Conclusions", p. 424, Table 11.1) 267

Fig. 11.2 Literacy, 1800–1900: UK, France and Japan (*Source* Steckel and Floud, "Conclusions", p. 424, Table 11.1) 268

Fig. 11.3	Attendance, Indian government-supported schools, 1852–1853 to 1913 (*Source* UK Parliament, *Statistical Abstract ... British India*, 1840–1865, 1884–1885 to 1894–1895, 1903–1904 to 1912–1913)	268
Fig. 11.4	Percentage of adult population with university degree, 1970–2015: France, the United States, Australia and Britain (*Source* Bowden, *Work, Wealth and Postmodernism*, Figure 8.12)	273
Fig. 11.5	Growth in real per capita GNP, the United States 1869–1878 to 1970 (constant 1958 prices) (*Source* US Department of Commerce, *Historical Statistics*, Series F-1-5)	280
Fig. 11.6	Union membership by occupational categories, 2017–2018: the United States, Australia and Canada (in percent) (*Note* Canadian and US figure for 2017. Australian figures for 2018. *Source* Bowden, "Trade Union Decline and Transformation", Figure 4)	284
Fig. 11.7	European birth rates, 1860–1913 (births per thousand) (*Source* Trebilcock, *Industrialization of the Continental Powers*, Table 7.12b)	289
Fig. 11.8	European death rates, 1860–1913 (births per thousand) (*Source* Trebilcock, *Industrialization of the Continental Powers*, Table 7.12c)	290
Fig. 11.9	Government spending as share of GDP, 1880–2019: United Kingdom, United States, France and Sweden (*Sources* Ortiz-Ospina and Roser, "Government Spending"; OECD, *General Government Spending 1970–2019*)	295
Fig. 11.10	Taxation as share of GDP, 1868–2019: United Kingdom, United States, France and Sweden (*Note* UK figures from 1868; French figures from 1870; Swedish figures from 1880; US figures from 1900. *Sources* Ortiz-Ospina and Roser, "Taxation"; OECD, *Global Revenue Statistics Database*)	296
Fig. 11.11	Government debt as share of GDP, 1995–2019: the United Kingdom, the United States, France and Sweden (*Source* OECD, *OECD-Data: General Government Debt*, 1995–2019)	298
Fig. 11.12	Government social expenditure as share of GDP, 1980 to 2017–2019: the United Kingdom, the United States, France, Sweden, Canada and Australia (*Source* OECD, *Social Expenditure—Aggregated Data*, 1980–2019)	299

xxxvi LIST OF FIGURES

Fig. 11.13 Annual changes in multifactor productivity, 2000–2019: France, the United Kingdom, the United States, Canada and Australia (*Source* OECD, *OECD-Data: Multifactor Productivity*, 1985–2019) 304

Fig. 11.14 Merchandise imports and exports, British India, 1849–1920 (British pounds sterling, millions) (*Sources* UK Parliament, *Statistical Abstract ... British India*, 1840–1865, 1885–1886 to 1894–1895, 1894–1895 to 1903–1904) 307

Fig. 11.15 Principal merchandise exports, British India, 1849–1919 (British pounds sterling, millions) (*Sources* UK Parliament, *Statistical Abstract ... British India*, 1840–1865, 1885–1886 to 1894–1895, 1894–1895 to 1903–1904) 308

Fig. 11.16 British merchandise imports by nation of origin, 1855–1900 (British pounds sterling, millions) (*Sources* UK Parliament, *Statistical Abstract ... United Kingdom*, 1853–1867, 1871–1885, 1886–1900) 309

Fig. 11.17 British merchandise exports by nation of destination, 1855–1900 (British pounds sterling, millions) (*Sources* UK Parliament, *Statistical Abstract ... United Kingdom*, 1853–1867, 1871–1885, 1886–1900) 310

Fig. 11.18 Imports and exports of treasure, British India, 1849–1920 (British pounds sterling, millions) (*Sources* UK Parliament, *Statistical Abstract ... British India*, 1840–1865, 1885–1886 to 1894–1895, 1894–1895 to 1903–1904) 312

Fig. 12.1 University graduates per year by academic discipline, British India, 1868–1913 (*Sources* UK Parliament, *Statistical Abstract ... British India*, 1867–1868 to 1876–1877, 1884–1885 to 1894–1895, 1903–1904 to 1912–1913) 323

Fig. 12.2 Indian and Chinese per capita GDP (2020 US dollars), 1960 to 2019–2020 (*Source* World Bank, World Bank Data—Development Indicators) 324

Fig. 12.3 Cotton textile output of the Indian mill and handloom sectors, 1900–1903 to 2018–2019 (in millions of square meters) (*Source* Clark, *Farewell to Alms*, Table 17.3; Indian Ministry of Textiles, *Report of the Office of the Textile Commissioner*, 2019–2020) 332

Fig. 12.4	Median hourly earnings, Australia, 2020 (Australian dollars) (*Source* Australia Bureau Statistics, *Characteristics of Employment, August 2020*, Table 3.2)	338
Fig. 12.5	Population and cereal production, low-income nations, 1961–2018 (population in tens of millions, cereals in million metric tons) (*Source* Calculated from World Bank, *Online Database—Indicators—Agricultural and Rural Development*)	344
Fig. 12.6	Growth in GDP per capita, by region, 1960–2020 (in 2020 US dollars) (*Note* Middle East/North Africa Figures 1965–2017 only. *Source* Calculated from World Bank, *Online Database—Indicators—Economy & Growth*)	345
Fig. 12.7	Growth in GDP per capita, OECD average, 1960–2020 (in 2020 US dollars) (*Source* Calculated from World Bank, *Online Database—Indicators—Economy & Growth*)	347

CHAPTER 1

Introduction: Civilization and Lived Experience

Is Algeria part of the West? Or, to be more exact, is it a part of the western civilization that gained a global ascendancy in the nineteenth and twentieth centuries, confronting societies everywhere with fundamental choices as to acceptance and rejection?

To such questions, those guided by Samuel Huntington's *The Clash of Civilizations and the Remaking of World Order* would argue a resounding "no". Declaring that the "West" was never a "universal civilization in any meaningful sense", Huntington went on to proclaim that "The survival of the West depends on ... Westerners accepting their civilization as unique and ... uniting to renew and preserve it against challenges from non-Western societies".[1] Among the civilizations that Huntington identified as rivals were not only Islam and China—its principal foes—but also Latin America and Europe's orthodox east.[2]

Operating from very different premises, the Egyptian Islamic theorist, Sayyid Qutb—whose writings inspired not only the Islamic Brotherhood to which he belonged, but also al Qaeda and the Islamic State

---

[1] Samuel Huntington, *The Clash of Civilizations and the Remaking of World Order* (New York: Simon & Schuster, 1996), 20–21.

[2] Ibid., 20, 26.

© The Author(s), under exclusive license to Springer Nature Switzerland AG 2022
B. Bowden, *Slavery, Freedom and Business Endeavor*,
Palgrave Debates in Business History,
https://doi.org/10.1007/978-3-030-97232-5_1

movements—came to similar conclusions as Huntington. An unbridgeable chasm separated the West from the deeply rooted cultural values of Islamic North Africa and the Middle East. For Qutb, the West was an intellectual and moral "rubbish heap". By contrast, "Islamic society" was "by its very nature, the only civilized society".[3] In his much-cited *Orientalism*, the critical theorist Edward Said also highlighted a chasm between the West and the Middle Eastern "Orient". In Said's estimation, the concept of the West only exists by positing its "identity" against an alien oriental "other", a contrast he believed was seminal to western "power" and its "authority over the Orient".[4]

If many perceive an unbridgeable chasm between the West and the societies of the Orient and the Islamic world, this is not how Albert Camus, one of the towering literary and intellectual giants of the twentieth century, perceived it. On the eve of the independence war that was to drive people of European ancestry into permanent exile, and while reflecting back on his life in Algeria, Camus recorded:

> I have passionately loved this land where I was born, I drew from it whatever I am ... Although I have known and shared every form of poverty in which this country abounds, it is for me the land of happiness, of energy, and of creation.[5]

Jacques Derrida, another Algerian born and raised intellectual, also refused to draw a sharp distinction between his North African homeland and the societies within which he spent his adult career. Declaring himself to be "a child of the Mediterranean, who was not simply French nor simply African", Derrida reflected at the end of his long life on how:

> ... my family was in Algeria before colonization, and it probably came from Spain ... I wouldn't contrast the East and the West, especially when talking

---

[3] Sayyid Qutb, *Milestones* (https://cryptome.org/2017/10/Milestones-Qutb.pdf), 155, 107. First published in 1964, *Milestones* was written in an Egyptian prison.

[4] Edward W. Said, *Orientalism*, 25th anniversary edition (New York: Vintage Books, 2003), 3, 5.

[5] Albert Camus, "Appeal for a Civilian Truce in Algeria, February 1956", in Albert Camus (trans. Justin O'Brien), *Resistance, Rebellion and Death: Essays* (New York: Vintage International, 1995), 140–141.

about Algeria ... the Arab and Muslim or Arabo-Muslim culture of Algeria and of the Maghreb is also a Western culture.[6]

Algeria has provided not only the modern world with some of its most significant intellectuals, it has also given sanctuary and voice to some of the West's most prominent critics. In the late 1960s and early 1970s, Algeria provided refuge to not only Eldridge Cleaver, co-founder of the American Black Panthers and his "government in exile", but also Timothy Leary, the counter-culture's leading proponent of LSD. Of the critics of the West who found a home in Algeria, however, none was more influential that the West Indies-born, French-educated psychiatrist, Franz Fanon. Becoming a leading spokesperson for the *Front de Libération Nationale* during the Algerian War of Independence, Fanon argued in his book *The Wretched of the Earth* that, "when the native hears a speech about Western culture he pulls out a knife".[7]

For Fanon, the societies created by the West in North Africa and elsewhere were marked by a fundamental "Manichaeism", a primeval struggle between the white "settler" on the one hand and the "native" on the other. In this world, Fanon argued, violence against the "settler"— whether male, female or child—was not only a means to an end, it was an essential end in itself. "Violence" was, Fanon concluded, "a cleansing force", the "practice of violence" unifying the colonial population over "the rotting corpse of the settler".[8] One of the most uncompromising foes that European colonialism ever faced, Fanon was nevertheless dismissive of efforts to create an "Arab" or "African" culture in opposition to the West, condemning these campaigns as ones destined to lead "into a blind alley".[9] In the diversity of Africa, there was, he concluded "no

[6] Jacques Derrida, "To Have Lived, and to Remember, as an Algerian", in Mustapha Chérif (trans. Teresa Lavender Fagan), *Islam and the West: A Conversation with Jacques Derrida* (Chicago, IL: University of Chicago Press, 2008), 31; Jacques Derrida, "East–West: Unity in Difference", in Mustapha Chérif (trans. Teresa Lavender Fagan), *Islam and the West: A Conversation with Jacques Derrida* (Chicago, IL: University of Chicago Press, 2008), 39.

[7] Franz Fanon, *The Wretched of the Earth* (Harmondsworth, UK: Penguin, 1967), 33.

[8] Ibid., 73–74.

[9] Ibid., 172.

common destiny to be shared between the national cultures of Senegal and Guinea". Or any other African society.[10]

Rather than pursuing the mirage of "African unity", Fanon believed that Algeria could forge through a torrent of blood a new "national culture", and a new "nation" state.[11] In other words, Fanon—the West Indian-born revolutionary of African descent—perceived no post-colonial future other than one based on the nation-state model that emerged in Europe during the eighteenth and nineteenth centuries.

This was not only Fanon's vision, it was also that pursued by post-independence Algeria, even as it expelled *en masse* its entire European population—some 1.4 million people or 13% of the Algerian total. As was the case with other post-colonial states, the structural formations of the modern Algerian state closely resemble those of metropolitan France with an elected president and a national assembly—albeit through elections of a dubious nature—overseeing western-style ministerial departments. Everywhere, the global legitimacy of western-style democratic elections is witnessed in the fact that even the most authoritarian of regimes (such as Iran, North Korea, the People's Republic of China) cloak their power in the pretense of free and fair elections.

In terms of the lived experience of the ordinary citizen, the accoutrements of a western-style existence pervade every nook and cranny of their existence. Commenting on the supposed generalized hostility to western modes of thinking and being in the Middle East, Christopher de Bellaigue correctly observes in his study of the "Islamic Enlightenment" that, "There is something wonderfully earnest and yet wholly irrelevant about Westerners demanding modernity from people whose lives are drenched in it".[12] In the Middle East, as elsewhere, access to the internet is now almost universal. By 2019, more than half the world's internet users—an incredible 2.3 billion people—were found in Asia. There were also far more internet users in Africa (522.8 million), and in Latin America

---

[10] Ibid., 188.

[11] Ibid., 196–197, 39.

[12] Christopher de Bellaigue, *The Islamic Enlightenment: The Modern Struggle Between Faith and Reason* (London, UK: Vintage, 2017), xx.

and the Caribbean (453.7 million), than there were in North America (327 million).[13]

Across the globe, in every society, the western-style system of primary, secondary and tertiary education has been embraced with enthusiasm. Even in Sub-Saharan Africa, long a laggard in the literacy stakes, the United Nations estimates that 80% of children were attending school by 2015.[14] The appeal of an education system modeled on western lines is found in unlikely sources. In his touching account of his pre-1914 childhood in rural Egypt, Sayyid Qutb—the intellectual driving force behind the Islamic Brotherhood—fondly recalls the secular school where he received his education. Qutb recorded in his evocative *Child From the Village*, that whenever he returned to his home village he always headed for his old school, feeling "again the awe he felt in his school days, and if he were asked his sweetest wishes, he would say that he wished he could again be a student in the sacred school, defending it from the *kuttab* [religious school] and the *kuttab* boys" (those trained in the religious school).[15] Among the many transformative effects of the school Qutb attended was that it "finally opened its doors to the girls of the village, so that they could study with the boys throughout the day".[16] The Nile Valley school of Qutb's childhood also provided a portal to a wider transformative western culture that was making itself felt in British-dominated Egypt. Qutb remembered "a feeling" toward his state-appointed teachers "that almost amounted to worship". For not only did they know "things that he didn't", they also led "a special kind of life whose true nature he could no more understand than he could that of ghosts or spirits".[17] To this mysterious western-infused world, with its novel ideas and gadgets, the young Qutb—like countless others—was drawn like a moth to the light of a candle.

---

[13] Mimwatts Marketing Group, *Internet Usage Statistics: The Internet Big Picture—World Internet Users and Populations Stats* (Mimwatts Marketing Group, 2019), https://www.internetworldstats.com/stats.htm.

[14] Antonio Guterres, *Report of the Secretary-General of the United Nations on the Work of the Organization* (New York: United Nations, 2017), 23.

[15] Sayyid Qutb (trans. John Calvert and William Shepherd), *Child from the Village* (Cairo, Egypt: American University of Cairo, 2005), 25.

[16] Ibid., 30.

[17] Ibid., 24.

What Is Modern Western Civilization?

If we are forced to conclude that the lived experiences of the Algerian populace—along with the other nations of the North African littoral—are drenched at many different levels in modes of being inherited from the dominant "western civilization", then it becomes equally impossible to draw a rigid demarcation line between this "western" civilization and most other societies on the planet. Can we, for example, exclude India—a parliamentary democracy that boasts not only a "British" legal system but also a larger English-speaking population than any other nation on the planet—from a place in the pantheon of modern "western" societies? Can we exclude, as Huntington would have us do, Latin American societies that boast not only a European as well as a Native American heritage, but also long and often bitter struggles for democracy and constitutional rights? If we are, however, to include India, Argentina and Brazil in the modern western pantheon alongside France, Britain and Australia then we are led in the direction of some fundamental questions:

- What are the characteristic features of the "western civilization" that came to dominate the globe, for better or worse, during the nineteenth and twentieth centuries?
- When, where and why did this civilization emerge?
- To what did the "western civilization" that came to dominate the globe owe its success?
- Did its initial successes rest on factors indigenous to societies such as England, the Netherlands, France and the United States? Or, alternatively, was it the case, as Fanon alleged, that the "West" owed its wealth to imperial theft and the back-breaking work of "millions of deported slaves": an argument recently replicated by Nikole Hannah-Jones, Jake Silverstein and others in the *New York Time*'s *1619 Project*.[18]

In re-examining the contested concept of "western civilization" this book differs from earlier studies in that it defines civilization not in cultural

---

[18] Fanon, *Wretched of the Earth*, 81; Nikole Hannah-Jones, "The idea of America", in Jake Silverstein (ed.), *1619 Project* (New York: *New York Times Magazine*, 8 August 2019), 14–26; Jake Silverstein, "1619—Editor's Note", in Jake Silverstein (ed.), *1619 Project* (New York: *New York Times Magazine*, 8 August 2019), 4–7.

terms, or even in narrow economic terms, but in terms of lived experience. For, as Camus argued in *The Myth of Sisyphus*, the defining characteristic of human existence—what Camus referred to as the noble absurdity of life—is found in its ordinariness, in the daily routines of living rather than in the "high" culture of aristocratic elites.[19] The most obvious attraction of the modern iteration of "western civilization"—which is, in fact, a "global civilization"—is found in the fact that the routines of modern life are more comfortable, freer and able to offer the ordinary citizen a greater range of intellectual, physical and social circumstances, including opportunities for economic advancement, than in any other contemporary or historic civilization. Yes, it is true that historic legacies ensure that our "western" civilization is comprised in large part of "hybrids" that are characterized by marked cultural and religious differences. Nevertheless, as even the most cursory glance around the modern workplace demonstrates, an Indian accountant or information technology specialist can leave their residence in Mumbai or Bangalore and take a job in London, New York or Sydney with little difficulty. For what unites the citizens of Mumbai, London, Paris, Buenos Aires and Los Angeles is more than commonalities of education, training, and a scientific approach to problems. Rather, as Camus observed, "the conditions of modern life impose ... the same quantity of experiences and consequently the same profound experience".[20] This is not to say that there are no fundamental differences between India and Britain. As we note constantly in this book, India's experience was not Britain's. India long rejected many features of western economic life, typically at the cost of its own economic progress. There is, nevertheless, far less of a gap between the experiences and beliefs of office workers in London and Mumbai today than those that exist between today's citizen of London and their medieval counterpart.

Perceived in this way, the iteration of western civilization that emerged around 1850 is understood as one that emerged from the cradle of the older civilization, but which is distinct from it. As such, the new iteration of western civilization is distinguished by five characteristic features: seminal characteristics that caused not only a material improvement in

---

[19] Albert Camus (trans. Justin O'Brien), "The Myth of Sisyphus", in Albert Camus, *The Plague, the Fall, Exile and the Kingdom, and Selected Essays* (New York: Everyman's Library, 2004), 489–605.

[20] Ibid., 542.

the human condition, but which also profoundly altered the intellectual, social and political circumstances in which life was lived. These five characteristic features are:

1. an energy-intensive economy
2. democracy
3. economic liberalism (that is, a preferencing of market-based mechanisms)
4. political liberalism (that is, a system of laws and social mores that entrench private ownership, freedom of speech, individual choice and political pluralism)
5. a powerful bureaucratic state that constantly threatens economic and political liberalism—and even democracy.

Of these five characteristic features, the emergence of a mechanized, energy-intensive economy provided the most obvious break with the pre-1850 world, transforming the nature of both work and home life. Whereas previously the great majority of the world's population dedicated their lives to immediate food requirements, either as farmers or hunter-gatherers, this was no longer the case after 1850. Instead, as mechanized agriculture took hold, an ever-shrinking percentage of the workforce fed the rest of the population with comparative ease. Consequently, an ever-increasing number led an urban existence as factory hands, managers, office workers, retail employees and so on. Home life was also transformed as electrification brought the energy-intensive economy inside the home in the form of washing machines, televisions, fridges, air-conditioning and internet connections.

The energy-intensive economy also brought with it unprecedented levels of physical mobility and interconnectedness.

Prior to the revolution wrought in the middle-third of the nineteenth century by steam-powered shipping, railroads and improved roads, most people lived and died within sight of the place where they were born. If a good was transported overland more than 20 miles (32 km), its transport costs often exceeded its production costs. Sea transport was also slow, expensive and dangerous. Long-distance trade was largely restricted to high-value, low-bulk commodities: sugar, tea, coffee, cotton, silk, wool, textiles, spices, wine and beer, salted fish and so on. This restricted both the size of markets and the level of market competition—and hence the

1 INTRODUCTION: CIVILIZATION AND LIVED EXPERIENCE 9

need for innovation. It also restricted the capacity of markets to support large cities, given the copious demands of urban centers for not only food but also fuel for cooking, heating, lighting and industrial purposes.

In Britain, the most industrialized society on the planet, London was the only city with more than 100,000 people in 1800. In the United States, only one city—New York—had more than 50,000, a total that it exceeded by barely 10,000. At the dawn of the nineteenth century, national populations were also extremely modest in both the Old and New World. Britain had fewer than nine million people. The United States' first census, conducted in 1790, identified fewer than 3.9 million people. Of these, 694,280 were slaves.[21] Not until the middle decades of the nineteenth century did emigration from the old European heartlands to the New World become a mass phenomenon. The record 369,980 who migrated to the United States in 1850, for example, was a 4.1-fold advance on the 1840 Figure (84,060), which was in turn a 3.6-fold increase on the 1830 number (23,322).[22] Technological and transport deficiencies in the pre-1850 world also restricted nutrition, health and life expectancy. In 1850, the typical Briton lived but 39.5 years, an advance of only 3.4 years on the 1800 figure. By 1900, however, the typical Briton lived 7.5 years longer than the 1850 norm. By 1950, they were living 19.5 years longer. In Japan, the first Asian society to embrace western-style modernization with enthusiasm, life expectancy rose from 38 years to 44 between 1850 and 1900, before advancing to 58 years in 1950.[23]

The transformation in everyday life in the pre-1850 iteration of western civilization always entailed more than comparative plenty and new patterns of interconnectedness. Positively, it also entailed democracy and economic and political liberalism. Of these three attributes, this study identifies economic and political liberalism—and associated *personal* freedoms—as the unique social attributes of the new civilization rather than democracy, which expresses the will of a *collective* majority. For,

---

[21] United States Bureau of Census, *First Census of the United States* (Baltimore, ML: United States Bureau of Census, 1978), 6–8.

[22] United States Department of Commerce, *Historical Statistics of the United States: Colonial Times to 1970* (Washington, DC: United States Department of Commerce, 1975), Series C89-199.

[23] Richard H. Steckel and Roderick Floud, "Conclusions", in Richard H. Steckel and Roderick Floud (eds.), *Health and Welfare During Industrialization* (Chicago, IL: University of Chicago Press, 1997), 424, Table 11.1.

unlike democracy, liberalism places the individual and individual choice—whether it relates to purchases, economic decisions, job selections or individual opinion and belief—at center stage. In essence, therefore, the new iteration of western civilization prioritized *individual* identity over expressions of *collective-based* identity, whether associated with social class, religious sect, race or ethnicity. What counted, in short, was what you were *capable of doing*, not *who you were*. By contrast, democratic majorities have often favored anti-liberal agendas. Sometimes these anti-liberal agendas have discounted individual worth because of perceived membership of this or that ethnic, racial, religious or political grouping. At other times, they have sought to preference members of this or that grouping at the expense of others. Even more commonly, anti-liberal agendas have involved state direction and control in ways that favor certain political agendas (for example, agricultural subsidies, child-care subsidies, renewable energy subsidies) that involve de facto financial transfers to one constituency at the expense of others.

Invariably, the modern bureaucratic state—which is as much a defining feature of the new iteration of western civilization as democracy and economic and political liberalism—was the beneficiary, if not the initiator of these anti-liberal agendas. Sometimes, as occurred in Nazi Germany and the Soviet Union, this involved a near total suppression of individual choices and rights.

More commonly, the modern bureaucratic state has grown by stealth. As we shall discuss in Part III, in the twenty-first century the economic and social footprint of the modern bureaucratic state assumed a scale and size that belied the vast academic literature on "neo-liberalism" and the supposed retreat of the state's influence. In 2020 in the United States, almost a fifth of the workforce was *directly* employed by government. Elsewhere, the percentage of the workforce in government employment was typically of even-greater proportions. Across the world's advanced economies, government spending typically represented 40 to 50% of Gross Domestic Product (GDP) even before the COVID-19 pandemic with its associated "stimulus" packages. Yes, it is true that the modern bureaucratic state has been a force for good. It provides law and order, assistance to the sick and needy, schools and hospitals and many other services without which modern life would be unimaginable. As every political operative understands, however, the state is also *always* a weapon, a mechanism for pursuing your agenda and for forestalling your opponent's political program. More fundamentally, the state by its very nature entails a *collective* process of decision making and resource allocation. It thus stands in perpetual opposition to the premise that resources are best allocated through market mechanisms and the individual choices that inform them.

It is easy to perceive economic and political liberalism as matters that are peripheral to everyday life. Any such conclusions, however, are profoundly misguided. For wealth benefits one little if one is arrested and sent to a *gulag* or labor camp, or if one is discriminated against—or has job rivals who are perpetually favored at your expense. If one looks to the modern world, it is certainly easy to identify societies that have willingly embraced the West's energy-intensive technologies, bureaucratic state structures and military formations while showing little respect for democratic norms or individual rights. Reflecting on the Middle Eastern experience, de Bellaigue notes the prevalence of "coercive moderniz-ers" who "set up new, modern institutions" while, at the same time, suffocating "human autonomy". Tragically, if predictably, the resultant societies resemble a "lobotomized" animal, one where "externally every-thing seemed all right while inside critical malfunctions were going on".[24]

In the contemporary world, the People's Republic of China stands at the forefront of these "coercive modernizers". Under the *hukou* system of household registration and internal passport control that remains the central plank in China's system of employment control, migrant workers spend their working lives in places where they have no legal right of resi-dence, and thus no entitlement to education, social security, health care, or any of the other rights that characterize life in a liberal democracy. As one Chinese worker is recorded as saying in Elly Leung's powerful recent study, *The (Re)Making of the Chinese Working Class*:

> I know my future – I'll be poor for the rest of my life ... illiterate people like me ... can only get low-wage jobs. Just like any other dagong [worker] ... we have to suffer because we have no "culture" in us ... that's why we do whatever our leaders want.[25]

---

[24] Christopher de Bellaigue, *The Islamic Enlightenment: The Modern Struggle Between Faith and Reason* (London, UK: Vintage Books, 2017), 18.

[25] Elly Leung, *The (Re)Making of the Chinese Working Class* (Cham, Switzerland: Palgrave Macmillan, 2021), 108.

If contemporary China is best perceived as a "hybrid" civilization, one that has embraced the "West's" production methods and lifestyles but not its guiding social and economic norms, what then of the question that began this chapter: "Is Algeria part of the West?" Like China, Algeria also represents an all-too-common "hybrid". Since independence, Algeria has willingly embraced the technological and even economic features of the new civilization (mechanization, an energy-intensive lifestyle, literacy, high standards of health). The Algerian regime has, however, been reluctant to grant its citizens the political and social liberties associated with the new civilization—a refusal that was seminal to both a long and brutal civil war (1991–2002) and the repression of the Algerian "Arab Spring" (2010–2012). Algeria is, in short, in a halfway house; a society that shares many economic, technological and even cultural characteristics with its former colonial master, France, but which is devoid of many of the personal and political freedoms that support "western-style" individualism and the economic dynamism that is its universal handmaiden.

1850 and the Dawn of a New Civilization

What was it that made the period around 1850 such a seminal divide in human history?

On the economic and work front many have previously identified the Industrial Revolution (c. 1760–1830) as the decisive turning point in human history, rather than some earlier or later date. It was the Industrial Revolution, Deane and Habakkuk observed, which "initiated the sustained upward movement of real incomes that the Western world now takes for granted".[26] Similarly, in the opinion of the great Italian economic historian, Carlo Cipolla, the "world in which we live and the problems we face would be unintelligible without reference to that grandiose change which we label the Industrial Revolution".[27] For Robert Allen, as well, it was the Industrial Revolution "that inaugurated

[26] Phyllis Deane and H.J. Habakkuk, "The Take-Off in Britain", in W.W. Rostow (ed.), *The Economics of Take-off into Sustained Growth* (London, UK: Macmillan, 1963), 63.

[27] Carlo M. Cipolla, *Before the Industrial Revolution*, second edition (London, UK: Routledge, 1981), xiii.

Fig. 1.1 Real wage of skilled building worker in southern England, 1264–1930 (1447 = 100) (*Source* Brown and Hopkins: "Seven centuries of ... builders' wage rates", Appendix B)

an era of industrial expansion and further technological innovation that changed the world".[28]

The Industrial Revolution certainly *initiated* a process of industrialization that was to become a hallmark feature of the new iteration of western civilization. It was not, however, until the middle of the nineteenth century that the Industrial Revolution's *potential* was realized in ways that profoundly altered the human condition outside a comparatively small part of Britain and, to a lesser degree, Belgium and the United States. Even in Britain it is easy to exaggerate the immediate economic and social impact of the Industrial Revolution. Figure 1.1— which traces the real consumption wage of a skilled building worker in southern England between 1264 and 1930—indicates how real wages fell rather than rose during the first half of the Industrial Revolution. It was not until 1850 that British real wages decisively broke clear of the derisory standard that prevailed during the seventeenth and eighteenth

---

[28] Robert C. Allen, *The British Industrial Revolution in Global Perspective* (Cambridge, UK: Cambridge University Press, 2009).

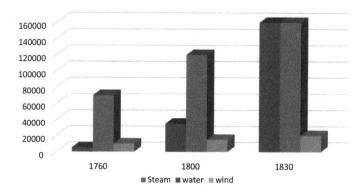

Fig. 1.2 Britain's installed horsepower, 1760–1830 (*Note* stationary machinery only. *Source* Allen, *British Industrial Revolution in Global Perspective*, Table 7.1)

centuries.[29] Although the steam engine was unquestionably a revolutionary technology, its expense and complexity initially limited its use, as did the voracious appetite for coal of the early models. Indeed, as Fig. 1.2 indicates, during the first half of the Industrial Revolution it was an expansion of water power—typically associated with the establishment of mills alongside the fast-flowing streams of the Pennines, a range of hills and mountains in northern England, that underpinned the growth in industrial output, not steam power. Even at the end of the Industrial Revolution (c. 1830), the installed horse-power equivalents produced by wind and water still exceeded that produced by steam.[30] Only in the second half of the nineteenth century did industry finally witness a cascading series of transformations associated with mechanization. Whereas in 1840 steam power provided Britain with energy equivalent to that produced by seven million adult male laborers, by 1870 it was generating the energy equivalent of 121 million. By 1896, steam power's output was equivalent to 411 million.[31]

[29] E.H. Phelps Brown and Sheila V. Hopkins: "Seven Centuries of the Price of Consumables, Compared with Builders' Wage Rates", *Economica*, Vol. 23, No. 92 (1956), 311–314, Appendix B.

[30] Robert C. Allen, *British Industrial Revolution in Global Perspective* (Cambridge, UK: Cambridge University Press, 2009), 173.

[31] Peter Vries, "Cotton, Capitalism, and Coercion: Some Comments on Sven Beckert's 'Empire of Cotton'", *Journal of World History*, Vol. 28, No. 1 (2017), 137.

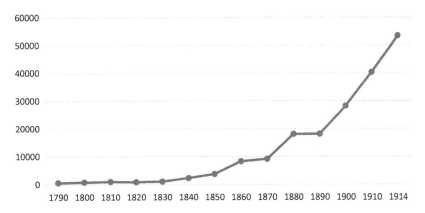

Fig. 1.3 Shipping tonnage at United States' ports, 1790–1914 (thousands of tons) (*Source* US Department of Commerce, *Historical Statistics*, Series 506–507)

Mechanization during the Industrial Revolution was also almost solely a factory phenomenon. Any significant improvement in transportation was largely due to canal construction. Not until the 1840s and 1850s were steam-powered ships and railroads a serious commercial force. In shipping, the scale of this transformation is indicated in Fig. 1.3, which traces the tonnage of ships (thousands of tons) recorded at port in the United States between 1770 and 1914. By 1880, the tonnage of ships at port was 16.4 times larger than it was in 1830.[32] This expansion in tonnage, it should be noted, severely understates the transformation which occurred, given the superior speed and greater durability of the iron-hulled, steam-powered ships that dominated the oceans after 1850.

The unprecedented mobility of people and goods that characterized the post-1850 world profoundly affected almost every society on the planet in ways that were both beneficial and pernicious—with many societies feeling these two effects simultaneously. Few were able to resist the temptations of a new iteration of western civilization. In the 1830s, for example, the portrait painter, George Catlin, found himself in "the great Sioux country" of the still-remote Northern Plains of America. Although

---

[32] United States Department of Commerce, *Historical Statistics of the United States: Colonial Times to 1970* (Washington, DC: United States Department of Commerce, 1975), Series Q 506–507.

the new industrial civilization was at this point still half born, Catlin found to his surprise that the Lakota (the Sioux) were already devoting much of their efforts toward the "spring trade" with the American Fur Company: a trade that saw an "incredible number of buffalo robes" exchanged for the "articles and luxuries of civilized manufacturers".[33] By 1880, however, this dynamic Lakota trading economy was in utter ruin, the victim of not only military defeat but also of a human tide of European migration. In the first five years of the 1850s, almost four times as many migrants disembarked in American ports (1.92 million) as were landed between the end of the War of Independence (1783) and 1819 (250,000).[34]

Other New World societies witnessed a similar process of displacement and settlement. In 1851, for example, Australia's European population was less than 180,000, 59% of whom were convicts, freed convicts or convict offspring.[35] By 1890, however, Australia was a complex urban society with a European population of more than three million. Melbourne, with half a million inhabitants, was the second-largest city in the British Empire. With the success of the independence struggles against Spain and Portugal, the societies of Latin America were also transformed as a trickle of European migration turned into a flood. Of the post-1850 South American experience, Braudel observed:

> Over vast areas, this immigration acted like a human bombardment, destroying the old social order – not overnight, but rapidly all the same. It began to fill the countryside.[36]

As the New World witnessed an inrush of immigrants, the Old World experienced the reverse. In a single decade (1881–1890), Germany lost 1.34 million citizens to overseas emigration. Between 1861 and 1910, Spain lost one-eighth of its population (2.5 million). During the same

---

[33] George Catlin, *Letters and Notes on the Manner, Customs and Conditions of North American Indians*, vol. 1 (New York: Dover Publications, 1973), 209.

[34] United States Department of Commerce, *Historical Statistics*, Series C 89–119.

[35] Russel Ward, *The Australian Legend*, second edition (Melbourne, AUS: Oxford University Press, 1966), 16, Table II.

[36] Fernand Braudel (trans. Richard Mayne), *A History of Civilizations* (London, UK: Penguin, 1995), 440.

period, almost one-fifth of Italy's population (6.4 million) left for the New World.[37]

The unprecedented mobility that characterized the post-1850 world points to the realization of the Industrial Revolution's economic potential. Was this realized potential, however, largely parasitic in nature, something that simply drew upon the slave plantations of the Americas? This was certainly the view of Franz Fanon. As Fanon expressed it:

> Europe is literally the creation of the Third World ... The ports of Holland, the docks of Bordeaux and Liverpool were specialized in the Negro-slave trade. And owe their renown to millions of deported slaves.[38]

Writing in the aftermath of World War II, the African American intellectual, W.E.B. Du Bois, articulated a similar conclusion. The "Negro race", Du Bois wrote, was "the foundation upon which the capitalist system has been raised". It was also, he concluded, African slave labor that produced the wealth "that caused the Industrial Revolution".[39] In the much-cited *1619 Project*, a near identical conclusion was proclaimed. It was upon the cotton plantations of the American South, Mathew Desmond declared, that "a capitalist economy" was first fashioned.[40] In recent years, a host of studies have similarly associated the wealth that (eventually) emerged from the Industrial Revolution with American slavery and plantation cotton.[41] Paradoxically, this was the same argument that underpinned the succession of the Confederate States of America in 1861, the successionists

---

[37] Clive Trebilcock, *The Industrialization of the Continental Powers, 1780–1914* (London, UK and New York: Longman, 1981), 310–311, Table 5.2.

[38] Fanon, *Wretched of the Earth*, 81.

[39] W.E.B. Du Bois, *The World and Africa: Color and Democracy* (Oxford, UK: Oxford University Press), 144.

[40] Mathew Desmond, "Capitalism", in Jake Silverstein (ed.), *1619 Project* (New York: *New York Times Magazine*, 8 August 2019), 34.

[41] Sven Beckert, "Emancipation and Empire: The World Wide Web of Cotton Production in the Age of the American Civil War", *American Historical Review*, Vol. 109, No. 5 (2004), 1405–1438; Sven Beckert, *Empire of Cotton: A New History of Capitalism* (London, UK: Penguin, 2017); Walter Johnson, *River of Dark Dreams: Slavery and Empire in the Cotton Kingdom* (Cambridge, MA: Harvard University Press, 2013); Edward Baptist, *The Half That Was Never Told: Slavery and the Making of American Capitalism* (New York: Basic Books, 2014). For a critical review see, Alan Olmstead and Paul W. Rhode, "Cotton, Slavery, and the New History of Capitalism", *Explorations in Economic History*, Vol. 67, No. 1 (2018), 1–17.

(wrongly) believing that the British economy could not survive without their cotton. It did. Thus, we are (wrongly) informed by Sven Beckert in his *Empire of Cotton: A New History of Capitalism* that "by 1830, one in six workers in Britain labored in cottons [manufacturing]", whereas in fact only one-sixth of the workforce labored in *manufacturing*. Beckert also (wrongly) asserts that by 1831 the cotton sector was responsible for 22.4% of the "value added" in the British economy.[42] In truth, as Peter Vries noted in a review of Beckert's book, "Cotton textile production … never amounted for more than 10% of Britain's GDP".[43] In terms of employment, cotton manufacturing remained a minority phenomenon. In 1830, at the very end of the Industrial Revolution, the "cotton-mill population of Great Britain … was perhaps one-eightieth of the total population".[44]

If we turn to an examination of United States exports during the Industrial Revolution (that is, 1760–1830) the modest contribution of cotton becomes even more apparent. Prior to 1802, by which time the Industrial Revolution was more than half over, there were no United States cotton exports. In four years—1808, 1809, 1811, 1812—the United States cotton exports were close to zero. In 1813 and 1814, during the War of 1812 (1812–1815), there were, once more, no United States cotton exports at all.[45] Yes, it is true that the United States *did* become the major source of supply to Britain's cotton mills after the War of 1812–1815. By this stage, however, British manufacturing was already diversified as industrial production soared upwards in pottery ware, iron smelting, woolen textiles and, above all, engineering. The significance of the Industrial Revolution is thus found in the fact that it was *not* confined to cotton. If it had been, the result would have been a humanity still leading a back-breaking pre-industrial existence simply to have the benefit of cheap cotton shirts and dresses.

If cotton's contribution to the global transformation that occurred during the nineteenth century has been exaggerated, we are still left with the argument that, at its heart, the new global civilization and

---

[42] Beckert, *Empire of Cotton*, 73.

[43] Vries, "Cotton, Capitalism, and Coercion", 132.

[44] J.H. Clapham, *Economic History of Modern Britain: The Early Railway Age 1820–1850* (Cambridge, UK Cambridge University Press, 1967), 54.

[45] Department of Commerce, *Historical Statistics*, Series U 274–294.

economic order that emerged c. 1850 rested on wealth generated by the Atlantic slave trade and the slave plantations of the New World. In 2020, this claim was reasserted by Leon Prieto and Simone Phipps, authors who have made significant contributions to the study of "Black" and "African American" management, including a Special Issue in the *Journal of Management History*, of which I am currently co-editor.[46] In Prieto and Phipps's estimation, "it is certain that capitalism and slavery are inextricably linked ... slavery played a central role in the economic development of Europe".[47]

If Prieto and Phipps's argument is true then we would expect to see it reflected in steadily rising European living standards that correlated with trends in the Atlantic slave trade, which reached a peak of intensity between 1750 and 1800. We would also expect that the societies most involved in the slave trade, namely Portugal and Spain, would have enjoyed markedly higher living standards than those societies that played little or no role in the slave trade, such as Italy, Austria or Poland. Between the sixteenth century and 1870, Portugal and Spain were responsible for the carriage of two-thirds of the African slaves transported to the Americas. Moreover, of the 11.3 million slaves who were transported, two-thirds were landed in Spanish or Portuguese colonies.[48] In Fig. 1.4, however, when, we look at the per capita output of Spain, Portugal, Italy and Holland (measured in 1990 dollars) between 1500 and 1800 it is difficult to ascertain a positive correlation between prosperity and involvement in the slave trade. Throughout the entire 300-year period, Portugal and Spain remained poor, economically backward societies. Even Italy, which was effectively excluded from the Atlantic economy, fared better. Neither Iberian society enjoyed anything approaching the prosperity of "Golden Age" Holland, a society whose wealth was largely obtained prior

---

[46] Leon Prieto and Simone T.A. Phipps, "Guest Editorial", *Journal of Management History*, Vol. 26, No. 3 (2020), 293–294.

[47] Leon C. Prieto and Simone T.A. Phipps, *Why Business Schools Need to Address Black History: It's Time to Decolonize the Business Curriculum* (Cambridge, MA: Harvard Business Publishing—Education, 18 February 2021), 2.

[48] Hugh Thomas, *The Slave Trade: The History of the Atlantic Slave Trade 1440–1870* (London, UK: Picador, 1997), 805.

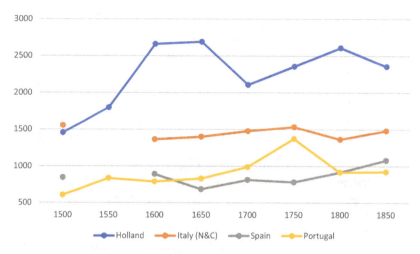

Fig. 1.4 Output per capita (1990 dollars), 1500–1850 (*Note* No figures for Spain and Italy for 1550. *Source* Palma and Reis, "From Convergence to Divergence", 6)

to its (very limited) eighteenth-century involvement in the Atlantic slave trade.[49]

To query the contribution of slavery to European prosperity and the rise of our modern "western" and global civilization is not to deny either the significance or horror of the Atlantic slave trade. As Sir Hugh Thomas noted in his encyclopedic study:

> In the first three and a quarter centuries of European activity in the Americas, between 1492 and 1820, five times as many Africans went to the New World as did white Europeans … Most of the great enterprises of the first 400 years of colonization owed much to African slaves.[50]

The fact that individual Europeans grew wealthy from the slave trade, however, is not the same as "Europe" growing rich from its spoils.

---

[49] Nuno Palma and Jaime Reis, "From Convergence to Divergence: Portuguese Economic Growth 1527–1850", *Journal of Economic History*, Vol. 79, No. 2 (2019), 500, Table 4. Note: dollars referred to are Geary–Khamis dollars, indicating purchasing parity with 1990 United States dollars.

[50] Thomas, *The Slave Trade*, 794.

As Palma and Reis conclude in their study of Portuguese circumstance between 1527 and 1850, years that approximate its involvement in the slave trade, "Over the long run, there was no per capita growth; by 1850 per capita incomes were not much different from what they had been in the early 1530s".[51] If the economic benefit of the slave trade for Europe was, at best, extremely modest, this in part reflects the fact that— until the post-1820 development of the United States cotton trade—the plantation economies only produced and transported small volumes of luxury products (sugar, tobacco, coffee), which were consumed by a tiny European elite. As such, they had little in common with the industrialized economy that emerged after 1850—an economy primarily directed toward servicing new, mass consumer markets. Despite the long history of slavery in the Americas, therefore, the New World's plantation economies proved a dead end. Only with their demise was a viable, capitalist and mechanized economic model entrenched in its place.

NOT ONLY ECONOMICS, BUT ALSO FREEDOM

It is tempting to associate the principles of democracy, individualism and personal freedom that characterized the modern iteration of western civilization with the legacies of ancient Athens and republican Rome. Certainly, if we look to the revolutionary movements of the late eighteenth century, we observe a universal tendency to not only justify political action through reference to the classics but also to drape the new republican societies in the symbolism of antiquity. As Bernard Bailyn noted in his study of the American Revolution: "The classics of the ancient world are everywhere in the literature of the Revolution". Typically, however, Bailyn also noted, such references were mere "window dressing". They were, Bailyn concluded, "illustrative, not determinative of thought".[52] In short, the revolutionary leaders of North America and elsewhere did not become democrats and proponents of individualism because they had reached out to the classics. Rather, they reached out to the classics because they were already democrats and proponents of individualism.

---

[51] Palma and J. Reis, "Convergence to Divergence", *Journal of Economic History*, Vol. 79, No. 2 (2019), 499.

[52] Bernard Bailyn, *The Ideological Origins of the American Revolution*, Fiftieth anniversary edition (Cambridge, MA: Belknap Press, 2017), 23–24, 26.

From where did the principles of democracy, individualism, and political and economic liberalism spring if not from the classics?

In part, as Marx and Engels indicated, it sprang from the nature of a bourgeois existence, a lifestyle built upon choices, risk and individual obtainment. Of the commercial middle class that emerged in the cities of medieval Europe, the great Belgium historian, Henri Pirenne observed that "freedom" was its "necessary and universal attribute". For, Pirenne observed, commercial life on a significant scale was incompatible with the fixed hierarchical structures of feudalism.[53] In his study of Renaissance Italy, Burckhardt came to similar conclusions. The merchant cities of Italy, he wrote, were unique in both their "municipal freedom" and their emphasis on individual identity. By 1300, he argued, "Italy began to swarm with individuality".[54] In successfully demanding passage of a *Bill of Rights*, or the *Act Declaring the Rights and Liberties of the Subject and Settling the Succession of the Crown* to give it its full title, the British parliament in 1689 also pointed to freedom's supposed long heritage. A host of rights—trial by jury, parliamentary representation, parliamentary free speech—were declared "the true, ancient and indubitable rights and liberties of the people". A similar viewpoint was articulated in William Blackstone's *Commentaries on the Laws of England in Four Books*, a mid-eighteenth-century study that redefined "common law" as it applied in not only Britain but also its New World colonies. Like the framers of the *Bill of Rights*, Blackstone located the protections of common law in a time "of higher antiquity than memory or history can reach".[55] Rooted in ancient tradition, this system of protection, Blackstone concluded, was such that "the moment" a "slave or negro" landed in England they fell "under the protection of the laws, and so became a freeman".[56]

If there is some truth in claims that freedom had an ancient heritage in the western tradition there is also much hyperbole, exaggeration and straight-out fabrication in such assertions. The fact that Britain fought

---

[53] Henri Pirenne (trans. Frank D. Halsey), *Medieval Cities: Their Origins and the Revival of Trade* (Princeton, NJ: Princeton University Press, 1952), 193–194.

[54] Jacob Burckhardt (trans. S.G.C. Middlemore), *The Civilization of the Renaissance in Italy*, second edition (New York, NY: Modern Library, 1954), 101–102.

[55] William Blackstone, *Commentaries on the Laws of England in Four Books*, Vol. 1 (Indianapolis, IN: Liberty Fund, 2010), 62.

[56] Ibid., 96.

a bloody Civil War (1642–1651) and experienced the Glorious Revolution of 1688 before the monarch (reluctantly) accepted the *Bill of Rights* suggests that the nation's "true, ancient and indubitable rights" were, in fact, highly contested. Under Britain's eighteenth-century parliamentary system, the exercise of power remained in the hands of a tiny minority. Few were able to vote. In Renaissance Italy, as Burckhardt willingly acknowledged, despotic rule was the norm, rather than the exception.[57] In Western Europe, prior to the Year of Revolutions (1848), the vast majority lived under authoritarian, monarchical regimes that maintained their hold on power at the point of a bayonet. In commerce and industry, even mid-eighteenth-century England—a society that rivalled the Netherlands in its economic and social dynamism—was far removed from a liberal *laissez-faire* economy. Instead, as Dan Wren and Art Bedeian observed in their iconic study, *The Evolution of Management Thought*, the British economy embodied the principles of "mercantilism", a system of state regulations and crony capitalism that "curbed private initiative, imposed elaborate bureaucratic controls, and fostered wars and trade rivalries that destroyed the very markets it [the state] was trying to gain".[58]

The principles of individualism, democracy and economic liberalism upon which the modern iteration of western civilization was founded were thus far from being "ancient" rights. Instead, as we discuss in Part II, they were based on novel, contested and revolutionary understandings as to the role of the state and of the individual citizen's relationship to it. In part, these new understandings involved a battle of ideas, a contest in which John Locke, Montesquieu, Voltaire, Jean-Jacques Rousseau and countless others faced exile and imprisonment for their beliefs. In part, it also grew out of lived experiences in both the Old and New World. Of North American circumstance, the French political theorist Alexis de Tocqueville believed that a spirit of democracy and individualism was an inevitable consequence of a frontier existence that demanded self-reliance. In the towns that dotted New England, he observed, "the affairs which affected everyone were discussed, as in Athens, in the public squares or

---

[57] Burckhardt, *Civilization of the Renaissance*, 101.

[58] Daniel A. Wren and Arthur G. Bedeian, *The Evolution of Management Thought*, seventh edition (Hoboken, NJ: Wiley, 2018), 27.

in the general assembly of the citizens".[59] The highly contested nature of these new political and economic understandings was such, however, that their ascent was always troubled. In Britain, the United States, Latin America, France and elsewhere, they rode to victory only through blood and fire. The ascent of an economic order premised on individualism and market exchanges also entailed a cultural revolution—one that placed self, family and material acquisition at center stage. In part, as Deidre McCloskey observed in reflecting upon the peculiarities of "bourgeois virtue", this entailed an ethic of greed. It also entailed, however, a belief that wealth was best obtained through exchange and persuasion rather than violence. A preference for market solutions also mandated "tolerance", a willingness to do business with anyone no matter what their ethnicity or religion.[60]

From the outset the political and economic principles upon which the modern iteration of western civilization was founded always contained multiple elements that were in many ways contradictory. Democracy, as a political system, rests on majority opinion. It can empower groups that are hostile as well as those who are favorably disposed to individualism, personal liberties and markets. Conversely, individualism and its institutionalized expressions, political and economic liberalism, rest on personal choices and personal protections: private property, freedom of assembly and speech and so on. Therefore, there is a creative but also a destructive tension built into the very fabric of our modern western civilization.

If we identify democracy and, more particularly economic and political liberalism, as seminal features of the new iteration of western civilization that emerged after 1850, why is it that we once more select the years around 1850 as the decisive turning point rather than 1688 and the British *Bill of Rights*, or 1776 (the American Declaration of Independence), or 1789 (the French Revolution)?

The reason is found in the fact that the achievements of the revolutionary movements of the late nineteenth century were largely rolled back after the Napoleonic Wars. Across continental Europe, absolutist monarchies reasserted their hold after 1815. While Britain's colonies boasted legislative councils, these were largely comprised of appointed members

---

[59] Alexis de Tocqueville (trans. Gerald E. Bevan), *Democracy in America, and Two Essays on America* (London, UK: Penguin, 2003), 23, 52.

[60] Deidre McCloskey, "Bourgeois Virtue", *American Scholar*, Vol. 63, No. 2 (1994), 181, 187.

drawn from colonial elites. It was not until 1856 and the granting of "self-government" to the Australian colony of New South Wales that one could point to something approaching representative democracy in any of Britain's colonies. Even in Britain itself, only 8% of the adult male population could vote prior to the electoral reforms of 1867. While the United States did maintain a unique republican form of representative democracy, this achievement was tainted by the continuation of large-scale slavery—a practice that is anathema to economic and political liberalism (although not necessarily democracy). The great turning point that moved democracy and economic and political liberalism to a permanent place at center stage was thus not the American and French Revolutions of 1776 and 1789, respectively—even if subsequent achievements were incomprehensible without reference to their example—but rather 1848—the Year of Revolutions. For, from 1848 onwards, it was clearly democracy, capitalism and individualism that was ascendant, and absolutism and aristocratic privilege that was in clear retreat.

NOT ONLY FREEDOM, BUT ALSO STATE POWER

The bureaucratic state is as much a part of the current iteration of western civilization as capitalism. This was not, however, always the case. In western civilization's medieval iteration, the power of the state sunk to its historic nadir. The feudal monarch was reduced to the status of a superior baron. The center of government was simply the place where the monarch and their retainers happened to be at any point in time. As Max Weber accurately observed, "political association" in the form of state power was "completely replaced by a system of relations of purely personal loyalty". In consequence, the authority of both the monarch and their subsidiary vassals was "reduced to the likelihood" that their personal vassals would "remain faithful to their oaths of fealty".[61] In a society built around personal relationships rather than monetary exchanges, the feudal monarch was almost totally devoid of reliable revenue streams. Even the monarch's personal estates offered up grain and pledges of loyalty rather than cash. Taxes that delivered the monarch more liquid revenues typically required parliamentary approval, which was only begrudgingly offered, usually with strings attached. To the extent that medieval society

---

[61] Max Weber (ed. Guenther Roth and Claus Wittich), *Economy and Society* (Berkeley, CA: University of California Press, 1978), 256.

possessed large reserves of cash and sophisticated systems of monetary exchange, these were in the hands of the nascent urban bourgeoise, rather than the state. Thus, whereas the feudal monarch stood at the apex of an agrarian society based upon personal relationships, the medieval bourgeoisie was the undisputed leader of a rival commercial culture based on monetarized relationships. "Never before had there existed", Pirenne observed, a class of people "so specifically and strictly urban as the medieval bourgeoisie".[62]

In the medieval world we can thus distinguish two rival political economies. Of these two political economies, the agrarian society headed by the monarch was always chronically short of cash. Conversely, bourgeois society had cash but suffered a deficit of political power. Invariably, this dynamic led to self-serving deals. In exchange for loans and other financial bequests offered up to feudal monarchs, the medieval bourgeoisie secured for itself an ever-increasing range of "privileges" or "freedoms". In detaching itself from feudalism's hierarchal obligations, however, the nascent bourgeoise also allowed the monarchical state to free itself from its reliance on aristocratic levies and services. In lieu of these feudal relationships the monarchy substituted monetarized relationships, professional armies and salaried bureaucracies, running up ever-larger debts with the banking houses of Italy, Germany and the Low Countries. If, however, the bourgeoisie and the nascent bureaucratic state existed in a symbiotic relationship with each other in the medieval and early modern eras, the state soon entered into an enduring relationship with another emerging social class—the university-educated salaried professional—in ways that freed it from its dependence on the bourgeoise. From the sixteenth century, as Braudel noted, the "corridors of political history" were "suddenly thronged" with "civil servants". "Their arrival", Braudel concluded, represented "a political revolution coupled with a social revolution", providing a new locus of power and prestige within western society.[63] Increasingly, as we discuss more fully in Chapter 8, the key symbiotic relationship that underpinned the growth of the bureaucratic state was that which existed between the state and the university,

[62] Henri Pirenne (trans. Frank D. Halsey), *Medieval Cities: Their Origins and the Revival of Trade* (Princeton, NJ: Princeton University Press, 1952), 131–132.

[63] Fernand Braudel, *The Mediterranean and the Mediterranean World in the Age of Philip II*, vol. 2 (New York, NY: Harper Torchbooks, 1975), 681.

rather than the older marriage of convenience between the state and the bourgeoisie.

From the mid-sixteenth century, the bureaucratic state and its institutional ally, the university, coexisted with capitalism in a state of tension. In a work that heralded the birth of the great era of British political and economic thought, Thomas Hobbes famously argued in the *Leviathan* that the "pact or covenant" between the bureaucratic state and private-sector industry was seminal to social and economic progress. Given that "covenants without the sword are but words and no strength", Hobbes concluded, the security that the state offered as its part of this covenant was only meaningful if the state exerted control over every aspect of life. And without such a covenant, Hobbes believed, there was "no place for industry, because the fruit thereof is uncertain". In consequence, "the life of man" would remain in the state in which it had always existed: "solitary, poor, nasty, brutish, and short".[64] Most of Hobbes's intellectual successors—John Locke, David Hume, Edmund Burke, Adam Smith, John Stuart Mill—perceived the modern state's ascent in far less benign terms. In his *Two Treatises of Government*, John Locke perceived in *every* form of government a latent, if not actual tyranny. For, Locke advised his readers:

> … wherever the power that is put in any hands for the government of the people and the preservation of their properties is applied to other ends … there it presently becomes tyranny, whether those that thus use it are one or many.[65]

As we explore in detail in Chapters 7 and 8, this Lockean suspicion of state power profoundly influenced the American Revolution and, through it, the democratic revolutions and movements that subsequently characterized both the New and Old Worlds. So powerful was Locke's influence, Bradley Thompson argues in his recent *America's Revolutionary Mind*,

---

[64] Thomas Hobbes (ed. A.P. Martinich), *Leviathan* (Peterborough, CAN: Broadway Press, 2002), 82.

[65] John Locke, *Two Treatises of Government* (London, UK: Thomas Tegg and Others, 1823), 193.

that the American Declaration of Independence can justly be considered nothing more than "an expression of Locke's mind".[66]

From the time of Locke's defining study at the end of the seventeenth century we can distinguish two markedly different schools of thought within the western tradition, one of which viewed the modern bureaucratic state as foe and the other as friend. Invariably, those who perceived the state as foe preferenced market solutions over state direction and control, and individualism over collective expressions of identity. Conversely, those who viewed the state as friend typically favored the opposite on both counts. Whereas those who favored markets over state direction primarily drew inspiration from the British empirical tradition (Locke, Hume, Smith, Mill, and so on), those who associated socially beneficial outcomes with the state drew on traditions of thought that can be traced back through Karl Marx to Georg Hegel and a central strand of German idealist thought. In giving voice to this latter tradition, Hegel declared that "all the worth which the human being possesses ... he possesses only through the State ... Society and the State are the very conditions in which Freedom is realized".[67]

Contrasting intellectual opinions of the state reflected another deep-seated tension that ran through the modern western civilization from its very inception. At the heart of this tension was a fundamental question: on what principles were the resources of the society to be allocated? Were they to be allocated according to individual preferences and market demand? Or, alternatively, were they to be allocated through the political process and state direction? While the benefits of the latter approach seem self-evident in the provision of services such as education and health care without regard to the financial capacity of the recipient, a reliance on politics rather than markets also leads in not only illiberal but also authoritarian directions. The "Jim Crow" laws that subjected African Americans to systematic discrimination in the wake of the Civil War (1861–1865) were the product of law and state direction, not market forces. Similarly,

---

[66] C. Bradley Thompson, *America's Revolutionary Mind: A Moral History of the American Revolution and the Declaration that Defined It* (New York and London: Encounter Books, 2019), 34.

[67] Georg Hegel (trans. J. Sibree), *Philosophy of History* (New York, NY: Dover Publications, 1956), 39, 41.

it is inconceivable that market forces and individual subscriptions could ever lead to the horrors of Auschwitz or Buchenwald. Such outcomes were the result of political decisions, not market forces.

ESCAPING HUMANITY'S ETERNAL CURSE—THE "MALTHUSIAN TRAP"

Of all the achievements of the new iteration of western civilization, none was arguably more significant than its capacity to break out of the "Malthusian trap" that had bound all previous civilizations. Developed by the English pastor, Thomas Malthus in 1798, the hypothesis behind the "Malthusian trap" is that the population of all societies will increase up to and ultimately beyond their "means of subsistence", leading to an eventual collapse in both living standards and population.[68]

The utility of Malthus's hypothesis is well demonstrated by the experiences of the Mayan civilization, arguably the most technologically advanced society to carve a place for itself in the Americas prior to the European conquests. Today, when we see images of the ruins of the Maya cities amid the jungles of Central America there is a tendency to see the Maya civilization as one that lived in harmony with nature. Indeed, when the second Star Wars movie (*Return of the Jedi*) was filmed, the ruined city of Tikal and its jungle environs was used as a backdrop to locate the forest moon of Endor and its population of Ewoks—an environmentally friendly people who helped defeat an advanced, evil technology. The association of the Maya, however, with environmental awareness is totally misplaced. Like other pre-industrial societies, the Maya developed their productive capacities to the maximum extent allowed by their technology. As recent paleo-archaeological studies have indicated, between 400 BC and AD 810 the Maya turned the jungle around them into open savannah and maize fields.[69] Repeatedly, they pushed their agricultural

---

[68] Thomas Malthus, *An Essay on the Principles of Population* (London, UK: J. Johnson, 1798), 106.

[69] Julia A. Hoggart, Mathew Restall, James W. Wood and Douglas J. Kennent, "Drought and Its Demographic Effects in the Maya Lowlands", *Current Anthropology*, Vol. 58, No. 1 (February 2017), 82–113; Mark Brenner, Michael F. Rosenmeier, David A. Hodell and James H. Curtis, "Paleolimnology of the Maya Lowlands: Long-Term Perspectives in Interactions Among Climate, Environment, and Humans", *Ancient Mesoamerica*, Vol. 13 (2002), 141–157; Richardson B. Gill, Paul A. Mayewski, John Nyberg, Gerald H. Haug and Larry C. Peterson, "Drought and the Maya Collapse", *Ancient Mesoamerica*,

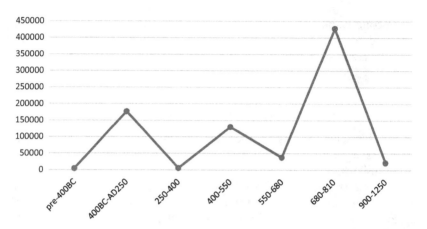

Fig. 1.5 Population history of Mayan Three Rivers Region, 400 BC–AD 1250 (*Source* Gill et al., "Drought and the Maya Collapse", Figure 5)

technology to the limits of what was possible, cultivating marginal hill country where the soil runoff is still detectable in the lakes of Central America. Figure 1.5—which traces the rise and fall of population in the Maya heartlands in the "Three Rivers Region" (modern-day Belize and Guatemala)—indicates that the result of living at the limits of one's technology proved disastrous. When a global "cooling" period in the eighth century heralded a prolonged drought in the Maya heartlands, a catastrophic societal collapse ensued. In reflecting on the Maya plight, Gill et al. observe that, "There was nothing they could do or could have done. In the end, the food and water ran out—and they died".[70] Only with the demise of the once great Mayan civilization—which had found itself caught in a remorseless example of the "Malthusian trap"—did forest regrowth return the society's geographic heartlands into overgrown jungle.

The experience of the Maya is not an isolated one. On the contrary, one of the characteristic features of all historic human civilizations is that, ultimately, they failed.

Vol. 18 (2007), 283–302; B.L. Turner II and Jeremy S. Sabloff, "Classic Period Collapse and the Maya Lowlands: Insights About Humanity-Environment Relationships for Sustainability", *PNAS*, Vol. 109, No. 35 (28 August 2012), 13908–13914.

[70] Gill et al., "Drought and the Maya Collapse", 297.

If failure, and an inability to break through an ecological and technological "Malthusian ceiling", was the destiny of historic civilizations everywhere, then the converse applies to the modern iteration of western civilization. Its greatest achievement is found in the fact that around 1850 it permanently escaped the "Malthusian trap" as a cascading series of productivity-enhancing gains overwhelmed the constraining effects of an accelerating increase in population. This historic achievement, however, was not preordained. There is little to suggest that medieval or early modern Europe, considered as a whole, was capable of escaping the clutches of the "Malthusian trap". On the contrary, even in England, as Fig. 1.1 indicated, the only sustained improvement in living standards prior to the nineteenth century occurred because of the "Black Death" of the fourteenth century, a disaster that allowed survivors to abandon marginally productive land. As population recovered, however, the validity of Malthus's theorem was revealed; living standards reached an all-time low in 1597, the year that Shakespeare's *Midsummer Night's Dream* was first performed.[71] In 1750, the circumstances of a skilled building worker in southern England were still worse than that enjoyed by his distant ancestor at the dawn of the fifteenth century.

Why were the earlier medieval and early modern iterations of western civilization so incapable of breaching the "Malthusian ceiling", an obstacle that the modern iteration of the same civilization breached with comparative ease in the latter half of the nineteenth century?

In looking for answers to this question, which go to the very heart of our understandings of the "West", we must first abandon the idea that Europe was a cultural and sociological monolith. Rather we can distinguish within Europe four distinct political economies, all of which were in trouble to a greater or lesser degree by 1750. These distinct political economies comprised the following:

Post- or semi-feudal/peasant subsistence agriculture: Although pre-revolutionary France is popularly regarded as "feudal", in fact small-scale peasant tenant farmers had long enjoyed effective tenure of their holdings. Despite this benefit, there is reason to believe that France c. 1750 was approaching, or had already reached, a "Malthusian ceiling". Of eighteenth-century France, Braudel concluded that, even when it "could

---

[71] E.H. Phelps Brown and Sheila V. Hopkins: "Seven Centuries of the Price of Consumables, Compared with Builders' Wage Rates", *Economica*, Vol. 23, No. 92 (November 1956), 296–314.

feed its own population, it could not feed it very well", offering the vast majority of its citizens only "a hierarchy of hardship".[72] On the eve of the French Revolution, Robert Fogel estimated, 20% of the population was only able to undertake three hours of light work a day, given their calorie intake.[73] Other European societies with similar economic structures c. 1750 included Catalonia, western Germany and Scandinavia.

Agricultural societies based around large estates where peasants worked as serfs or in serf-like circumstances: Dire as circumstances were in peasant-dominated France, they were far worse in those areas dominated by vast estates, worked either by serfs, or by peasants whose condition was little better than that of a serf (southern Spain and Portugal, southern Italy, Austria–Hungary, Prussia and the German east, Poland and Russia). In Italy, a grinding process of peasant impoverishment was an inevitable result of what has been referred to as the "abrasive juxtaposition of great estates and micro-plots". At the end of the nineteenth century, two-thirds of the population of Reggio Emilia—which was by no means Italy's poorest region—were drawing charity. In Spain, the great estate was a product of the *Reconquista*, becoming a mechanism for social polarization and the debasement of an agricultural workforce who typically labored on behalf of absentee landlords. In 1900 a third of Spanish agricultural land was still owned by only 0.1% of the population.[74] It was this economic model that was transported to the New World in the form of the *encomienda*, a vast estate worked by Indian peasants under serf-life conditions; a model that quickly morphed in the Caribbean Basin and Brazil into the large commercial plantation worked by imported African slaves.[75]

Economies built around long-distance commerce and finance: With the emergence of the "Atlantic" economy in the sixteenth century,

[72] Fernand Braudel (trans. Siân Reynolds), *The Identity of France: People and Production* (London, UK: Fontana Press, 1991), 382.

[73] Robert W. Fogel, "The Conquest of High Mortality and Hunger in Europe and America: Timing and Mechanisms", in Patrice Higonnet, David S. Landes and Henry Rosovsky (eds.), *Favorites of Fortune: Technology, Growth, and Economic Development Since the Industrial Revolution* (Cambridge, MA: Harvard University Press, 1991), 45–46.

[74] Trebilcock, *Industrialization of the Continental Powers*, 332, 328.

[75] John Hemming, *The Conquest of the Inca* (London, UK: Macmillan, 1970), 145–148; Allen Wells, *Yucatan's Gilded Age: Haciendas, Henequen, and International Harvester* (Albuquerque, NM: University of New Mexico Press, 1985), 9, 19–20; Thomas, *The Slave Trade*, 96–98, 104–106.

the center of European commerce and finance decisively shifted from Italy to the Netherlands and England. As early as 1500, some 44% of Netherlands' population was associated with non-agricultural pursuits.[76] London's population also grew ten-fold between 1500 and 1700 as the city rivalled Amsterdam as a trading and financial center.[77] By the 1760s, the three million inhabitants of Britain's North American colonies could be counted alongside Great Britain's home population of eight to nine million as members of this commercialized economy. By 1800, the Netherlands and England also boasted Europe's highest literacy rates. Sixty-eight percent of the Dutch population were literate, as were 53% of England's citizens. By contrast, in Italy—the main hub for trade in the medieval and Renaissance periods—only 22% were literate in 1800.[78] Despite such achievements, however, it is easy to exaggerate both the scale and social impact of the Dutch and English commercial revolutions. In absolute terms, the tonnage carried by their merchant fleets was miniscule. In the early 1600s, the total carrying capacity of Europe's entire merchant fleet is estimated at no more than 600,000–700,000 tons.[79] This equates to the capacity of just four modern capesize ships (that is, they are too large for the Panama or Suez canals—dead weight, up to 175,000 tons), vessels that act as the workhorses of the modern merchant marine.[80] Even in 1789, when carrying capacity stood at 3.4 million tons, Europe's carrying capacity was still derisory by later industrial standards, equating to twenty modern capesize ships.[81] As the experience of Renaissance Italy had demonstrated, there is no reason to assume that commercial success led either in the direction of industrialization or a breaching of the "Malthusian ceiling". In the wake of the Renaissance, Italy went

[76] Robert Allen, "Progress and Poverty in Early Modern Europe", *Economic History Review*, Vol. 56, No. 3 (2003), 408; Bas J.P. van Bavel and Jan Luiten van Zanden, "The Jump-Start of the Holland Economy During the Late-Medieval Crises, c.1350–c.1500", *Economic History Review*, Vol. 58, No. 3 (2004), 503–532.

[77] Ralph Davis, "English Foreign Trade, 1770–1774", *Economic History Review*, Vol. 15, No. 2 (1962), 285–303; Allen, *British Industrial Revolution in Global Perspective*, 16.

[78] Allen, "Progress and Poverty", 408.

[79] Fernand Braudel (trans. Sian Reynolds), *Civilization and Capitalism, 15th–18th Century: The Structures of Everyday Life* (London, UK: Collins, 1981), 362.

[80] G. Polo, "On Marine Transport Costs, Evolution, and Forecasts", *Ship, Science and Technology*, Vol. 5, No. 10 (2012), 1–31.

[81] Braudel, *Capitalism and Material Life*, 265.

backwards economically, not forwards. Similarly, in the Netherlands, the society's "Golden Age" (1570–1870) was "followed by a period of technological stagnation, characteristic of Malthusian economies".[82] In the late 1700s, life expectancy at birth in London—"the largest, busiest, and wealthiest metropolis in the world"[83]—was but 23 years.[84]

Emerging Industrial Economy Model: Of all the factors that worked to maintain a "Malthusian ceiling", none was arguably more significant than a near universal reliance on wood: wood for heating, cooking, houses, ships, plows, charcoal for iron smelting and a myriad of other uses. In Paris on the eve of the Revolution it is estimated that the city burned 2 tons of wood per inhabitant per year; a demand that remorselessly stripped ever-more distant forests.[85] In the mid-eighteenth century only three regions showed evidence of reducing their dependency on wood and moving toward an energy-intensive industrial economy: the Netherlands, England and southern Belgium. The fact that two of these regions—the Netherlands and England—were also Europe's most commercialized is more coincidental than causal. The commercial success of the Netherlands was primarily dependent upon its maritime prowess, whereas its industrial capacity was associated with its peat bogs. In England, the focal point for the emerging energy-intensive economy was not London and the south-east, but rather the Tyne and Wear valleys, the world's preeminent source of coal. By 1710, it was probable that the "entire production of the rest of the world did not perhaps amount to much more than a sixth of that of Great Britain".[86]

In considering the overall performance of the four European political economies that existed c. 1750, the evidence to support claims that any of them were riding a wave of prosperity underpinned by slave labor in the Americas, foreign commerce or any other factor is underwhelming.

Evidence of the dire circumstances that European societies found themselves in is indicated in Fig. 1.6. Drawn from Broadberry and

---

[82] Gregory Clark, *A Farewell to Alms: A Brief Economic History of the World* (Princeton, NJ: Princeton University Press, 2007), 93.

[83] Cipolla, *Before the Industrial Revolution*, 293.

[84] Clark, *A Farewell to Alms*, 93.

[85] Fernand Braudel (trans. Sian Reynolds), *The Wheels of Commerce: Civilization and Capitalism, 15th–18th Century*, vol. 2 (London, UK: Collins, 1982), 367.

[86] John Nef, *The Rise of the British Coal Industry*, vol. 2 (London, UK: Frank Cass & Co., 1932), 187.

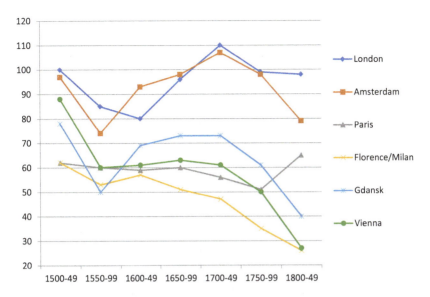

Fig. 1.6 Real consumption wage index for unskilled building laborers, 1500–1849 (London, 1500–1549 = 100) (*Source* Broadberry and Gupta, "The early modern great divergence", 7)

Gupta's comparative study, Fig. 1.7 traces the fluctuations in the real wage of unskilled building laborers located in the four political economies we have considered: Paris (semi-feudal and subsistence farming), Florence and Milan (combination of subsistence farming and large estates), Gdansk, Vienna (large estates), Amsterdam (commerce and finance) and London (both commerce and finance, and emerging economy).[87] As is self-evident, building laborers who earned a living in societies associated with either subsistence farming (Paris), large estates (Gdansk, Vienna) or a combination of the two (Florence and Milan) witnessed a deterioration in their real wage. While the Parisian situation improved after 1800, that found in Florence and Milan, Gdansk and Vienna did not. Although Amsterdam and London outperformed their more rurally oriented counterparts throughout the entire 350-year period, real wages in both cities were declining by 1750. While real wages in London stabilized after 1800,

---

[87] Broadberry and Gupta, "The Early Modern Great Divergence", 7.

those in Amsterdam did not. There was, in short, little to suggest that "Europe" or the "West" was on the verge of decisively breaking-through the "Malthusian ceiling" that condemned most to a life of privatization. That a new iteration of western civilization was able to achieve this result was thus a surprising development, one that developed from a unique combination of economic and social attributes that gained general sway in the middle decades of the nineteenth century.

THE WINTER OF WESTERN CIVILIZATION?

In his *Decline of the West*, Oswald Spengler concluded, as has been previously noted, that the modern industrialized iteration of western civilization was a continuation of an earlier manifestation of western civilization, but distinct from it. Spengler also believed, however, that this new industrialization iteration was not so much a culmination of the West's historic potential but rather a final decay. If the centuries between AD 900 and AD 1100 represented the West's springtime, a time associated with Germanic myth and spiritual independence, then the nineteenth and twentieth centuries were a cultural and spiritual winter.[88] On every front, Spengler lamented, one could detect a cultural failing, a loss of dynamism and "existence without Inner Form". Socially, "the position of the individual vis-à-vis the State" was increasingly circumscribed. Even "Nature" was "exhausted, the globe sacrificed" to a "Faustian" pact with the machine.[89]

A fifth of the way through the twenty-first century, the sense that we are living in the winter of a fading civilization has arguably never been more pronounced. Increasingly, in both academia and the wider society, we are informed that western civilization embodies not freedom and human progress but rather racism, environmental degradation, and exploitation and inequality on an unprecedented scale. We thus read that every supporter of western civilization has "blood" on "their hands",[90]

---

[88] Oswald Spengler (trans. Charles Francis Atkinson), *The Decline of the West*, revised edition (New York: Alfred A. Knopf, 1927), 506, Table 2.

[89] Ibid., 48, 469–70, 505.

[90] Nick Riemer, "Weaponising Learning", *Sydney Review of Books* (12 June 2018), 6, 11, https://sydneyreviewofbooks.com/essay/weaponising-learning/.

1 INTRODUCTION: CIVILIZATION AND LIVED EXPERIENCE   37

that "the white dominant culture" is premised on an "essential racism",[91] that "whiteness is the institutionalization of European colonialism",[92] that "life on Earth is in crisis", that we are facing "crop failure", "mass extinction" and "social and ecological collapse".[93]

In the face of such condemnations and doom-laden prophecies it is useful to provide some balance. By the 1930s, as noted in Fig. 1.1, the real wages of British workers were infinitely superior to those found in any previous epoch. It is also a fallacy to believe that the benefits of increased prosperity are confined to a fortunate few in the "first world". As we note in our final chapter, the World Bank estimates that between 1961 and 2018 the population of "low-income countries" rose 2.8-fold to 6.3 billion. During the same period, cereal output in this category of nations rose more than 5.2-fold to 2.2 billion metric tons. Evidence of a generalized improvement in the human condition is also found in the United Nations' Human Development Index (HDI)—an index supplemented by estimates of historic circumstance undertaken by Nicholas Crafts and others. Giving weight to life expectancy and levels of education as well as per capita GDP, a cross-national perusal of HDI outcomes—such as provided in Fig. 1.7—is revealing for two reasons. Most obvious is the universal advance, indicative of a sustained, global improvement in the human condition. Second, we can observe a marked closing of the gap between leaders and laggards.[94]

[91] Ruth Frankenberg, *White Women, Race Matters: The Social Construction of Whiteness* (Minneapolis, MN: University of Minnesota Press, 1993), 14.

[92] Birgit Brander Rasmussen, Eric Klinenberg, Irene J. Nexica and Matt Wray, "Introduction", in Birgit Brander Rasmussen, Eric Klinenberg, Irene J. Nexica and Matt Wray (eds.), *The Making and Unmaking of Whiteness* (Durham, NC: Duke University Press, 2001), 13.

[93] Extinction Rebellion, *This Is an Emergency*, https://rebellion.global/ [accessed 18 December 2021].

[94] Nicholas Crafts, "The Human Development Index 1870–1999: Some Research Estimates", *European Review of Economic History*, Vol. 6, No. 2 (2002), 395–405; United Nations Development Programme, *Human Development Report, 2019* (New York: New York Development Programme, 2019), Table 2. Historic HDI calculations are also found in: Richard Floyd and Bernard Harris, "Health, Height, and Welfare: Britain, 1700–1980", in Richard H. Steckel and Roderick Floud (eds.), *Health and Welfare During Industrialization* (Chicago, IL: University of Chicago Press, 1997), 91–126.

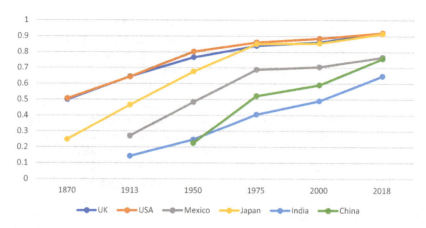

Fig. 1.7 Human Development Index, selected countries, 1870–2018 (*Sources* Crafts, "Human Development Index 1870–1999", 396—for years 1870–1975; United Nations Development Programme, *Human Development Report, 2019*, Table 2—for years 2000–2018)

Of all the changes wrought by the new civilization on the economic front, few proved as momentous as those in relation to slavery and the slave trade.

In reflecting upon the new patterns of work heralded by the Industrial Revolution, the Austro-British management historian Sidney Pollard correctly observed that the need "to control" highly mobile workforces "without powers of compulsion … was not only one of the marked characteristics of the new capitalism, but one of its seminal ideas".[95] Such principles seem innocuous enough. In the early nineteenth century, however, they conflicted with accepted norms of work and economic organization almost everywhere. Nowhere was this more obvious than in relation to the hoary institution of slavery. Accordingly, if one has to choose the seminal event that defined the new iteration of western civilization there is good reason to choose Britain's abolition of the slave trade in 1807 rather than either the American Declaration of Independence (1776) or the French Declaration of Rights (1789).

---

[95] Sidney Pollard, *The Genesis of Modern Management: A Study of the Industrial Revolution in Great Britain* (London, UK: Edward Arnold, 1965), 6–7.

For although, in the popular imagination, slavery is associated with the cotton plantations of the American South, human bondage was in truth endemic in the New World as well as the Old, long before Columbus discovered the Americas. In recording life in pre-conquest Aztec society in their native Nahuatl, for example, adult survivors of this once great civilization remembered the revered place in which "slave traders" were held, and the elaborate procedures that they undertook to maximize the price obtained "in the market place".[96] Of the circumstances that prevailed in Africa in the year that Britain abolished the slave trade, Thomas observed in his history of the Atlantic trade, "There were ... more slaves in Africa in 1807 than in the Americas ... Among the Ashanti, the most powerful of the kingdoms in Guinea, every man of property had slaves".[97] Yes, it is true that Britain did not abolish slavery in its own colonies until 1834. But, even before the passage of the anti-slave trade legislation, an increasingly urbanized, literate and mobile population had come to see involvement in slavery as the domain of the morally bereft. Nor was the passage of the British anti-slave law a token gesture. Immediately the new legislation came into effect a naval squadron was dispatched to Africa, empowered to intercept slave ships of whatever nationality. By 1870, when Spain ended Cuba's slave trade—the last significant destination for Atlantic slavers—an estimated 200,000 slaves had been freed by the British-led squadrons.[98]

The fact that the new iteration of western civilization entailed freedom and the abolition of slavery does not mean that it did not also bring destruction, loss and wrenching dislocation in its wake. Across the globe, traditional modes of existence as a villager or hunter-gatherer were subject to utter destruction. Even today, the circumstances of Indigenous communities within the most prosperous societies leave much to be desired. Writing of the Australian situation in 2021, Jacinta Price—a Warlpiri woman who currently serves as Deputy Mayor for Alice Springs, the gateway to the iconic Uluru (Ayer's Rock)—laments the fact that the Indigenous school attendance rate (63%) in Australia's remote and very remote areas was "below countries such as Zambia (69%) and war-torn

[96] Fray Bernardino de Sahagun, ed. (trans. Charles E. Dibble and Arthur J.O. Anderson), *Florentine Codex: Book 9—The Merchants* (Salt Lake City, UT: University of Utah Press, 1959), 23–24.

[97] Thomas, *Slave Trade*, 559–560.

[98] Ibid., 784.

Iraq".[99] Of the domestic violence that is rampant in Australian Indigenous communities, Price observed in an earlier study, "Ngajurlangu – 'Me Too'":

> My Aboriginal sisters, aunts, mothers, nieces and daughters live this crisis every day. There is not a woman in my family who has not experienced some kind of physical or sexual abuse at some time in her life. And none of the perpetrators were white.[100]

For many (if not most) Indigenous people, as well as for much of the wider society, the culprit responsible for the disadvantage that Price describes is unquestionable; it is a western civilization that can never deliver justice to Indigenous peoples. Significantly, this is not a viewpoint shared by Price and many other Indigenous leaders in Australia. Pointing to the violence she and other female family members have suffered, Price asserts the fact that:

> Aboriginal women and children are Australian citizens and they must be able to make the same choices as other citizens. Aboriginal activists campaigned for decades for my people to have the full rights of citizens. Now we have them ... If Australian citizens are in danger of abuse and neglect they deserve to be protected, not on the basis of their culture, but on the basis of their human rights.[101]

Whether one agrees with Price's analysis or not it points to the key cultural, social and political difference between the modern iteration of western civilization and most other historic and contemporary societies: it is premised on individual expressions of identity, on equality before the law, and an unmediated relationship between the individual and a state-endorsed system of rights and obligations. The most *fundamental* choice involved in accepting or rejecting the new iteration of western civilization has thus *always* entailed a choice between collective and individual identity. Do you *primarily* see yourself as Warlpiri, Lakota or African American in ways that permanently align your sense of identity with the

---

[99] Jacinta Nampijinpa Price, *Worlds Apart: Remote Indigenous Disadvantage in the Context of Wider Australia* (Sydney, AUS: Centre for Independent Studies, 2021), 2.

[100] Jacinta Nampijinpa Price, "Ngajurlangu—Me Too", *Meanjin* (Summer 2018), 132.

[101] Price, "Ngajurlangu—Me Too", 135.

collective interests of these group-based expressions of identity? Or, alternatively, do you believe your identity is unique, something personal to you?

Even within the old western heartlands the idea that each individual has, or should have, a unique set of concerns and interests that are distinct from any collective has always been contested. In the late nineteenth and early twentieth centuries, many identified their interests with socialist movements. In the 1930s, Germany's Nazi regime propagated a race-based sense of collective identity, persuading many Germans that they had more in common with their Swedish "Aryan" counterparts than their Jewish or Polish neighbors. In the twenty-first century, new expressions of identity associated with race, ethnicity, gender and sexual preference hold increasing sway.

Reflecting on these trends in 1994, Christopher Lasch lamented that the United States had become "a nation of minorities". Central to this development (which is now evident in virtually every advanced economy), Lasch observed, was the belief that each "minority" is victim to "white Eurocentric males", a "dominant" group that imposes its "self-serving readings on everybody else". Also seen as a foe "is western culture as a whole ... the very notion of a common tradition or common civic language".[102] Increasingly, collective expressions of identity are embedded into the very fabric of society. In the Californian State Board of Education's *Ethnic Studies Model Curriculum*, for example, students are advised that one's "personal identity" is a product of "group identification" and the "intersectionality" of the "social groups" one belongs to on the basis of "race", "ethnicity", "sex, religion, class, ability or disability, age, sexual orientation, gender identity", and so on.[103] In their highly influential *Critical Race Theory: An Introduction*, Delgado and Stefancic similarly insist that "old-fashioned" concepts of "merit" be erased in favor of policies that facilitate "upward mobility for minority populations", that "minority viewpoints and interests" be "taken into account, as though by second nature, in every major policy decision".[104]

---

[102] Christopher Lasch, *The Revolt of the Elites and the Betrayal of Democracy* (New York, NY: W.W. Norton & Co., 1995), 17, 12, 133.

[103] California State Board of Education, *Ethnic Studies Model Curriculum: Introduction and Overview* (Sacramento, CA: California State Board of Education, 2021), 16.

[104] Richard Delgado and Jean Stefancic, *Critical Race Theory: An Introduction* (New York and London: New York University Press, 2001), 132.

There is an obvious historic precedent for the institutionalized preferencing of group-based manifestations of identity—Ottoman Turkey and the *millet* system that granted legal and cultural autonomy to each major religious and ethnic group within Turkish society (for example, Greek Orthodox, Armenian Christians, and so on). In recent years the Turkish *millet* system has been idealized as a model expression of "multiculturalism". We are thus informed that it "liberated the non-Muslim groups from the homogenizing logic of majority identity", that it embodied "liberality and tolerance", that it was premised on a benign rejection of cultural "sameness".[105] In truth, each *millet* was an intellectual and spiritual prison. As an individual, it was impossible to have ideas that were at odds with those mandated by one's *millet*. Nor could one behave in ways that were at odds with those of the *millet*. Rather than embody multiculturalism and mutual respect, the *millet* system also institutionalized group-based division and rivalry. The appearance of harmony existed only so long as the iron hand of the Ottoman state kept every group in its allotted place. Once the authority of the Ottoman state fell away, each *millet* sought to defend its interests and restrict those of its rivals. The result was the savage Balkan wars of the early twentieth century and the Armenian Genocide.

On every front we can today witness what this book refers to as the "milletization" of society. Increasingly, individuals are expected to conform to the perceived interests of the identity group, or *millet*, to which they belong. People who do not may find themselves condemned as prisoners of "white [male] identity politics" and "white [male] racial framing".[106]

As in late nineteenth century Turkey, there is today no iron hand to restrain intergroup rivalry and the competition for jobs, university places and political and social power. Accordingly, there is a divisive intergroup struggle. In proclaiming opposition to the dominant "white establishment", for example, Delgado and Stefancic's work on *Critical Race*

---

[105] Ebubekir Ceylan, "The *Millet* System in the Ottoman Empire", in Judi Upton-Ward (ed.), *New Millennium Perspectives in the Humanities* (Provo, UT: Brigham Young University Press, 2002), 246; Karen Barkey and George Gavrilis, "The Ottoman *Millet* System: Non-territorial Autonomy and Its Contemporary Legacy", *Ethnopolitics*, Vol. 15, No. 1 (2016), 24; Halil Inalcik, *The Ottoman Empire: The Classical Age 1300–1600* (London, UK: Weidenfeld and Nicolson, 1973), 7.

[106] Joe R. Feagin, *The White Racial Frame: Centuries of Racial Framing and Counter-framing*, third edition (New York and London: Routledge, 2020), 272.

Theory calls on each identity group "to marshal every conceivable argument, exploit every chink, crack, and glimmer of interest convergence" in their struggles for self-expression and empowerment.[107] In the opinion of Feagin, Delgado and Stefancic and like-minded thinkers, all "minority" groups (such as African Americans, Hispanics, Asian Americans, Muslims, gays) share a commonality or "intersectionality" of interests in ways that ensure unity against the dominant "white" culture.

Such beliefs are, at best, naïve. Once jobs and other means of advancement are allocated based on group membership, rather than merit, an unseemly rivalry between "minorities" becomes inevitable. In the US legal case, *Students for Fair Admissions Inc. v President & Fellows of Harvard College,* for example, the Students for Fair Admissions—a body largely composed of Asian Americans and Americans boasting a Pacific Islander ancestry—pointed to Harvard's "invidious discrimination against Asian Americans". "Each year", it was noted, "Harvard admits and enrolls essentially the same percentage of African Americans, Hispanics, whites, and Asian Americans even though the application rates and qualifications for each racial group have undergone significant change over time". Thus, whereas Asian Americans now comprise up to 46% of academically qualified applicants, they never make up more than 18% of enrolled students.[108] Lodged in 2014, and currently before the US Supreme Court, the Students for Fair Admission's complaint is but one of many such cases working their way through the American legal system.

The growing *milletization* of society is both a cause and a symptom of the loss of dynamism that is now evident in virtually every advanced economy. As a social and cultural trend, the *milletization* of society diminishes the role of markets and hence the need for innovation. It shifts the focus of activity from the individual to the collective, undermining individual initiative and entrepreneurship. At the same time, *milletization* feeds on the problems that were evident long before the COVID-19 pandemic that began in 2020: stagnant real wages, stagnant or declining multifactor productivity and falling levels of labor force participation. Confronted with such problems it is easy to conclude that one's personal difficulties are due to systematic discrimination. It is also easy to conclude

---

[107] Delgado and Stefancic, *Critical Race Theory*, 133.

[108] District of Massachusetts (Boston Division) District Court, *Students for Fair Admissions Inc. v President & Fellows of Harvard College* (Boston, MA: District of Massachusetts (Boston Division) District Court, 2014), 4, 70.

that the problems that beset us are best redressed by state mandates and further curtailments of market forces in favor of the "disadvantaged"— "solutions" that diminish even further the need for innovation, individual initiative and entrepreneurship.

Amid the problems that beset us are we thus, as Spengler believed, people born into the winter of a fading civilization that is doomed to a downward spiral that can only end in cultural extinction?[109] Or, alternatively, does another springtime beckon, a renaissance associated with a reassertion of the principles upon which the modern iteration of western civilization was built: individualism, a preferencing of individual choice and markets, entrepreneurship, economic and political liberalism? Neither outcome is preordained. Rather, as in the past, the outcomes that prevail will result from the choices we make.

---

[109] Spengler, *Decline of the West*, 44, 39.

PART I

The Quests that Created a New Western Civilization (and Destroyed Others): Crops, Climate, Calories

The transition from hunter-gathering to an existence based around settled agriculture was one of the defining shifts in the human experience. It was upon the raising of crops—most particularly wheat, rice and corn—that the civilizations of the Old World and New were built. Agrarian-based civilizations were, however, profoundly affected by the crops they raised, each bringing with it its own set of benefits and perils. Everywhere, agricultural societies found themselves exposed to climatic change to a far greater extent than were hunter-gathering communities. Agricultural societies also found it difficult to break out of a "Malthusian trap" as increases in output produced more people rather than improved living standards. As increased population outstripped available resources, moreover, every gain in population eventually led to a decline in living standards and, ultimately, a collapse in population. The typical result was a bitter cycle of population collapse, recovery and collapse. In exploring this conundrum, Part 1 traces how a new iteration of western civilization arose from this challenge.

CHAPTER 2

The 3-Cs: Crops, Climate, Calories

On 12 April 1961, the Soviet cosmonaut Yuri Gagarin became the first person to orbit the Earth. What he saw beneath him was both awe-inspiring and troubling. For while Gagarin's education had emphasized Soviet superiority in all things, it was plainly evident that the night-time skies of the West were filled with city lights, whereas those of Russia and the Eastern Bloc were largely shrouded in darkness. If Gagarin had orbited the Earth 160 years earlier, in the midst of what we think of as the Industrial Revolution, he would have witnessed a world where night-time darkness was an almost universal attribute. Only London, a city of one million people that had long sourced its lighting and heating from coal, would have stood out. Elsewhere in Britain the only twinkling would have come the new industrial cities of the north (Liverpool, Manchester, Birmingham), none of which could boast a population of 100,000. In North America, little would have attracted his attention. New York, the continent's largest city, was home to barely 60,000. If Gagarin's orbit had taken place a century further back, the sources of night-time light would have been fewer and fainter. Even London would have appeared but dimly. For, despite its coal-fired hearths, London in 1700 was home to only 500,000 people. Any further back in time and Gagarin would have passed over a world where almost total darkness enveloped night-time life.

© The Author(s), under exclusive license to Springer Nature
Switzerland AG 2022
B. Bowden, *Slavery, Freedom and Business Endeavor*,
Palgrave Debates in Business History,
https://doi.org/10.1007/978-3-030-97232-5_2

48   B. BOWDEN

Writing of the lived experience that characterized medieval Europe, the French historian, Marc Bloch, recorded:

> ... behind all social life there was a background of the primitive, of submission to uncontrollable forces, of unrelieved physical constraints ... The wild animals that that now only haunt our nursery tales – bears and, above all, wolves – prowled in every wilderness.[1]

In trying to understand the ways in which civilizations have grappled with the problems of forging a living from the natural world, the historian of today enjoys advantages over those of yesteryear. Foremost among these are advances in the study of diet and skeletal health, forensic anthropology, climatology, and of comparative well-being across cultures and civilizations.

Our understanding of fluctuations in real wages also benefits from the platform created by the International Scientific Committee on Price History. Established in 1929, and funded by the Rockefeller Foundation, this Committee created an extensive European database, recording the real wage of building workers, both skilled and unskilled, between the thirteenth and twentieth centuries.[2] In building on the Committee's work, historians have used two methodologies. The first of these, which replicates the work of the Committee, is based on a constant basket of consumables (which includes rent, food, heating, clothing and so on). Real wages are then expressed as an index, which compares what percentage of the basket a person could purchase at one point in time with another.[3] The second methodology is based on the concept of a "grain wage". This estimates how many kilograms of wheat, or the calorific equivalent in other grains, a worker could buy if they spent all their income on grain purchases.

Compared with these estimations of real wages, the calculation of an historic GDP per capita is a more difficult proposition. Not only does it

---

[1] Marc Bloch (trans. L.A. Manyon), *Feudal Society*, Second edition (London, UK: Routledge & Kegan Paul, 1962), 72.

[2] For history of the Committee, see Arthur H. Cole and Ruth Crandall, "The International Scientific Committee on Price History", *Journal of Economic History*, Vol. 24, No. 3 (1964), 381–388.

[3] The most notable estimate of real wages to emerge from the Committee was, E.H. Phelps Brown and Sheila V. Hopkins: "Seven Centuries of the Price of Consumables, compared with Builders' Wage Rates", *Economica*, Vol. 23, No. 92 (1956), 296–314.

require a population estimate, it also requires a valuation of all the goods and services produced during a year—calculations that can never be more than "guesstimates".

Collectively, studies of fluctuations in health, life expectancy, height and real wages have cast doubt on assumptions as to the superiority of living standards in pre-industrial Western Europe when compared to elsewhere. After studying changes in the height of indentured servants emigrating to colonial America, John Komlos, for example, concluded that "the height of the lower segment of the English population was probably beginning to decline *prior* to the beginning of the Industrial Revolution".[4] Such indicators, Komlos added, were proof of "an incipient Malthusian crisis" in which "agricultural output and food imports did not keep pace with ... the number of mouths to feed".[5]

If the "anthropometric history" that Komlos helped pioneer caused a questioning of the pre-industrial West's supposed material advantages, so too has the "Great Divergence Debate" initiated by Kenneth Pomeranz. For in seeking to contradict his argument that there were few fundamental differences between Europe and the advanced civilizations of Asia prior to 1800,[6] Pomeranz's opponents came to conclusions that were in many ways more substantive than those made by Pomeranz himself. Thus, whereas Pomeranz emphasized similarities between Europe and Asia in terms of "sophisticated agriculture, commerce, and nonmechanized industry",[7] Allen et al.'s study of real wages pointed to commonalities of misery. Even in the early decades of the nineteenth century, Allen et al. conclude, it "was only England and the Low Countries that pulled ahead of the rest"—a finding which they correctly suggest "calls into question the fundamental tenet of the large 'rise of the West' literature that sees western Europe – as a whole – surpassing the rest of the world in the early modern era".[8]

---

[4] John Komlos, "A Malthusian Episode Revisited: The Height of British and Irish Servants in Colonial America", *Economic History Review*, Vol. 46, No. 4 (1993), 780.

[5] John Komlos, "The Secular Trend in the Biological Standard of Living in the United Kingdom, 1730–1860", *Economic History Review*, Vol. 46, No. 1 (1993), 7364.

[6] Kenneth Pomeranz, *The Great Divergence: China, Europe, and the Making of the Modern World Economy* (Princeton, NJ: Princeton University Press, 2000), 1.

[7] Ibid., 12.

[8] Robert C. Allen, Jean-Pascal Bassino, Debin Ma, Christine Moll-Murata and Jan Luiten Van Zanden, "Wages, Prices, and Living Standards in China, 1738–1925: In

The shift in the ways in which the lived experience of the pre-industrial West has come to be perceived is exemplified by the conclusions articulated in Gregory Clark's *A Farewell to Alms: A Brief Economic History of the World*. Guided in part by the new studies emerging from anthropometric history, Clark argues that even in comparatively "wealthy societies such as eighteenth-century England or the Netherlands" most of the population "managed a material lifestyle equivalent to that of the Stone Age".[9] Yes, Clark willingly conceded, the transformations initiated by the Industrial Revolution did irreversibly alter the human condition *after* 1800. In Clark's opinion, however, the circumstances that prevailed after the Industrial Revolution should not blind us to pre-industrial reality.[10]

If there is evidentiary support for Clark's conclusions there is nevertheless also room for caution. The debate as to the state of living standards around the time of the Industrial Revolution is, after all, long and tortured. In many ways, Clark's conclusions merely return us to our point of departure, Malthus's *Essay on the Principles of Population*, a study in which it was argued that any significant population increase invariably overstrains resources, reducing "real" wages "to the level of subsistence". As Malthus himself explained it, "The natural inequality of the two powers of population and of production" are such that no society "can escape from the weight of this law"—a "law" that perpetually gives "human life a melancholy hue".[11] In other words, every society eventually confronts a "Malthusian ceiling" that causes per capita gains in productive capacity and wealth to stall in the face of rising population pressures on scant resources. The fact that mass misery was a lived reality in early nineteenth-century Britain should not, however, blind us to evidence of not only economic progress but also substantial alterations in lived experience. As noted in this book's introduction, real wages for unskilled laborers in London and Amsterdam in the late sixteenth and early seventeenth centuries began an ascent that put them on a fundamentally different trajectory to that found in Southern and Central Europe. While it is

Comparison with Europe, Japan, and India", *Economic History Review*, Vol. 64, No. 1 (2011), 38.

[9] Gregory Clark, *A Farewell to Alms: A Brief Economic History of the World* (Princeton, NJ: Princeton University Press, 2007), 1.

[10] Ibid., 30–31.

[11] Thomas Malthus, *An Essay on the Principles of Population* (London, UK: J. Johnson, 1798), 10, vii–viii.

true that real wages in both London and Amsterdam were *falling* by the latter half of the eighteenth century, the circumstances of unskilled laborers in these commercial metropolises were nevertheless far superior to those found elsewhere. In both cities in 1750–1799, real wages were almost three times higher than those obtained in Florence and Milan, and almost double those received in Vienna.[12]

The contradictory evidence before us is also apparent when we consider the most basic issue in lived experience: life expectancy. In this domain, work in forensic archaeology allows us to broaden our field of inquiry from early modern Europe and Asia to include societies found in both European antiquity and pre-Columbian America. In considering pre-Columbian America, however, we must first remind ourselves of the extraordinary achievements of its civilizations. In the early seventh century AD, Teotihuacan in Central Mexico boasted a population of at least 120,000, making it the sixth-largest city in the world. Large urban concentrations also characterized the Moche civilization of coastal Peru (c. AD 100–AD 800), the Maya (c. 500 BC–c. AD 930), the Aztecs (c. 1345–1521), the Inca (c. 1250–1533), the *pueblo*-dwelling communities of the North American southwest (c. AD 800–present) and the agricultural societies of the Mississippi Valley (c. AD 800–AD 1600).

All these societies benefited from operating in an environment that was virtually free of the infectious epidemics that continually devastated Eurasian populations. We would therefore expect that these societies would have boasted healthy populations; however, this was not the case. Instead, Fig. 2.1—which considers life expectancy in Roman Egypt (both urban and rural), medieval Italy, Beijing (c. 1644–c. 1739), Teotihuacan (c. AD 600), the Pre-Columbian Dickson Mound communities of the Illinois Valley of the United States (c. AD 800), England (1550–1599 and 1750–1799) and London (1750–1799) when compared with those currently enjoyed in Peru and the United States—indicates there was remarkably little variation in life expectancy across time and across civilizations.[13] Invariably, life expectancy was less in towns and greater in the

---

[12] For details, see Stephen Broadberry and Bishnupriya Gupta, "The Early Modern Great Divergence: Wages, Prices and Economic Development in Europe and Asia, 1500–1800", *Economic History Review*, Vol. 49, No. 1 (2006), 7: Table 3.

[13] Figures for Roman Egypt, Medieval Italy, Beijing, England and London are drawn from Clark, *A Farewell to Alms*, 94–95, Table 5.2, Table 5.3; figures for Teotihuacan and Dickson Mounds from Rebecca Storey, "An Estimate of Mortality in a Pre-Columbian

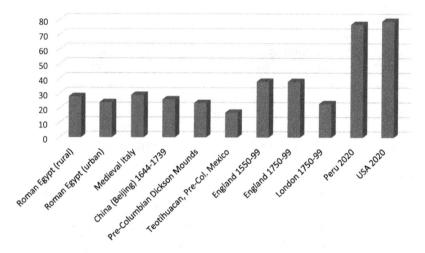

Fig. 2.1 Life expectancy in pre-industrial and modern populations (*Sources* Clark, *Farewell to Alms*, Tables 5.2, 5.3; Storey, "Mortality in a Pre-Columbian Urban Population", Tables 6, 9; UN Development Programme, *Human Development Report 2020*, Table 1)

countryside, seeming proof of Malthus's observation that "great cities" were "the graves of mankind". In 1750–1799, life expectancy in London (23 years) was 15 years less than that enjoyed by England as a whole (38 years). In pre-Columbian Teotihuacan, life expectancy was a miserable 17 years, its public sewerage system incapable of protecting its population from malnourishment and contaminated water.[14] To the extent that there is a stand-out performer across time and space it is pre-industrial England. The fact that England's life expectancy failed to improve across the two centuries between 1550–1599 and 1750–1799, however, is also indicative of a society that had reached a "Malthusian ceiling".

What is it that explains not only the incapacity of the historic "West" but of all civilizations to break through a Malthusian ceiling that

Urban Population", *American Anthropologist*, Vol. 87, No. 3 (1983), 526, 528, 530, Table 6, Table 9; figures for modern-day Peru and the United States from United Nations Development Programme, *Human Development Report 2020* (New York: United Nations Development Programme, 2020), 341–342, Table 1.

[14] Storey, "Mortality in a Pre-Columbian Urban Population", 522, 532.

condemned the vast majority in *every* pre-industrial society to a premature death? The answer, it is suggested, is found in the interrelationship of the 3-Cs: crops, climate and calories. If crops (most particularly wheat, rice and corn) were the backbone of civilizations, climate acted as the destroyer of not only crops but of entire civilizations. At the same time, in every civilization, the search for new sources of calorific energy—not only for human energy but also for heating, cooking, smelting and manufacturing—acted as the driver of human endeavor and innovation.

Through its exploration of the ways in which the 3-Cs fostered, destroyed and transformed civilizations, Part 1 engages in three principal tasks:

- In Chapter 3, we explore the ways in which wheat, rice and corn (maize) both underpinned and bound the settled societies of Eurasia, North Africa and the Americas. Despite the bounty provided by these three crops, the limited yields that they provided ensured that *every* pre-industrial society that relied upon them was caught in a "Malthusian trap" in which population and per capita income moved in an inverse relationship.

- In examining the ways in which climate constantly threatened both crops and the civilizations that depended upon them, in Chapter 4 we pay special heed to two underlying variables—the North Atlantic Oscillation and the El Niño–Southern Oscillation. While the former held the societies of the Atlantic littoral zones in its paw, bringing alternating patterns of warm and cold to Western Europe and fluctuating cycles of rain and drought to Central America, the latter controlled the monsoon rains of the Indian and Pacific Oceans. In the case of the Maya civilization of Central America, climatic variation was utterly destructive, rendering damage from which the society never recovered. By contrast, the damage inflicted on Western Europe's medieval civilization in the fourteenth century was both destructive and transformative, creating an "early modern" commercial civilization that was neither "medieval" nor "modern".

- For this "early modern" civilization, as we observe in Chapter 5, the pursuit of new forms of calorific energy (wind, water, peat, coal) proved troublesome but also rewarding, ultimately offering humanity a way out of the "Malthusian trap" that had previously bound it, creating a new, industrializing iteration of "western" civilization.

In short, we can perceive across time and space a common struggle, by societies everywhere, to provide for the needs of their population. Like other civilizations, the medieval iteration of western civilization faltered in the face of these challenges, just as the western civilization of classical antiquity had faltered. Where, however, the civilization of classical antiquity experienced a near total collapse, the medieval iteration of western civilization was transformed into a more technologically sophisticated and inquiring society that gave birth to a new, early modern iteration of western civilization. As this civilization also found itself pressing against a technological Malthusian ceiling in the eighteenth century, a small part of it—initially associated with industrializing Britain and, to a lesser degree, the Netherlands—provided new solutions to old problems, becoming the basis for a new metal-intensive and energy-intensive civilization.

By happenstance, these technological and economic breakthroughs occurred in those parts of the early modern western civilization that were also associated with emerging patterns of representative democracy, individual rights and liberties, and a free-market version of capitalism. Theoretically, the decisive breakthroughs associated with iron making, coal production, machine-tool manufacturing and shipping could equally have come from more authoritarian European societies. If such an outcome would have eventuated, it would have produced a profoundly different iteration of "western" civilization to the one that eventually prevailed.

CHAPTER 3

Crops and the Shaping of Civilizations

The most fundamental task of any society is one of ensuring the biological survival of its members; a challenge which in the final analysis comes down to the provision of calories. And, although the minimum caloric intake needed to ensure physical survival is in the range of 1,200 to 1,500 calories—far less than the 3,500 calories typically consumed each day in the modern world—such an intake needs to be exceeded by a reasonable margin if a worker is to make a productive contribution. Historically, hunter-gatherer societies obtained calories from a diversity of sources: animal game, fishing, wild fruit and vegetables. Settled, urbanized societies, however, demanded a more reliable source of calories.

Invariably, in every civilization across the Eurasian, American and African continents, urban societies relied on the performance of three grain crops: wheat (predominant in Europe, North Africa, the Middle East, northern India, northern China); rice (southern India, southern China, Southeast Asia); and corn or maize (the Americas). Even today, these three grains dominate global agriculture and food chains. In 2019–2020, corn was the most prolific crop with a production total of 1,116 million metric tons, followed by wheat (764 million metric tons) and rice

© The Author(s), under exclusive license to Springer Nature Switzerland AG 2022
B. Bowden, *Slavery, Freedom and Business Endeavor*,
Palgrave Debates in Business History,
https://doi.org/10.1007/978-3-030-97232-5_3

55

(496 million metric tons). Barley, principally used for beer production and animal feed, came a poor fourth with 156 million metric tons.[1]

Yes, it is true, that certain New World crops, most particularly potatoes, began to make a significant contribution to some regional diets by the eighteenth century. In Europe, Flanders, and more particularly Ireland, adopted the potato with enthusiasm. However, although an acre of potatoes could deliver twice the calories as an acre of wheat or rice, it suffered from several problems. Not only did it have a lower protein content than wheat, its bulk and short storage life also made it unsuitable for long-distance transport and urban storage. While all early modern societies had a range of other foods available to them, these were invariably in much shorter supply (and hence more expensive) than grain. In pre-revolutionary France, calories obtained from bread were eleven times cheaper than those from meat and six times cheaper than those found in eggs.[2]

Recently, Pomeranz and others have also attempted to make the case that the rising European prosperity c. 1800 owed much to the plantation produce of the Americas.[3] Evidence in support of this argument is underwhelming. In 1800, the only plantation foodstuff with calorific value was sugar. In England, where 150,000 tons were imported, this amounted (at most) to 1.2–1.5 ounces per person per day (7–10 teaspoons). Even if this bounty was evenly distributed it would have only provided the addition of somewhere between 100 and 160 calories per day. The price of sugar in 1800, however, ruled out such an equitable distribution. In his study of the global sugar trade, Sidney Mintz concluded that sugar remained a rarity in working-class pantries in the early nineteenth century, consumption being restricted to the addition of the occasional teaspoon of brown

---

[1] M. Shanbandeh, "Grain Production Worldwide 2019/20, by Type", *Statista*, https://www.statista.com/statistics/263977/world-grain-production-by-type/ [accessed 30 March 2021].

[2] Fernand Braudel (trans. Sian Reynolds), *Civilization and Capitalism, 15th–18th Century: The Structures of Everyday Life* (London, UK: Collins, 1981), 133.

[3] Kenneth Pomeranz, *The Great Divergence: China, Europe, and the Making of the Modern World Economy* (Princeton, NJ: Princeton University Press, 2000); Khali Gibram Muhammed, "Sugar", in Jake Silverstein (ed.), *1619 Project* (New York: *New York Times Magazine*, 8 August 2019), 70–77.

sugar or treacle to cups of tea or coffee.[4] Only after 1850 did sugar make "a significant calorific contribution" to the "working class diet".[5]

It was not sugar but alcohol that remained the principal dietary supplement in the Old World. In Paris in the 1780s, every man, woman and child was consuming an average of one-third of a liter (l) of wine a day. The 300 calories that this provided was not an inconsequential addition to the overall calorific intake given that the average adult consumed only 2,000–2,300 calories a day (inclusive of alcohol).[6] Elsewhere in the Old World—the Middle East, northern Europe—beer provided both an additional source of calories and a safer alternative to water as a source of fluid, given the polluted nature of streams and wells. In the beer-drinking societies of northern Europe a revolution in brewing in the late 1500s allowed for the cheap production of "small beer" (that is, a low alcohol beer). Cheaper to make than traditional beer, "small beer" provided poor families with a new source of "daily nourishment".[7] Such was the enthusiasm among English families for "small beer", who plied their children with ale from an early age, that it goes a long way to explaining the comparatively long life expectancy that we noted in Chapter 2.

If alcohol (and an associated cultivation of grapes, barely and hops) was frequently a calorific supplement, it nevertheless remained the case that wheat, rice and corn persisted as the dietary backbone of civilizations. Each, however, also brought peculiar problems that posed potential threats to the civilizations that depended upon them.

WHEAT

In Europe, North Africa, the Middle East and northern India the key to survival and prosperity revolved around the annual wheat harvest. As a grain, wheat had several advantages. A kilogram (2.2 lbs.) of wheat contained approximately 3,000 calories. As a hard grain, wheat was easily stored and transported. This made it well suited to the needs of urban

---

[4] Sidney Mintz, *Sweetness and Power: The Place of Sugar in Modern History* (New York: Vintage, 1985), 148.

[5] Ibid., 149.

[6] Fernand Braudel (trans. Siân Reynolds), *Structures of Everyday Life: Civilization and Capitalism 15th–18th Century* (London, UK: Collins, 1982), 237, 129–131.

[7] John U. Nef, "Prices and Industrial Capitalism in Germany, France and England 1540–1640", *Economic History Review*, Vol. 7, No. 2 (1937), 168.

populations, where large stocks had to be maintained to ensure survival between one harvest and the next. Typically baked fresh each day given the short shelf life of flour, wheaten bread varied in quality but typically delivered 1,000 calories to a 1 lb. loaf (2,200 calories per kg).[8] As a product, it should be noted, the bread consumed in the medieval and early modern periods little resembled the soft white staple that is now a ubiquitous item on the supermarket shelves. Instead, most ate a heavy bread containing large quantities of bran and, more often than not, flour made from cheaper grains (mainly rye).[9]

Wheat also benefited from the fact that it could be grown by individuals boasting little capital. In this it differed markedly from rice, where high yields were dependent upon irrigation. Peasant agriculture in medieval Europe also profited from two technological innovations that were absent in antiquity. The first of these was the heavy wheeled plow. Unlike the swing-plow—which remains in use in parts of India and the Middle East and resembles a curved stick suspended from a single ox-drawn shaft—the wheeled plow allowed farming of the heavy soils in northern Europe's river valleys. The second advance, which was key to the first, was the use of shoulder-harnesses on horses. Given that a horse using a shoulder-harness could exert a pulling power equivalent to four oxen, this innovation represented a significant productivity improvement.[10]

The incorporation of animals into cereal cultivation also provided a ready source of manure and supplementary calories in the form of milk, butter and cheese. Every year, Braudel estimated, the typical peasant proprietor in both medieval and early modern Europe dug around fifty cartloads of manure into their fields.[11] European farmers also profited from wheat's association with a three-field cultivation system. Given over to wheat one year and mixed crops (predominately oats) the next,

---

[8] Braudel, *Structures of Everyday Life*, 130–131.

[9] Ibid., 136–145.

[10] Charles Parain, "The Evolution of Agricultural Technique", in M.M. Postan (ed.), *The Cambridge Economic History of Europe*, Vol. 1 (Cambridge, UK: Cambridge University Press, 1966), 144.

[11] Fernand Braudel (trans. Sian Reynolds), *The Identity of France: People and Production* (London, UK: Fontana Press, 1991), 341. Note: Braudel gives a figure of 150 cart loads but this is calculated over a triennial calendar.

before being left for pasture (fallow) in the third, the three-field rotation provided a buffer against the potential failure of the wheat crop.[12]

Despite its multiple advantages, pre-industrial wheat cultivation was also associated with problems and perils. As a crop, it placed a heavy demand on both the soil and the cultivator. Every planting led to a large-scale loss of nitrogen and other soil nutrients, compelling most farmers to adopt the triennial field rotation system, noted above. Effectively, this meant that it took 3 acres of farmland to grow 1 acre of wheat. Wheat also placed constant, brutal, demands on farming households. Planted in northwestern Europe in autumn (from September to October), the main wheat crop was harvested in ensuing summer (between July and August). In early spring (March), a second field was sown with "lesser cereals" (such as oats, barley) along with beans and lentils. At all times, manure had to be dug into the soil, weeds chipped out and animals tended.[13] For all this effort, wheat gave the cultivator—and the societies that depended on it—a meagre return. Nowhere in the pre-industrial world did wheat yields remotely approach that found on twenty-first-century farms, where each seed typically returns 75–100 grains at harvest time.[14] In France in the eleventh century, a planted seed only returned three grains at harvest time, one of which had to be held over as seed for the ensuing harvest. While yields improved over time the results were hardly impressive. Even in early modern England and the Netherlands between 1750 and 1820, where agricultural productivity was higher than elsewhere, yields averaged only 10.6 grains for every one sown.[15]

The modest improvements apparent in pre-industrial yields in England cast doubt on the benefits of the supposed "agricultural revolution" associated with the eighteenth-century "enclosure movement" (which was the replacement of unfenced "common land" with fenced "private fields"). Taught to generations of school children as an essential component of Britain's Industrial Revolution, the "agricultural revolution" is

---

[12] Braudel, *Structures of Everyday Life*, 114–120.

[13] Braudel, *The Identity of France*, 339–348.

[14] Jeff Edwards, *Estimating Wheat Grain Yield Potential* (Ferguson, OK: Oklahoma State University, 2017), 1–2.

[15] Braudel, "The Identity of France", 179; Braudel, "Structures of Everyday Life", 123.

60 B. BOWDEN

dismissed by Clark as "myth".[16] More kindly, Allen declares the benefits of the "enclosure movement" to be "hopelessly overstated".[17] Far from improving, England's agricultural productivity was falling in the eighteenth century's final quarter, which are the years associated with the first half of the Industrial Revolution.[18] Low wheat yields meant that even in good years the price of wheaten bread was high relative to income, with high calorific alternatives (fish, meat, dairy) being even more expensive. Consequently, a large percentage of the population who lived in the Eurasian wheat belt were forced to resort to alternatives that had lower calorific values, subsisting on soups and gruels made from oats, barley and vegetables. In times of shortage, however, when the price of wheat went up, everything else went up as well, spelling catastrophe.

Inevitably, the combination of a dietary dependence on wheat (whether direct or indirect) and low yields manifested itself in two outcomes, both of them disastrous. The first of these is found in a population where a large proportion, if not the majority, was chronically malnourished. In reflecting upon the French experience prior to the 1860s, Braudel lamented "the tragic inadequacy of agricultural production".[19] In England, it is estimated that between 1787 and 1796 the average daily calorific intake was only 2,322 calories—approximately two-thirds of the modern average. England's "rural poor" consumed only 1,508 calories per day. In Paris on the eve of the Revolution (1789), the average person's calorific intake was on a par with England's.[20] Everywhere, malnourishment left people prone to disease, contributing to the pattern of premature death we noted in Chapter 2.

If wheat's modest yields left many hungry even in good times, an even-greater peril was the all-too-common failure of the harvest. France witnessed thirteen *nationwide* famines in the sixteenth century, eleven

[16] Gregory Clark, *A Farewell to Alms: A Brief Economic History of the World* (Princeton, NJ: Princeton University Press, 2007), 238.

[17] Robert C. Allen, *The British Industrial Revolution in Global Perspective* (Cambridge, UK: Cambridge University Press, 2009), 64.

[18] Ibid., 60, Figure 3.2.

[19] Braudel, *The Identity of France*, 382–383.

[20] Gregory Clark, Michael Huberman and Peter H. Lindert, "A British Food Puzzle", *Economic History Review*, Vol. 48, No. 2 (1995), 223; Clark, *A Farewell to Alms*, 50, Table 3.6.

in the seventeenth century and sixteen in the eighteenth.[21] By 1800 a rapid increase in population size was placing an almost universal pressure on food supplies. In the century between 1701 and 1801, England's population rose from 5.06 million to 8.66 million—a 71.1% increase. In the ensuing 50 years it almost doubled, growing from 8.66 million to 16.74 million. Across Europe as a whole, similar increases were observed, with the continent's population (including European Russia) rising from 100 million in 1650 to 140 million in 1750 (a 40% increase), before adding a further 47 million between 1750 and 1800 (a 33.6% increase). In the ensuing half century, Europe's population grew by an additional 79 million to 266 million (a 42.2% increase).[22]

Under the ever-increasing weight of numbers, evidence of a looming Malthusian crisis is found on many fronts. In Britain, although "real wages went up" between 1770 and 1814, food consumption "stagnated or even declined".[23] Perhaps the best indicator of the looming crisis is found in average skeletal heights. As Fig. 3.1 indicates, between 1770 and 1850 the

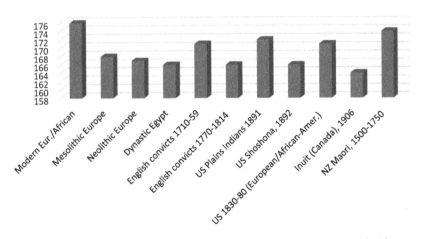

Fig. 3.1 Adult male height: pre-industrial societies (in centimeters) (*Sources* Clark, *Farewell to Alms*, Tables 3.8, 3.9; US Department of Health and Human Services, *Anthropometric Reference Data*, Table 11)

---

[21] Braudel, *The Identity of France*, 384.
[22] Braudel, *Structures of Everyday Life*, 42.
[23] Clark, Huberman and Lindert, "British Food Puzzle", 215.

average height of English adult male convicts was a full 5 cm (2 inches) shorter than that recorded between 1710 and 1759. Standing 166 cm (5 feet, 4 inches), the English convict of the early nineteenth century was also no taller than the average recorded among skeletal remains from dynastic Egypt.[24]

Why was wheat's performance in both the medieval and early modern worlds so consistently lackluster, given that today the same crop feeds countless millions?

First and most significantly, wheat-farming remained a labor-intensive activity whereby planting and harvesting was reliant on human and animal power rather than mechanization, as increasingly became the New World norm after 1850. Secondly, reliance on locally acquired animal manure as a fertilizer constrained attempts to improve yields. Not until the importation of *guano* (bird droppings) from Chile and Peru in the 1840s, and the manufacture of artificial fertilizers in the second half of the nineteenth century, was the barrier to higher yields overcome. Finally, until the 1850s the "tyranny of distance" limited access to the broad acres of the United States and Canadian west, the Argentine Pampas and the Australian interior. In England, for example, 86% of food was homegrown in 1800. A century later, only 46.9% was grown domestically.[25] Even the achievements of New World farmers in the nineteenth century, it should be noted, owed more to extra acres sown than yields per acre. Prior to the 1840s, when New England farmers were the main source of national supply, the United States struggled to meet demand. Indeed, between 1830 and 1840 the United States was a wheat importer rather than an exporter. Corn and oats, not wheat, provided the bedrock of the American diet. At the end of the nineteenth century, when the vast expanses of Kansas and Minnesota flooded the world markets with wheat, yields per acre were still lackluster. Whereas the typical British wheat farm yielded 32.4 bushels (973 kg) per acre at the turn of the century, their American

---

[24] Clark, *A Farewell to Alms*, 57–59, Table 3.8, Table 3.9; United States Department of Health and Human Services, *Anthropometric Reference Data for Children and Adults: United States 2015–2018* (Hyattsville, ML: National Center for Health Statistics, 2021), 15, Table 11.

[25] Calculated from Clark, Huberman and Lindert, "British Food Puzzle", 220, Table 1.

competitor was producing less than half, at 13.7 bushels (411 kg) per acre.[26]

Even in the late 1930s, wheat yields in the United States—and adjacent Canada—were among the world's worst. From 1936 to 1938, when the United States and Canadian wheat farms yielded 690 kg and 650 kg per acre, respectively, British farms yielded 2,230 kg per acre. Even India performed better, its farms yielding 730 kg per acre.[27] Despite their low per-acre yields, however, Canadian and American farmers—along with their low-yield, broadacre counterparts in Australia, Argentina and the Ukraine—dominated world markets by the end of the nineteenth century.

Invariably, mechanization was the key to the success of broadacre farming. Writing in 1892, Thorstein Veblen observed that the twine-bind harvester (a type of harvester that cut and bound the sheaves of wheat), which was a ubiquitous feature of North American wheat farms by the 1880s, could "cut and bind twelve acres and upwards in a day". The impact of this technology on farm productivity was profound. In 1850, an American wheat farmer typically expended 62.4 hours per acre; however, by the mid-1890s those farmers using "the most advanced machine methods" were spending only 3.1 hours per acre.[28] Aided by such methods, American Midwest production (505 million bushels) on the eve of World War I was nine times that of Britain's harvest (56 million bushels) and equivalent to half the combined production of Western, Southern and Central Europe (1,024 million bushels). Canada's production (208 million bushels) was four times that of Britain and Australia's output (152 million bushels) three times as much.[29]

RICE

If wheat's "unpardonable fault" in the pre-industrial world was its low yield, no such allegation could be made against paddy-grown rice.[30] In the decades around 1700, it is estimated that Europe's most productive

[26] Albert Perry Bingham, "The Development of Wheat Culture in North America", *The Geographical Journal*, Vol. 35, No. 1 (1910), 42, 56.

[27] Thorstein Veblen, "Price of Wheat Since 1867", *Journal of Political Economy*, Vol. 1, No. 1 (1892), 85; Colin Clark, *Conditions of Economic Progress*, second edition (London, UK: Macmillan, 1951), 225.

[28] Ibid., 221, 224.

[29] C. Knick Harley, "Western Settlement and the Price of Wheat 1872–1913", *Journal of Economic History*, Vol. 38, No. 4 (1978), 866, Table 1.

[30] Braudel, *Structures of Everyday Life*, 121.

wheat fields in England and the Netherlands were typically producing 700 kg of wheat per hectare. By comparison, a hectare of rice paddy in South China and Vietnam in 1750 was yielding 3,000 kg of unhusked rice per annum. Although husking would have reduced the edible amount to 2,100 kg, it nevertheless left the rice cultivator with three-fold advantage over their English or Dutch counterparts. The calorific advantage would have been even higher, given that a kilogram of rice provides up to 3,500 calories, whereas wheat typically delivers 3,000 calories a kilogram.[31]

The superiority of paddy-grown rice over wheat rested on multiple factors. Typically, its yield in terms of seeds sown was 60% higher. More significantly, an acre of rice paddy invariably returned two harvests a year, whereas an acre of land given over to wheat only delivered a harvest every second or third year due to the need for crop rotation and periods of "fallow". Rice cultivation was also compatible with the growing of vegetable crops that could be planted adjacent to flooded paddy fields. Among the most notable of these were groundnuts, sweet potatoes and corn. Obtained from the Portuguese in the 1500s, these crops underpinned an "agricultural revolution" in South China; a revolution associated with both the geographic expansion of Chinese agriculture and rising productivity.[32] Recent comparative studies also suggest that Chinese, Japanese and Indian peasants were as innovative as their European counterparts in raising productivity during the early modern period.[33] By 1800, Li and van Zanden conclude, agricultural productivity in China's Yangzi delta "was at about the same level as in the Netherlands and England".[34]

The ultimate proof of rice's productive bounty is found in the population increases that it allowed. Between 1300 and 1750, Europe's population grew by 75% to 140 million. During the same period the Chinese population rose from 72 to 270 million, a 275% increase.

---

[31] Ibid., 51, 130.

[32] Ibid., 44.

[33] Ho-fung Hung, *The China Boom: Why China Will Not Rule the World* (New York: Columbia University Press, 2015), 15–33; Allen et al., "Wages, Prices and Living Standards in China", 8–38; Bozhong Li and Jan Luiten van Zanden, "Before the Great Divergence": Comparing the Yangzi delta and the Netherlands at the Beginning of the Nineteenth Century", *Journal of Economic History*, Vol. 72, No. 4 (2012), 956–989; Prasannan Parthasarathi, *Why Europe Grew Rich and Asia Did Not: Global Economic Divergence 1600–1850* (Cambridge, UK: Cambridge University Press, 2011).

[34] Li and van Zanden, "Before the Great Divergence", 956.

Japan's growth was even more spectacular, its population rising more than five-fold (from 6 to 31 million).[35]

A bountiful provider, rice has nevertheless been described as "an even more tyrannical and enslaving crop than wheat".[36] To achieve harvests in both early summer (June) and late autumn (November), fields had to be manured, plowed, flooded, tended and drained not once, but twice. Given the time frames imposed by these demands, rice seedlings for the next harvest had to be nurtured simultaneously with field cultivation.[37] While water buffalo were an invaluable aid to plowing, the rice farmer was still confronted with a larger array of labor-intensive tasks than their wheat-cultivating counterpart. At planting time, the rice farmer could not simply scatter seeds in furrows. Instead, each seedling had to be laboriously transplanted. Above all, irrigation channels had to be dug, levee banks constructed and water channeled through fields.

As a mode of existence, rice farming was inherently a far more collectivist activity than wheat cultivation. Whereas a wheat farmer could go about their activities whether or not their neighbor chose to follow their example, this individualistic approach was never a viable option in the rice paddies. For if the irrigation system collapsed, everything collapsed. In China, this manifested itself in what Hung refers to as the "paternalist state", one which in the seventeenth and eighteenth centuries constantly "intervened in the agrarian economy", instigating "a massive state-planned migration program" that moved vast numbers "to the newly reclaimed agricultural land in the periphery".[38]

Possessing a limited understanding of the intricacies of the Chinese economy, classical economists such as Adam Smith and John Stuart Mill had a very dim view of this system of centralized direction and its effects. In Smith's opinion, China was undoubtedly "one of the ... most fertile, best cultivated, most industrious ... countries in the world".[39] Despite such attributes, Smith continued, China suffered from "laws and institutions" that offered no "liberal reward" for labor and initiative, thereby

---

[35] Clark, *A Farewell to Alms*, 267.

[36] Braudel, *Structures of Everyday Life*, 141.

[37] Ibid., 151.

[38] Hung, *The China Boom*, 27, 19.

[39] Adam Smith (ed. Andrew Skinner), *The Wealth of Nations* (London, UK: Penguin Classics, 1999), 174.

condemning the society to stagnation and a "beggarly" state.[40] For Mill, as well, the society's inability to instill an "effective desire of [individual] accumulation" was its unpardonable fault, producing a state of "insufferable wretchedness".[41] Although it is now apparent that the Chinese economy was far more sophisticated than Smith and Mill suspected, Hung nevertheless concludes that "the Qing state's paternalist disposition prevented ... the rise of a strong domestic capitalist class".[42] In the long-run, this stultified economic growth. As a result, the Chinese economy was under strain long before the Opium War of 1839–1842; a conflict that heralded a destructive period of western intervention and Chinese political disintegration. An early indicator of China's economic malaise was the so-called 'White Lotus' rebellion of 1796 and 1804; a rebellion instigated by an "overburdened" peasantry that swept through China, aggravating "social dislocation and disintegration".[43] In the ensuing repression, millions died.

Evidence that the major rice-producing regions of East and South Asia were by 1800 facing a Malthusian crisis similar to that confronting much of Europe at the same time is indicated in Fig. 3.2, which considers the kilograms of wheat—or the calorific equivalent in rice—that an unskilled laborer from various European locations, southern India and the Yangzi delta of China could have purchased c. 1800 if they spent all their wage on grain. Working on the same assumption, that is, a person spends all of their income on wheat at the prevailing price, a modern comparison is provided by the United Nations' measure of extreme poverty (US$1.90, 2011 prices). As is evident, the 3 kg of wheat equivalent that a laborer in the Yangzi delta could have purchased c. 1800 meant that they were "richer" than their counterpart in Milan (2.54 kg). By comparison, a laborer from southern India (2.32 kg) was marginally worse off. Unskilled laborers in both the Yangzi delta and southern India were, however, also significantly worse off than their counterparts in non-metropolitan England (5 kg), Paris (4.5 kg) and Madrid (4.1 kg).[44] In reality, what we

[40] Ibid., 174–176.

[41] John Stuart Mill, *Principles of Political Economy* (New York: Prometheus Books, 1999), 185.

[42] Hung, *The China Boom*, 32.

[43] Ibid., 33.

[44] Clark, *A Farewell to Alms*, 48–49, Table 3.4, Table 3.5; United Nations Development Programme, *Goal No. 1: No Poverty* (New York: United Nations Development

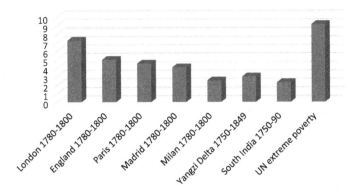

Fig. 3.2 Purchasing power of unskilled laborers, kilograms of wheat or rice equivalent (*Sources* Clark, *Farewell to Alms*, Tables 3.4, Table 3.5; UN Development Programme, *Goal No. 1*)

are talking about in every circumstance is not the variations in wealth but rather degrees of misery.

The fact that there is today far more wheat grown across the globe (764 million tons) than rice (496 million tons) points to rice's inherent limitations. A labor-intensive crop, it proved less amenable to mechanization than wheat. Dependent on irrigation to reach its productive potential, it was also less geographically adaptable. Although Asia boasts vast plains, these have largely remained the domain of pastoralists or of dry-land crops such as wheat and millet. Rice never found an equivalent of wheat's Kansas or Manitoba—lands of few people but of endless grain fields.

Corn

In Book 11 of the so-called *Florentine Codex*, titled "Earthly things" in which the survivors of the Aztec Empire wrote in their native Nahuatl, corn from distant "dry lands" is described as "our sustenance, product of the fields". The kernels of this dry-land corn are also described as

Programme, 2021), https://www.undp.org/content/undp/en/home/sustainable-development-goals/goal-1-no-poverty.html [accessed 2 April 2021].

"slender, small, hard". As such they were totally unlike the "soft, feather-like, long, spongy" kernels grown in "the *chinampas*", the "irrigated lands" close to the Aztec capital of Tenochtitlan, the site of modern-day Mexico City.[45]

The recollections of the Aztec survivors, written down in the mid-sixteenth century, point to both the adaptability of corn and its centrality to the existence of not only the Aztec but also of all the settled societies of pre-Columbian America. Corn was grown by the *pueblo*-dwelling peoples in what is now the United States' southwest, by the Inca in high valleys of the Andes, and by the Maya in the tropical lowlands of Central America. Some, such as the Maya, relied on dry-land cultivation and natural rainfall. Others, such as the Inca, relied on complex irrigation systems. The Aztec harnessed the productive power of both their own *chinampas* and the dry-land fields of their conquered, tributary peoples. Everywhere, corn cultivation relied on the same three basic ingredients: simple planting processes, the provision of water (whether irrigated or natural) in the key growing periods, and labor-intensive cultivation techniques.

By comparison with both wheat and rice farming, the cultivation of corn offered some obvious advantages. In terms of calorific content, corn was comparable to rice (3,500 calories per kg). It also offered much higher yields than either wheat or rice. In colonial Mexico, dry-land corn fields yielded 70 to 80 kernels for each one sown. Intensively farmed irrigated fields returned 800 kernels for each seed.[46] A short growing season of around 80 days also allowed for two crops each year. As a garden crop, corn did not necessitate the extensive plowing found in both wheat and rice farming. Instead, planting required little more than a sharpened stick, although the Inca farmed corn with foot plows, "long poles hardened at the point and equipped with foot-rests and handles".[47]

The high calorific return of corn for invested effort ensured the crop a ready reception in the Old World. In Africa, corn was first introduced by Portuguese slave traders in the sixteenth century. By the eighteenth century it had become a staple of the West African diet along with manioc (cassava), another South American crop. Underpinned by these

---

[45] Fray Bernardino de Sahagun, ed. (trans. Charles E. Dibble and Arthur J.O. Anderson), *Florentine Codex: Book 11—Earthly Things* (Salt Lake City, UT: University of Utah Press, 1959), 282.

[46] Braudel, *Structures of Everyday Life*, 161.

[47] John Hemming, *The Conquest of the Inca* (London, UK: Macmillan, 1970), 58.

new sources of nutrition, it is estimated that by 1700 West Africa's population was growing at an annualized rate of 1.7%, more than offsetting the depredations of the slave trade.[48] In southern Europe, corn was also taken up with enthusiasm from the mid-sixteenth century. In Italy it was largely consumed as *polenta* and in France as *millasse*. By the early 1700s corn had become the primary staple of Southern Europe's poor, providing "a much cheaper source of calories than wheat bread".[49] By the eighteenth century, corn was also widely grown in Japan and China, becoming a staple of the northern Chinese diet alongside millet, wheat and sorghum.[50]

Despite its comparative bounty, reliance on corn entailed perils that were in many ways more dangerous than those associated with wheat and rice. Comparatively low in protein, corn also lacks niacin, leading to endemic pellagra and chronic diarrhea.[51] In pre-Columbian America a corn-dominant diet was also linked to chronic tooth decay.[52] On the basis of a comparative study of skeletal health, Steckel et al. also observed how pre-Columbian populations that were engaged in corn cultivation—such as the Maya and the *pueblo* people of what is now the United States southwest—suffered degenerative bone lesions similar to those experienced by African American slaves.[53]

In part, the poor skeletal health of the corn-farming populations of pre-Columbian America reflected the fact that they undertook their labors without the assistance of technologies that were commonplace in the Old World. Nowhere did Native American farmers operate with the benefit of either draught animals or metal tools. The lack of wheeled vehicles also made transport a labor-intensive endeavor. The absence of livestock common to Eurasia and Africa (cows, pigs, goats) denied the settled populations of the Americas a ready source of protein. In the case of the Inca, Hemming observed that, despite the grandeur of their cities

[48] Hugh Thomas, *The Slave Trade: The History of the Atlantic Slave Trade 1440–1870* (London, UK: Picador, 1997), 115, 796.

[49] Allen, *British Industrial Revolution*, 30.

[50] Braudel, *Structures of Everyday Life*, 167.

[51] Allen, *British Industrial Revolution*, 31.

[52] Richard H. Steckel, Jerome C. Rose, Clark Spencer Larsen and Phillip L. Walker, "Skeletal Heath in the Western Hemisphere from 4000 BC to the Present", *Evolutionary Anthropology*, Vol. 11 (2002), 150.

[53] Ibid., 153.

and irrigated terraces, "everyday life" for the "common people" was one of privation and "a steady struggle for subsistence".[54] There is little reason to conclude that the plight of the other settled populations of the Americas was much better. In observing the agricultural practices of the Mandan people of the Upper Missouri River in the early 1830s, for example, George Catlin noted how an over-reliance on "corn and some pumpkins and squashes" left the tribe "oftentimes" in a "state of starvation".[55] In eking out a subsistence existence from the soil, Catlin also observed, the Mandan little resembled their bison-hunting neighbors, the "Sioux" (Lakota) and the "Crow", peoples who exploited to the fullest a lifestyle built around European-introduced horses. Not only was the "stature" of these meat-eating horsemen "considerably above that of the Mandans", Catlin concluded, it was also evident that "at least one-half of their warriors [were] of six feet or more in height".[56] Catlin's observations as to the remarkable differences in heights of the corn-eating Mandan and their bison-eating neighbors were not idle ones. As Fig. 3.1 indicated, the Native American populations of the Northern Plains were significantly taller than other historic populations. In their study into skeletal health, Steckel et al. also found the "health index" for the "equestrian nomads from the North American Great Plains" to be far superior to that found in most other Native American populations.[57]

If a corn-based diet was associated with endemic health problems, it was also the case that a reliance on corn posed existential threats to entire civilizations. For, by comparison with either wheat or rice, corn is a soft crop. Unless carefully dried and kept free of moisture, it is poorly suited to long-term storage or long-distance transport. Consequently, corn-based economies were more reliant on the immediate harvest than societies that hitched their fortunes to either wheat or rice. In areas of dry-land cultivation, the perils of a dependency on corn manifested itself most clearly in times of drought. A thirsty crop when young, even comparatively short periods of rain deficiency can have a devastating impact on the resultant harvest. In 2001, for example, a one-year drought caused the loss

---

[54] Hemming, *Conquest of the Inca*, 60.

[55] George Catlin, *Letters and Notes on the Manner, Customs and Conditions of North American Indians*, Vol. 1 (New York: Dover Publications, 1973), 121, 123.

[56] Ibid., 208.

[57] Steckel, Rose, Larsen and Walker, "Skeletal Heath in the Western Hemisphere", 152.

of 80% of Guatemala's corn crop.[58] Where Native American civilizations attempted to counter the effects of drought on their cornfields through elaborate irrigation systems, it was flood rather than drought that imperiled their survival. In describing the Moche civilization that flourished in the Peruvian coastal lowlands between AD 100 and AD 800, Brian Fagan observed that, "Over many centuries, the coastal valley populations steadily rose … until the only way to feed everyone was through massive, highly organized irrigation systems that used every drop of water that cascaded downstream during the spring mountain thaw".[59] Well adapted to drought, the Moche's achievements were undone by severe El Niño events that dumped up to a year's worth of rain in twenty-four hours, washing away not only crops and homes but also the structural basis of an entire way of life.

Despite corn's climatic and storage vulnerabilities, it was arguably the crop's very bounty that posed the most insidious threat to those who relied on it. Easy to grow, and providing cultivators with a wealth of cheap calories, corn was well suited to maintaining large populations at a bare subsistence level. As such, dependency on corn directed entire societies toward a "Malthusian trap" in which large populations constantly teetered on the edge of demographic catastrophe. Whereas even short-term fluctuations brought starvation and suffering, long-term variations in temperature or rainfall acted as the destroyer of entire civilizations. In this, corn-based societies were arguably more exposed than their wheat and rice-reliant counterparts. But they were, however, hardly unique in their dependency on the vagaries of climate for survival.

[58] Julia A. Hoggart, Mathew Restall, James W. Wood and Douglas J. Kennent, "Drought and Its Demographic Effects in the Maya Lowlands", *Current Anthropology*, Vol. 58, No. 1 (2017), 92.

[59] Brian Fagan, *Food, Famines and Emperors: El Nino and the Fate of Civilizations* (New York: Basic Books, 1999), 124–125.

CHAPTER 4

Climate: The Destroyer of Civilizations, and How Early Modern Europe Rose from Catastrophe

Writing during what we think of as the Industrial Revolution, Thomas Malthus reflected on the misery that he witnessed among England's laboring poor. In doing so, he made a blistering attack on Adam Smith and his support for capital investment in commerce and manufacturing. In Malthus's opinion, as with the French physiocrats (Richard Cantillon, Francois Quesnay, Etienne Bonnet de Condillac), the only members of society who were engaged in "productive" labor were those employed in "agriculture" and "grazing".[1] By contrast, he argued, "manufacturing labor" was "unproductive", producing only "silks, laces, trinkets, and expensive furniture" that benefited "the vanity of a few rich people".[2] Accordingly, if society was to improve the lot of the laboring majority it needed to abandon industrialization, embracing instead "the state of mixed pasture and tillage"—pursuits which he believed would always be the hallmarks of "the most civilized nations".[3]

Superficially, the appeal of Malthus's logic is obvious. If people do not have enough to eat, then the priority needs to be immediate food

[1] Thomas Malthus, *An Essay on the Principles of Population* (London, UK: J. Johnson, 1798), 30.

[2] Ibid., 104–105.

[3] Ibid., 17.

© The Author(s), under exclusive license to Springer Nature
Switzerland AG 2022
B. Bowden, *Slavery, Freedom and Business Endeavor*,
Palgrave Debates in Business History,
https://doi.org/10.1007/978-3-030-97232-5_4

73

production. The more farmers there are, the greater the amount of food. There were, however, serious flaws in Malthus's thinking. Fewer people employed in transport meant a lessening of the society's capacity to import food and ship it to places of need when the inevitable harvest failure occurred. Fewer people in manufacturing meant fewer goods to trade for foodstuffs that could be grown more profitably and securely in other locations. A lack of investment in manufacturing meant not only fewer "silks" and "laces" but also fewer metal goods, plows and machines that could till the soil more efficiently. Above all, the view that a society should place all its eggs in the rural basket exposed it, and all its members, to the historic vagaries of climate; vagaries that have acted as the destroyers of civilizations since time immemorial.

Invariably, what the farmers of every civilization wanted from the climate was warmth, rain and predictability. Tragically, none of these could ever be relied upon.

In our modern world, global warming is the great fear, a recent Intergovernmental Panel on Climate Change (IPCC) associating it with higher levels of poverty and reduced opportunities for "sustainable development".[4] The IPCC also points to "human-induced warming" of "approximately 1° Celsius … above pre-industrial levels", the degree of warming being expressed relative "to the 1850–1900 period" which is "used as an approximation of pre-industrial temperatures".[5] The 1850–1900 period was, however, no more typical of the "pre-industrial" past than any other. Instead, climate research points to an enormous variation in climatic experiences over time. Based on a study of Iberian pollen records, Desprat, Goñi and Loutre, for example, identify six distinct European climatic periods across the last three millennia:

- a cooling period that lasted from c. 975 BC–250 BC
- the "Roman Warm Period" (c. 250 BC–c. AD 450)
- the "Dark Ages Cooling Period" (c. AD 450–c. AD 950)
- the "Medieval Warm Period" (c. AD 950–c. AD 1400)

---

[4] V.P. Masson-Delmotte, H.O Zhai, D. Pörtner, J. Roberts, P.R. Skea, A. Shukla, W. Pirani, C. Moufouma-Okia, R. Péan, S. Pidcock, J.B.R. Connors, Y. Matthews, X. Chen, M.I. Zhou, E. Gomis, T. Lonnoy, M. Maycock, Tignor, and T. Waterfield (eds.), *Global Warming of 1.5 °C. An IPCC Special Report* (Geneva, Switzerland: Intergovernmental Panel on Climate Change, 2018), 58.

[5] Ibid., 51.

- the "Little Ice Age" (c. 1400–c. 1850)
- the modern warm period (c. 1850–).[6]

The cut-offs for such time periods are, admittedly, inherently arbitrary; AD 400, for example, would appear a better date to mark the commencement of the "Dark Ages Cooling Period" than AD 450, given that the Western Roman Empire's political demise was heralded by the mass crossing of the frozen Rhine by Germanic invaders on New Year's Eve in AD 406. Similarly, the rapid deterioration of the European climate after AD 1300 suggests that this date is a better marker of the border between the "Medieval Warm Period" and the "Little Ice Age" than AD 1400.

Invariably, colder weather was associated with the retreat of agriculture and the civilizations that depended upon it, whereas a warmer climate was associated with the reverse. In Carole Crumley's estimation, the "Dark Ages Cooling Period" (c. AD 400–AD 850) saw the climatic border between the continental and Mediterranean weather zones migrate southward from the vicinity of Hamburg to the North African coast, an outcome associated with a catastrophic collapse in both agricultural output and population.[7] Berglund's study of various climatic markers (for example, tree rings, lake levels, and so on) in Scandinavia and Central Europe, supports such findings, pointing to large-scale reafforestation as a result of agricultural abandonment during the "Dark Age Cooling period".[8] By contrast, warmer weather was invariably associated with better times, driving the size of the harvest upward and the cost of grain down. In medieval and early modern England, it is estimated that a 1 °C rise in the seasonal weather temperature depressed prices by about 10%, with the associated boost to nutrition fueling a 0.1% rise in the rate of

[6] Stéphanie Desprat, Maria Fernada Sánchez Goñi and Marie-France Loutre: "Revealing Climatic Variability of the Last Three Millennia in Northern Iberia Using Pollen Influx Data", *Earth and Planetary Science Letters*, Vol. 213, No. 1 (2003), 63–78.

[7] Carole Crumley, "The Ecology of Conquest: Contrasting Agropastoral and Agricultural Societies Adaption to Climate Change", in Carole Crumley (ed.), *Historical Ecology: Cultural Knowledge and Changing Landscapes* (Santa Fe, NM: School of American Research Press, 1994), 192–195.

[8] Bjorn E. Berglund: "Human Impact and Climate Changes—Synchronous Events and a Causal Link?" *Quaternary International*, Vol. 105, No. 1 (2003), 7–12.

population increase.[9] It was not only Europeans, however, who regarded a cold climate as "a persistent visitor, dangerous and devastating".[10] If we read the Aztec account of "Earthly things", written by survivors of the European conquest, it is evident that they too regarded cold with dread. When it "becomes cold", the Aztec recounted, where "ice lies forming a surface" one finds a place where "Misery abounds ... there is death from hunger ... there is freezing; there is ... the chattering of teeth".[11] Everywhere, cold climate demanded more heating, more clothes and a greater expenditure of calories. In short, it made sources of food more essential than in warm weather, while making their acquisition more difficult.

Even more than the societies located around Mediterranean and the Atlantic, the economies of Asia and the Pacific have long hitched their fortunes to the vagaries of climate. In India and, indeed, most of South and East Asia, it was drought rather than cold that posed the primary threat to not only human life but also entire societies. Of Indian agriculture, it has long been said that it is a "gamble on the monsoon".[12] When the monsoon failed, catastrophe historically ensued. Writing of the disastrous famine of 1899–1900 that killed up to 4.5 million people, the British Viceroy reported how the normally rich farmland of the Deccan had become a place of "dismal, sun-cracked, desert-charged earth ... No water in the wells; no water in the rivers".[13] In pre-Columbian America, drought and flood also presented existential threats. In discussing the "brutal drought" that struck the Yucatan Peninsula between AD 760 and AD 930, Gill et al. observed that it caused "devastation on a scale rarely

[9] Ronald D. Lee, "Short-Term Variations: Vital Rates, Prices, and Weather", in E.A. Wrigley and R.S. Schofield (eds.), *The Population History of England, 1541–1871: A Reconstruction* (Cambridge, MA: Harvard University Press, 1981), 398.

[10] Fernand Braudel (trans. Sian Reynolds), *Civilization and Capitalism, 15th–18th Century: The Structures of Everyday Life* (London, UK: Collins, 1981), 245.

[11] Fray Bernardino de Sahagun, ed. (trans. Charles E. Dibble and Arthur J.O. Anderson), *Florentine Codex: Book 11—Earthly Things* (Salt Lake City, UT: University of Utah Press, 1959), 106.

[12] The adage appears to have derived from a 1909 statement by Sir Guy Wilson, a British administrator in India, that "estimating [agriculture] in this country is largely a gamble in rain".

[13] Cited, Brian Fagan, *Food, Famines and Emperors: El Nino and the Fate of Civilizations* (New York: Basic Books, 1999), 12.

suffered in world history", effectively destroying the great Mayan civilization of Central America.[14] The large *pueblo* communities of the Chaco Canyon of what is now New Mexico, which provided an urban home to an estimated 5,500 residents in AD 1130, also suffered from brutal societal-destroying drought. For about fifty years, the Canyon suffered an almost total failure of life-supporting rain. By the early thirteenth century the *pueblos* were abandoned, never recovering their former glory.[15]

It was not only cold, drought and flood that threatened survival in the world's historic civilizations. Equally perilous was the unpredictable nature of the climate. For cold, drought and flood were inherently unpleasant climatic phenomena rather than being deadly. Where they became perilous was through their capacity to either shorten the growing season or inhibit a harvest. Conversely, rain and sunshine were only beneficial when they came at the right time. Societies everywhere sensed, in the climate, powers that were beyond human comprehension. In the Old Testament, the fate of the harvest is ultimately in God's hands, not those of his human creations, Jeremiah advising his flock that:

> Let us now fear Yahweh our God, who gives rain, of autumn and of spring, at the right season, and reserves us the weeks appointed for harvest.[16]

Similarly, in *The Iliad*, Zeus, the most powerful of the Greek Gods, is described as "the Gatherer of the Clouds", the master of the "wide heaven" and of "clear air and clouds".[17] In dynastic Egypt, the supernatural powers of the Pharaohs were reflected in their capacity to deliver the all-important Nile flood, any failure of the flood and the ensuing harvest attributable to weakness in the monarch's divine capacity.

The view of the ancients that climate is determined by forces greater than any human capacity was well founded. The belief that these forces are beyond the capacities of rational human inquiry was not. Admittedly,

[14] Richardson B. Gill, Paul A. Mayewski, John Nyberg, Gerald H. Haug and Larry C. Peterson: "Drought and the Maya Collapse", *Ancient Mesoamerica*, Vol. 18 (2007), 288.

[15] Fagan, *Food, Famines and Emperors*, 173–176; Alan Taylor, *American Colonies: The Settling of North America* (London, UK: Penguin Books, 2001), 12–14.

[16] Henry Wansbrough (ed.), *The New Jerusalem Bible* (London, UK: Darton, Longman & Todd, 1985), 1305, Jeremiah, 5: 28.

[17] Homer (trans. Andrew Lang, Walter Leaf and Ernest Myers), *The Iliad* (London, UK: Macmillan Collector's Library, 2020), 313–314.

the drivers behind the Earth's movement in and out of centuries-long cooling and warming periods remain unclear. Alterations in the Earth's long-term orbit and tilt are no doubt key factors, as are variations in the Sun's solar intensity. What has nevertheless become increasingly clear in recent decades is that the key climatic events of the last two millennia— Europe's continued slide in and out of warming and cooling periods, the devastating droughts that destroyed the Maya, the success or failure of the Indian and western Pacific monsoons—are *not* random, unconnected events. Instead, they are correlated. Prolonged cooling periods in Europe correspond to long years of drought in Central America. Devastating floods in California and Peru are closely linked to droughts and the failure of the monsoons in East Asia, India and northern Australia. If we are to understand the historic fate of civilizations, including the rise and fall of the various iterations of western civilization, then a comprehension of the forces behind these climatic correlations is essential.

As with many complex matters, the key driver behind correlated alterations in the Earth's climate is surprisingly simple: warm, moist air tends to rise while dry air tends to sink. In terms of global climate, this climatic law manifests itself in the tendency of moist air to rise around both the Equator (the Intertropical Convergence Zone) and the sub-Arctic/sub-Antarctic around latitudes 60° north and 60° south, and to descend—devoid of moisture—at the poles and around latitudes 30° north and 30° south. As rising air creates low depressions, and hence storms and rain, it is thus the tropics and the subarctic regions that experience the wettest weather. Conversely, dry conditions are associated with descending air and high-pressure weather systems. In each Hemisphere, moreover, this pattern of rising and descending air is associated with three self-contained "cells", two of which (the Hadley cell, and the midlatitude or Ferrel cell) result in currents of dry, descending air around latitudes 30° north and south. It is these latitudes that are home to most of the world's deserts (including the Sahara, the Arabian and Australian deserts). By contrast, the propensity of air to rise at the junction of the Polar cells and Ferrel cells, at about latitudes 60° north and 60° south, causes the Earth's subarctic and subantarctic regions to be the home of endlessly circulating low depressions and freezing storms.

If the atmospheric cells were rigidly confined to their latitudes the world would witness only modest climate variations. The Earth's tilt and its annual journey around the Sun, however, contribute to a number of oscillations, the most important of which are the North Atlantic

Oscillation and the El Niño–Southern Oscillation. Invariably, it is these oscillations that have acted as the principal destroyers of civilizations.

THE NORTH ATLANTIC AND EL NIÑO–SOUTHERN OSCILLATIONS

In Europe, North Africa and Central America the key driver of climate is the North Atlantic Oscillation, and central to this phenomenon is the movement of the Bermuda-Azores High. During the European summer, this high moves north, establishing itself over the Azores. In this position it blocks the movement of rain-bearing low depressions into the Mediterranean basin, causing the region's characteristically dry summers. By July and August, even London, Paris and Berlin enjoy the benefits of dry, warm weather. As it moves south, however, rain-bearing low depressions move into the Mediterranean. In northern Europe this retreat allows for an inrush of cold northerly airstreams. The southward migration of the Bermuda-Azores High is also associated with a southerly retreat of the Intertropical Convergence Zone, bringing drought-like conditions to Central America that typically last from November to May.

Significantly, the seasonal association of cold European weather with dry conditions in Central America is a pointer to a far deadlier correlation, one that results from the Bermuda-Azores High remaining to the southwest of its normal position for extended periods. When this happens, Europe suffers from an unusual cold that can last for centuries. At the same time, the Caribbean Basin finds itself in the grip of prolonged droughts.

In the Indian and Pacific Oceans, the interconnected nature of climatic events was revealed through inquiries into the cause of monsoon failure. Long a mystery, the causal mechanism behind the frequent monsoon failures was first suggested in the 1920s by the British scientist, Gilbert Walker. Identifying what became known as the Southern Oscillation, Walker observed the tendency of air pressure in the western Pacific adjacent to Australia to move in an inverse direction to that detected in the Indian Ocean. In other words, monsoon failures were not random. Rather, they were the product of interconnected oceanic changes. In 1959, a clearer understanding emerged when a link was identified between the El Niño and La Niña weather patterns of South America and those of monsoon-reliant Asia and Australia. In "normal" years the cool waters off the coast of Peru and Chile are drawn inexorably northwestwards, ultimately strengthening the trade winds and the rising columns of moist air that drive the Asian monsoons. As a result, Asia and Australia experience wet seasons while dry conditions prevail along the South American and Californian coast. In El Niño years, however, this pattern is driven into reverse as warm water from East Asia migrates southwestwards toward South America, causing monsoon failure in both Asia and Australia and flooding rain in South America and California. Even the North Atlantic Oscillation is impacted as cool descending air causes drought in the Caribbean Basin (see Fig. 4.1). The global interconnectedness of climate patterns was further highlighted in 1999 with the discovery of the so-called Indian Ocean Dipole, an event associated

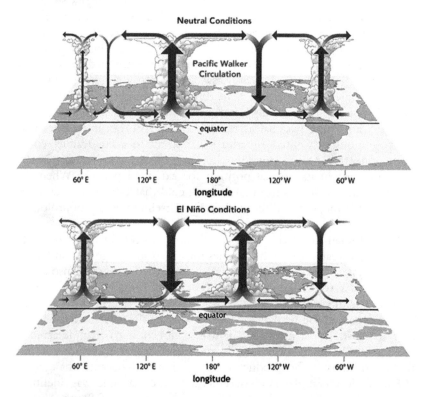

Fig. 4.1 El Niño–Southern Oscillation weather patterns (*Source National Aeronautics and Space Administration*)

with an upswelling of cool water along the Indonesian coast that drives a reversal of the trade winds underpinning the Indian monsoon. While typically occurring in parallel with El Niño conditions, Indian Ocean Dipole events also occur independently of it, a propensity that makes the Indian monsoon a particularly unreliable source of life-supporting rain.[18]

The extent to which the El Niño–Southern Oscillation and the Indian Ocean Dipole held the pre-industrial societies of Asia and Australia hostage is becoming increasingly clear. As a recent study published in *Nature* indicates, the "Asian and Australian summer monsoons both experienced their driest mean conditions of the last millennium during the seventeenth century", resulting in a climatic disaster caused by an "extreme" variation in the Indian Ocean Dipole.[19] Reaching "peak" intensity in 1675, the study continues, the failure of the monsoons was associated with a "crisis in tropical Asia, involving widespread mortality" and the "simultaneous failures of rice crops in India and Thailand".[20] In short, there is no reason to believe that the monsoon-exposed rice farmers of southern India and China ever enjoyed a bucolic lived experience that was fundamentally different from that found in pre-industrial Europe and pre-Columbian America. Throughout the Indo-Pacific, the vagaries of climate made harvest failure a regular occurrence.

In the case of India, the failure of the monsoon caused disastrous famines in 1344–1345, 1631, 1685–1688, 1770, 1789, 1792 and 1830–1831.[21] Accordingly, statements such as those made by Parthasarathi—including that "the advanced areas of the [Indian] subcontinent were ... relatively famine-free in the eighteenth century", and that it was British rule that was responsible for "nineteenth-century India" descending "into levels of poverty that were unprecedented"—are in need of serious

---

[18] Nerilie J. Abram, Nicky M. Wright, Bethany Ellis, Bronwyn etc. Dixon, Jennifer B. Wurtzel, Mathew H. England, Caroline C. Ummenhofer, Belle Philibosiean, Sri Yadawati Cahyarini, Tsai-Luen Yu, Chuan-Chou Shen, Hai Cheng, R. Lawrence Ewards and David Heslop: "Coupling of Indian-Pacific Climate Variability over the Last Millennium", *Nature*, Vol. 579 (19 March 2020), 385.

[19] Abram et al., "Coupling of Indian-Pacific Climate Variability over the Last Millennium", 389, 387.

[20] Ibid.

[21] Fagan, *Food, Famines and Emperors*, 7–10.

qualification.[22] Indeed, far from causing the disruption of an economy well-adjusted to the climate, the British system of railroads and improved internal communications were a salvation, allowing the importation of foodstuffs into famine-affected areas. Since the disastrous food shortages of 1899–1900, India has experienced only one national famine (in 1943–1944), a disaster that was attributable in no small part to a breakdown in the wartime transport systems.

THE MAYA: A CIVILIZATION IN A TERMINAL MALTHUSIAN TRAP

Few people in the human experience have struggled as valiantly against the effects of climate change as the Maya, a contest that ended in the early tenth century with the total collapse of their civilization. Indigenous to a subtropical land that was historically covered by verdant rainforest, the Maya's environment was always far more challenging than it superficially appeared. As we have previously noted, the Maya lowlands of Central America are situated at the northern extremity of the Intertropical Convergence Zone, a location that produces a highly obvious dry season (November–April) and wet season (May–October). Less obvious, but equally consequential, was the region's exposure to extreme climate variation due to both the North Atlantic Oscillation and the El Niño–Southern Oscillation. A geological underlay of limestone karst is another less obvious hindrance to sustainable agriculture. Causing the disappearance of much of the received rainwater into underground streams, this geology has left the northern Yucatan largely devoid of surface rivers and lakes.[23]

From an inhospitable natural environment, the Maya forged a classical period civilization (c. AD 250–900) whose achievements rivaled those of the Old World. Although the Mayan world was fractured into competing city-states, this did little to hinder cultural and economic effervescence. By the eighth century Mayan settlements, "large and small", were distributed across the Yucatan Peninsula and modern-day Guatemala,

[22] Prasannan Parthasarathi, *Why Europe Grew Rich and Asia Did Not: Global Economic Divergence 1600–1850* (Cambridge, UK: Cambridge University Press, 2011), 6, 224.

[23] Julia A. Hoggart, Mathew Restall, James W. Wood and Douglas J. Kennent: "Drought and Its Demographic Effects in the Maya Lowlands", *Current Anthropology*, Vol. 58, No. 1 (2017), 83.

Honduras and Belize. Larger city-states, such as Tikal and Calakmul, "exceeded populations of 50,000 and maintained large amounts of monumental architecture, elite residences, markets, reservoirs, and manipulated seasonal wetlands".[24] Caracol, in modern-day Belize, boasted a population in excess of 100,000.[25] Internally, the residential areas in each Mayan city were organized around private courtyards, each surrounding structure used for a distinct purpose (for example, kitchens, domiciles, religious ritual).[26] Unique to pre-Columbian America, the Maya also developed "a complex system of hieroglyphic writing with a true phonetic component".[27]

Paradoxically, the fact that we know so much about the Maya is primarily due not to their achievements but rather to the circumstances of their collapse, whereby a whole civilization suddenly abandoned all they had created. Until the 1970s most explanations operated on the not unreasonable assumption that the Maya of the classical period inhabited a tropical rainforest similar to that which we witness today. It was also assumed that the classical-period Maya farmed the soil using the same slash-and-burn agricultural practices that have long been the norm among their descendants. Seen from this perspective the abandonment of the great Mayan cities after AD 760 was not as disastrous as appearances suggested. Living largely in harmony with their environment, the Maya simply returned to the jungle, focusing on their traditional slash-and-burn agriculture rather than on the construction of grand architecture.[28] To the extent that the classical-period Maya interfered with the environment, one pioneering paleolimnological study concluded, this involved

---

[24] B.L. Turner II and Jeremy A. Sabloff: "Classic Period Collapse of the Central Maya Lowlands: Insights About Humanity—Environment Relationships for Sustainability", *PNAS*, Vo. 109, No. 35 (2012), 13910.

[25] Ibid.

[26] T. Kam Manahan: "The Ways Things Fall Apart: Social Organization and the Classic Maya Collapse of Copan", *Ancient Mesoamerica*, Vol. 15 (2004), 111–112.

[27] Cecil H. Brown: "Hieroglyphic Literacy in Ancient Mayaland: Inferences from Linguistic Data", *Current Anthropology*, Vol. 32, No. 4 (1991), 489.

[28] Mark Brenner, Michael F. Rosenmeier, David A. Hodell and Jason H. Curtis, "Paleolimnology of the Maya Lowlands: Long-Term Perspective on Interactions Among Climate, Environment, and Humans", *Ancient Mesoamerica*, Vol. 13 (2002), *142–143*; Fagan, *Food, Famines and Emperors*, 12.

84   B. BOWDEN

the fostering of the rainforest rather than its destruction.[29] The idea that
the Maya built their civilization while remaining stewards of the forest
faltered, however, on the quandary of how a low-density forest population could have built and supported complex cities that housed tens
of thousands; a puzzle that continued to make the Maya collapse "one
of the great controversies of archaeology".[30] In consequence, the Maya
lowlands and adjacent areas of the Caribbean Basin were subject to a
host of paleolimnological studies that involved analysis of pollen and silt
deposited in lakebeds and oxygen-isotopes in shell carbonate. The picture
that emerged from these studies was the reverse of what had traditionally
been argued.

Far from being unchanging, the climate of the Maya lowlands was
inherently unstable. Subject to 208-year cycles of rain and drought,
the long-term sustainability of rainforest was also eroded by a climatic
backdrop associated with three millennia of gradual drying.[31] Far from
being stewards of the forest, the Maya systematically "converted tropical lowland forest into an agricultural, savanna-like landscape".[32] From
around 1000 BC the early Mayans engaged in a process of extensive
land clearance that was gradually extended to the less fertile hillsides. As
agricultural intensity increased, a massive layer of silt and clay—the so-
called "Maya clay"—built up in lakebeds as the result of soil runoff.[33]
By the late classical period (c. AD 700), the amount of aboreal pollen
being deposited in lake sediment fell to 10 percent of pre-cultivation
levels, indicating an almost total destruction of the original rainforest.[34]
Supported by the intensive cultivation of corn, population levels in the
"Three Rivers" region of the central Maya lowlands soared from an estimated 4,000 people in 400 BC to a peak of 427,760 souls in the late

[29] Ursala M. Cowgill, G. Evelyn Hutchinson, A.A. Racek, Clyde E. Goulden, Ruth
Patrick and Matsuo Tsukada: "The History of Laguna de Petenxil, a Small Lake in
Northern Guatemala", *Memoirs of the Connecticut Academy of Arts and Sciences*, Vol.
17 (1966), 1–126.

[30] Fagan, *Food, Famines and Emperors*, 140.

[31] Brenner et al., "Paleolimnology of the Maya Lowlands", 148–152; Gill et al.,
"Drought and the Maya Collapse", 294–295.

[32] Brenner et al., "Paleolimnology of the Maya Lowlands", 145.

[33] Ibid., 146–147.

[34] Turner II and Sabloff, "Classic Period Collapse of the Central Maya Lowlands",
13910.

seventh century AD.[35] In addition to large cities such as Tikal, Calakmul and Copan, rural hamlets became an "ubiquitous" feature of the Maya lowlands, "complete with house-lot orchard gardens".[36] As the Maya population rose, fell, and then climbed to new heights, immense pressure was placed on all available resources, be they natural or cultivated. "The sheer size of the population and plastered surfaces in the heartland", Turner and Saboff conclude, "would have required large amounts of fuel for cooking and preparing mortar, placing large demands on forest biomass and water, especially during the latter stages of the dry season".[37]

A sophisticated society with advanced literary and mathematical skills, the Maya would no doubt have appreciated the extent to which they were pushing resources to the limit and taken all possible measures to alleviate the problems they confronted. Despite this, Maya society collapsed not once but four times: in AD 150–200 (the Preclassical Abandonment), AD 536–AD 595 (the Classic Hiatus), AD 760–930 (the Classic Collapse) and AD 1450–1454 (the Postclassical Abandonment). In the "Three Rivers" region (modern-day Guatemala and Belize), the population fell from 17,400 to 5,370 in the Preclassical Abandonment, before reaching a new peak of 130,320 in the early sixth century AD. Then, during the Classical Hiatus it plummeted to 37,761 before rebounding to an all-time peak of 427,760. From this demographic height the population then collapsed irretrievably, the region boasting a population of only 21,480 by the tenth century.[38]

Having pushed their society to its calculated limits the Maya were undone by the unseen effects of the North Atlantic Oscillation and the movement of the Bermuda-Azores High, an atmospheric system whose lengthy southerly placement continually blocked the seasonal migration of the rain-bearing Intertropical Convergence Zone. Each of the four periods of demographic disaster in the Maya lowlands was triggered by Oscillation-induced droughts of unusual severity. Of these four droughts, the so-called Post Terminal Drought, associated with the Classical Collapse of c. AD 760, was not only the most severe of the four, it

[35] Gill et al., "Drought and the Maya Collapse", 289, Figure 5.

[36] Turner II and Sabloff, "Classic Period Collapse of the Central Maya Lowlands", 13910.

[37] Ibid.

[38] Gill et al., "Drought and the Maya Collapse", 186, 289, Figure 5.

was "the most severe of the last 7,000 years".[39] Lasting from AD 750 to AD 1060, with a limited hiatus between AD 870 and AD 920, its severity ensured a societal collapse that was not only severe but it was final in terms of the Mayan people's capacity to construct a highly organized civilization.

It is superficially attractive to regard the Maya Collapse as a salutary lesson in environmental stewardship, of the need to restrict one's ambitions to those dictated by one's natural surrounds. This, however, is a spurious conclusion. Like people everywhere, the Maya wanted the best material and social circumstances for both their families and the wider society. Through back-breaking work they created a civilization that was "intensive in kind" and a "millennia in the making".[40] Admittedly, the Maya had many unsavory attributes, their embrace of human sacrifice and slavery being faults common to most Mesoamerican civilizations. Mayan society was also highly hierarchical. It is almost certain that the monumental stone inscriptions produced in the Mayan cities were meant to be read *at* the populace, not *by* them.[41] Despite such failings, the Maya nevertheless strived with every skill and resource that they possessed to overcome the obstacles before them. Tragically, these resources were never enough and were never going to be enough. Their reliance on corn provided cheap calories but inevitably led the society in the direction of a classic Malthusian trap. Even if the Maya had pushed food production higher than they did it would have merely driven population upward to a higher ceiling, creating additional corpses for the inevitable crunch. The fact that the pre-Columbian Maya civilization rose and fell, rose and fell, rose and fell, points to its inherent failings. Confronted with a classic Malthusian trap, the society not only failed to escape it, it fell apart.

Tragically, the demographic cycle of drought-induced famines, and of population recovery and collapse, continued into the European colonial era and beyond. Drought-induced famines saw the population of the Mexican state of Yucatan fall by 50% in 1666, 20% in 1736, and 40% in 1773. In the "great famine" of 1765–1769 the Indigenous Maya

---

[39] Ibid., 294.

[40] Turner II and Sabloff, "Classic Period Collapse of the Central Maya Lowlands", 13910.

[41] Stephen Houston and David Smart: "On Maya Hieroglyphic Literacy", *Current Anthropology*, Vol. 33, No. 5 (1992), 589–593.

witnessed almost total crop failures in 1769, 1773 and 1776.[42] As in pre-Columbian times, "the rapid decomposition of maize" restricted both storage and the transport of corn from less effected regions.[43] To thus conclude in relation to the Maya, as Lovell and Lutz did, that European contact was responsible for the "greatest destruction of lives in human history", is hyperbole. Sadly, the Maya were well accustomed to a great destruction of life, long before the first European arrived on the scene. Not until the arrival of the railroad in rural Yucatan in 1881 was the cycle of demographic recovery and collapse finally broken. By this stage, as Allen Wells noted, steam-powered shipping "drew Merida, the commercial center of the state, closer to New Orleans, New York, and Chicago than to Mexico City".[44] When the Maya's crops failed in six successive seasons between 1881 and 1886 the population was therefore spared the normal pattern of demographic collapse as the state government imported "huge grain shipments to feed the starving populace".[45] The intrusion of steam-powered shipping and railroads into the Maya's Yucatan heartlands also allowed for new commercial forms of agriculture that involved the growing of fibrous henequen for use in manufactured twine. As such, it offered the Maya an alternative to their traditional subsistence lifestyle for the first time. Amid the crop failures of the 1880s, it was an alternative that was accepted *en masse*, Wells observing how, "With the destruction of each successive crops, peasants abandoned their plots, fled to the northwest, and accepted employment on henequen plantations".[46]

EUROPE: CLIMATE AND TRANSFORMATIVE MALTHUSIAN TRAPS, AD 350–1500

If climate often acted as the destroyer of civilizations, it was not destiny. The Maya rose again and again from famine-induced demographic

---

[42] Hoggart, Restall, Wood and Kennent, "Drought and Its Demographic Effects", 89, 94.

[43] Ibid., 97.

[44] Allen Wells, *Yucatan's Gilded Age: Haciendas, Henequen, and International Harvester, 1860–1915* (Albuquerque, NM: University of New Mexico Press, 1985), 6–7.

[45] Ibid., 94.

[46] Ibid., 94.

collapse. What did appear the immutable human condition in the pre-industrial world, however, was a lived experience where the mass of the population shared a state of material misery. Nevertheless, it is a characteristic feature of Malthusian traps that each demographic collapse opens up new social possibilities. Poor farmland can be abandoned in favor of better land. Fewer people also means that there is less pressure on woodland, allowing more timber for construction and heating. The aftermath of a demographic crisis also provides the possibility for new social and economic directions. A shortage of labor, for example, not only increases the bargaining power of the laboring poor vis-à-vis societal elites, it also incentivizes technological innovation and greater capital intensity. Most societies, however, squander the opportunity to move in a new direction. Western Europe in the fourteenth, fifteenth and sixteenth centuries is an exception. Confronted with the worst demographic collapse in human history in terms of the number of lives lost, Western Europe gradually abandoned its medieval past, creating a distinctly new civilization built around commerce, long-distance trade and scientific inquiry. In short, a fundamentally new civilization—early modern Europe—emerged from the demographic ruins of medieval Europe, which was itself the creation of an earlier demographic crisis that had destroyed the West of classical antiquity.

In the millennia between AD 350 and 1350, Europe suffered not one but two demographic crises, the first corresponding to the Dark Ages Cooling Period (c. AD 400–AD 950) and the second to the Little Ice Age (c. 1300–1850). From each of these crises, a profoundly different civilization emerged from that which preceded it. As Europe's population reached its demographic nadir between the sixth and tenth centuries, the inevitable result of the first of these crises was a society that turned in on itself, focusing on subsistence and survival. As Henri Pirenne observed, each rural community became "a little world on its own. It lived by itself and for itself".[47] In England, J. C. Russell estimated that the entire country boasted only 726,000 inhabitants in AD 856.[48]

As population plummeted down toward "the minimum density that would enable human life to go on", the vibrant urban centers of Roman

---

[47] Henri Pirenne (trans. Frank. D Halsey), *Medieval Cities: Their Origin and the Revival of Trade* (Princeton, NJ: Princeton University Press, 1925), 46.

[48] J.C. Russell, "Late Ancient and Medieval Population", *Transactions of the American Philosophic Society*, Vol. 48, No. 3 (1958), 98.

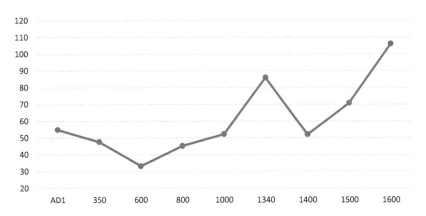

Fig. 4.2 European population, AD 1–1600 (*Sources* Russell, "Late ancient and medieval population", Table 152; Cipolla, *Before the Industrial* Revolution, 4, Table 1.1)

antiquity fell into ruin.[49] As late as 1086, by which time England's population had risen to 1.1 million, London provided a home to only 17,800 inhabitants.[50] Across Europe as a whole, as Fig. 4.2 indicates, population fell to an estimated 33.2 million in AD 600, 40% less than the total that lived on the continent during the reign of Augustus.[51] Whereas the societies of Greek and Roman antiquity were urbane in terms of culture and political power, the Western European civilization that emerged c. AD 800 was unmistakably rural in orientation. Whereas the Greek and Roman worlds were largely secular in their approach to inquiry and philosophy, the ideas that prevailed in Europe between the ninth and fourteenth centuries—and which were literally held with religious faith—were associated with a single institution, the Catholic Church. The feudal Europe that emerged during the ninth century was also inherently collectivist, far removed from the individual ethos of classical Greece. As North and Thomas accurately observed, "Feudal law

---

[49] Braudel, *The Identity of France*, 107.
[50] Russell, "Late Ancient and Medieval Population", 105, 69.
[51] Ibid., 148, Table 152.

did not recognize the concept of land ownership".[52] Instead, in theory at least, feudalism involved the replacement of *property* relationships— which can be expressed in monetary terms—by *personal* relationships based on "vassalage" and an interlocking system of interdependent social obligations.

Of the medieval civilization that reached its apogee around 1300, Barbara Tuchman observed that, "People of the Middle Ages existed under mental, moral, and physical circumstances so different from our own as to constitute almost a foreigncivilization."[53] Braudel went further, arguing that not only did feudalism create "the first European civiliza-tion"—as against earlier Mediterranean civilizations—it was also the case that "Feudalism built Europe".[54] In other words, through its creation of a political economy that embraced most of Western and Central Europe, feudalism transformed "Europe" from a vague geographic concept into a cohesive cultural entity with shared values and beliefs. Consequently, a traveler going about their business in medieval Europe "felt as much at home in Lübeck as in Paris, in London as in Bruges".[55] Boosted by the return of benign climatic conditions associated with the Medieval Warming Period (c. 950–c. 1300), this culturally cohesive European society made extraordinary advances from the tenth century. Everywhere the forests and wild animals that had advanced during the Dark Ages Cooling Period were driven back. In France, half the forest was destroyed between AD 1000 and 1350.[56] By the beginning of the second millen-nium the demographic losses suffered between AD 1 and AD 600 were largely recouped, Europe's population subsequently soaring to a peak of 85.9 million in 1340—a 259% gain from the nadir reached c. AD 600.[57] Amid accelerating demographic expansion, England's population rose from 1.1 million in 1086 to possibly four million in 1250. Then, in the

[52] Douglass C. North and Robert Paul Thomas, *The Rise of the Western World* (London, UK: Cambridge University Press, 1973), 63.

[53] Barbara W. Tuchman, *A Distant Mirror: The Calamitous 14th Century* (New York: Ballantine Books, 1978), xiv.

[54] Fernand Braudel (trans. Richard Mayne), *A History of Civilizations* (London, UK: Penguin, 1993), 312–313.

[55] Ibid., 315.

[56] Braudel, *The Identity of France*, 140.

[57] Russell, "Late Ancient and Medieval Population", 148, Table 152.

ensuing half century, it may have added another million.[58] In France, the population more than trebled between 1086 and 1346, growing from 5.2 to 17.6 million.[59]

The extraordinary demographic gains that characterized medieval Europe during the first three centuries of the second millennium are suggestive of an innovative and dynamic society that belied its rural roots. Among the technological innovations that medieval Europe possessed, but which the world of antiquity did not, were the heavy wheeled plow, the horseshoe, the horse collar, the horse stirrup, wheelbarrows, mechanical clocks, spectacles and the spinning wheel. Tragically, the innovation and toil of medieval Europe tended to increase population at the expense of living standards, leading the society into the same sort of Malthusian trap that the Maya repeatedly faced; a trap whereby frantic additions to population merely added to the corpses when the inevitable climate-induced demographic crunch finally occurred.

As with the demographic catastrophes experienced by the Maya, it was a change in climate that acted as the harbinger of doom for medieval Europe. In 1303 and from 1306 to 1307 the Baltic Sea froze over. In 1315, amid incessant rain, crops failed all over Europe. For the next fifteen years a series of bitterly cold winters caused repeated harvest failures. With the onset of the Little Ice Age, however, the very circumstances in which everyday tasks were undertaken were also profoundly changed for the worse for the next five centuries. In the depths of the Little Ice Age, experienced between 1500 and 1700, Europe's mean annual temperature was 1.5 °C colder than during the Medieval Warming Period. In England, the growing season in 1500 was three weeks shorter than the medieval norm. By 1700, it was five weeks shorter.[60] During the reign of Louis XIV, the "Sun King" (1643–1715) the weather was so cold that wine froze in the glass at the royal table.[61]

Discomforting as such changes were, they were not in themselves typically fatal. For, as in every pre-industrial society, "it is not starvation that kills; rather, it is nutritional deficiencies that contribute to

---

[58] Jón Steinsson, *Malthus and Pre-industrial Stagnation* (Berkeley, CA: University of California, Berkeley, 8 June 2020), 26, https://eml.berkeley.edu/~jsteinsson/teaching/malthus.pdf [accessed 11 April 2021].

[59] Russell, "Late Ancient and Medieval Population", 105.

[60] Fagan, *Food, Famines and Emperors*, 183, 194.

[61] Braudel, *The Identity of France*, 245.

increased susceptibility to disease".[62] Proof of this adage is found in the horrific toll inflicted on Europe by the "Black Death", the bubonic plague outbreak that struck Europe in 1347. Described by Guy Bois as Europe's "Hiroshima" moment,[63] the effects of cold, famine and disease combined to drive the continent's population below the level obtained in AD 1. Even in 1500, more than 160 years after the first outbreak of plague, Europe's population was still 18 percent lower than it had been in 1347.[64]

Disastrous as it was for medieval Europe, the demographic catastrophe was a boon for survivors. Everywhere, as North and Thomas accurately observed in their study into *The Rise of the Western World*, labor shortages "made the landlord worse off" and "improved the bargaining strength of the worker".[65] Evidence of these effects is found in Fig. 4.3, which traces changes in the real wages of skilled building workers in southern England between 1264 and 1597, measured against a basket of consumables (food, rent, clothing, heating, and so on). What is most significant about the rise and fall of real wages during this period is how it constantly moves in an inverse direction to the trend in population as identified in Fig. 4.2. As population continued to rise in the years prior to 1300, real wages fell. When demographic gains faltered between 1300 and 1347, real wages began to recover. As the faltering in population growth turned into a calamitous collapse after 1347, real wages soared. By 1500, real wages were 2.4 times higher than they had been in 1300. Then, as the population's recovery gained steam after 1500, real wages collapsed, falling to an all-time low in 1597.[66]

Nowhere in history can we find a clearer example of the operation of a Malthusian trap than that witnessed in Europe during the centuries on either side of 1347. If, however, the ascent in real wages between 1347 and 1500 disguised unimaginable suffering on a vast scale, so the decline of real wages after 1500 masked a new intellectual and economic vibrancy.

[62] Hoggart, Restall, Wood and Kennent, "Drought and Its Demographic Effects", 98.

[63] Cited, Braudel, *The Identity of France*, 127.

[64] Russell, "Late Ancient and Medieval Population", 148, Table 152.

[65] North and Thomas, *The Rise of the Western World*, 13.

[66] E.H. Phelps Brown and Sheila V. Hopkins: "Seven Centuries of the Price of Consumables, Compared with Builders' Wage Rates", *Economica*, Vol. 23, No. 92 (1956), 311–314, Appendix B.

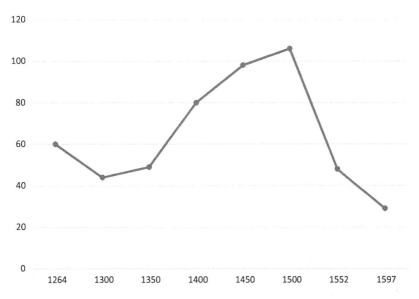

Fig. 4.3 Real wages of skilled building workers in southern England, 1264–1597 (1447 = 100) (*Source* Brown and Hopkins, "Seven centuries of ... builders' wage rates", Appendix B)

By decreasing the value of landed wealth and increasing the value of labor, the demographic crisis of the fourteenth century accelerated the substitution of monetarized dealings for feudal personal relationships. Across Western and Central Europe, commercially oriented cities increasingly asserted a set of individualistic cultural values that were profoundly different from those that had underpinned the Middle Ages.

Of the merchants of Venice, Pirenne observed, "No scruple had any weight with the Venetians. Their religion was a religion of business men".[67] Similarly, in his defining study of the Renaissance, Jacob Burckhardt famously declared this new business class to be the flagbearer of an entirely "new civilization", one that acted "as competitor" to the "whole culture of the Middle Ages, which was essentially clerical".[68] This new

---

[67] Pirenne, *Medieval Cities*, 86.

[68] Jacob Burckhardt (trans. S.G.C. Middlemore), *The Civilization of the Renaissance in Italy*, second edition (New York: The Modern Library, 1954), 148.

civilization, Burckhardt continued, manifested itself "not only in political life, in religion, art, science", but also in "its characteristic stamp on social life". For, as moneyed wealth became the key to the success, "Birth and origins were without influence, unless combined with leisure and inherited wealth".[69]

In science, what was revolutionary was not so much the new understandings of the cosmos expounded by Copernicus and Newton. Instead, it was the principles of inquiry based on "theory, hypothesis and factual reporting"; an approach that has been described as "the most pregnant feature of Western civilization", that is, the one that opened up the most possibilities.[70]

Technological advances were no less revolutionary. In 1440, Gutenberg's invention of the printing press based on movable metal type opened the door to mass literacy. Improvements in cannon and firearms manufacture made European armies of the early modern era far deadlier propositions than their medieval counterparts—as the peoples of Asia, Africa and the New World discovered to their cost. A new-found ability to calculate latitude and a new type of ship, the three-masted caravel, opened up the oceans to European expansion. "And that", Carlo Cipolla, correctly observed, "changed the course of world history".[71]

THE RISE OF EARLY MODERN EUROPE: ANOTHER TRAP?

If we look at the economic, demographic and technological trajectories that are apparent in early modern Europe in the early 1500s we can ascertain two underlying currents: one tugging the society toward another Malthusian trap and the other in the direction of commercial success and global expansion. This tug-of-war was witnessed at two obvious levels: in the contrast between the commercial growth and vigor of the Dutch and English economies and the stagnation apparent elsewhere, and the divergent trends even within Dutch and English societies.

In the sixteenth and early seventeenth centuries, Spain was the dominant European power. The military and political strength of the Spanish

[69] Ibid., 265–266.

[70] A. Rupert Hall, *The Scientific Revolution 1500–1800: The Formation of the Modern Scientific Attitude*, second edition (Boston, MA: Beacon Press, 9162), 387.

[71] Carlo M. Cipolla, *Before the Industrial Revolution: European Society and Economy, 1000–1700*, second edition (Cambridge, UK: Cambridge University Press, 1981), 177.

Hapsburgs, however, rested on fragile economic foundations. Increasingly, Spain was bled dry in support of foreign ventures. Although Spain's vast empire in the Americas and the profits of the Atlantic slave trade enriched individual Spaniards, they did not enrich the broader Spanish society. In 1750, per capita output ($783)—measured in constant 1990 US dollars—was lower than it had been in 1500 ($846). In Italy, per capita output in 1750 ($1,533) was also less than that obtained in 1500 ($1,553).

By contrast, the Dutch economy was transformed between 1500 and 1650, per capita output almost doubling to $2,691.[72] Although largely excluded from the Atlantic trade by the mercantilist policies of France, Britain and Spain, the Netherlands dominated North Sea fishing and the Baltic trade. In every year between 1550 and 1650 most of the ships entering the Baltic were Dutch. In some years the figure stood at 85 percent as the Netherlands imported Baltic timber and grain, which was then re-exported all around Europe.[73] Profiting immensely from its monopolization of trade with the Dutch East Indies (Indonesia), the Netherlands also benefited from its plentiful peat supplies, a boon that allowed for the energy-intensive manufacture of beer, glass and bricks. Accordingly, during the seventeenth century—the Dutch "Golden Age"—the economy of the Netherlands "was surely the wealthiest in Europe".[74]

Between 1650 and 1750 the English economy followed a similar trajectory as per capita output grew by 182 percent to $1,695. Until 1700, English prosperity still rested on traditional export staples, most particularly wool and woolen manufactures.[75] After 1700, however, the importation and re-export of plantation produce from the Americas predominated. Between 1771 and 1775, for example, Britain imported 278 million pounds (lbs.) of tobacco from the Americas and re-exported

---

[72] Nuno Palma and Jaime Reis: "From Convergence to Divergence: Portuguese Economic Growth 1527–1850", *Journal of Economic History*, Vol. 79, No. 2 (2019), 500, Table 4.

[73] Cipolla, Before the Industrial Revolution, 271.

[74] Jan Leuten van Zanden, "The 'Revolt of the Early Modernists' and the 'First Modern Economy': An Assessment", *Economy History Review*, Vol. 55, No. 4 (2002), 631.

[75] Ralph Davis: "English Foreign Trade, 1770–1774", *Economic History Review*, Vol. 15, No. 2 (1962), 285–303.

230 million lbs.[76] Sugar was even more profitable. In 1773, imports from the sugar island of Jamaica were worth five times more than that obtained from all of Britain's thirteen North American colonies.[77] By the latter decades of the eighteenth century, Britain was also heavily involved in the slave trade, annually transporting 50,000 slaves to the Americas.[78]

If the English and Dutch economies were unquestionably the most dynamic in Europe by the latter half of the sixteenth century, we should nevertheless not exaggerate their achievements. Per capita output in the Netherlands stalled after 1650. Yes, it is true, as Allen argues, that wages in London and Amsterdam were significantly higher than elsewhere in the eighteenth century.[79] The Industrial Revolution, however, was associated with northern England, not London—and certainly not Amsterdam. There is also no reason to assume that commercial success associated with the importation of tobacco and sugar led toward investments in coal mining and mechanized manufacture. For the most part it did not. Contrary to what has been recently asserted, there is also little to suggest that involvement in the slave trade was "central" to subsequent success and prosperity.[80] Instead, participation in the slave trade was a gamble that enriched some but ruined others. "In the last sixty years of British slaving", Thomas estimated, "the annual returns seem to have been less than 10 per cent".[81] Nor was England the dominant force in textile manufacture that it became after 1800. On the contrary, England found itself steadily losing business to imported Indian textiles during the first half of the eighteenth century. Not until the 1790s was the landed price of Indian cotton textiles dearer than those produced domestically.[82]

[76] Ibid., 297.

[77] Hugh Thomas, *The Slave Trade: The History of the Atlantic Slave Trade 1440–1870* (London, UK: Picador, 1997), 479.

[78] Ibid., 540.

[79] Robert Allen: "Progress and Poverty in Early Modern Europe", *Economic History Review*, Vol. 56, No. 3 (2003), 403–443.

[80] Leon C. Prieto and Simone T.A. Phipps, *Why Business Schools Need to Address Black History: It's Time to Decolonize the Business Curriculum* (Cambridge, MA: Harvard Business Publishing—Education, 18 February 2021), 2.

[81] Thomas, *The Slave Trade*, 443.

[82] Stephen Broadberry and Bishnupriya Gupta, "Lancashire, India, and Shifting Competitive Advantage in Cotton Textiles, 1700–1850", *Economic History Review*, Vol. 62, No. 2 (2009), 295.

The underlying tug-of-war between the forces leading toward another Malthusian trap and rising per capita prosperity is also evident when we switch our focus from national trends to those existing within British society. In terms of real wages and living standards, we are confronted with contradictory evidence at almost every turn. Thomas Malthus, writing in 1798, noted on one hand the comparative well-being of "labourers of the South of England" who had become "accustomed to eat fine wheaten bread".[83] Yet, he also lamented how "the pressure of distress" on "the lower classes of society" was "so deeply seated that no human ingenuity can reach it".[84] Robert Allen argues that England's "high wage economy" experienced a "northern spread" during the eighteenth century.[85] However, he also concedes that "[r]eal wages grew very little in Britain during the Industrial Revolution"—a conclusion that necessarily implies that real wage growth had stalled by 1800.[86] Whereas Allen argues that it was "technological innovation" that finally allowed British society an escape from "Malthusian economics",[87] Clark concludes that England's "technological advance ... in the latter half of the eighteenth century ... created only a larger population without generating any [per capita] income gains".[88] Certainly, eighteenth-century England led the world in scientific research. Yet, very little of this research aided technological innovation, the typical inventor on the Industrial Revolution being an artisan, some of whom—such as James Hargreaves—were functionally illiterate.[89] Everywhere, the long wintery grip of the Little Ice Age continued its hold on ordinary life. In 1684, the ground in parts of southern England froze to a depth of more than a meter.[90]

[83] Thomas Malthus, *An Essay on the Principles of Population* (London, UK: J. Johnson, 1798), 42.

[84] Ibid., 30.

[85] Robert C. Allen, *The British Industrial Revolution in Global Perspective* (Cambridge, UK: Cambridge University Press, 2009), 44.

[86] Ibid., 41.

[87] Ibid., 128, 135.

[88] Gregory Clark, *A Farewell to Alms: A Brief Economic History of the World* (Princeton, NJ: Princeton University Press, 2007), 30.

[89] Allen, *British Industrial Revolution*, 265.

[90] Fagan, *Food, Famines and Emperors*, 197.

Between 1693 and 1700, a third of the population of the Scottish Highlands died of hunger, a contemporary recording that, "For seven years the calamitous weather continued", the population perishing in their thousands "from weakness, cold, and hunger".[91]

How to make sense of this contradictory evidence, some of which points one way and some of which leads in the opposite direction? The simplest (and best) answer is to conclude that both bodies of evidence are accurate. Certainly, there is every reason to suspect that, by 1750, England's commercial success was no longer capable of sustaining increases in national income commensurate to the gains in population. Thus, whereas England's population grew at an annualized rate of 0.7 percent across the course of the eighteenth century, the per capita growth in national output between 1700 and 1750 was only 0.24%. By contrast, in the preceding half century (1650–1700), per capita output grew at an annualized rate of 1.24%.[92]

In the final analysis, England's eighteenth-century commercial success was too narrowly based to ensure avoidance of another Malthusian crisis. For, despite Britain's maritime superiority, its reliance on wind power and wooden hulls ensured a continued orientation toward low-weight, high-value freight, such as tobacco and sugar. Although the textile industry survived behind protective tariffs, the superiority of Indian cottons had eroded what were once lucrative exports. In short, there is every reason to suspect, as Komlos concluded, that in 1750 England confronted "an incipient Malthusian crisis", one that it only avoided "at the last minute".[93]

[91] Ibid., 198.

[92] Calculated from Palma and Jaime Reis, "From Convergence to Divergence", 500, Table 4.

[93] Komlos, "Secular Trend in the Biological Standard of Living", 143, 141.

CHAPTER 5

The Eternal Challenge: Calorific Expenditure and the Emergence of an Industrialized Civilization

In the popular imagination, calories are associated with food intake and, to a lesser degree, exercise expenditure. In truth, calories are simply a measure of energy. Calories are expended by animals as well as humans. Animals also consume calories, often competing with humans for the same sources of calorific intake. Calories are also expended in heating, cooking and manufacturing. Typically, the latter forms of calorific expenditure use the energy stored in inanimate objects (such as wood, coal, gas, oil, and so on) with the energy being released through the process of combustion. Where oil and gas are burned the measure of energy expenditure is typically British thermal units (BTU), rather than calories. Energy can also be harnessed from wind and water for mechanical purposes (for example, transport, machinery). Generally, these forms of harnessed energies are expressed as either kilowatts or horsepower per hour (hp·h). These latter forms of measurement are also applied to mechanized energy more generally.

Of the naturally occurring sources of energy the easiest to harness, and typically the most abundant, was human muscle power. Highly flexible and adaptable to many tasks, humans are nevertheless inherently puny.

© The Author(s), under exclusive license to Springer Nature
Switzerland AG 2022
B. Bowden, *Slavery, Freedom and Business Endeavor*,
Palgrave Debates in Business History,
https://doi.org/10.1007/978-3-030-97232-5_5

Typically, an adult can exert no more than 0.03–0.04 hp.[1] By comparison, a horse can exert up to 0.6 hp.[2] In terms of pulling power, a horse's performance also exceeds that which can be garnered from oxen by a factor of four or five.[3] Accordingly, in pre-industrial societies the use of horses in agriculture is typically associated with comparatively high productivity, and reliance on oxen with low productivity. Horses are also more reliable and adaptable than either water power or wind power, which are of little use when the water freezes over, or the wind does not blow. Such boons, however, come at a high cost. Typically, it takes 2 acres of managed pasture (0.8 hectares) to support a single horse for a year, and up to 30 acres of natural grassland (12 hectares).[4] Even in Northern Europe, which is a region of abundant meadows and forest, this was difficult to achieve. In Greek and Roman antiquity, the comparative rarity of horses is indicated by the fact that the Greek phalanx and the Roman legions were constructed around soldiers on foot, not horsemen. Where horses were maintained, the onset of inclement weather required not only stabling but also the provision of alternative sources of feed, such as oats. Both required a reallocation of scarce resources from human to animal consumption. In urban locales, the problems involved in stabling and feeding horses multiplied inexorably. On the eve of the Revolution, Paris—a city of about 500,000 inhabitants—boasted only 21,000 horses.[5]

Depending on the geography and climate, water and wind offered a viable alternative to animal power for a range of industrial purposes. Perfected in Europe in the second century AD, the watermill became a ubiquitous feature of medieval and early modern life.[6] England's Domesday Book records that, in 1086, 3,000-odd communities were

---

[1] Fernand Braudel (trans. Sian Reynolds), *Civilization and Capitalism, 15th–18th Century: The Structures of Everyday Life* (London, UK: Collins, 1981), 337.

[2] Ibid.

[3] Charles Parain, "The Evolution of Agricultural Techniques", in M.M. Postan (ed.), *The Cambridge Economic History of Europe*, vol. 1. (Cambridge, UK: Cambridge University Press, 1966), 144.

[4] Extension Horses, *How Much Land Do I Need for a Horse*, https://horses.extension. org/ [Accessed 16 April 2021].

[5] Braudel, *Structures of Everyday Life*, 350.

[6] Andrew Wilson, "Machines, Power and the Ancient Economy", *Journal of Roman Studies*, Vol. 92, No. 1 (2002), 1–32.

operating 5,264 watermills, principally to grind grain.[7] By the late eighteenth century, Western Europe featured more than 500,000 watermills, making it the society's most important source of inanimate power.[8] From the fourteenth century the large winged windmill also became a feature of the Western European landscape, France possessing 20,000 by the end of the fifteenth century.[9] The significance of water and wind for medieval and early modern industry should not be understated. As late as 1830—a year traditionally seen as marking the end of the Industrial Revolution—wind and water generated more motive power in Great Britain than did steam power.[10] But neither should it be exaggerated. In Great Britain, a society that had exploited water power for more than a millennium, water power generated a miniscule 70,000 hp in 1760, a total that would have been vastly overshadowed by animal power. Wind's contribution was even more inconsequential, providing only 10,000 hp.[11] It is thus evident that the vast number of watermills and windmills that characterized the medieval and early modern European landscape belied their feeble output. Watermills typically generated 2 hp, 5 hp at the most. Few windmills generated more than 5 hp, the great tower mills of the Netherlands being an exception, producing up to 30 hp.[12]

Wind and water's potential was more obvious in transport. By the sixteenth and seventeenth centuries, Western European ships were plying the Indian and Pacific Oceans as well as the Atlantic. Between 1600 and 1786, the tonnage of Europe's merchant marine grew roughly five-fold, from around 650,000 tons to almost 3.4 million tons.[13] Although Japan and China pursued policies of maritime exclusion in the early modern era, substantial non-European shipping fleets also plied the Indian Ocean

[7] Douglass C. North and Robert Paul Thomas, *The Rise of the Western World* (London, UK: Cambridge University Press, 1973), 44.

[8] Carlo M. Cipolla, *Before the Industrial Revolution: European Society and Economy, 1000–1700*. Second edition (Cambridge, UK: Cambridge University Press, 1981), 97.

[9] Fernand Braudel (trans. Sian Reynolds), *The Identity of France: People and Production* (London, UK: Fontana Press, 1991), 145.

[10] Robert C. Allen, *The British Industrial Revolution in Global Perspective* (Cambridge, UK: Cambridge University Press, 2009), 177.

[11] Ibid., 173, Figure 7.1.

[12] Braudel, *Structures of Everyday Life*, 233; Fernand Braudel (trans. Richard Mayne), *A History of Civilizations* (London, UK: Penguin, 1993), 374.

[13] Braudel, *Structures of Everyday Life*, 362.

102   B. BOWDEN

and the waters around South-East Asia. In 1841, a total of 24,497 native Indian craft were recorded as entering Indian ports alongside 171 from the Gulf states. It was not only the number but also the tonnage of the Indian craft that was impressive. In 1841, this amounted to 590,692 tons, a total roughly equivalent to Europe's entire fleet in the early seventeenth century.[14]

As with wind and water's contribution to industry, it is important that we neither understate nor exaggerate their maritime contribution. Until the advent of the railways, water transport was the only financially feasible mechanism for long-distance shipment. On land, the cost of horse-drawn transport rapidly consumed the value of the goods being shipped, an iron rule that applied as much to the nineteenth century as it did in the twelfth. In late nineteenth-century Australia, it was calculated that a ton of wheat could be hauled only 15 miles (25 km) across land before its value was fatally eroded.[15] Cheap by comparison with landed transport, the inherent failings of water-borne transport nevertheless restricted communication and economic expansion on every front. As noted in this book's introduction, in 1786—when the Industrial Revolution was more than a quarter of a century old—the tonnage of the entire European fleet equated to only twenty modern capesize ships (deadweight, up to 175,000 tons). Even this comparison overstates the usefulness of the pre-industrial shipping fleet. Reliance on the prevailing trade winds severely restricted the number of journeys that could be undertaken. In 1700, it took six months to sail from London to Calcutta, allowing only one return voyage a year.[16] Wood construction and exposure to the elements also meant that ships typically survived only a few years. Given the expense and risks, few volunteered for maritime crossings. In 1820 only 8,385 immigrants to the United States braved the Atlantic crossing. Twenty years later the annual total was still only 23,322.[17]

[14] Parliament of the United Kingdom, *Statistical Abstract Relating to British India, 1860 to 1869* (London, UK: George E. Eyre & William Spottiswoode, 1870), Figure 14.

[15] Edward Shann, *Am Economic History of Australia* (Cambridge, UK: Cambridge University Press, 1948), 292.

[16] Niall Ferguson, *Empire: How Britain Made the Modern World* (Melbourne, AUS: Penguin Books, 2008), 25.

[17] United States Department of Commerce, *Historical Statistics of the United States: Colonial Times to 1970—Bicentennial Edition* (Washington, DC: United States Department of Commerce, 1975), Series C 25–75.

For the Indigenous peoples of Australia and New Zealand the winds of the Southern Ocean provided better protection than spears and battle-axes, neither witnessing a European settler prior to 1788. "Sailors who had spent a life at sea in the Baltic and Mediterranean and North Sea or in the North Atlantic Ocean", Geoffrey Blainey reflected, "did not appreciate the strength and staying power of the westerlies in the chill waters of the southern hemisphere".[18] Waves were typically "mountainous", exacting a heavy toll on ships and crew.[19]

If wind and water offered only limited succor to human endeavors in manufacturing and transport, a reliance on wood for construction, heating and smelting acted as an even-greater barrier to improvement in the human condition. For, in the final analysis, as Carlo Cippola accurately noted, "Civilisations before the eighteenth century were civilizations of wood and charcoal."[20] Wood was used to build not only homes but also ships, carts, bridges, watermills and tools. By contrast, iron remained a relative rarity. In the first two decades of the eighteenth century, the annual output of iron in Great Britain—an unquestioned leader in the field—only amounted to between 24,000 and 25,000 tons.[21] Much of the iron that was cast, moreover, was used for cannon and other military purposes. In consequence, iron was used only sparingly in tools and equipment. The metal blades on plowshares were so thin that on clay or stony soil they only penetrated to a depth of 10–12 cm (4–5 inches), a fact that goes a long way to explaining the low productivity of pre-industrial agriculture.[22] It was in relation to heating, industrial manufacturing and smelting, however, that the problems associated with a reliance on wood manifested themselves in its most serious form. For even basic heating consumes enormous amounts of calorific energy. To raise the temperature of 1 lb. (0.43 l) of water by 1°Fahrenheit (0.56 °C), for example, one will typically expend 40,320 calories or 160 BTUs. Invariably, in pre-industrial societies this heating requirement was met by burning wood, each person

---

[18] Geoffrey Blainey, *The Tyranny of Distance: How Distance Shaped Australia's History* (London, UK: History Book Club, 1968), 38.

[19] Ibid., 40.

[20] Cipolla, *Before the Industrial Revolution*, 266.

[21] Philip Riden, "The Output of the British Iron Industry Before 1870", *Economic History Review*, Vol. 30, No. 3 (1977), 443, Table 1.

[22] Braudel, *The Identity of France*, 254–255.

requiring—the estimates vary according to both economic circumstances and the calculations of individual historians—between 0.33 tons and 0.5 tons per annum for their own personal heating and cooking.[23] This basic need placed a heavy demand on woodland. In Paris, Braudel estimated, 2 million tons of wood was consumed each year simply for charcoal and firewood on the eve of the Revolution (1789).[24] In Guangdong in southern China, such was the demand for wood that the area under forest fell from 9 million hectares in 1753 to 4.88 million hectares a century later.[25] During the course of the eighteenth century, one-sixth of England's remaining woodland disappeared.[26]

In the early eighteenth century, across Eurasia and Africa, every civilization confronted the same basic conundrum. Productivity in agriculture, manufacturing and transport suffered from a shortage of smelted iron and an over-reliance on fast disappearing timber. To increase iron output, however, one needed to convert vast reserves of wood to charcoal. Yes, it is true, that England had long experimented with coal-derived coke as a substitute for charcoal. However, the impurities in coal, most particularly sulfur, caused insoluble problems until the mid-1700s.[27] In short, civilizations everywhere found themselves in a technologically induced Malthusian trap; one that had pressed on all agricultural societies from time immemorial, but which nevertheless presented itself more acutely as woodlands vanished.

The explanation as to how Britain, and ultimately the world, escaped from the vicious circle that once confronted it owes a great deal to John Ulric Nef, a Chicago-based economic historian with an obsessive interest in English history. In Nef's estimation, the key to Britain's Industrial Revolution was found in the inexorable rise of the nation's coal industry. As production rose from 200,000 tons in 1560 to 3 million tons in 1681, Nef argued, England swiftly transitioned to an energy-intensive

---

[23] For a discussion of various estimates, see Kenneth Pomeranz, *The Great Divergence: China, Europe, and the Making of the Modern World Economy* (Princeton, NJ and Oxford, UK: Princeton University Press, 2000), Appendix C.

[24] Braudel, *Structures of Everyday Life*, 367.

[25] Pomeranz, *The Great Divergence*, Appendix C.

[26] Allen, *British Industrial Revolution*, 96.

[27] Ibid., 221–222.

economy fundamentally different to any other.[28] "Compared with the high mounds besides the collieries in Durham and Northumberland", Nef noted, "the piles of coal besides the chief French pits resembled anthills".[29] This achievement also meant that Britain was better placed than any rival to exploit the two key technological breakthroughs of the eighteenth century, coke-smelted iron and steam power—both of which used copious amounts of coal.[30] Admittedly, many of the details of Nef's argument have been challenged in recent years. Some, most particularly Robert Allen, have challenged Nef's belief that England faced an incipient timber crisis in the sixteenth century, arguing that this only became manifest in the eighteenth century.[31] Allen also demonstrates that it took a considerable time for coal to assert a decisive price advantage in key markets, such as London.[32] Despite such quibbles, however, Nef's central argument—that Britain's early success in coal mining underpinned its subsequent industrial superiority—has stood the test of time. As Fig. 5.1 indicates, the comparatively high price of coal in London owed more to transport expenses than production costs. Despite this obstacle, however, coal was far cheaper than either wood or charcoal by the seventeenth century, an outcome that caused London to be the first metropolis to source its energy needs from the burning of coal. It was, however, England's north—in Northumberland, Durham and Lancashire—where coal's price superiority exerted itself to the fullest.[33] And, consequently,

---

[28] John U. Nef, *The Rise of the British Coal Industry*, vol. 1 (London, UJ: Frank Cass, 1932), 1920; John U Nef, *War and Human Progress: An Essay on the Rise of Industrial Civilization*, second edition (New York: Norton & Co., 1963), 8–10.

[29] John U. Nef, "The Industrial Revolution Reconsidered", *Journal of Economic History*, Vol. 3, No. 1 (1943), 18.

[30] John U. Nef, "The Progress of Technology and the Growth of Large-scale Industry in Great Britain, 1540–1640", *Economic History Review*, Vol. 5, No. 1 (1934), 3–34; John U. Nef, "Prices and Industrial Capitalism in Germany, France and England, 1540–1640", *Economic History Review*, Vol. 7, No. 2 (1937), 155–185.

[31] M.W. Flinn, "Timber and the Advance of Technology", *Annals of Science*, Vol. 15, No. 2 (1959), 109–120; G. Hammersley, "Crown Woods and the Exploitation in the Sixteenth and Seventeenth Centuries", *Bulletin of the Institute of Historical Research*, Vol. 30, No. 82 (1973), 136–161; Allen, *British Industrial Revolution*, 84–96.

[32] Allen, *British Industrial Revolution*, 84–90.

[33] Ibid., 99, Table 4.2; R.C. Allen, "Why the Industrial Revolution Was British: Commerce, Induced Invention, and the Scientific Revolution", *Economic History Review*, Vol. 64, No. 2 (2011), 365–366.

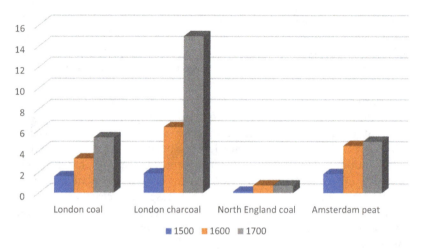

Fig. 5.1 Price of energy in grams of silver, 1500–1700 (*Source* Allen, *British Industrial Revolution*, Table 4.2)

it was here that the Industrial Revolution of the 1760–1830 period was forged.

Initially, the new energy-intensive economy was confined to a handful of industries: cotton and woolen textiles, pottery and iron making. By the 1830s, however, as the Industrial Revolution (or, rather, its first stage) came to an end, a more far-reaching transformation occurred due to interconnected revolutions in agriculture, transport and manufacturing. As iron and (after 1850) steel production soared upward, the door was opened to a transport revolution associated with railroads and iron, and steel-hulled ships. As transport costs fell, a truly integrated global market emerged. By the 1870s, Kevin O'Rourke observed, Europe was both benefiting and suffering from a New World "grain invasion". It drove down not only food costs but also land prices as it rendered much of the European farm sector uncompetitive.[34] Manufacturing, in turn, benefited from both falling input costs (grains, cotton, wool, silk, indigo,

---

[34] Kevin O'Rourke, "The European Grain Invasion, 1870–1913", *Journal of Political Economy*, Vol. 57, No. 4 (1997), 775–801.

minerals) and also expanded markets that facilitated mechanized production in domains that had hitherto been the preserve of artisans and the household sector: clothing, boot and shoes, furniture, and so on.

In few places did the interconnected revolution in agriculture, manufacturing and transport in the middle third of the nineteenth century have a more enduring impact on the human condition than in the United States. From the outset, American success was built on exploiting both European-derived and home-grown technologies to the fullest. As early as 1840, the United States operated 3,200 miles (5,120 km) of railroad track—a length that was more than twice as long as that found in Europe.[35] In the ensuing decades, America's railroads assumed a scale and scope for which there was no historical precedent. During the 1880s, a record 75,000 miles (12,000 km) were laid down, "by far the greatest amount of railroad mileage ever built in any decade in any part of the world".[36] By the 1890s, Alfred Chandler famously observed, the "great railway systems" of the United States were not only the nation's "largest business enterprises", they were also the largest anywhere in the world.[37] In addition to facilitating rural settlement, the railroads also underpinned a large-scale expansion of America's engineering and metal industries. On the eve of the Civil War, the railroads were absorbing 22% of the nation's pig iron output for rails alone. They were also responsible for 60% of the nation's installed horsepower.[38] What was unique about the United States' manufacturing, however, was not so much its achievements in heavy engineering as its capacity to bring mechanized production to a range of everyday consumer items: stoves, tobacco, ready-made clothing, and boot and shoe manufacture. In 1860, the value adding in stovemaking alone was equal to that of iron railroad rails.[39] In ready-made clothing, the invention of the Howe (1846) and Singer (1851) sewing machines revolutionized production. In boot and shoe manufacture, the

[35] Daniel Walker Howe, *What Hath God Wrought: The Transformation of America, 1815–1848* (Oxford, UK: Oxford University Press, 2007), 563,

[36] Alfred D. Chandler, Jr., *The Visible Hand: The Managerial Revolution in American Business* (Cambridge, UK: Cambridge University Press, 1977), 171.

[37] Ibid., 204.

[38] W.W. Rostow, "Leading Sectors and the Take-off", in W.W. Rostow (ed.), *The Economics of Take-off into Sustained Growth* (London, UK: Macmillan, 1963), 5.

[39] Douglass C. North, "Industrialization in the United States", in W.W. Rostow (ed.), *The Economics of Take-off into Sustained Growth* (London, UK: Macmillan, 1963), 53.

108   B. BOWDEN

patenting of the Blake McKay sole-sewing machine (1864) had a similar effect, largely displacing the artisanal shoemaker who had been a ubiquitous feature of village life since time immemorial. By 1860, boot and shoemaking employed more American workers than any other manufacturing sector. Ready-made men's clothing stood alongside cotton textiles in second place.[40]

Equally revolutionary were American advances in farm mechanization. In the 1860s the self-rake reaper, which left cut sheaves for hand-bundling, was the most revolutionary item of farm machinery. For every harvester operator, however, the self-rake required four or five laborers to gather up the cut grain. Then, in 1879, these tasks were made redundant by the patenting of the twine-binding harvester that both cut and bound the farmer's crops. Built in vast numbers at ever-lower costs by the Deering Harvester Machine Company and the McCormick Harvesting Machine Company, the new harvester "was an advance over the self-rake", Thorstein Veblen observed in 1892, "such as anyone who has not seen both machines in use on the wheat fields of the West will scarcely appreciate". Whereas, previously, four to five adults were required for harvesting, with the new machine "a boy" could do the work unaided.[41]

If by the dawn of the twentieth century the United States was the unchallenged leader in consumer goods and agricultural machinery, in Europe the newly forged nation of Germany became an industrial powerhouse through a focus on capital intensity, industrial research and high-productivity farming. By 1872, Clive Trebilcock noted, "a single German university, that at Munich, contained more graduate research chemists than all English universities put together".[42] Whereas British industry on the eve of World War I was still based on the family firm, and that of the United States on the multiunit corporation, the cartel was the characteristic institution of German business. It was, Trebilcock noted, "a collectivist and co-operative form of industrial activity" that provided a "safe environment for investment".[43] By 1907, Germany was the world's largest chemical producer, responsible for 80% of the world's

[40] Ibid., 49, Table1.

[41] Thorstein Veblen, "Price of Wheat Since 1867", *Journal of Political Economy*, Vol. 1, No. 1 (1892), 83, 85.

[42] Clive Trebilcock, *The Industrialization of the Continental Powers, 1780–1914* (London, UK and New York: Longman, 1981), 63.

[43] Ibid., 68.

industrial dyes.[44] It was also the world's largest exporter of electrical products. Only the American corporate giants of Du Pont (chemicals) and General Electric (electricals) rivaled the dominant German firms in size and market share, a rivalry in electricals that came to an end in 1907 when General Electric and the German A.E.G. agreed to divide the world market between themselves.[45] Where, in the United States, the symbiotic relationship between agriculture and manufacturing in the nineteenth century was embodied in the twine-binding harvester that became the key to low-cost, broadacre cultivation, in Germany the exploitation of the nation's ground-breaking work in chemicals resulted in a high-yield rural sector. By 1910–1913, the typical German farmer was applying 50 kg of fertilizer per hectare annually, a level that "was exceeded by no other large country". German fertilizer rates were almost double those of Britain (28 kg) and almost four times those of Italy (14 kg). As a result of such efforts, as Fig. 5.2 indicates, German agricultural productivity soared, rising 190% between 1841 and 1900.[46]

By the first decade of the twentieth century, the basis for a fundamentally different mode of existence was evident on many fronts in ways that bore increasingly little resemblance to that which had characterized the human condition a century earlier.

Slavery, Agriculture, Industry and Capital Intensity

The ready availability of human labor, and the comparative expense of alternatives, resulted in historic production systems that were labor-intensive rather than capital-intensive. In the oldest surviving comprehensive text on farm management, Cato the Elder (234 BC–149 BC) provided guidance to his Roman contemporaries as to the efficient running of a *latifundia*, or slave estate. In buying a new estate, Cato advised, one should always look for one with "few tools". For when one

---

[44] Ibid., 47.

[45] V.I. Lenin, "Imperialism, the Highest Stage of Capitalism", in V.I. Lenin, *Selected Works*, vol. 1 (Moscow, UUSR: Foreign Languages Publishing House, 1946), 694.

[46] Trebilcock, *Industrialization of the Continental Powers*, 434, Table 7.5a.

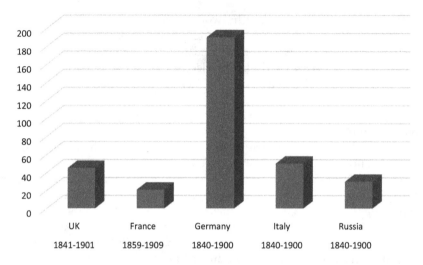

Fig. 5.2 Agricultural productivity, percentage increases, 1841 to 1900–1901 (*Note* French figures are for period from 1841 to 1909. *Source* Trebilcock, *Industrialization of the Continental Powers*, 434, Table 7.5a)

observed this, you knew "it is not an expensive farm to operate".[47] On days of inclement weather that restricted working hours, Cato also advised that, "the Slaves' rations shall be cut down as compared with what is allowed when they are working".[48]

Significantly, in advising against the use of "tools", Cato used the word "operate" rather than "purchase". For, as we have already noted, one of the typically overlooked features of pre-industrial equipment was that it was almost always made of wood. This made tools and equipment comparatively cheap to purchase. However, it also guaranteed constant repair and replacement. In Bologna in the thirteenth century, for example, the equipment required by a one-household workshop in the silk and wool trade was amortized within a year. In other words, equipment had to be replaced on an annual basis.[49] Where large-scale manufacturing existed

---

[47] Cato the Elder, "De agricultura", in A Virginian Farmer, *Roman Farm Management: The Treatises of Cato and Varro* (New York: Macmillan, 1913), 22.

[48] Ibid., 25.

[49] Cipolla, *Before the Industrial Revolution*, 203–204.

it typically entailed the construction of *buildings* where the flow of material and work could be coordinated, rather than the purchase of *machinery* to facilitate production. Even in the late eighteenth century the typical Genovese silk factory—one of Europe's most mechanized industries—spent 87% of its fixed capital on buildings and only 13% on machinery.[50] In agriculture, livestock rivaled buildings as the prime capital expense, investment in the two being intertwined. One late seventeenth century estimate calculated that the value of English livestock at 25% of the value of the nation's agricultural land.[51] Unfortunately, livestock's high value in pre-industrial society largely reflected the cost of animals rather than their widespread availability. In Italy in the seventeenth century the cost of a cow equated to 100 work days for the typical laborer.[52] Of the horses or oxen required to pull a wheeled plow in medieval Europe, North and Thomas observed that their expense was "prohibitively large for any single family".[53] Similarly, in reflecting upon the French experience, Braudel observed that "the great majority did not own either a horse or a pair of oxen".[54] Consequently, in medieval villages, most peasants only worked their plots by "pooling their resources to make up a team".[55] Even in the late eighteenth century the stock of animals in Europe was limited. At best, there was one horse for every thirteen people, and one ox for every eight. In terms of motive power, this equated to 0.065 hp per capita.[56] In classical antiquity, and even in the medieval period, this ratio would have been far lower.

Low levels of capital intensity, and the short life expectancy of the equipment that did exist, led inevitably to labor-intensive work practices, including the use of slavery.

In pre-industrial societies, human labor had many advantages over animal power. Humans ate less than horses and could be stabled in smaller

---

[50] Ibid., 105.

[51] Ibid., 99–100.

[52] Cipolla, *Before the Industrial Revolution*, 101–102.

[53] North and Thomas, *Rise of the Western World*, 30.

[54] Braudel, *The Identity of France*, 257.

[55] North and Thomas, *Rise of the Western World*, 30.

[56] Calculated from Braudel, *Structures of Everyday Life*, 350, 42. Braudel estimated that there were 14 million horses and 24 million oxen and a European population of 187 million. A horse is estimated at providing 0.6 hp and an ox a quarter of this.

dwellings. They were also more flexible. Like everything else, however, the price of labor fluctuated up and down over time. As a rule of thumb, labor shortages led to the displacement of unfree work relationships by ones that favored the laboring majority. The demographic crisis associated with the fall of the Western Roman Empire, for example, led to the collapse of slave-operated *latifundia*. Keen to incentivize their remaining workforce, landowners opted for the system of sharecropping that we know of as serfdom. In other words, landholders surrendered day-to-day control of their workforce in return for a share of their tenant's output as well as the promise of labor at the lord's behest for specified purposes. Similarly, the demise of serfdom was heralded by the demographic crisis of the fourteenth century as feudal lords willingly accepted monetarized payments in lieu of peasant vassaldom.

The relationship between slavery and comparative freedom cannot, however, simply be reduced to a matter of supply and demand. In Roman Egypt in the fourth century AD, for example, the cost of unskilled waged labor has been described as "almost derisory".[57] Despite this fact, slavery in Roman Egypt remained commonplace. Conversely, slaves were hardly ever cheap, either to purchase or maintain. In classical Athens, where a series of military victories lowered the purchase price, a slave cost a sum equivalent to that earned by a skilled worker over 180 days. In Rome in the first century AD the price was 3.6 times higher.[58]

Why would a person pay a large sum for a slave, and take on responsibility for their maintenance, when labor costs could be cheaply outsourced to either day-labor or self-supporting peasant households? Four explanations present themselves.

First, slavery and unfree labor tended to advance when normal market mechanisms were unhinged by a mass influx of low-cost captive labor. This situation prevailed in both classical Athens and Republican Rome. Of the Roman experience, Hopkins observed that, "Poor soldiers were engaged in capturing their own replacements", prisoners of war and their descendants comprising up to 40% of Italy's population in the first century

---

[57] R.P. Duncan-Jones, "Two Possible Indices of the Purchasing Power of Money in Greek and Roman Antiquity", *Publications de l'Ecole Francaise de Rome*, Vol. 37, No. 1 (1978), 162.

[58] Ibid., 162–163.

BC.[59] A similar situation prevailed in the Ottoman Empire and northern Africa between the sixteenth and nineteenth centuries. In 1810, a single raid by the West African Oyo Empire against the neighboring Mahi netted 20,000 captives; unfortunates who were sold into bondage at Lagos' vast slave markets.[60] Of the Muslim states of the Sahel, Thomas noted that, "By about 1780 most … depended on slave labour. There were slaves in households, in workshops, in the fields".[61]

The second circumstance that facilitates slavery is where market mechanisms cannot supply the labor required for commercialized agriculture. This is clearly the situation that applied in the Americas after 1500, because European impact caused "the complete collapse of the [native] population of the Caribbean".[62] It is also the situation that prevailed in Republican Rome as urban growth demanded agricultural surpluses that were beyond the ability of subsistence farms.[63] For, as Cato realized, one of the *latifundia*'s advantages was that it could farm a greater range of crops than a peasant household, switching labor from one to the other across the seasons.[64] This allowed for extremely high labor utilization, Plutarch recording that Cato's slaves were "either busy or asleep".[65]

A third circumstance that facilitated slavery was where isolation or danger made work highly unattractive. In classical Athens, for example, the largest slave workforce was found at the Laurion silver mine, a place of misery that funded the city's naval expansion and subsequent prosperity. In the 1930s, de facto slave labor also worked the remote Kolyma goldfield in eastern Siberia, the output of which was largely responsible for the Soviet Union's financial survival.[66] Located in one of the world's most

---

[59] Keith Hopkins, *Conquerors and Slaves* (Cambridge, UK: Cambridge University Press, 1978), 104.

[60] Hugh Thomas, *The Slave Trade: The History of the Atlantic Slave Trade 1440–1870* (London, UK: Picador, 1997), 561.

[61] Ibid., 379.

[62] Ibid., 96.

[63] Hopkins, *Conquerors and Slaves*, 106.

[64] Cato the Elder, "De agricultura", 25.

[65] Plutarch (trans. Robin Waterfield), *Roman Lives* (Oxford, UK: Oxford World Classics, 1999), 28–29.

[66] Stephen Kotkin, *Stalin: Waiting for Hitler* 1929–1941 (London, UK: Penguin Books, 2017), 133, 599; Tim Tzouliadis, *The Forsaken: From the Great Depression to*

114 B. BOWDEN

inhospitable regions, the Kolyma Gulag exacted a horrific toll. Accordingly, as Tzouliadis notes, "the deaths of the Gulag's victims became the *cause* as well as the effect of Stalin's mass repressions" [emphasis in original], the regime's existence resting on its capacity to replenish lost labor through new arrests.[67]

The final circumstance that favored slavery was associated with an inability to recruit skilled labor regarded as sufficiently loyal. Following the Roman conquest of Greece in the second century BC, most wealthy families engaged educated Greek slaves as administrators, advisors and tutors.[68] Similarly, in the Ottoman Empire and its offshoots, slaves not only filled senior administrative positions but also served as the soldiery for elite military units (such as the Janissaries, Mamluks and so on). Bought at birth, such individuals knew nothing other than a life of state service.

As discussed more fully in Part 2, one of the peculiarities of Western European history is that from the seventh century AD, society witnessed a progressive and unbroken movement toward freer forms of labor. From the fall of the Western Roman Empire until the twelfth century this involved the abandonment of slavery in favor of serfdom, and from the fourteenth century (if not earlier) it manifested itself in the displacement of serfdom by personal property ownership and waged labor.

If there was a generalized movement toward freer forms of labor and property ownership in Western Europe, there was nevertheless considerable variation in the overall European experience. By 1700, as rule of thumb, freer and more dynamic circumstances applied in Northwest Europe, while less free conditions prevailed in Southern and Eastern Europe. As noted in the introduction, in Spain and Portugal the large estate worked by serf-like workforces was a product of the *Reconquista*, a practice that morphed in the New World into the *encomienda* labor system, worked by subjugated Indian peasants. In Eastern Europe, the commercialization of agriculture to supply growing Western European demand evoked a similar response to that witnessed in Republican Rome. In what has been described as Europe's "second serfdom", a once-free

---

the Gulags—Hope and Betrayal in Stalin's Russia (London, UK: Little, Brown, 2008), 170.

[67] Tzouliadis, *The Forsaken*, 175.

[68] Plutarch (trans. Rex Warner), *Fall of the Roman Republic*, revised edition (London, UK: Penguin Classics, 2005), 112.

peasantry ended up working for "the good will and pleasure of the lord".[69] Similarly, in Italy the emergence of a commercially oriented system of large estates existed alongside a peasantry surviving in a state of impoverishment and "proletarianization", increasingly reduced to the status of landless laborers.[70] In Russia, a pact between the Muscovite state and the *boyar* elite resulted in a similar process of subjugation, the *boyars* accepting state service as a condition for their peasantry's enserfment.[71]

As the lived experiences of the peasantry in much of Southern and Eastern Europe slid backward, the achievements of Dutch and English farmers demonstrated the connection between private property rights and economic achievement. A "swampy and inhospitable" land of marshes and peat bogs in the tenth century, the transformation of what became Holland began when the region's feudal lords offered peasants "their freedom and almost absolute, exclusive property rights ... as a stimulus to settle".[72] When land subsidence caused an agricultural crisis in the fourteenth century the agricultural population were granted long-term loans to fund windmills and land reclamation.[73] As population pressure began to mount, the region's farmers sought out supplementary income from fishing, trade and a range of "proto-industrial" activities (such as beer-making, brickmaking, clothing manufacture, and so on).[74] Increasingly, supplementary sources of income became the primary means of support. By 1622, 60% of the population of Holland—the most urbanized Dutch province—were townsfolk, turning Amsterdam, Rotterdam and Delft and their surrounds into "the marvel of the world".[75] From the seventeenth century, English agriculture and industry increasingly emulated

---

[69] Fernand Braudel (trans. Sian Reynolds), *The Wheels of Commerce: Civilization and Capitalism, 15th–18th Century* (London, UK: Collins, 1982), 262, 265.

[70] Trebilcock, *Industrialization of the Continental Powers*, 332.

[71] Bradley Bowen, "Work and Society in the Orthodox East: Byzantium and Russia, AD 450–1861", in Bradley Bowden, Jeffrey Muldoon, Anthony Gould and Adela McMurray (eds.), *The Palgrave Handbook of Management History*, vol. 2 (Cham, Switzerland: Palgrave Macmillan, 2020), 1117–1123.

[72] Bas J.P. van Bavel and Jan Luiten van Zanden, "The Jump-start of the Holland Economy During the Late-Medieval Crisis, c.1350-c.1500", *Economic History Review*, Vol. 58, No. 3 (2004), 504.

[73] Ibid., 521.

[74] North and Thomas, *Rise of the Western World*, 112–113.

[75] van Bavel and van Zanden, "The Jump-start of the Holland Economy", 503.

their Dutch neighbors and rivals. In 1625, English labor productivity, measured in terms of the non-agricultural population each farm worker could support, was 0.8, a level little different from that found in France, Spain and Italy. By 1750, it rivaled the Netherlands as each farm worker supported 1.8 people outside agriculture.[76] Central to the English performance was a decline in farm employment. As people migrated to the cities, new crops (sainfoin, clover, turnips) raised output on land that had been previously left fallow.

In considering the achievements of Dutch and English agriculture, it is once more important that we neither understate nor exaggerate the achievements that were obtained. Yes, it is true that in 1800 the agricultural productivity of England and the Low Countries was far superior to that found in the rest of Europe. Nevertheless, England, Belgium and the Netherlands were all witnessing *declining* levels of farm productivity by 1800.[77] This suggests that the dynamic that had fostered agricultural improvement in these countries had hit a technological ceiling that restricted further gains. Only with mechanization and artificial fertilizers was agricultural productivity resuscitated.

Despite the stagnation of British agriculture by about 1800, its society nevertheless witnessed an acceleration of urbanization as factory demand sucked new labor from the countryside. As we have previously noted, the combination of these tendencies raised the prospect of a classic Malthusian trap until food supply was rescued by a recovery in agricultural productivity and, more particularly, North American imports. Increasingly, however, mass urbanization with all its perils and potential became the defining hallmark of industrializing societies, distinguishing them from economies that remained wedded to pre-industrial norms and techniques. The results of this process are shown in Fig. 5.3, which indicates the percentage of the workforce engaged in agriculture in the United States and various European nations between 1841 and 1901, measured against that recorded in the Indian census of 1901. As is evident, in the United Kingdom (including Ireland) farm jobs made up only one-fifth of jobs in 1841 and only 9% in 1901. By contrast, circumstances in Spain and Italy were not dissimilar to India. In 1901, Russian society remained overwhelmingly rural and poverty-stricken. France and, more particularly

[76] Allen, *British Industrial Revolution*, 60, Figure 3.2.

[77] Ibid., 60, Figure 3.2.

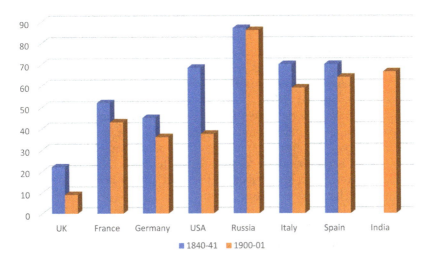

Fig. 5.3 Percentage of labor-active population engaged in agriculture, 1841 and 1901 (*Note* No Indian figure for 1841. *Sources* Trebilcock, *Industrialization of the Continental Powers*, Table 7.5b; Parliament of UK, *Statistical Abstract Relating to British India, 1894–1895 to 1903–1904*, Table 18, Clark, *Conditions of Economic Progress*, 404)

Germany, represented intermediate cases, with their societies witnessing the same process of urbanization that Britain experienced half a century earlier. It was the United States, however, which witnessed the most rapid process of urbanization between 1840 and 1900. Whereas 68.4% of the American population worked the land in 1840, by 1900 only 37.5% of the workforce were found in farm jobs. In terms of occupational structure, this put the United States on par with Germany where 36% of the workforce were engaged in agriculture at the dawn of the twentieth century.[78]

---

[78] Trebilcock, *Industrialization of the Continental Powers*, 435, Table 7.5b; Parliament of the United Kingdom, *Statistical Abstract Relating to British India, 1894–1895 to 1903–1904* (London, UK: Her Majesty's Stationary Office, 1904), Table 18: Occupations of Population—Census of 1901; Colin Clark, *Conditions of Economic Progress*, second edition (London, UK: Macmillan, 1951), 404.

118   B. BOWDEN

Although in *nineteenth-century* Britain, France, Germany and the United States the decline in farm employment *did* indicate industrialization and profound transformation, we should nevertheless be wary of assuming that this was the *pre-industrial* norm. Instead, everywhere in the pre-industrial world the border between agriculture and manufacturing was blurred. Most households spun cloth, made their own clothes and fashioned their own furniture. Invariably, such activities also provided a supplementary source of income. For the merchant–manufacturer catering for large-scale markets there were a number of benefits to using this home-based workforce. Not only did it mitigate the need for capital investment, it also avoided the stricter work practices enforced by the town-based guilds. Accordingly, this system of "putting-out" or "proto-industrialization"—whereby the merchant–manufacturer coordinated the flow of raw materials and semi-finished goods from one workshop to the next—dominated production in pre-industrial Europe. In Florence, in the mid-fourteenth century, there were, within a 60-km (50-mile) radius of the city, an estimated 60,000 individuals producing for the cloth trade.[79] Across Europe, proto-industrialization remained the norm well into the nineteenth century. Writing of the French experience between 1800 and 1830, Trebilcock noted that, "The great majority of enterprises ... remained small", relying on workers "who were part peasant and part artisan".[80] In the United States as well, "household manufacture" still overshadowed factory employment and output well into the 1820s.[81]

Traditionally, business and economic historians have perceived a large proto-industrial sector as a necessary stepping stone on the path to full industrialization.[82] Such an argument is also increasingly difficult to sustain, as is the belief that proto-industrialization was an area of endeavor where pre-industrial Europe had an advantage over other Eurasian societies. By 1750, the more economically developed regions of

[79] Braudel, *Wheels of Commerce*, 299.

[80] Trebilcock, *Industrialization of the Continental Powers*, 142.

[81] North, "Industrialization in the United States", 46–47.

[82] Franklin F. Mendels, "Proto-industrialization: The First Phase of Industrialization", *Journal of Economic History*, Vol. 32, No. 1 (1972), 241–261; Peter Kriedt, Hans Menick and Jurgen Schumbohn (trans. Beate Schempp), *Industrialization before Industrialization* (Cambridge, UK: Cambridge University Press, 1981); Pomeranz, *The Great Divergence*, 15.

Japan, China's Yangtze Delta and northern India (most notably Gujarat) boasted levels of proto-industrialization comparable to that found in parts of the Netherlands.[83] Everywhere, however, proto-industrialization was associated with the same pre-industrial attributes: low levels of capital intensity, low productivity and a reliance on natural sources of energy that generated little in the way of horsepower. Rather than seeing high levels of Asian and European proto-industrialization as proof of common economic advancement, therefore, one is better advised to see it as evidence of a technological Malthusian trap that ensnared societies, whatever their cultural and political attributes. There is no evidence that early leadership in the proto-industrial stakes guaranteed a more rapid transition to full-scale industrialization. In 1500, for example, 22% of the Italian population was urban with another 16% engaged in non-agricultural pursuits (mining, home manufacturing, and so on). Three hundred years later the level of urbanization was unchanged while those engaged in non-agricultural activities had advanced by only four percentage points.[84] Rather than improving, Italian living standards fell steadily from the seventeenth century, producing a country where "starvation wages" were the norm.[85]

Transport and the Suffocation of Markets

In his most influential study, *The Visible Hand*, Alfred Chandler observed that nineteenth-century railroads were responsible for a:

> ... volume of economic activities ... that made administrative coordination more efficient and more profitable than market mechanisms ... In many sectors of the economy the visible hand of management replaced what Adam Smith referred to as the invisible hand of market forces.[86]

---

[83] Pomeranz, *The Great Divergence*, 12; Li and van Zanden, "Before the Great Divergence", 966; Prasannan Parthasarathi, *Why Europe Grew Rich and Asia Did Not: Global Economic Divergence 1600–1850* (Cambridge, UK: Cambridge University Press, 2011, 4–5.

[84] Robert Allen, "Progress and Poverty in Early Modern Europe", *Economic History Review*, Vol. 56, No. 3 (2003), 408, Table 1.

[85] Trebilcock, *Industrialization of the Continental Powers*, 332.

[86] Chandler, *The Visible Hand*, 8, 1.

120   B. BOWDEN

At the same time, Chandler argued that:

> As long as the processes of production and distribution depended on the traditional sources of energy – on man, animal, and wind power – there was little pressure to innovate. Such sources of energy simply could not generate a volume of output in production and number of transactions in distribution large enough to require ... new business forms and practices.[87]

Chandler's observations accurately sum up the transformation in both business organization and economic circumstance that occurred during the middle decades of the nineteenth century. As a revolution in transport allowed firms access to larger markets, the need for increased output created larger firms. More accessible markets also facilitated greater competition; an inter-firm rivalry was often waged in markets that were located far away from places of manufacture. This is a very different situation to that which typically prevailed in the pre-industrial world. Everywhere in the pre-industrial world the "tyranny of distance" suffocated markets, competition, and the need for innovation.[88] Given the cost of transport, most markets were local. Where competition did occur in the pre-industrial world it largely involved luxury goods, most particularly textiles (woolens, silks, cotton). On occasion, admittedly, this competition for luxury markets had profound consequences. In the sixteenth and seventeenth centuries, for example, English and Dutch exports of lightweight, colored woolens drove Italian woolen fabrics out of the market, forcing the Italian city-states to focus on silk.[89] Similarly, in the eighteenth century, English woolens were driven out of their traditional European markets by high-quality cotton goods from India, Daniel Defoe lamenting how, "Almost everything that used to be wool or silk, relating either to the dress of the women or the furniture of our houses, is supplied by the Indian trade".[90] For the ordinary person, however, such changes in luxury fashion meant little. Their needs were met closer to home.

---

[87] Ibid., 14.

[88] The "tyranny of distance" is a concept popularized in, Geoffrey Blainey, *The Tyranny of Distance: How Distance Shaped Australia's History* (London, UK: History Book Club, 1968).

[89] Allen, "Progress and Poverty", 412.

[90] Ralph Davis, "English Foreign Trade, 1770–1774", *Economic History Review*, Vol. 15, No. 2 (1962), 286, 294.

The suffocating effects of the tyranny of distance on markets and innovation were most obvious in land transport.

When thinking of pre-industrial land transport there is an invariable tendency to think of horse-drawn vehicles. However, as we have previously noted, horses were a comparative rarity even in societies such as France that boasted an abundance of meadows. Given the demands of agriculture, even fewer were available for transport. Where they were available, the cost of feed and maintenance was high. In mid-nineteenth-century Australia, the official daily ration for horses engaged on government business was 10 lbs. of oats, 4 lbs. of bran, 4 lbs. of wheat straw, and 12 lbs. of hay.[91] Such expenses reserved the use of horses to society's wealthier members and to those forms of transport and communication where speed was essential. Even here the results were slow and haphazard. In the early eighteenth century, it still took two to three weeks for a letter to travel from Paris to Venice, a speed that effectively ruled out rapid responses to distant market events.[92] With horses reserved for priority customers, most everyday freight was hauled by oxen, animals who could survive by eating grass along the verge of roadways. Most oxen, however, were small and malnourished, so it typically took a team of six to haul a ton of cargo.[93] To add to the woes of the carrier, roads were universally terrible despite the expense that their maintenance incurred. In pre-revolutionary France no activity was more hated by the peasantry than the *corvée des routes*, which required them to spend from six to thirty days a year on the upkeep of local roads, supplying not only their labor but also wagons and animal teams.[94] Although there was an improvement in Western European roadways in the second half of the eighteenth century, progress should not be exaggerated. Even with a fast carriage, and traveling on a major roadway, a French traveler in the vicinity of Paris could only progress some 50 km (30 miles) a day.[95] In Antebellum America (between the War of 1812 and the Civil War of 1861), travel times were typically longer. When the noted Senator, Henry Clay, first traveled from

---

[91] Blainey, *The Tyranny of Distance*, 123.

[92] Braudel, *Structures of Everyday Life*, 426–427, Maps 2–3.

[93] Blainey, *The Tyranny of Distance*, 123.

[94] Georges Lefebvre (trans. R.R. Palmer), *The Coming of the French Revolution* (Princeton, NJ: Princeton University Press, 1947), 9.

[95] Braudel, *The Identity of France*, 473.

Lexington, Kentucky to Washington, DC in 1806, the 535-mile (861-km) journey took him three weeks. By 1846, traveling by rail, the journey took just four days.[96]

The uncertainty and expense of animal-drawn transport had two principal effects. On one hand it sustained what North and Thomas referred to "as a hodge-podge of local markets dominated or controlled by monopoly privileges".[97] On the other hand, it created a demand for luxuries (including spices, fine cloth, sugar, coffee) that were locally unobtainable. It was the logic of the second circumstance that underpinned the most profitable trading ventures, Pirenne noting that, "To get high prices it was necessary to seek afar the products which were there found in abundance, in order to be able to resell them at a profit in places where their rarity increased their value."[98]

Involving high risk as well as the rewards of large profits, sea-borne transport in the early modern era was able to move from luxuries into bulk commodities that delivered high returns. In the Dutch "Golden Age" (1588–1672), the prosperity of the Netherlands rested on a new type of ship, the *fluyt*. Employing fewer crew members because of its complex system of pulley and blocks, the *fluyt* gave the Dutch a new-found capacity to tap Baltic supplies of grain and timber—products that were perennially in short supply in Western Europe.[99] Typically, the Dutch obtained Baltic grain through a two-way exchange process, Adam Smith noting with admiration the ways in which "the Dutch merchant … carries the corn of Poland to Portugal, and brings back the fruits and wines of Portugal to Poland".[100] The Baltic grain trade's profitability, however, belied its modest scale. In 1649, it is estimated that Danzig, the Baltic's principal grain port, exported—in what was a bumper year—around 132,000 tons of grain, a total that would today comfortably fit into a single modern-day capesize ships (deadweight, up to 170,000

---

[96] Howe, *What Hath God Wrought*, 564–565.

[97] North and Thomas, *Rise of the Western World*, 153.

[98] Henri Pirenne (trans. Frank. D. Halsey), *Medieval Cities: Their Origin and the Revival of Trade* (Princeton, NJ: Princeton University Press, 1925), 122.

[99] Cipolla, *Before the Industrial Revolution*, 274–275.

[100] Adam Smith, *An Inquiry into the Nature and Causes if the Wealth of Nations* (London, UK: W. Strahan and T. Cadell, 1776), Smith, *Wealth of Nations*, Book II, Chap. V, para. 30.

tons).[101] Given these constraints there is little evidence that European grain trade grew significantly in the course of the eighteenth century. Consequently, the sea-borne grain trade probably never supplied more than 1–2% of Europe's consumption.[102] The rest was locally acquired.

If the Baltic grain and timber trade remained the core business of the Netherlands, in England more ships plied the sea between the northern coal fields and London than any other route, bringing in the vast tonnages of coal that kept homes in the metropolis warm and industrial furnaces fueled. As Adam Smith advised readers in his *The Wealth of Nations*, "The coal trade from Newcastle to London ... employs more shipping than all the [remaining] carrying trade of England".[103] By 1790, an incredible 10 million tons was being mined and transported annually, overshadowing the trade in any other commodity.[104] Providing a cheap source of energy to both the householder and the manufacturer, the expansion of the coal trade nevertheless confronted an apparently insoluble problem. As Smith well realized, coal was a commodity whose "bulk" was high but whose "value" was low, the "coal trade from Newcastle to London" was only viable because the two ports were sited "at no great distance" from each other.[105] Accordingly, the cheap energy that coal provided was only available to coastal ports and the comparative handful of businesses located on the coalfields themselves.

The ingenuous if capital-intensive solution to this problem was the pioneering British canal system. Movement of coal was its primary purpose, the inaugural Bridgewater canal linking the coalfields of the Midlands to Manchester in 1761. Like Britain's roadways, the canals relied on animal power, horses pulling the barges from roadways built along canal banks. It was far easier, however, for a horse to pull floating cargo. On a normal roadway a horse could pull (at best) a two-ton wagon, whereas along a canal the same horse could pull 50 tons. As a result, the Bridgewater Canal's opening caused the price of coal in Manchester to plummet by more than 75%; a fall that suddenly made feasible a whole

---

[101] Braudel, *Structures of Everyday Life*, 127.

[102] Ibid.

[103] Smith, *Wealth of Nations*, Book II, Chap. V, para. 30.

[104] Nef, *Rise of the British Coal Industry*, 19–20.

[105] Smith, *Wealth of Nations*, Book II, Chap. V, para. 30.

range of energy-intensive industries.[106] Soon replicated elsewhere, canals were the marvel of the pre-railroad age. In France, there were 4,000 km (2,500 miles) of canals by 1843, a four-fold advance on that found in 1800.[107] In the United States, the scale of canal-building dwarfed even that of Great Britain, with the opening of the Eerie Canal providing a cheap transport link between New York and the Midwest. In 1859, most low-value bulk freight shipped between the American West and the East was still going by canal.[108]

Although canals brought cheaper transport costs to some inland areas, such benefits only disguised systematic problems that continued to suffocate the growth of markets and firm specialization. Not only was canal traffic slow, ruling out its use for the transport of perishables, it was also subject to the vagaries of the weather. In dry periods, water levels were maintained with difficulty. In winter, canals froze.

Even more systematic problems were deeply entrenched in sea-going transport, difficulties that were as apparent in the Arabian Sea as the North Sea. As noted earlier, in 1841 there were 24,497 native Indian craft plying the coastal trade of the Subcontinent. The average tonnage of these vessels, however, was only 24.1 tons, a weight that can easily be hauled by a single semi-trailer on today's roads.[109] Although the Arabian sea-going vessels entering Indian ports were much larger, the average tonnage was still only 176 tons. Even the British ships that cleared customs in India—boats that had braved several oceans on their voyage—averaged only 364.2 tons.[110] Although shipping was on the cusp of a steam-powered revolution in 1841, the fact that such vessels still dominated the waves points to the depths of the Malthusian technological trap that characterized early modern shipping. In Europe, timber shortages added to the shipping industry's woes, guaranteeing United States dominance in construction after 1800. To move from wood to iron in the eighteenth century required, however, large-scale increases in iron output. In

---

[106] Phyllis Deane and H. H. Habakkuk, "The Take-off in Britain", W.W. Rostow (ed.), *The Economics of Take-off into Sustained Growth*, (London, UK: Macmillan, 1963), 72.

[107] Braudel, *Identity of France*, 477.

[108] Albert Fishlow, *American Railroads and the Transformation of the Ante-Bellum Economy* (Cambridge, UK: Harvard University Press, 1965), 284.

[109] Parliament of the UK, *Statistical Abstract Relating to British India, 1860 to 1869*, Table 14.

[110] Ibid.

1750, this was constrained by shortages of wood-derived charcoal. Even if iron-hulled ships were constructed, they needed an alternative source of power if they were to reduce their dependency on wind. Despite the invention of Newcomen's steam engine in 1712, this appeared an unlikely prospect. Early steam engines consumed copious amounts of coal, effectively limiting their use to coalfields and factories supplied by canal or sea from nearby deposits. Accordingly, when Robert Fulton began the world's first steamboat service between New York and the state capital of Albany he relied on wood to fire the boilers, not coal; a practice soon replicated by the steamboats that began to ply the Mississippi and Ohio rivers. Wood-fired boilers, however, were impractical for sea-voyages. In short, it appeared in the mid-eighteenth century that sea-borne transport had hit a technological Malthusian ceiling that was as difficult to penetrate as that witnessed on the land.

ENERGY, IRON AND ESCAPING THE MALTHUSIAN TRAP

In reflecting upon the problems of pre-industrial societies, the noted Italian economic historian, Carlo Cipolla, observed that the "main bottleneck" that each one faced "was the strictly limited supply of energy".[111]

To fully understand the significance of this insight we need to extend our understanding of "energy" from heating and cooking to encompass, as we have in this chapter, other applications, such as agricultural work, transport, manufacturing and metal smelting. For many of these applications, as has been noted, there were alternatives to burning carbon in form of wood, peat or coal. Wind could power windmills and the grinding of grain as well as the movement of ships. Animals could be harnessed to factory machines in addition to plows. There was, however, no alternative to the burning of wood, peat or coal when it can to household heating and cooking. Nor was there any alternative when it came to a range of industrial purposes: brickmaking, glassmaking, baking, brewing, and so on. It was, however, in relation to the smelting of iron that shortfalls in the supply of carbon-based energy became most apparent. For it was iron smelting, far more than any other manufacturing activity, that shaped economic activity and labor productivity. As the nineteenth-century American historian Lewis Morgan correctly noted:

[111] Cipolla, *Before the Industrial Revolution*, 113.

> The production of iron was the event of events in human experience, without a parallel, and without an equal ... Out of it came the metallic hammer and anvil, the axe and the chisel, the plough with the iron point, the iron sword; in fine, the basis of civilization.[112]

The key to everything else, iron could not be forged or smelted without the high temperatures generated by the burning or either charcoal or coke, a task that posed fundamental problems no matter which way you approached it.

If one forged iron by hand, hammering a lump of iron into the desired shape—as was the norm in antiquity and even medieval Europe—the consumer was presented with wrought iron. Composed of pure iron, wrought iron benefited from being highly malleable. It was, however, inherently soft. Hand manufacturing also ensured that it remained a scarce commodity. By contrast, the smelting of cast iron in blast furnaces—a technique perfected in China in the fifth century BC but only adopted in Europe in the early medieval period—demanded the addition of charcoal as a flux. This produced metal that was not only more plentiful but also harder. Cast-iron manufacture, however, brought with it a set of new difficulties. Invariably the iron produced contained too much residual carbon, an outcome that made cast iron inherently brittle. The large blasts of air that the furnaces demanded also necessitated bellows so large that only waterwheels could drive them—an outcome that made iron smelting a seasonal activity that could only occur in conjunction with fast-flowing streams. More fundamentally, blast furnaces demanded enormous quantities of wood, making them the perennial destroyer of forests. In the seventeenth century a typical blast furnace, producing only few hundred tons of iron per year, consumed the wood output of a 2,000-hectare forest every two years.[113] Unsurprisingly, few could resist the temptation to push production beyond the capacity of woodlands to recover. In China, it is estimated that iron output in AD 1100 was 20% higher than that subsequently found in Europe in 1700. Such was the demand on the forests, however, that much of China's rice region

---

[112] Lewis Henry Morgan, *Ancient Society* (New York: Henry Holt and Company, 1878), 43.

[113] Braudel, *Wheels of Commerce*, 270.

"became a great clear-felled zone", causing a collapse in output.[114] By the early seventeenth century, European iron production was dominated by England, Sweden and Russia, nations that still boasted more plentiful forests than their continental rivals.[115] Circumstances were particularly favorable in Russia, which benefited from rich iron deposits in the heavily forested Ural Mountains. As late as the 1820s, Russian production still exceeded that of other European nations.[116] British increases in iron output, however, soon petered out. Between 1710 and 1720 the average annual output (24,000 tons) was almost identical with that obtained in the mid-seventeenth century (23,000 tons).[117] As British production faltered that of its distant North American colonies assumed greater significance. Benefiting from seemingly endless forests that allowed charcoal burning without restraint, by 1750 the American colonies were responsible for 14% of the world's (feeble) production.[118]

A simple comparison highlights the vast gulf that separated even mid-eighteenth-century England—a society about to enter the Industrial Revolution—from the circumstances that became commonplace in the middle of the ensuing century. Between 1847 and 1848 alone, Britain's railroads placed orders for 400,000 tons of iron running rails.[119] Yet, as we noted in the preceding paragraph, Britain's average annual output between 1710 and 1720 averaged only 24,000 tons.[120]

As Fig. 5.4 indicates, the change, when it came, occurred suddenly and dramatically. Across the first decade of the nineteenth century the average annual output of the British iron was more than eight times higher than it had been 40 years earlier, commencing an ascent that made iron goods a ubiquitous feature of modern life.[121]

---

[114] E.L. Jones, *The European Miracle: Environments, Economies, and Geopolitics in the History of Europe and Asia*, second edition (Cambridge, UK: Cambridge University Press, 1987), 4.

[115] Braudel, *Wheels of Commerce*, 325; Nef, "The Progress of Technology", 9–12.

[116] Vladimir I. Lenin, "The Development of Capitalism in Russia", in Vladimir I. Lenin (ed.), *Collected Works*, vol. 3 (Moscow, USSR: Progress Publishers, 1964), 485.

[117] Riden, "British Iron Industry Before 1870", 448, 455.

[118] Jones, *European Miracle*, 4.

[119] John H. Clapham, *Economic History of Modern Britain: the Early Railroad Age* (Cambridge, UK: Cambridge University Press, 1967),

[120] Riden, "British Iron Industry Before 1870", 455.

[121] Ibid.

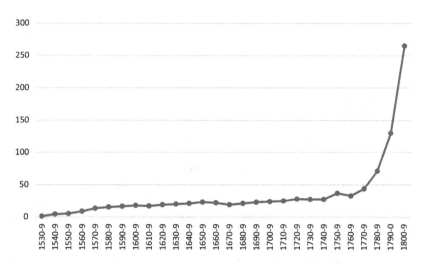

Fig. 5.4 Average annual British output (thousands of tons), by decade (*Source* Riden, "British iron industry before 1870", 448, 455)

What turned Britain's early supremacy in coal production into a corresponding supremacy in iron output were two technological breakthroughs.

The first of these stemmed from England's Coalbrookdale ironworks. Here, between 1709 and 1755, three generations of the Darby family (each of whom were named Abraham), perfected the reduction of coal into coke, thereby removing hydrocarbons and other impurities that damaged smelted iron.[122] In a country that boasted plentiful supplies of coal but diminishing reserves of woodland, the impact of this revolution was immediate. Whereas less than 10% of British iron was produced with coal-derived coke in 1750, by century's end its use was almost universal.[123]

The second breakthrough was obtained by Henry Cort in 1785, who perfected a technique for reducing the carbon content of coke-produced iron, and therefore its brittleness, by "puddling" or stirring the molten metal. Of Cort and his iron-making process, a noted Edinburgh academic

---

[122] Allen, *British Industrial Revolution*, 217–237.
[123] Ibid., 229, Figure 4.

soon observed, "he is a plain Englishman without science but by dint of natural ingenuity and a turn of experiment has made such a discovery as will undoubtedly give to this island the monopoly of that business".[124] In the short term, this prediction proved accurate. As Fig. 5.4 clearly indicates, the 1780s represented an historic divide in British iron production, heralding in a period of exponential growth that was to continue well into the twentieth century. In the long term, however, Britain's participation in a free-market economy ensured that its "monopoly" of the "puddling" process was short-lived. What Cort and the Darby family's technological breakthroughs did ensure, however, was that supremacy in iron (and subsequently) steel output would pass to regions that enjoyed ready access to large coal reserves. At the end of the nineteenth century the top iron producers, measured in kilograms of iron per head, were Britain (16 kg), the United States (12 kg), Belgium (11 kg) and Germany (9.9 kg), each of which possessed large coal reserves.[125]

Although revolutionary, the technological breakthroughs in iron production brought no immediate solution to the world's energy problems, be they ones associated with home heating or the powering of ships. Increased iron output required greater volumes of coal. Greater coal production, however, necessitated deeper mines. Deeper mines required machines to pump out water, raise and lower mining crews, and lift out the ore. In 1800, however, Britain possessed only 2,500 steam engines. Second-placed Belgium boasted just 100.[126] In the United States, coal production faced peculiar hurdles. Although Pennsylvania and West Virginia possessed vast deposits these were often composed of anthracite coal, rather than the bituminous material that was the norm elsewhere. Composed of almost pure carbon, anthracite coal is hard to burn. Accordingly, as Chandler noted, "anthracite coal owners expended a great deal of technological and entrepreneurial energy and skills to find ways to make this fuel useable".[127] Not until the early 1830s were these

---

[124] Cited Ibid., 246.

[125] Boris Ananich, "The Russian Economy and Banking System", in Dominic Lieven (ed.), *The Cambridge History of Russia*, vol. 2 (Cambridge, UJ: Cambridge University Press, 2006), 415.

[126] Ibid., 162–163.

[127] Alfred D. Chandler, Jr., "Anthracite Coal and the Beginnings of the Industrial Revolution in the United States", *Business History Review*, Vol. 46, No. 2 (1972), 151.

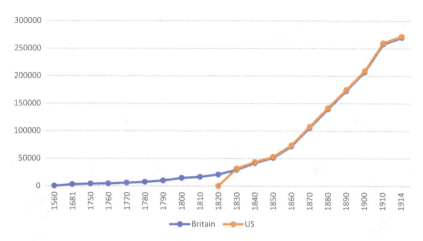

Fig. 5.5 British and United States coal production (thousands of tons), 1560–1914 (*Sources* Riden, "British iron industry before 1870", Tables 1–2; Pollard, British coal production, 1750–1850"; UK Department of Business, Energy & Industrial Strategy, *British Coal Data 1853–2018*; US Department of Commerce, *Historical Statistics*, Series M 76–92)

efforts rewarded with success, allowing a mass, if belated, transition from charcoal to coal.

The scale and timing of the nineteenth-century energy revolution is clearly indicated in Fig. 5.5. In Britain it took 290 years to raise production from 200,000 tons to 50 million tons. It took, however, only a further 20 years to surpass 100 million tons. In the United States, the increases were even more extraordinary, production going from 4,000 tons in 1820 to 52.8 million tons in 1850, after which output rose in parallel with that of the United Kingdom.[128] At the dawn of the twentieth century these two Anglo Saxon powers remained the world's

---

[128] Riden, "British Iron Industry Before 1870", 443, 448, 455; Sidney Pollard, "A New Estimate of British Coal Production, 1750–1850", *Economic History Review*, Vol. 33, No. 2 (1980), 212–235; United Kingdom Department of Business, Energy & Industrial Strategy, *British Coal Data 1853–2018* (London, UK: United Kingdom Department of Business, Energy & Industrial Strategy, 2019); United States Department of Commerce, *Historical Statistics of the United States: Colonial Times to 1970—Bicentennial Edition* (Washington, DC: United States Department of Commerce, 1975), Series M 76–92.

undisputed leaders in terms of coal output, a placement that underpinned their success in other areas of business endeavor.

Despite its many gifts, the consumers of coal's calorific bounty have long regarded it with ambivalence. Although whole regional economies became dependent on it for their survival, coal mining was always hard, dangerous work. Notwithstanding the fact that 1 ton of coal generated as much calorific energy as 2.5 tons of wood, few preferred burning coal fumes to that of wood smoke.[129] Commenting on the fair held on the frozen Thames in 1684, one observer lamented how the "fuliginous steame of the Sea Coal" prevented one from seeing across the street.[130] Although heavy particles are filtered out by modern coal-fired power-houses, the burning of coal nevertheless contributes more than its fair share of carbon dioxide to the atmosphere. Accordingly, the continued use of coal, and its carbon-based cousins, oil and natural gas, has become one of the most polarizing issues of our times. For many, coal is an existential matter of planetary survival. For others, coal is an existential matter of jobs and regional economic survival. Despite such polarizing debates, however, increasing levels of coal production have remained a hallmark feature of the industrialized civilization that emerged in the first half of the nineteenth century.

It remains a characteristic feature. In 1978, when few worried about global warming, global coal consumption amounted to almost 2.35 billion tons per year. Twenty-two years later, amid the rapid industrialization of China and India, annual consumption stood at more than 3.3 billion tons—an increase of some 900 million tons. By 2013, annual consumption was 5.6 billion tons—an increase of 2.3 billion tons over the 2000 figure.[131] In 2021, amid the Glasgow COP26 Climate Change Conference and an associated push for "net zero emissions" by 2050, the International Energy Agency reported that with "electricity demand" soaring, "global coal power generation" was set to reach "10,350 terawatt

---

[129] Braudel, *Identity of France*, 522.

[130] Cited, Brian Fagan, *Food, Famines and Emperors: El Nino and the Fate of Civilizations* (New York: Basic Books, 1999), 198.

[131] International Energy Agency, *Coal Information: Overview—Statistics Report*, July 2020 (Paris, FRA: International Energy Agency, 2020), https://www.iea.org/reports/coal-information-overview [Accessed 21 April 2021]. Note: Coal production figures are considerably above those for consumption due to considerable wastage in processing and transport.

132   B. BOWDEN

hours ... a new all-time high". At the same time, "overall coal demand" was "close to the record levels it reached in 2013 and 2014".[132] In practical terms, it is evident, the environmental campaign to "decarbonize" the world's economy has had only one significant effect: it has accelerated the outsourcing of high-value, energy-intensive manufacturing to the new rising industrial powers, most notably India and China; an outsourcing that has dealt a devastating blow to the working-class communities of North America, Europe and Australasia.

If increased iron and coal output laid the basis for an energy-intensive economy the fulfillment of its promised bounty was initially fraught, requiring the creation of new industries virtually from scratch.

Central to the future mechanization of manufacturing, agriculture and shipping—as well as the creation of an entirely new industry in the shape of the railroads—was the establishment of a machine-tools and engineering industry. It was not, however, until the establishment of Matthew Boulton and James Watt's Soho foundry in 1785 that factories were even offered a rotary engine capable of driving other machines. Earlier models were designed only with pumping water in mind. Unfortunately, the Boulton and Watt engine had a voracious appetite for coal, consuming 8.8 lbs. (4 kg) of coal for each horsepower generated.[133] Consequently, persuading textile mill owners to abandon England's upland streams—which drove their machinery free of charge—was no easy task. The main selling point for steam engines was an ability to relocate closer to markets and the comforts of city life, Boulton advising one early potential customer that his firm's engines were "certainly very applicable to the driving of cotton mills, in every case where the convenience of placing the mill in a town, or ready-built manufactory, will compensate for the expense of coals".[134] If some mill owners were persuaded by such arguments, the scale of the highly profitable Boulton and Watt operation should not be overstated. In their first fifteen years of operation

---

[132] International Energy Agency, *Coal 2021: Analysis and Forecast to 2024* (Paris, FRA: International Energy Agency, 2021), 6.

[133] Allen, *British Industrial Revolution*, 164.

[134] Cited, Paul Mantoux, *The Industrial Revolution in the Eighteenth Century: The Outline of the Beginning of the Modern Factory System in England* (London, UK: Jonathan Cape, 1961), 334.

(1785–1800), the Soho factory sold and installed a total of 332 machines (slightly less than two per month, on average).[135]

In 1830, despite steady improvements in steam-engine technology, the total installed horsepower of Great Britain was still extremely modest, amounting (as previously noted) to 160,000 hp. To put this in perspective, a modern ocean-going cruise liner typically boasts engines that generate between 50,000 and 84,000 hp.

A highly specialized industry initially associated with the pain-staking crafting of parts, the engineering sector's greatest advance in the wake of the invention of the steam engine came from an unlikely source: the machine shop of Eli Whitney's gun factory in the American state of Connecticut. A farmer's son who studied at Yale University before turning his mind to invention and engineering, Whitney labored in his gun factory between 1798 and his death in 1825, seeking to perfect the use of interchangeable parts. In firearm manufacture, interchangeable parts had two obvious advantages. First, it simplified production by allowing the incorporation of a single part into multiple weapons. Second, it allowed for ease of battlefield repair as soldiers took parts from one damaged gun to repair another.[136] Subsequently adopted by the government's armories at Springfield and Harper's Ferry before being embraced by firm after firm in the private sector, interchangeable parts transformed first American, then global manufacturing.

Despite Whitney's technological breakthrough, the pace of progress was slow during the first half of the nineteenth century. In the United States, for example, the Springfield Armory with 250 workers was, Chandler noted, "for decades the largest metalworking establishment in the country".[137] The slow growth of engineering, in turn, resulted in a shipping industry that remained reliant on wind well into the nineteenth century. While much famed, the first generation of ocean-going steamers were, in many ways, floating white elephants. Isambard Kingdom Brunel's famed *SS Great Western*, first floated in 1837, required sails not only for auxiliary power but also for stabilization, so that its paddle wheels maintained contact with the water. Even in the comparatively calm waters of the North Atlantic, the paddle wheels of the early steamers were at risk

---

[135] Allen, *British Industrial Revolution*, 172.

[136] Howe, *What God Hath Wrought*, 532–535.

[137] Chandler, *The Visible Hand*, 72.

134   B. BOWDEN

of being torn from their sides by any passing storm. On the Southern Ocean voyages to Australia, they had little hope of survival. Invariably, profitability rested on a high-paying passenger and mail service rather than freight operations. As one maritime historian observed in relation to the Cunard Line's paddle-steamers of the early 1840s:

> … all the steamers put together could only handle a very small proportion of the steady flood of westerly trade and the sailing ships still carried the great bulk of it. They [the sailing ship operators] professed to have a great contempt for the "steam wagons", and maintained that they would never be a serious competitor to sail.[138]

Such were the failings of the early steamers that they soon found themselves overshadowed by a final great flowering of the age of sail, embodied in the American-made "clipper". The "America clipper was", Blainey admiringly recorded, "the consummation of centuries of shipbuilding, the most glamorous ship that ever went with the wind".[139] Although the "clippers" ruled the waves for only a decade, they could venture where no paddle-wheeler dared, taking the'49-ers around the Horn to the goldfields of California and would-be Australian prospectors across the sweeps of the Southern Ocean.

As Fig. 5.6 indicates, the transformation of shipping into a mechanized industry, capable of swiftly carrying passengers and cargo around the globe, was a product of the second half of the nineteenth century rather than the first. Whereas in 1849 only 2.5% of Britain's deep-sea maritime fleet was undertaken by steamers, by 1882 steam-powered ships were dominant in terms of carrying capacity.[140] As in iron making, a series of technological innovations were behind the advance of steam shipping. High-pressure marine engines dramatically reduced coal consumption. Condensers converted salt water into fresh, mitigating the need for large stores of water. Greater production of iron and steel allowed for all-metal construction. No innovation, however, was more important than

---

[138] Frank C. Brown, *A Century of Atlantic Travel, 1830–1930* (Boston, MA: Little, Brown & Co., 1930) 42.

[139] Blainey, *Tyranny of Distance*, 182.

[140] Parliament of the United Kingdom, *Statistical Abstract of the United Kingdom 1840–1853* (London, UK: George Edward Eyre and William Spottiswoode, 1954), 20, Table 19.

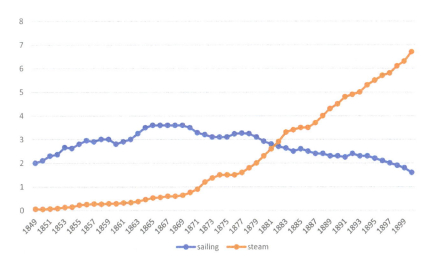

Fig. 5.6 British merchant fleet engaged in foreign trade, 1840–1900: sailing and steam-powered (millions of tons) (*Source* Parliament of the UK, Statistical Abstract 1840–1853, 20, Table 19)

the replacement of paddle wheels by underwater propellers, a technology that was not only more efficient but also safer, allowing the second-generation fo steam-powered ships to travel into the roughest and most remote oceans.

More Than "Modernization"

The steam-powered ships that traversed the oceans in the second half of the nineteenth century conveyed more than agricultural produce, immigrants and factory goods. Alongside other forms of mass communication—railroads, telegraphs, newspapers, political and literary journals—they also knitted together a new civilization.

In looking to the character of this new global civilization it is a mistake to see its impact as simply economic and technological (that is, as "modernization"), just as it is an error to perceive the "West's" impact simply in terms of culture and politics. The two were inseparably intertwined. Indeed, the greatest selling point of the new iteration of western civilization was the association of its political and cultural attributes (including individualism, democracy, and freedom) with an obvious capacity to change one's material circumstances for the better. Inevitably, even those who opposed the advance of the new civilization through force of arms (such as the Indigenous peoples of the North American plains, the New Zealand Māori, the Zulu and Matabele of Southern Africa, and others) found the new civilizations material artifacts to be irresistible temptations. Everywhere, settled agricultural societies could also see that the "West" had escaped the technological and material Malthusian trap within which they were still ensnared; a trap that caused, even in 1850, the great bulk of humanity to live a brutally hard existence at a level barely above subsistence.

In short, it was the new civilization's demonstrated capacity to deal with the 3-Cs (crops, climate, and calorific energy expenditure) that provided the *foundation* of its appeal. Without this foundation, success on other fronts is inconceivable. The new civilization offered more, however, than machine-made clothes and metallic goods. In the age-old struggle between tyranny and democracy, it offered new models for democratic government. In the battle between slavery and freedom, it supported freedom. Why this was so, and the complex and fraught ways it became so, is therefore as important to the rise of the (new) "West" as its economic and technological successes.

PART II

Freedom, Slavery and the Rise
of an Industrialized Western Civilization

A consideration of the nature of freedom and slavery brings us to the most important issues in the history of western civilization. What, however, do we mean by freedom? How important was political and economic freedom to the rise of the new industrialized iteration of western civilization? What role did slavery play? Why was slavery a characteristic feature of many New World societies when it had been virtually extinct in Western Europe itself during the medieval era? Why, after profiting from slavery and the Atlantic slave trade, did Great Britain and the United States turn against these practices with such vigor during the nineteenth century? What, in fact, do we even mean by the term "slavery"? It is to these seminal questions—ones that are central to debates as to the nature of western civilization—that Part 2 speaks.

CHAPTER 6

Time, Scale and Understandings of Western Civilization

In any area of study there is a tendency to speak of any given experience, industry or time period as if it existed in isolation from other events, industries or time periods. What is lost is not only the interactions between one industry and another—and the ways in which an event in one time period made possible or constrained those in ensuing decades or centuries—but also a sense of proportion. This leads to an exaggeration or understatement of one aspect of the historical experience and a corresponding understatement or exaggeration of others. Nowhere is this more apparent than in the debates relating to freedom and slavery.

It is the fundamental thesis of this book that there was a profound transformation in the lived experience of humanity around the year 1850, an alteration in the human condition associated with not only improved living standards but also unprecedented advances in both transport and production. In reflecting upon the transformative nature of the Industrial Revolution, the Italian economic historian, Carlo Cipolla, located its central dynamic in the transition from "biological energy" (wood, charcoal, and animal and human muscle power) to artificial or "non-biological" energy (coal, gas, oil, nuclear). It was "the discovery and exploitation of this new Eldorado of energy sources", Cipolla concluded, that underpinned advances in every aspect of production: steam power,

© The Author(s), under exclusive license to Springer Nature
Switzerland AG 2022
B. Bowden, *Slavery, Freedom and Business Endeavor*,
Palgrave Debates in Business History,
https://doi.org/10.1007/978-3-030-97232-5_6

139

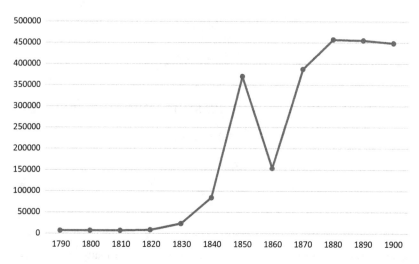

Fig. 6.1 Immigration to the United States, 1790–1900 (*Source* US Department of Commerce, *Historical Statistics of the United States*, Series C 89–119)

the mechanization of agriculture and industry, iron and steel production, and so on.[1]

Everywhere, the new energy Eldorado underwrote a revolution in transport as well as manufacturing. Associated with iron-hulled vessels and, subsequently, steam-powered railroads and shipping, this nineteenth-century transport revolution facilitated the movement of goods and people on an unprecedented scale. In Europe, as noted in Chapter 4, Spain lost one-eighth of its population to emigration between 1870 and 1910. In Italy, almost one in five left for the New World. By contrast, as Fig. 6.1 reveals, the United States witnessed immigration on an unprecedented scale in the decades after 1840; a wave of humanity that profoundly altered the demographic, cultural and sociological structure of American society. In 1850, the number of individuals who stepped ashore (369,980) was a 4.4-fold advance on the 1840 figure (84,060), which

---

[1] Carlo Cipolla, "The Discussion of the Paper of Professor Kuznets", in W.W. Rostow (ed.), *The Economics of Take-Off into Sustained Growth: Proceedings of a Conference Held by the International Economic Association* (London: Macmillan/St Martin's Press, 1963), 316.

was in turn a 3.6-fold increase on the 1830 number (23,322).[2] Interrupted by the Civil War (1861–1865), immigration assumed ever-greater significance in the second half of the nineteenth century. Similar trends were evident in other New World societies, most particularly Argentina, Australia, Brazil, Canada, New Zealand and South Africa.

In industry after industry, the mid-to-late nineteenth-century energy and transport revolution upended long-standing supply chains, creating highly specialized regional economies that drew upon cheaper transport costs and new production methods. Historically, for example, woolen textiles had provided Britain with its primary source of exports. As mechanization allowed a large-scale increase in output that paralleled the expansion of cotton textiles, factory demand soon outstripped the supply capacity of local wool producers. By the early nineteenth century, even the supply provided by Spain and Germany—Europe's leading wool producers—was inadequate. Fortuitously, British textile producers were able to draw on New World suppliers in New Zealand and, more particularly, Australia.[3] As Fig. 6.2 indicates, the volume of wool imported from Australasia in the second half of the nineteenth century dwarfed earlier import volumes. Consequently, in Britain, Australasian imports allowed an exponential increase in production. In Australia, it created a unique New World society whereby "an extraordinary high labor productivity" in the pastoral sector delivered a standard of living "considerably above" that of Great Britain.[4]

The reforging of western civilization in the aftermath of the Industrial Revolution was characterized by more than simply a technologically driven revolution in manufacturing and transport. It also required new forms of work organization, new forms of management and a new type of worker. In the new industrial factories, railroads and mines the old artisanal and peasant modes of work proved incompatible with work

---

[2] United States Department of Commerce, *Historical Statistics of the United States: Colonial Times to 1970* (Washington, DC: Department of Commerce, 1975), Series C 89–119.

[3] J.H. Clapham, *Economic History of Modern Britain: Free Trade and Steel 1850–1886* (Cambridge, UK: Cambridge University Press, 1967), 6; Simon Ville, "The Relocation of the International Market for Australian Wool", *Australian Economic History Review*, Vol. 45, No. 1 (2005), Table 3; C.H. Knibbs, *Commonwealth of Australia Yearbook, 1908* (Melbourne, AUS: Commonwealth of Australia Government Printer, 1909), 293.

[4] N.G. Butlin, *Investment in Australian Economic Development 1861–1900* (Canberra, AUS: Australian National University Press, 1972), 5.

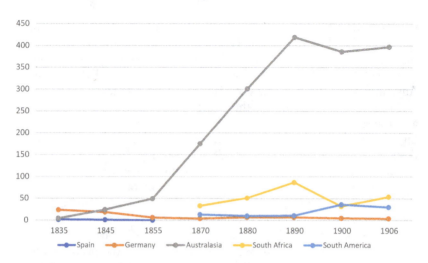

Fig. 6.2 British wool imports, 1835–1906 (in millions of lbs.) (*Sources* Clapham, *Economic History of Modern Britain: Free Trade and Steel*, p. 6; Ville, "International market for Australian Wool", Table 3; Knibbs, *Commonwealth of Australia Yearbook*, 1908, p. 293)

regimes that demanded timeliness, discipline and strict adherence to management-decreed labor processes. Similarly, the mobility, literacy and urban orientation of the new industrial era was incompatible with slavery, rooted as it was in modes of work that were little changed since the days of the late Roman Republic.

If the business-driven revolution in work and daily existence created a profound alteration in the nature and scale of western enterprises, there nevertheless remains a tendency to discuss matters relating to freedom and slavery without reference to this transformation. Instead, one is led to believe that the economic success of western civilization was due to slavery and the resultant profits obtained in a handful of industries, most particularly cotton and sugar. In the *1619 Project*, for example, Mathew Desmond locates in the cotton fields "of Georgia and Alabama … the birthplace of America's low-road to capitalism".[5] Similar claims are made on behalf of plantation-grown sugar. This "white gold", Khalil

---

[5] Mathew Desmond, "Capitalism", in Jake Silverstein (ed.), *1619 Project* (New York, NY: *New York Times Magazine*, 2019), 32.

Muhammad asserted in the *1619 Project*, "fueled the wealth of European nations".[6] In like fashion, James Walvin observes that slave-grown cotton and sugar acted as "the center of a massive global empire".[7]

Overlooked in such accounts are the modest productive obtainments typically secured by slave-based plantations despite an inordinate expenditure of not only human labor but also of life. Constantly, underachievement is dressed up as an extraordinary result. Commenting on the slave-based economy of "Carolina" (which consists of modern-day North and South Carolina and eastern Georgia), Alan Taylor, for example, traces the ways in which rice production "surged from 400,000 pounds in 1700 to about 43 million in 1790", making the region the British Empire's "great rice colony".[8] In truth, this level of production was little to boast about. In 1700, Carolina's rice production equated to a mere 179 tons; a tonnage that would barely fill nine modern-day 20-foot containers. In 1740, despite an extraordinary expenditure of labor and lives, production only equated to 32,589 tons; an output that would today only one-sixth fill a single capesize bulk freighter (dead weight, up to 175,000 tons). A similar lack of awareness as to the small-scale, pre-industrial nature of slave-based production characterizes Walvin's discussion of sugar. In the late eighteenth century, Walvin observes, the French colony of Saint-Domingue (modern-day Haiti) was the source of half the world's sugar, "producing an astonishing 60,000 tons". To achieve this result, the French had landed 800,000 African slaves, of whom 600,000 were still alive in 1789.[9] The "astonishing" tonnage to which Walvin refers, however, would only one-third-fill a modern-day capesize ship. Won at enormous cost, such tonnages added little to the material enrichment of Europe, even if they financially enriched a comparative handful of plantation owners and investors.

Of the plantation produce of the Americas, only cotton achieved industrial-scale output. As Fig. 6.3 indicates, however, even this result was obtained belatedly in the decades immediately preceding the Civil

---

[6] Khalil Gibram Muhammad, "Sugar", in Jake Silverstein (ed.), *1619 Project* (New York, NY: *New York Times Magazine*, 2019), 72.

[7] James Walvin, *Resistance, Rebellion & Revolt: How Slavery Was Overthrown* (London, UK: Robinson, 2019), 50.

[8] Alan Taylor, *American Colonies: The Settling of North America* (London, UK: Penguin, 2002), 237.

[9] Walvin, *Resistance, Rebellion & Revolt*, 33, 74–75.

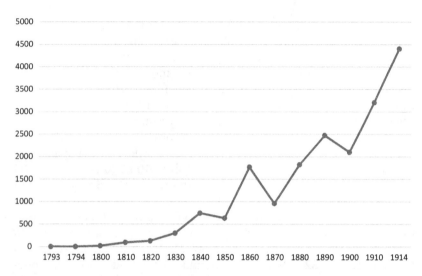

Fig. 6.3 The United States cotton exports, 1793–1914 (millions of lbs.) (*Source* US Department of Commerce, *Historical Statistics of the United States*, Series U 274–294)

War. Accordingly, as Olmstead and Rhode recently observed, "US cotton played no role in kick-starting the Industrial Revolution, which began decades before the South's cotton commenced arriving on Britain's docks".[10] Yes, it is true that United States *did* became the principal supplier of cotton to Britain's textile mills between 1818 and the Civil War. As Olmstead and Rhode suggest, however, there is a tendency to conflate the post-1818 American dominance of the global raw cotton market with the entire period of European industrialization.[11] In fact, the region that became the main cotton-producing area in the American South—the Black Belt region of Georgia, Alabama and western South Carolina, named for its black earth—remained under the control

---

[10] Alan L. Olmstead and Paul W. Rhode, "Cotton, Slavery, and the New History of Capitalism", *Explorations in Economic History*, Vol. 67, No. 1 (2018), 3.

[11] See, for example, E.J. Hobsbawm, *Industry and Empire* (Harmondsworth, UK: Pelican, 1969), 56–59; Nikole Hannah-Jones, "The Idea of America", in Jake Silverstein (ed.), *1619 Project* (New York, NY: *New York Times Magazine*, 2019), 16–18; Desmond, "Capitalism", 34–35; Walvin, *Resistance, Rebellion & Revolt*, 45.

6 TIME, SCALE AND UNDERSTANDINGS OF WESTERN CIVILIZATION   145

of the Creek and Cherokee peoples until 1815–1816. Only with the eviction of these Native American peoples, and the region's subsequent colonization by slave plantations, was the United States belatedly guaranteed a dominant position in the global market. Eventual United States success in the international cotton trade also rested on short-staple cotton (*Gossypium hirsutum*), a different species to the superior long-staple native America variety (*Gossypium barbadense*) popularly referred to as "Sea Island cotton". It was also botanically different to the high-tensile strength cotton (*Gossypium arboretum*) supplied by India, a variety that was key to India's production of high-class "muslin" fabrics. Easier to grow in the South's humid environment short-staple cotton was, however, more difficult to process than its long-staple cousin due to the presence of a mass of green seeds within the cotton boll. Not until 1794 and the invention of the "cotton gin", which stripped the seeds from the boll, did short-staple cotton become an economically feasible proposition. Once achieved, American dominance in the raw cotton market was, moreover, never as secure as it superficially appeared. To the dismay of the rebel Confederated States, Britain had surprisingly little difficulty in acquiring alternative supplies from Egypt and India during the American Civil War (1861–1865). In 1872, India and Egypt were still supplying almost half of Britain's (expanded) cotton needs.[12] Accordingly, statements such as that by Walvin—who concludes that, "By the mid-nineteenth century it was clear that Lancashire ... would be lost without American cotton"[13]—are as misguided today as they were on the eve of the Civil War.

While it is undeniable that cotton textiles did become *one* of the key generators of both wealth and employment in not only Britain but also the United States, we should nevertheless neither understate nor exaggerate cotton's significance. By 1851, the British cotton textiles employed 527,000 people, more than any other single industry. This total, however, represented only 16.7% of the manufacturing workforce and but 6.5% of

[12] In 1872, Britain imported 625.5 million lbs. from the US, and 443.2 million lbs. and 177.6 million lbs. from India and Egypt, respectively. In 1859, it imported 961.7 million lbs. from the US and 250.3 million lbs. from India and 24.5 million lbs. from Egypt, respectively. United Kingdom Parliament, *Statistical Abstract of the United Kingdom 1853–1867* (London, UK: George R. Eyre and William Spottiswoode, 1868), 50, Table 16; United Kingdom Parliament, *Statistical Abstract of the United Kingdom 1871–1885* (London, UK: George R. Eyre and William Spottiswoode, 1886), 74, Table 29.

[13] Walvin, *Resistance, Rebellion & Revolt*, 49.

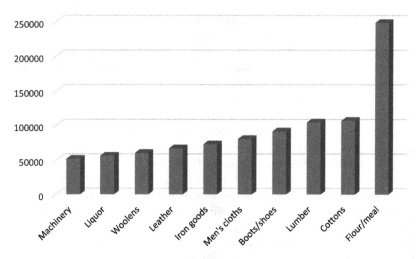

Fig. 6.4 Leading US manufacturing industries, 1860: value of product (*Note* Value in historic US dollars. *Source* North, "Industrialization in the United States", p. 49, Table 1)

the overall labor force.[14] In the case of the United States, as Figs. 6.4 and 6.5 indicate, the cotton industry was but one of several expanding areas of employment and wealth creation on the eve of the Civil War. In terms of value of output, it was overshadowed by grain processing for flour and meal. In terms of employment, it occupied second place behind boot and shoe manufacture. Other industries, most notably lumber-milling and men's clothing, were of a comparable size in terms of either value or employment.[15]

By 1860, cotton textiles had also lost any claim to being an industrial pace setter in Britain. Increasingly, engineering, steel, chemicals, ship-building and railroads acted as the prime drivers of industrial activity. The advent of the railroad also facilitated the emergence of entirely new

---

[14] Clapham, *Free Trade and Steel*, 24; Colin Clark, *The Conditions of Economic Progress* (London, UK: Macmillan, 1951), 408.

[15] Douglass C. North, "Industrialization in the United States (1815–60)", in W.W. Rostow (ed.), *The Economics of Take-Off into Sustained Growth: Proceedings of a Conference Held by the International Economic Association* (London: Macmillan/St Martin's Press, 1963), 49, Table 1.

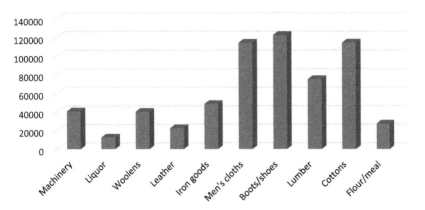

Fig. 6.5 Leading US manufacturing industries, 1860: employment (*Source* North, "Industrialization in the United States", p. 49, Table 1)

industries: industrial-scale meat packing, mail-order retail, refrigerated fruit and vegetables, for example. Even during its Industrial Revolution heyday, Deane and Habakkuk observed "it is difficult to see how the cotton industry could have *led* [emphasis in original] the [British] national economy in any meaningful sense of the word".[16] At the dawn of the nineteenth century, by which time the Industrial Revolution was more than half over, cotton's contribution to Britain's national income was a modest 4–5%.[17] Not until 1800 did cotton textiles finally surpass woolens in their contribution to British exports.[18]

If we are to look for the source of the transformation that caused the reforging of western civilization during the middle decades of the nineteenth century, we are best advised to consider the role of freedom and business innovation rather than the proceeds of slavery, which were extremely modest in comparison. For, as Sidney Pollard observed, the

---

[16] Phyllis Deane and H.J. Habakkuk, "The Take-Off in Britain", in W.W. Rostow (ed.), *The Economics of Take-off into Sustained Growth: Proceedings of a Conference Held by the International Economic Association* (London: Macmillan/St Martin's Press, 1963), 72.

[17] Ibid., 70.

[18] E.A.G. Robinson, "The discussion of the paper of Professor Habakkuk and Miss Deane", in W.W. Rostow (ed.), *The Economics of Take-Off into Sustained Growth: Proceedings of a Conference Held by the International Economic Association* (London: Macmillan/St Martin's Press, 1963), 340.

Industrial Revolution was first and foremost a "managerial revolution" rather than a "technological revolution", one that involved "improvements in organization ... interchangeability of parts, control of raw material stocking and supply".[19] And central to this "managerial revolution", underpinning everything else, was the existence of a legally free workforce that management had to incentivize and motivate if it was to achieve its objectives. It was this dynamic, Pollard concluded, which defined "the new capitalism".

[19] Sidney Pollard, *The Genesis of Modern Management: A Study of the Industrial Revolution in Great Britain* (London, UK: Edward Arnold, 1965), 102.

CHAPTER 7

What Is Freedom? What Is Slavery?

What Is Freedom?

In his most influential book, *The Social Contract*, the French philosopher, Jean-Jacques Rousseau, famously observed that:

> Man is born free; and everywhere he is in chains. One thinks himself the master of others, and still remains a greater slave than they.[1]

The "freedom" of which Rousseau spoke appears, at first glance, to solely concern the "natural rights" that find expression in both the American *Declaration of Independence* and the French *Declaration of the Rights of Man and the Citizen*. Whereas the former declared "Life, liberty and the pursuit of happiness" were "inalienable rights", the latter proclaimed that "liberty, property, security and resistance to oppression" were "the natural and imprescriptible rights of man". In inspiration, these understandings are largely attributable to John Locke. Writing in 1689, Locke asserted

---

[1] Jean-Jacques Rousseau (trans. G.D.H. Cole), "The Social Contract", in Jean-Jacques Rousseau (ed. G.D.H. Cole), *The Social Contract and Discourses* (London, UK: J.M. Dent and Sons, 1950), 1.

© The Author(s), under exclusive license to Springer Nature Switzerland AG 2022
B. Bowden, *Slavery, Freedom and Business Endeavor*,
Palgrave Debates in Business History,
https://doi.org/10.1007/978-3-030-97232-5_7

149

150   B. BOWDEN

that "all men", when in a "state of nature", enjoy "equality" and "perfect freedom".[2]

In writing about the nature of freedom, however, Rousseau clearly had something in mind other than "natural rights". As the opening sentence of *The Social Contract* made clear, what primarily concerned Rousseau was whether it was possible to enjoy freedom as part of a "civil order", one premised on people "as they are and laws as they might be".[3] In considering this problem, Rousseau argued that "civil liberty" could never be commensurate with the "natural liberty" that people (supposedly) experienced in their "natural state", that is, in societies operating in the wild, free of the confines of civilization. Instead, in becoming members of a "civil" society people trade their "natural liberty" for something very different: namely, a "civil liberty" that was always and necessarily (in Rousseau's opinion) constrained by "the general will".[4] Seen from this perspective, the full exercise of individual freedom was *never* possible in *any* organized society.

Inevitably, this highly abstract understanding of freedom attracted critics. In the eighteenth century the most prominent of these were British political theorists, most notably Edmund Burke. As a "metaphysical abstraction", Burke argued in his *Reflections on the Revolution in France*, "liberty ... may be classed among the blessings of mankind".[5] However, he suggested, the concept of "liberty" was meaningless when considered apart from economic, social and legal "circumstances". It was, in other words, concrete laws and social conventions that protected freedom, not abstractions. Conversely, freedom removed from social context could prove a menace rather than a benefit. If a sensible person met an escaped murderer, Burke observed by way of example, they would hardly "congratulate him on the recovery of his natural rights". Instead, they would flee.[6]

[2] John Locke, *Two Treatises of Government* (London, UK: Thomas Tegg and Others, 1823), 106.

[3] Rousseau, "The Social Contract", 1.

[4] Ibid., 19.

[5] Edmund Burke, *Reflections on the Revolution in France* (Hamilton, Canada: McMaster University, nd), 7, https://socialsciences.mcmaster.ca/econ/ugcm/3ll3/burke/revfrance. pdf.

[6] Ibid.

For *both* the proponents and critics of the concept of "natural rights" there was *always* a profound difference between *abstract* understandings of liberty and the *civil* or *actual* freedoms that people enjoyed as citizens. "Natural rights" may provide "civil" laws and even constitutional provisions with an underlying intent and moral legitimacy. But they can never be one and the same thing, given the propensity of one person's "natural" rights to impinge upon those of others. In the case of the United States, for example, philosophical principles of "natural rights" find expression in the *Declaration of Independence* of 1776. By contrast, practical or actual freedoms are embodied in the Federal Constitution of 1789, as well as in state and federal legislation and common law. This patchwork of law—which reflected the origins of the United States as a federation of legally distinct colonies or states—resulted in significant differences in the rights enjoyed even by adult white males. Commenting on these differences in 1830, Tocqueville noted that voting rights in Maryland and South Carolina were only conferred on adult (white) males boasting 50 acres of farmland. Significant asset tests were also imposed in Massachusetts, Connecticut, Rhode Island, New Jersey and North Carolina. In contrast, Vermont, Illinois, Indiana, Kentucky, Louisiana, Missouri and Alabama imposed no property restrictions.[7]

Nowhere was the gulf between *abstract* "natural rights" and *actual* "civil rights" more evident than in the legal treatment of slavery.

In Britain, the curtailment of slavery was initially a matter of common law rather than parliamentary statute. In 1770, a jury ruled that Thomas Lewis, a slave resident in England, could not, as a British resident, legally be the property of anyone. He was thus entitled to the same freedom as any other Briton. Two years later, slavery was effectively declared illegal within the British Isles when Lord Mansfield declared James Somerset, another resident slave, a free man.[8] Significantly, both these historic judgments were guided by Sir William Blackstone's highly influential *Commentaries on the Laws of England*. Expressing a view that became a cornerstone of common law, Blackstone recorded in 1753 that the English "spirit of liberty" was so "deeply implanted" that even "a slave or a negro, the moment he lands in England, falls under the protection

[7] Alexis De Tocqueville (trans. Gerald E. Bevan), *Democracy in America and Two Essays on America* (London, UK: Penguin Books, 2003), 842.

[8] Thomas Clarkson, *The History of the Abolition of the African Slave-Trade by the British Parliament*, vol. 1 (London, UK: Longman, Hurst, Rees and Orme, 1808), 73–77.

of the laws, and so far becomes a freeman".[9] In other words, Blackstone was asserting that British "liberty" stemmed not from legislative decree but rather from legal precedent and immemorial tradition. Despite slavery being effectively illegal in the British Isles from 1772, however, Parliament did not abolish the Atlantic slave trade until 1807. Slavery in the colonial British Empire persisted until 1834. In North America, the advance of abolitionism was even more hesitant. Not until 1804 did all the Northern states boast abolitionist legislation. In the South, it took a Civil War (1861–1865) and the passage of the Thirteenth Amendment to bring slavery to an end.

Why was *legal* freedom extended to the slave population of the British Empire and the United States in such a hesitant fashion? In the case of the United States, Nikole Hannah-Jones's much-cited article in the *1619 Project* provides a simple answer to this question: the nation was founded upon a lie. According to Hannah-Jones, the "founding ideals of liberty and equality" recorded in the American *Declaration of Independence* "were false when they were written"; they were principles cynically expressed by beneficiaries of slavery who had little intention of extending freedom to people of a different race.[10]

Overlooked in Hannah-Jones's conclusion is a problem that impacts not only African Americans but everyone who lives within a democratic society: the inherent tension between individual rights on the one side and laws that reflect the common consent of the majority on the other. For if a majority supports slavery, or any other form of social oppression, on what basis can a democracy reject it? What slavery in the United States contradicted was not so much democracy as emerging understandings of economic and political liberalism: a system of belief that placed the individual rather than the group at center stage. For in a "liberal" society that gives pride of place to individual choice and liberty, it is impossible for slavery to co-exist side by side with free forms of labor and business for any extended period of time. Each poses an existential threat to the other. Whereas slavery threatens to undercut the wages and profits of free workers and firms, freedom threatens slavery simply through its presence as an alternative.

[9] Sir William Blackstone, *Commentaries on the Laws of England in Four Books*, vol. 1 (Indianapolis, IN: Liberty Fund, 2010), 127.

[10] Nikole Hannah-Jones, "The Idea of America", in Jake Silverstein (ed.), *1619 Project* (New York, NY: *New York Times Magazine*, 2019), 14.

In reflecting upon the "tyranny of the majority" in the wake of his tour of America's democracy, Tocqueville concluded that it was not only in its laws that democratic majorities encroached on individual liberty. Even more insidious, Tocqueville argued, was the impact of majority opinion upon "independence of thought and real freedom of debate".[11] Whereas absolutist regimes dealt with dissent through arrests and imprisonment, democracies imposed a "civilized despotism" through social conventions and norms.[12] Bolstered by popular support, democratic governments also showed, Tocqueville believed, a disturbing tendency to encroach upon "the minor things of life". In doing so, he continued, the democratic state "does not tyrannize but it inhibits, represses, drains, snuffs out" and "dulls" the imagination.[13]

As Tocqueville's insights highlighted, it is evident that freedom entails much more than democracy, equality before the law and a legal right to free speech. It also entails psychic independence, a sense of individual identity, and a capacity to think and act in ways that are at odds with majority-dictated norms.

In the history of western civilization, no one has paid greater heed to matters relating to self and individual freedom than Friedrich Schelling and Friedrich Nietzsche.

Part of the German idealist tradition that emerged in reaction to the rationalism of the French Revolution, both Schelling and Nietzsche were loath to impose any restriction on individual freedom. In doing so, they resolutely opposed the system of "civil" restraints advocated by not only Burke but also Rousseau. As noted a few paragraphs earlier, Burke, in delineating the logical limits of freedom gave the light-hearted example of the escaped murderer as representing a type of "liberty" that no sensible person would advocate. For Schelling, however, and subsequently for Nietzsche, a person's "capacity for good and evil" was no light-hearted matter. Rather, Schelling observed in his *Philosophical Investigations into the Essence of Human Freedom*, it was the most important issue "in the entire doctrine of freedom".[14] Where everyone before him—with the

[11] De Tocqueville, *Democracy in America*, 292, 297.

[12] Ibid., 297.

[13] Ibid., 808, 806.

[14] F.W.J. Schelling (trans. Jeff Love and Johannes Schmidt), *Philosophical Investigations into the Essence of Human Freedom* (New York, NY: State University of New York Press, 2006), 22.

exception of the Marquis de Sade—had seen evil as something to be constrained, Schelling argued that a capacity for evil is the ultimate expression of human freedom. Operating on the assumption that God is an entity solely for good, Schelling logically concluded that it is only humanity's "capacity for evil" that allowed a form of freedom that "must have a root independent of God".[15] Unwilling to see "complete freedom" restrained by God, Schelling was even less enthusiastic about societal restraints. For the moment one accepted *any* restraint on a person's capacity for evil then one also restricts individual freedom. Abandoning the belief in God that imposed a divine restraint on Schelling's analysis, Nietzsche pushed this "doctrine of freedom" to its logical conclusion. Where individuals erred, Nietzsche argued in *Beyond Good and Evil* was in allowing morality to act as a guide to action. Calling for "the self-overcoming, of morality", he reasoned that genuine freedom involved acting solely as one saw fit, unencumbered by allegiances to one's nation or one's friends.[16]

In our modern world, this Nietzschean emphasis on self, identity and resistance to social norms finds cogent expression in postmodernist understandings, most particularly those inspired by Michel Foucault. For Foucault, as with Nietzsche, oppressive social norms and conventions were located in every aspect of life—the "fundamental codes of culture", the ways in which "power and knowledge are joined together" through "discourse", in the "disciplinary" nature of society.[17] In his *Madness and Civilization*, Foucault also argued that oppression occurred through "reason's subjugation of non-reason" and the suppression of "desire and murder, of cruelty and the longing to suffer".[18]

There is an undeniable truth to the Nietzschean and Foucauldian beliefs that social norms and conventions impose restraints on individual

[15] Ibid., 24.

[16] Friedrich Nietzsche (trans. R.J. Hollingdale), *Beyond Good and Evil: Prelude to a Philosophy of the Future* (London, UK: Penguin Classics, 1990), 64, 70.

[17] Michel Foucault, *The Order of Things: An Archaeology of the Human Sciences* (New York, NY: Vintage Books, 1994), xx; Michel Foucault (trans. Robert Hurley), *The History of Sexuality—An Introduction* (New York, NY: Pantheon Books, 1978), 94; Michel Foucault (trans. Alan Sheridan), *Discipline and Punish: The Birth of the Prison* (New York: NY: Vintage Books, 1991), 308.

[18] Michel Foucault (trans. Richard Howard), *Madness and Civilization: A History of Insanity in the Age of Reason* (Mew York, NY: Pantheon Books, 1965), 9, 221.

liberty, on one's capacity to act as one sees fit. What also needs to be recognized, however, is that just as a majority consensus in a democracy is incompatible with total individual freedom, so it is that total individual freedom is incompatible with democracy. This is something that Nietzsche, logical to a fault, fully realized. For if any individual is given the capacity to exert their will without restraint this necessarily involves that person's domination of others. As Nietzsche expressed it, "Few are made for independence – it is a privilege of the strong".[19]

Freedom, it is evident, is a slippery and potentially dangerous concept. As a social construct based upon explicit and implicit freedoms, a democracy can only function by imposing restraints on individual behavior and by prioritizing majority concerns. At the same time, a democracy loses its creative motive force if individual liberties and minority interests go unprotected. In a democratic society it is the state and its elected representatives who are tasked with this delicate balancing act. Yet, the state itself has also long revealed itself to be the biggest threat to individual liberties, ever willing to advance its own institutional objectives.

WHAT IS SLAVERY?

In 2015, the British parliament passed a *Modern Slavery Act* that compelled firms to report what steps they were taking to mitigate the use of "slavery, servitude or forced or compulsory labour". Emulated by more than thirty countries, the Act's definition of slavery and servitude included all forms "of exploitation where a person is subject to force, threats or deception".[20] In the Australian *Modern Slavery Act 2018*, modeled on its British counterpart, "modern slavery" was defined in similar broad terms, including:

> ... eight types of serious exploitation: trafficking in persons; slavery; servitude; forced marriage; forced labour; debt bondage; deceptive recruiting for labour or services; and the worst forms of child labour.[21]

[19] Nietzsche, Beyond Good and Evil, 60.

[20] Parliament of the United Kingdom, *Modern Slavery Act 2015* (London, UK: Parliament of the United Kingdom, 2015), s.1, s.3, Explanatory notes.

[21] Parliament of the Commonwealth of Australia, *Commonwealth Modern Slavery Act* (Canberra, AUS: Parliament of the Commonwealth of Australia, 2018), 8.

156   B. BOWDEN

Well meaning, these definitions of slavery—and the conflation of "slavery" with "serious exploitation"—are wrong-headed. Yes, it is true that the *working* circumstances of people engaged in "forced labor" can have a passing resemblance to working conditions suffered under slavery. What is profoundly different, however, is the *legal* circumstances of slaves, which causes them to be regarded as complete outsiders, people denied membership of the society within which they live and work. To ignore or downplay this legal distinction is to gloss over the truly barbaric nature of slavery when compared to other forms of exploitative labor.

In discussing slavery in ancient Rome, Plutarch described slaves as "living tools".[22] Nowhere in the whole canon of western civilization do we find a better definition.

As a "living tool", a Roman slave was no different to a plow or an ox. They could be bought and sold, looked after or neglected, fed or left to starve. They could be placed in positions of comparative comfort and then, at a whim, be subjected to floggings and mutilation. In providing advice to his fellow Romans as to the efficient running of an estate, Cato the Elder, for example, recommended that plantation owners should always sell off "old and sick slaves" along with "the old cattle, the worn-out oxen".[23] This equation of slaves with animals is also observed in Plutarch's commentary on Cato's purchasing practices. Typically, Plutarch recorded that Cato bought:

> ... prisoners of war who were still young enough to be reared and trained, as young hounds and horses are.[24]

In managing his household slaves, Cato revealed the same brutal managerial efficiency that characterized his rural estates. As "soon as a meal was over", Plutarch recounted:

---

[22] Plutarch (trans. Rex Warner), *Fall of the Roman Republic* (London, UK: Penguin Classics, 2005), 112.

[23] Cato the Elder, "*De Agricultura*", in A Virginia Farmer (ed.), *Roman Farm Management: The Treatise of Cato and Varro* (New York, NY: Macmillan, 1913), 25.

[24] Plutarch (trans. Robin Waterfield), *Roman Lives* (Oxford, UK: Oxford University Press, 1999), 28.

7 WHAT IS FREEDOM? WHAT IS SLAVERY? 157

... he would punish any of slaves whose service had been in any way slip-shod or whose preparations had been at all careless by beating them with a leather strap.[25]

In reading such accounts it is easy to imagine Cato as a sadistic monster. In fact, throughout the history of the Roman Republic, Cato the Elder was regarded as the very embodiment of Roman values, a person whose private life was characterized by thrift and hard work and whose public life was noted for its incorruptibility and moral virtue. Cato could treat his slaves as he did because they were regarded by the whole society as little more than animals.

If one turns from descriptions of slavery in Roman antiquity to accounts of slave life in the American South during the early nineteenth century, one reads depictions that are almost identical. In describing circumstances in the stables of a Colonel Lloyd, for example, the great African American abolitionist, Frederick Douglass, recounted:

> They [the stable hands] never knew when they were safe from punishment. They were frequently whipped when least deserving, and escaped whipping when most deserving it ... Colonel Lloyd could not brook any contradiction from a slave. When he spoke, a slave must stand, listen, and tremble.[26]

Often, slaves in the American South were comparatively well-treated. Certainly, on average, they enjoyed better conditions than their compatriots elsewhere in the Americas, a fact reflected in much higher survival rates. As James Walvin noted in a recent study: "From the 1720s North America's slave population began to diverge from Brazil and the Caribbean ... to expand by natural increase, while elsewhere it grew only because of ever more African imports".[27] Evidence of this comparative benevolence is easily found. In reflecting upon his time as a Baltimore house slave, Douglass recorded:

[25] Ibid., 29.

[26] Frederick Douglass, *Narrative of the Life of Frederick Douglass: An American Slave* (Boston, MA: Anti-slavery Office, 1846), 17.

[27] James Walvin, *Resistance, Slavery & Revolt: How Slavery was Overthrown* (London, UK: Robinson, 2019), 43.

A city slave is almost a freeman, compared with a slave on the plantation, and enjoys privileges altogether unknown to the slave on the plantation.[28]

While some American slaves enjoyed comparatively good living conditions, their legal circumstances nevertheless did not differ in any fundamental way from that of Cato's slaves. They were perpetually subject to the whim of their master. Recalling the unhappy situation in the home of his neighbor, Mrs. Hamilton, Douglass described beatings not dissimilar to those inflicted by Cato the Elder on his house-slaves. Mrs. Hamilton, Douglass remembered:

> ... used to sit in a large chair in the middle of the room, with a heavy cowskin by her side, and scarce an hour passed during the day but was marked by the blood of one of these slaves.[29]

Cato's views on slavery also bear more than passing similarities to those expressed by Supreme Court Chief Justice Roger Taney in his ruling in the *Dred Scott v Sandford* case of 1857. A slave who had lived for many years in the free state of Illinois, Scott's circumstances became a test as to the legitimacy of slavery, the case having slowly worked its way up through lower courts. In handing down the Court's decision, which confirmed Scott's status as a slave by seven to two, Taney infamously declared that African slaves were "beings of an inferior order, altogether unfit to associate with the white race ... and so far inferior, that they had no rights which the white man was bound to respect". The court also ruled that slaves were "unambiguously property".[30] Although Scott was soon freed by his Southern owners, Taney's ruling polarized opinion in ways that made civil war ever-more likely. In famously repudiating Taney's opinion in his public debates with Stephen Douglas—his rival for the presidency in 1860—Abraham Lincoln declared:

> I combat it as having a tendency to dehumanize the negro—to take away from him the right of ever striving to be a man. I combat it as being one of the thousand things constantly done in these days to prepare the public

---

[28] Douglass, *Life of Frederick Douglass*, 34.

[29] Ibid., 35.

[30] James M. McPherson, *Battle Cry of Freedom: The Civil War Era* (New York, NY: Oxford University Press, 2003), 171–74.

7 WHAT IS FREEDOM? WHAT IS SLAVERY? 159

mind to make property, and nothing but property, of the negro in all the States of this Union.[31]

In thinking of slavery there is a temptation to restrict one's vision to the two circumstances that Frederick Douglass experienced: the plantation slave and the house slave. Slavery, however, encompassed a much wider range of activities, some better and some worse than those experienced by Douglass. Arguably the worst experiences were those suffered in pre-Columbian America at the hands of the Aztec Empire and the other Mesoamerican civilizations. Typically, these slaves were used for ritual sacrifices rather than manual labor. In recording the "days of old" in their native Nahuatl, Aztec survivors recalled how, after a sacrifice:

> ... They cooked him [the slave] in a[n] "olla". Separately, in an "olla" they cooked the grains of maize. They served [his flesh] on it ... No chili did they add to it; they only sprinkled salt on it. ... all [the host's] kinsmen ate of it.[32]

At the other end of the historic spectrum were the highly educated slaves who occupied bureaucratic positions in the Roman and Turkish empires, both in private businesses and government administration. In the Roman Republic, the conquest of Greece in the second century BC brought a flood of highly literate slaves into the Roman slave markets. The business operations of Crassus, Rome's wealthiest citizen, Plutarch recounted, boasted slaves "of the highest quality – readers, secretaries, silversmiths, stewards". Crassus even assembled a slave workforce of 500 "architects and builders", using them to rebuild fire-ravaged premises he had acquired on the cheap.[33] During the reign of Claudius in the first century AD, highly educated slaves occupied key positions in the imperial bureaucracy. Slave bureaucrats were an even-more characteristic feature of the Ottoman Empire between the fifteenth and nineteenth centuries. As Christopher de Bellaigue observed, "The annals of [Turkish] empire

---

[31] Abraham Lincoln, *Seventh Joint Debate Between Abraham Lincoln and Stephen A. Douglas* (Altona, IL: 15 October 1858).

[32] Fray Bernardino de Sahagun (trans. Charles E. Dibble and Arthur J.O. Anderson), *Florentine Codex: Book 9—The Merchants* (Salt Lake City, UT: University of Utah Press, 1959), 67.

[33] Plutarch, *Fall of the Roman Republic*, 112.

were full of slaves who had risen to ministerial office or become top commanders".[34]

If the legal position of Crassus' slave architects and stewards was as precarious as that of his plantation slaves, the bureaucrats of the Ottoman Empire occupy a gray area between freedom and slavery. These were people who not only exercised political power but who also accumulated property on a considerable scale. Should we consider these officials to be slaves in any meaningful sense? Probably not. Another gray area is presented by the Turkish *janissary* corps, the elite army units forcibly recruited through a "child levy" or "blood tax" imposed on the Balkans' Christian population. Torn from their families and forced into a life of military service, these people arguably were slaves in the classic sense even though they obtained a salary for their services. The Sub-Saharan Africans dragged in chains across the Sahara and forced into military service by the Arab sultanates of North Africa, suffered a similar plight. More problematic are the *Mamluks*, the slave soldiers who exercised an iron control over Egypt until their power was smashed by Napoleon at the Battle of the Pyramids. Given their political power, this military elite is better regarded as a social caste rather than a true slave population.

Shades of gray are also evident when we look at the many categories of indentured and bonded labor that worked in the fields, plantations and workshops of the New World.

Before 1776, of the 450,000 immigrants of European ancestry who arrived "voluntarily" in what was to become the United States, it is estimated that almost half were indentured servants.[35] Most of this indentured labor was destined for the plantations of Virginia and Maryland. Of the 120,000 immigrants who arrived in this region during the seventeenth century, an estimated 90,000 were indentured servants.[36] In return for payment of their voyage across the Atlantic, indentured laborers and servants worked for between four and seven years without pay under conditions that differed little from slavery. Regarding the circumstances in the Chesapeake colonies, Alan Taylor notes that:

---

[34] Christopher de Bellaigue, *The Islamic Enlightenment: The Modern Struggle Between Faith and Reason* (London, UK: Vintage, 2017), 189.

[35] Christopher Tomlins, "Reconsidering Indentured Servitude: European Migration and the Early American Labor Force, 1600–1775", *Labor History*, Vol. 42, No. 1 (2001), 9.

[36] Alan Taylor, *American Colonies: The Settling of North America* (London, UK: Penguin, 2001), 142.

7 WHAT IS FREEDOM? WHAT IS SLAVERY? 161

Planters readily resorted to the whip, convinced that only fear and pain could motivate servants ... Until their terms expired, the servants were fundamentally property rather than people. Masters readily bought and sold the contracts of servants. Some masters even transferred servants to pay off gambling debts.[37]

Although in theory the indentured servants of seventeenth-century America enjoyed the protection of the law, this was often conspicuous by its absence. In 1634, two Virginian servants, Elizabeth Abbott and Elias Hinton, were beaten to death by their masters. In one beating, Abbott suffered 500 blows of the lash. Despite the publicity that surrounded their deaths, no prosecution ensued.[38] Significantly, the African slaves who arrived in Virginia between 1619 and 1660 were treated in near identical fashion to their indentured European counterparts, Edmund Morgan observing:

> There is no evidence during the period before 1660 that they [African slaves] were subjected to a more severe discipline than other servants ... Black men and white serving the same master worked, ate, and slept together, and together shared in escapades, escapes and punishments.[39]

Exploited as they were, the indentured servants of colonial North America were not slaves. Theoretically at least, they remained under the full protection of law. At the completion of their indenture, they could look forward to a life as either a waged laborer or a small-scale property owner. In this, it should be noted, the circumstances of African slaves who arrived before 1660 more closely resembled that of their indentured counterparts than that of subsequent generations of slaves. Arriving into a society where indentured servitude rather than slavery was the societal norm, many were treated as de facto servants. Some were placed on indentured contracts with the promise of freedom as a means of incentivizing labor. Others were freed after serving terms comparable to that of their white counterparts.[40] Only with petering out of the supply of indentured

[37] Ibid., 143.

[38] Edmund S. Morgan, *American Slavery, American Freedom* (New York, NY: W.W. Norton & Co., 1975), 127.

[39] Ibid., 154–155.

[40] Ibid., 155–156; Taylor, *American Colonies*, 154.

servants after 1700 do we witness not only a tightening of the conditions of slave bondage but also a massive growth in North American slavery, the number of slaves in the Chesapeake region growing from 13,000 to 150,000 between 1700 and 1750.[41]

As the supply of indentured servants diminished it was not only African slaves who filled the void. Transported convicts from Britain and Ireland also arrived in increasing numbers. Between 1718 and 1775, 54,500 convicts arrived in chains; a total that represented 10 percent of the entire European immigrant cohort.[42] Subject to unpaid forced labor for up to fourteen years, many (if not most) were "subject to the same treatment as slaves".[43] Floggings and other forms of brutalization were imposed as a matter of course. Despite such treatment, this is another group that should not be considered as slaves. Theoretically, the law restricted the punishments that could be inflicted upon them. At the end of their sentence, they enjoyed opportunities similar to those of other American immigrants.

If we turn to colonial Australia, convict and indentured labor was even more significant. In 1851, convicts, freed convicts and their descendants still represented 59% of the Australian population.[44] Again, these people were far removed from slavery, despite the floggings and brutality that many endured. Numerically dominant, they created what Russel Ward referred to as a unique "national mystique", one characterized by egalitarianism and hostility to authority.[45] More problematic is the circumstances of the 61,160 Melanesians imported into the northern colony of Queensland between 1863 and 1901.[46] Much of this work-force labored under circumstances that bore physical resemblance to that of the slave-workforces of the Americas. Engaged in back-breaking labor on sugar plantations, most were housed in segregated barracks and huts. Expressing an increasingly popular view as to the status of

[41] Taylor, *American Colonies*, 154.

[42] Tomlins, "Reconsidering Indentured Servitude", 9; Taylor, *American Colonies*, 315.

[43] Taylor, *American Colonies*, 315.

[44] Russel Ward, *The Australian Legend*, second edition (Melbourne, AUS: Oxford University Press, 1966), 16, Table II.

[45] Ibid., 1–2.

[46] Raymond Evans, Kay Saunders and Kathryn Cronin, *Exclusion, Exploitation and Extermination: Race Relations in Colonial Queensland* (Sydney, AUS: Australia and New Zealand Book Co., 1975), 167.

this workforce, Australia's public broadcaster declared in 2020 that the enslavement and "trafficking" of "South Sea Islander people" is "well documented".[47] There is some truth to such assertions. Between 1863 and 1868, hundreds were subject to "blackbirding", whereby they were either kidnapped or (more likely) traded for guns by Melanesian chiefs. At the most, however, this involved only 900 individuals, less than 1.5% of the Melanesian total.[48] After 1868, virtually all Melanesians arrived with three-year contracts. Even those who arrived during the "blackbirding" era enjoyed the protection of British law. As Australia's greatest statistician, Timothy Coghlan, observed:

> These men had the same civil rights as other persons. If they chose to remain in Queensland, they were free to take any employment offered them.[49]

Among all the differences between the Melanesian experience and that suffered by American slaves there is one that speaks volumes: Melanesians were invariably armed to the teeth. For in coming to Queensland, most were motivated by the prospect of purchasing rifles that could be used back home to advance their clan's military standing. The scale of these purchases horrified many. After witnessing the huge number of rifles held in one district, a concerned official warned: "The white employer or overseer is more or less at their mercy".[50]

As noted in the introduction to this book, the economic imperative behind slavery is found in the fact that human labor typically provided the most plentiful and flexible source of energy in pre-industrial agricultural societies. Slavery, therefore, provided a useful supplement to a society's productive capacity. Normally, slaves came from one or two sources. Internal supplies could be generated by condemning criminals or debtors

---

[47] Australian Broadcasting Corporation, *Scott Morrison Says Comments Were About New South Wales Colony, Apologises for Causing Offence*, 12 June 2020, https://www.abc.net.au/news/2020-06-12/pm-apologises-offence-caused-slavery-comments-clarifies-remarks/12348716 [accessed 1 July 2021].

[48] Evans, Saunders and Cronin, *Exclusion, Exploitation and Extermination*, 168.

[49] T.A. Coghlan, *Labour and Industry in Australia*, vol. 3 (Melbourne, AUS: Macmillan, 1969), 1301.

[50] Evans, Saunders and Cronin, *Exclusion, Exploitation and Extermination*, 206.

164   B. BOWDEN

to slavery. External supplies, which were more useful in boosting a society's wealth, were garnered from either prisoners of war or by purchasing slaves captured by others. Historically, the latter was far more important than the former.

By drawing slaves from outside, a society could readily draw a distinction between its citizens' comparatively privileged position and those working under servitude, their "living tools".

In antiquity, the victorious Greeks drove the survivors of Troy into slavery. When Sparta captured Plataea during the Peloponnesian War—the city-state whose soldiers died with its own at Thermopylae—it massacred the men and enslaved the women. In Rome, every military victory brought a new wave of slaves into the labor force. By the first century BC, this motley collection of Africans, Greeks, Celts and Germans represented 40 percent of the Italian population.[51] In the Mediterranean Basin in the fifteenth and sixteenth centuries it was religion that "was overwhelmingly the marker of otherness that deemed one 'enslavable', not race".[52] If, in Europe, slavery had long fallen into abeyance, it nevertheless prospered in the Iberian "war zone" between the Muslim and Christian worlds. During the *Reconquista*, many aristocratic Christian households boasted Muslim slaves. In the Muslim world, where, as Hugh Thomas observed, slavery was regarded "an unquestionable part of human organization", the enslavement of the "other" continued on a much grander scale.[53] Prohibited by religious edict from enslaving fellow Muslims, the Islamic societies of North Africa and the Middle East circumvented this restriction by targeting people of other faiths. Throughout the Middle Ages, Thomas discerned:

> ... at all the Muslim Mediterranean courts ... there were gathered together, as in an international brigade of servitude, Greek, Slav, German, Russian, Sudanese, and black slaves.[54]

---

[51] Keith Hopkins, *Conquerors and Slaves* (Cambridge, UK: Cambridge University Press, 1978), 9.

[52] Samia Errazzouki, "Between the 'Yellow-Skinned Enemy' and the 'Black-Skinned Slave': Early Modern Genealogies of Race and Slavery in Sa'dian Morocco", *Journal of African Studies* (2021), 3, https://doi.org/10.1080/13629387.2021.1927557.

[53] Hugh Thomas, *The Slave Trade: The History of the Atlantic Slave Trade 1440–1870* (London, UK: Picador, 1997), 37.

[54] Ibid., 38.

In 1591, the Islamic prohibition on enslaving fellow Muslims was abandoned with the Moroccan conquest of the Sub-Saharan Songhai Empire; a conquest that saw a steady stream of Muslim Africans dragged across the Sahara for sale in the North African slave markets. Samia Errazzouki refers to this development as an "historic rupture" in the Muslim world, "the moment that race superseded religion as the factor that justified enslavement" across North Africa.[55] In 1415, another fateful development occurred with the Portuguese capture of the Moroccan port of Ceuta, opposite Gibraltar. As Portuguese ships pushed southwards along the African coast, they found fortune through bypassing traditional caravan routes, buying slaves from West African chieftains and selling directly into the North African slave markets.[56] Once engaged in this trade it was but a short step for Portugal to redirect its cargoes toward its own possessions in the Atlantic.

From the sense of "otherness" that characterized slavery in the Mediterranean "war zone", there thus emerged a new, heightened expression of "otherness" in the Atlantic slave trade. Driven, as slavery always is, by economics, this new manifestation of an age-old practice created both perpetual rifts and enduring bonds in the complex societies of the Americas. Thrown together as master and slave, the fates of these hitherto alien populations drawn from Western Europe and Sub-Saharan Africa were to be, henceforth, intertwined. As the new industrialized iteration of western civilization emerged in the first half of the nineteenth century, this racial and social tension added a new complexity to the enduring human struggle for freedom.

---

[55] Errazzouki, "Race and Slavery in Sa'dian Morocco", 8–9.
[56] Thomas, "Atlantic Slave Trade", 51–52.

CHAPTER 8

Freedom, Democracy and Individualism: Cause of Business Success or Mere Correlation?

The association of the "West's" economic success with freedom, democracy and individualism is so pervasive that it can be considered a truism. But is it true? If so, what are the causal mechanisms that link freedom, democracy and individualism with economic achievement? Where there is a clear link is not between democracy and economic success, but rather between individualism and successful business endeavor. It was the interaction of these two factors that underpinned the Industrial Revolution and humanity's escape from the series of Malthusian traps that had hitherto condemned most to misery.

The tenuous connection between business creativity and democracy was highlighted by Joseph Schumpeter, who noted the inherent tension between individual interests on one hand and the "common good" on the other. Often, expressions of "common good" are articulated in backward-looking conformity.[1] Accordingly, innovators are often pilloried rather than praised. When word got out that James Hargreaves had invented his revolutionary "spinning jenny", the Lancashire community in which he lived—fearing for their jobs—smashed both his machines and furniture.

---

[1] Joseph A. Schumpeter, *Capitalism, Socialism and Democracy*, third edition (New York, NY: Harper Perennial, 1950), 250–257.

© The Author(s), under exclusive license to Springer Nature Switzerland AG 2022
B. Bowden, *Slavery, Freedom and Business Endeavor*,
Palgrave Debates in Business History,
https://doi.org/10.1007/978-3-030-97232-5_8

167

Moving to a new community, Hargreaves received an identical reception.[2] In trying to understand the link between innovation, democracy and economic success we should also note that in a capitalist society a pursuit of profit does not necessarily act as a spur to innovation. Often the reverse applies. Every existing industry has an interest in restraining competition and innovation. This creates powerful collective interests that actively oppose change. Indeed, it was against this tendency—which in the eighteenth century manifested itself in the practice of "mercantilism"—that Adam Smith directed *The Wealth of Nations*. Commenting on the Royal Charters that guaranteed firms an exclusive monopoly, Smith lamented how "this prerogative ... seems to have been reserved rather for extorting money from the subject than for the defence of the common liberty".[3]

An inability to identify a *direct* link between democracy, political liberty and western economic success has, unsurprisingly, caused some to doubt any connection at all.

In assessing the factors that gave rise to the Industrial Revolution, Robert Allen, for example, concludes that "representative government had a negligible effect on [economic] development in early modern Europe". Often, Allen concludes, absolutist regimes were as effective in encouraging investment and economic growth as representative democracies.[4] This line of thinking leads to two conclusions, both unwarranted. First, in the so-called "Great Divergence Debate", it has fostered the belief that—prior to the Industrial Revolution—Western Europe boasted no political or social attributes that were economically superior to those found in the advanced societies of South and East Asia. Seen from this perspective, the "West's" economic "divergence" from the rest of the world reflects mere "geographic accident", that is, the West's capacity to move to an energy-intensive economy was largely due to its more easily exploited coal reserves.[5] A more sinister interpretation, long associated

---

[2] Robert C. Allen, *The British Industrial Revolution in Global Perspective* (Cambridge, UK: Cambridge University Press, 2009), 191–192.

[3] Adam Smith (ed. Andrew Skinner), *The Wealth of Nations*, vol. 1 (London, UK: Penguin Classics, 1999), Book X, Part II, para. 17.

[4] Allen, *British Industrial Revolution*, 129, 5.

[5] Keith Pomeranz, *The Great Divergence: China, Europe and the Making of the Modern World* (Princeton, NJ: Princeton University Press, 2000), 62. See also, Prasannan Parthasarthi, *Why Europe Grew Rich and Asia Did Not* (Cambridge, UK: Cambridge

with Marxists and anti-colonialists, locates the West's post-1760 success in its exploitation of the non-European colonial world. For Vladimir Lenin, this "imperialist" phenomenon was nothing more than "parasitism", a process through which Europe and North America drained the rest of the world of its wealth.[6] Similarly, for Franz Fanon, the West Indies-born leader of the Algerian Revolution, "the wealth of the imperial countries" was obtained by gorging on "the gold and raw materials of the colonial countries".[7]

If one cannot identify linkages between democracy, political liberty and the economic success of the modern West one would be forced to concede more than long-held business beliefs. One would also have to conclude that there is nothing inherently politically progressive in modern capitalism. However, the fact that liberal-democratic societies *have* proved themselves more economically and socially successful than others suggests more than mere correlation.

The key to understanding the causal (if indirect) links between democracy and economic success is to focus on what liberal democracies have historically restrained rather than empowered, namely corporate monopolies, state domination and, most threateningly, the alliance of the state with a coterie of favored corporate giants. Where liberal democracies have failed to achieve this objective, the result has been either state-centered Marxist dictatorships or, more commonly, fascist or quasi-fascist regimes characterized by an alliance of an authoritarian state and oligopolistic big business (for example, Mussolini's Italy, Francoist Spain, Peronist Argentina, Nazi Germany). The fact that liberal democracies have, in large part, achieved their objectives on this front is no accident. Rather, it is embedded in the *form* of democracy that was integrated into the very structure of the industrialized West in the early to mid-nineteenth century. This was *not* simply associated with majority rule. It was also associated with "liberalism", that is, "a legal order geared to the defense of private

---

University Press, 2011), 2–3; Bozhong Li and Jan Luiten van Zanden, "Before the Great Divergence: Comparing the Yangzi Delta and the Netherlands at the Beginning of the Nineteenth Century", *Journal of Economic History*, Vol. 72, No. 4 (2012), 956–989.

[6] V.I. Lenin, "Imperialism, the Highest Stage of Capitalism", in V.I. Lenin, *Selected Works*, vol. 1 (Moscow, USSR: Foreign Languages Publishing House, 1946), 717–718.

[7] Franz Fanon, *The Wretched of the Earth* (Harmondsworth, UK: Penguin, 1967), 81.

property and the civic rights of those recognized as citizens".[8] Shorn of its "liberalism", democracy per se loses its capacity to either incentivize innovation or restrain anti-competitive behavior, either by corporate behemoths or encroaching state power. That liberalism *was* a defining feature of the democratic societies that emerged in the late eighteenth and early nineteenth centuries was also no accident. Instead, it was a product of a prolonged intellectual and political struggle waged by the intellectual heirs of John Locke, Adam Smith, and John Stuart Mill; a struggle that found concrete expression in both the American constitutional republic and the liberal parliamentary system of Britain and its colonial offshoots. In summing up the central intellectual debate of his time, John Stuart Mill recorded:

> One of the most disputed questions ... in political science ... relates to the proper limits of the functions and agency of governments ... And when the tide sets so strongly towards changes in government and legislation, as a means of improving the condition of mankind, this discussion is more likely to increase than to diminish in interest.[9]

In the light of the COVID-19 pandemic, when governments everywhere assumed virtual wartime powers over every aspect of life, this debate assumes renewed significance. Even before the pandemic, the state's footprint had taken on unprecedented peace-time significance. In 2019, on average one-third of GDP in OECD countries went to taxes. In France, taxes consumed 45.4% of GDP. Even in the United States, a society historically renowned for its suspicion of state intervention, taxes represented a quarter of GDP. Government spending was even more significant. In 2019, United States government spending represented 38.1% of GDP. In the United Kingdom, government expenditure accounted for 41.1% of GDP. French government spending was equivalent to 55.2% of GDP.[10] Everywhere, this trend belied the popular

---

[8] Stephen Kotkin, *Armageddon Averted: The Soviet Collapse, 1970–2000* (Oxford, UK: Oxford University Press, 2001), 143.

[9] John Stuart Mill, *Principles of Political Economy* (New York, NY: Prometheus Books, 2004), 727.

[10] OECD, *Revenue Statistics 2020—The United States* (Paris, FRA: OECD, 2021), https://www.oecd.org/tax/revenue-statistics-united-states.pdf [accessed 8 July 2021]; OECD, *Data—General Government Spending* (Paris, FRA: OECG, 2021), https://data.oecd.org/gga/general-government-spending.htm [accessed 8 July 2021].

narrative as to the supposed advance of "neo-liberalist" policies at government expense. Yes, it is true that governments have shown a proclivity to outsource services. Invariably, however, such services are still paid for by the government. The effect of this is to arguably increase rather than diminish the state's power, creating a pool of corporate entities (rent-seekers) who profit from government largesse.

The tendency for the modern iteration of western civilization to oscillate has been a liberal capitalist model and one that can be described as "corporatist" (where business success rests on collusion with the state) points to a fundamental but easily overlooked fact. The rise of the industrialized iteration of western civilization is not only associated with innovation and business endeavor, it is also characterized by more powerful states. In large part, the history of western civilization has revolved around a perpetual contest between these two tendencies.

GREEK AND ROMAN ANTIQUITY: BOUNDED INDIVIDUALISM, BOUNDED FREEDOM

Speaking of the glory of ancient Greece, Thomas Carlyle, lamented:

> Greece, where is it? Desolate for thousands of years; away, vanished ... Like a dream; like the dust of King Agamemnon! Greece was; Greece, except in the words it spoke, is not.[11]

Vanished though it may be, the ideals of Athens in the fifth century BC still inspire. Articulating these ideals in his famed funeral oration, the Athenian leader at the time of the Peloponnesian War, Pericles, is recorded as saying:

> Our constitution is called a democracy because power is in the hands not of a minority but of the whole people ... when it is a question of putting one person before another in positions of public responsibility, what counts is not membership of a particular class, but the actual ability which the man possesses.[12]

---

[11] Thomas Carlyle, *On Heroes, Hero-Worship, and the Heroic in History* (New Haven, CT: Yale University Press, 1840), 92.

[12] Thucydides (trans. Rex Warner), *History of the Peloponnesian War* (Harmondsworth, UK: Penguin, 1972), 145.

172   B. BOWDEN

Entrusting the running of their society to majority consent, the Athenian democracy also reveled in an individualistic spirit that had no equal, Pericles boasting:

> ... our city is an education ... each single one of our citizens, in all the manifold aspects of life, is able to show himself the rightful lord and owner of his own person.[13]

If the Athens of classical antiquity glorified its individualism and democratic norms, this failed to translate into business or economic innovation. Commenting upon the generalized tendency in Greek antiquity to bury money in the ground, Scott Meikle observed that this was a logical strategy given the dearth of investment opportunities. There was, he added, "no credit instruments of any kind". Nor was there "a significant pool of unattached [free] labour". Manufacturing was undertaken by "craftsmen producing in workshops of very restricted scale, and by chattel-slaves".[14] In the absence of significant technological innovation, there were only two sure pathways through which the Greek city-states could accumulate substantial pools of wealth: steal from others or enslave them (or, preferably, achieve both goals simultaneously). This fundamental fact was, arguably, better understood by the ancients than by modern-day commentators. The Athenian democracy of the fifth century BC, and its material achievements, would also have been impossible without the slave-operated silver mines at Laurion and the tribute exacted from the Delian League. The latter, initially an anti-Persian alliance, had by 454 BC been reduced to tributary status, forced to pay the Athenian state 600 talents (1.56 tons) of silver a year.[15] In defending Athens' need to go to war to defend its imperial domination, Pericles conceded that the Athenian "empire is now like a tyranny". However, to surrender this prize, Pericles lamented, would reduce Athens "to ruin".[16]

Paradoxically, it was the Athenian struggle to maintain its empire that caused its ruination as Athens crashed to its defeat in the Peloponnesian

---

[13] Ibid., 147, 149.

[14] Scott Meikle, "Modernism, Economics and the Ancient Economy", in Walter Schiedel and Sitta von Reden (eds.), *The Ancient Economy* (New York, NY: Routledge, 2002), 241–242.

[15] Thucydides, *Peloponnesian War*, 132.

[16] Ibid., 161–162.

War. Collectively, the obvious failings of the Greek economy—the absence of formalized credit arrangements, subsistence agriculture, a lack of technological innovation and a propensity for internecine warfare—caused the whole society to rest on fragile foundations. By the middle of the second century BC, Polybius was reporting that the old Greek heartlands were suffering from "a general decrease of the population", a desertion of cities, and falling "agricultural production".[17] In the final analysis, the Greek incapacity to break through its Malthusian ceiling pointed to the bounded nature of Greek freedom and individualism. In the numerically small Greek city-states, the number of citizens who concerned themselves with large-scale profit accumulation was inconsequential. In Athens, leisurely participation in political affairs rested on a veritable army of slaves, amounting to some 30% of the total population. This made Athens one of only five western cultures that can truly be considered a "slave society", wherein slaves represented at least a third of the population; the other four being Rome, the American South prior to the Civil War, and nineteenth-century Brazil and Cuba.[18]

Unlike Periclean Athens, the Roman Republic in its pre-imperial heyday was structured around the primacy of law rather than unbridled democracy. In exploring the reasons for this abiding commitment to legal norms, the ancient Greek historian, Polybius, located it in the society's "mixed constitution". Articulating a view that countless others were to take up, Polybius argued that Rome managed to combine the best from "three kinds" of "political constitutions: monarchy, aristocracy and democracy".[19] Whereas democracy tended to degenerate into "mob rule", Polybius concluded, Rome avoided this fate by vesting executive power in annually elected consuls (who were, in effect, de facto monarchs) and legislative and administrative review in a quasi-aristocratic senate. Together, these monarchical and aristocratic elements checked the power of Rome's popular assembly. Conversely, the assembly restrained both consuls and the senate.[20] In the European Age of Enlightenment in the eighteenth century, this idealized Roman model exerted a near-irresistible

---

[17] Polybius (trans. Ian Scott-Kilvert), *The Rise of the Roman Empire* (London, UK: Penguin Classics, 1979), 537.

[18] Keith Hopkins, *Conquerors and Slaves* (Cambridge, UK: Cambridge University Press, 1978), 101.

[19] Polybius, *Roman Empire*, 312, 304.

[20] Ibid., 304, 310.

attraction. Nowhere was this more evident than in Britain's North American colonies. As Bernard Bailyn noted, among the pre-revolutionary population that enjoyed "any degree of education", a knowledge of Roman antiquity "was universal".[21] They "rejoiced in the freedom of Rome's republic and ... lamented its decline and fall when freedom was destroyed by the power of imperial despots".[22] Prior to the American Revolution, they perceived in George III another power-hungry dictator. After it, they sought to build a new, idealized republic on American soil.

Historically, there has been a tendency to explain Rome's decline in political and military terms. According to this narrative, Rome's decline can be traced to the displacement of the idealized constitution of Polybius' imagination by the quasi-military dictatorship of the Caesars, and the ultimate failure of the imperial legions to defend the frontiers. In truth, Rome's decline had far more to do with the suffocation of innovation and enterprise through its embrace of war and slavery as a means of achieving economic objectives.

Even more than in classical Greece, prosperity in Rome was premised on the principle that the surest way to obtain wealth was through either stealing it from others or by enslaving one's enemies. "From the Second Punic War onwards", Howgego observed, "Rome laid its hands by stages on the stored-up wealth of the whole of the Mediterranean."[23] The greatest cities of the Mediterranean basin—Carthage, Syracuse, Athens, Jerusalem—were sacked. Plutarch records that "so much money" was plundered from Macedonia in 167 BC "that the [Roman] people were exempt from taxes".[24] Military victories also flooded the labor market with slaves, displacing the traditional peasant farmer with the ubiquitous slave-operated *latifundia*. Reflecting upon this trend, the Roman historian, Appian, observed:

> ... the ownership of slaves brought them [the rich] great gain from the multitude of their progeny, who increased because they were exempt from

---

[21] Bernard Bailyn, *The Ideological Origins of the American Revolution*, 50th anniversary edition (Cambridge, MA: Belknap Press, 2017), 23–24.

[22] Ibid., xiii.

[23] Christopher Howgego, "The Supply and Use of Money in the Roman World, 200BC to AD300", *Journal of Roman Studies*, Vol, 82, No. 1 (1992), 4.

[24] Plutarch (trans. Robin Waterfield), *Roman Lives* (Oxford, UK: Oxford University Press, 1999), 74.

military service. Thus certain powerful men became extremely rich and the race of slaves multiplied throughout the country.[25]

Economically, the *latifundia* enjoyed a number of advantages over subsistence peasant agriculture. Whereas peasant farms typically restricted themselves to the farming of wheat, a few vines and vegetables, the *latifundia* cultivated an array of crops on a commercial scale, switching labor from one to another as the season required. In the long run, however, the use of slaves in not only agriculture but also mining and manufacturing curtailed innovation. While it is true that Rome demonstrated unprecedented virtuosity in logistics and construction, in other domains it remained perpetually backward. Rome never developed the capacity to cast iron. Roman agriculture and transport were constrained by an absence of the soft leather collars that would have allowed for the efficient harnessing of horses.[26] Roman cities, far from being centers for production and innovation, enjoyed a largely parasitic relationship with the countryside. In Rome itself, "what we should nowadays call the middle classes vegetated in semi-starvation within sights of the almost incredible opulence of a few thousand".[27]

As long as Rome could plunder new reserves of loot and slaves the fragility of its economic achievements could be disguised. When supply faltered, however, the whole society unraveled. Long before the invading German tribes crossed the frozen Rhine on the last day of AD 406, the death knell of the Roman economy was effectively sounded by the Antonine Plague of AD 165–AD 180. Suddenly confronted with severe labor shortages, production collapsed on every front. Suggestive of the generalized decline in both mining and metal manufacturing, analysis of Greenland's ice cores indicates a marked decrease in lead isotypes attributable to Roman atmospheric pollution from AD 170. A collapse in mining activity is also indicated by changes in the composition of Roman coins. By AD 250 the Roman denarius, once composed of almost pure

[25] Appian (trans. Horace White), *Roman History: The Civil Wars* (Cambridge, MA: Loeb Classic Library/Harvard University Press, 1913), Book 1, 7.

[26] Charles Parain, "The Evolution of Agricultural Technique", in M.M. Postan, *The Cambridge Economic History of Europe* (Cambridge, UK: Cambridge University Press, 1966), 125–179.

[27] Jerome Carcopino (trans. E.O. Lorimer), *Daily Life in Ancient Rome* (New Haven, CN: Yale University Press, 1940), 66.

176   B. BOWDEN

silver, boasted a silver content of only 40%. Twenty years later the figure was 4%.[28]

The unraveling of Roman society had profound consequences for not only western civilization but also for the potent rivals that emerged from Rome's ashes. For one of the most significant, if easily overlooked, legacies of Rome's failure was the shattering of a single Mediterranean world and its replacement by three, often competing, cultural entities: a feudal Catholic Christendom in the West; a Greek and Slavic Orthodox culture in the Balkans and Eastern Europe; and an Islamic civilization in North Africa and the Middle East.

THE PREMODERN WEST: INDIVIDUALISM AS AGENT OF STATE ABSOLUTISM—SCHOLARLY AND ARISTOCRATIC INDIVIDUALISM

Amid the collapse of Roman Empire in the fifth century AD—and the accompanying collapse of economic and cultural institutions (slavery, secular education, imperial bureaucracies, and so on)—there emerged four new forms of individualism that were to reshape western civilization: bourgeois; aristocratic; peasant; and scholarly. Although business and economic historians have paid greatest heed to the former, it is arguable that the scholarly individualism initially forged in the medieval monasteries was equally influential.

The association of intellectual leadership with a religious elite was hardly unique. Mesopotamian city-states, Pharaonic Egypt, Old Testament Israel and Zoroastrian Persia all vested intellectual leadership in religious authorities. In China, knowledge of Confucianism was the portal through which one became a member of a political as well as an intellectual elite. There were, nevertheless, features of medieval religious life that were unusual. Rather than retreating into spiritual reflection, monasteries and religious orders were the great managerial and technological innovators of the medieval age. Of the Benedictine monasteries that became a model for others, it has been observed that they:

[28] Andrew Wilson, "Machines, Power and the Ancient Economy", *Journal of Roman Studies*, Vol. 92, No. 1 (2002), 25–27.

... were the missionary centres, not only of faith, but of the fundamental arts of civilization. They were a great economic factor in the new Europe ... manual labour, that had once been considered suitable only to slaves, bore with it no stigma of degradation ... That principle of itself was a valuable contribution to human progress.[29]

As the Benedictines lost their innovative zeal, other religious orders assumed their position at the cutting edge. In the High Middle Ages (c. AD 1000–c. AD 1250), Kieser notes:

The Cistercians became the leading force in advancing technical progress ... they considerably improved the techniques of smelting, glass production and agriculture ... Their workshops resembled factories in which water-driven machinery were widely applied.[30]

A second unusual feature of the medieval religious orders was not only their effective autonomy from the central church bureaucracies but also their internal democracy. Official positions were typically elected. General assemblies, both at a monastic and transnational level, determined organizational priorities.[31] The medieval religious orders were also peculiar in extending education, and even a religious career, to women. Almost a third of all the monasteries ever established by the Catholic Church were run by female orders.[32]

Among the contributions of the medieval monasteries and religious orders to western civilization none was more consequential than a peculiar offshoot: the university. Like monasteries, the early universities were initially staffed by the religious orders. Even where lay staff were recruited, universities continued the monastic practice of confining membership to unmarried men who congregated with their students in semi-autonomous "schools". For those of humble means and in search of individual recognition, the university offered an alternative path to business success. As

---

[29] Dom Justin McCann, *Saint Benedict* (London, UK: Sheed and Ward, 1937), 100.

[30] Alfred Kieser, "From Asceticism to Administration of Wealth: Medieval Monasteries and the Pitfalls of Rationalization", *Organization Studies*, Vo. 8, No. 2 (1987), 112.

[31] Peter Wirtz, "Governance of Old Religious Orders: Benedictines and Dominicans", *Journal of Management History*, Vol. 23, No. 3 (2017), 259–77.

[32] Gitte Greater and Katja Rost, *Structural Effects of Sex-Ratios and Power Distribution on the Survival Rates of Female Monasteries* (Vancouver, CAN: Paper presented to the Academy of Management, 2015).

178 B. BOWDEN

Compayré recorded, "Great was the number of those who, destitute of all resources, joyfully braved privations ... in order that they might penetrate at last into the sanctuary of knowledge".[33] From the outset, municipal authorities—anxious to foster the new centers of learning—guaranteed universities a very large latitude in terms of freedom of speech. Consequently, far more than the monastery, the university allowed a flourishing of scholarly individualism, one observer noting the academic tendency "to talk about everything, discuss everything, intervene in everything".[34]

The scholarly individualism of the medieval and Renaissance university profoundly influenced the practice of freedom, in both positive and negative ways.

Like the Benedictine and Cistercian monasteries before them, universities were outwardly looking institutions. They systematized new business understandings and grappled with problems that had previously restrained business endeavor. Writing in the mid-thirteenth century, St Thomas Aquinas, a Dominican friar at the University of Paris, put forward cogent arguments that legitimized commercial interest rates—hitherto condemned as "usury"—as something a lender "may lawfully demand".[35] At the University of Perugia in the late fifteenth century, Luca Pacioli, a Franciscan friar, popularized "the accounting system used in Venice".[36] Built around double-entry bookkeeping, this system was seminal to the medieval "commercial revolution" with its bank credits and long-distance trade. What was nevertheless most revolutionary about the university was the pursuit of knowledge for its own sake. In 1541, giving voice to this sentiment in his revolutionary study of the solar system, Copernicus suggested that every "philosopher" should "endeavor to seek the truth in all things, to the extent permitted to human reason by God".[37]

[33] Gabriel Compayré, *Abelard and the Origin and Early History of Universities* (New York, NY: Charles Scribner's Sons, 1910), 266.

[34] Cited, Ibid., 290.

[35] Saint Thomas Aquinas, *Summa Theologica* (Fairfax, VA: Christian Classics Ethereal Library, George Mason University, n.d.), Q. 72, Article 2, https://www.ccel.org/ccel/a/aquinas/summa/cache/summa.pdf.

[36] Luca Pacioli, *Accounting Books and Records: Summa de Arithmetica, Geometria, Proportioni et Proportionalita* (Seattle, WA: Pacioli Society, 1994), 2.

[37] Nicholas Copernicus (trans. Edmund Rosen), *Six Books on the Revolutions of the Heavenly Spheres* (Baltimore, ML: John Hopkins University Press, 2008), 4.

If the universities and scholarly individualism were seminal to the dynamism of the new iterations of western civilizations that emerged from medieval Europe, they also contained more sinister seeds associated with absolutism, state power and the suppression of private initiative. For, invariably, large sections of the scholarly elite that the universities created found themselves drawn toward the old Platonist belief that political power was best vested in the educated and the wise so that they could act as "guardian and ruler" of common humanity.[38]

For a business historian it is always easy to fall into the trap that ensnared Karl Marx and Frederick Engels, both of whom believed that reference to the rise of capitalism explains everything else in modern history.[39] This is a mistake that no one living in Europe between 1500 and 1800 could have made as the princely state assumed unprecedented power. As Schumpeter observed:

> ... the prince came to personify the state and the nation from the sixteenth century on. He succeeded in subjecting all classes to his authority – the nobility and the clergy not less than the bourgeoisie and peasantry.[40]

At the core of this princely power was the symbiotic relationship between the new absolutist state and the universities that supplied it with career bureaucrats. In large part, as Henry Karmen noted, it can be said that the "universities existed ... to serve the state ... It was they, that turned out, year after the year, the administrative elite of both Church and state".[41] Scholastically, it was their training in canon and civil (statute) law that groomed university graduates for a civil service career. At the University of Salamanca, the great recruiting ground for the Spanish bureaucracy, almost all the 2,000 to 3,000 students who graduated each year between 1570 and 1640 boasted degrees in canon law. Other universities, most

---

[38] Plato (trans. Desmond Lee), *The Republic*, second edition (London, UK: Penguin, 2003), Book IX, para. 590 (d), 591 (a).

[39] Karl Marx and Frederick Engels, "Manifesto of the Communist Party", in Karl Marx and Frederick Engels, *Selected Works*, vol. 1 (Moscow, USSR: Foreign Languages Publishing House, 1951), 34–38.

[40] Joseph A. Schumpeter, *History of Economic Analysis* (London, UK: Routledge, 1954), 142.

[41] Henry Kamen, *The Iron Century: Social Change in Europe 1550–1600* (New York, NY: Praeger Publishers, 1971), 288.

notably those at Leiden (Netherlands) and Padua (Italy) specialized in civil or statute law, attracting graduates from all over Europe. Eighty-two percent of the 1,600 German students who studied at Padua each year between 1580 and 1600 studied law. At Oxford and Cambridge, canon and statute law were also the most popular courses by a considerable margin.

Significantly, even though British courts operated on the basis of common law—not Roman civil law—neither Oxford nor Cambridge offered courses in common law until 1758, when Oxford created its Vinerian Professorship in English (formerly Common) Law. This made university graduates near-useless when it came to representing clients before a court. Conversely, a university law degree became almost mandatory for those interested in a political or civil service career. Many aspired to obtain university professorships not because they were interested in scholarship but because they expected to be recruited from such posts to serve in the highest positions in the realm. At the University of Salamanca, one chair in canon law had to be filled sixty-one times in the course of the seventeenth century as the beneficiaries of the appointment moved across to the Spanish bureaucracy, underlining "the extent to which the university had become little more than a stepping stone to office".[42]

As the absolutist state harnessed and redirected the scholarly individualism that had emerged from the university it also reshaped—and came into conflict—with other forms of individualism rooted in the aristocracy, bourgeoisie and peasantry.

Initially, the new absolutist state was primarily directed against the aristocracy, a class for whom individual honor and military prowess represented their *raison d'être*. As a class, the aristocracy was both the essential prop of the monarchical feudal state and the cause of its perpetual weakness. In both war and peace, the monarchy relied upon the aristocracy for troops, supplies, the maintenance of law and order and what passed for administrative support. At the same time, however, the aristocracy typically enjoyed a closer relationship to the monarchical state's subsidiary vassals than did the monarchy did itself. Every monarch lived in fear of aristocratic rebellion. As a class, moreover, the aristocracy was defined by birth, not by innovation and accumulated wealth. Of Italy's Neapolitan aristocrats, Jacob Burckhardt observed that their defining characteristics

---

[42] Ibid., 195–196, 198, 289, 296.

were their "contempt for work" and their "passion for titles".[43] In terms of economic and social progress, Europe's nobility were role models of the worst sort. Across the medieval and early modern eras, Braudel observed, the "rich bourgeoisie" were "irresistibly drawn towards the aristocracy"—with their lifestyle of "careless indolence" and contempt for social inferiors, "as if towards the sun".[44]

Fearing their aristocratic vassals, Europe's monarchs constantly sought to undermine their social and military power. Everywhere, Schumpeter recorded, absolutist states sought to maximize "public revenue" through increased taxation.[45] Militarily, this allowed for the replacement of aristocratic-led feudal levies with professional armies. Administratively, it involved the displacement of aristocratic power with "civil servants". In commenting on this transformation, Braudel identified "a political revolution coupled with a social revolution", one that catapulted the so-called "new men" who staffed the absolutist state into prominence. Invariably, Braudel concluded, these officials were people "of humble origin", men who had no natural affinity with the hereditary aristocracy.[46] Such conclusions are, however, truer of the sixteenth century than the seventeenth. At Oxford in 1571, graduating commoners outnumbered the nobility and gentry by 54 to 35. By 1600, however, commoners were outnumbered by 142 to 110. Such trends were replicated across Europe as the nobility gained control of university education as a means of securing positions of wealth and influence in the state bureaucracy. In Spain, in particular, "the sons of the poor were crowded out". Even the University of Geneva became a haven not of the rising bourgeoisie but of the aristocracy, a "resort of the Calvinist nobility of Germany and France".[47]

As the aristocracy cemented its control over higher education—and, hence, the civil service—income from public office assumed increasing importance. In 1617, for example, the Marshal d'Ancre, one of France's leading aristocrats, drew only one-seventh of his wealth from the land.

---

[43] Jacob Burckhardt (trans. S.G. Middlemore), *The Civilization of the Renaissance in Italy*, second edition (New York, NY: The Modern Library, 1954), 269.

[44] Fernand Braudel, *The Mediterranean and the Mediterranean World in the Age of Philip II*, vol. 2 (New York: Torchbooks, 1975), 729, 725.

[45] Schumpeter, *History of Economic Analysis*, 143.

[46] Braudel, *Age of Philip II*, 681.

[47] Kamen, *Iron Century*, 293.

The rest came from "offices and other sources of government revenue" derived from the French state. In England, in 1613, the Earl of Rutland, one of the nation's preeminent nobles, obtained only 5% of his income from the land. Most of the rest came from state "pensions and public office".[48]

The educated aristocratic elites not only siphoned off state wealth, they also absorbed wealthy non-aristocratic elements. Whenever they obtained money, aspiring bureaucrats and bourgeoisie would buy landed estates and titles, joining the aristocracy in what Thorstein Veblen described as a "leisure class", people of "high-bred manners" who consumed "freely and of the best, in food, drink, narcotics, shelter, services, ornaments, apparel, weapons and accoutrements, amusements, amulets, and idols or divinities".[49] Yes, it is true that these aristocratic elites also participated in business ventures. Their participation was, however, often conducted in ways that were destructive of both competition and innovation. Preying on the absolutist state's money shortages, they bought Royal Charters, monopolies, and the right to collect taxes. Entrenched in the "mercantilist" policies pursued by European governments, these practices benefited the rich at the public's expense. In France, the aristocracy infamously used its power to exempt itself from taxes. Far from retreating, the French aristocracy's power was resurgent by the time of the French Revolution. From 1781, Lefebvre recorded, "four quarterings of nobility were required to obtain a commission [in the army] without passing through the ranks". In 1789, all France's bishops were aristocrats.[50] Elsewhere, the aristocracy's influence was even more pervasive—and destructive. Nowhere was this more evident than in Eastern Europe, where the nobility enriched itself by operating vast grain estates that serviced rising Western European demand. In the process, a once-free peasantry was reduced to servitude. In Poland, the number of days a week that the peasant was required to work on their lord's estate rose from one in 1519 to six in 1600.[51]

[48] Ibid., 140–41.

[49] Thorstein Veblen, *The Theory of the Leisure Class*, second edition (New York, NY: B.W. Huebsch), 75, 73.

[50] Georges Lefebvre (trans. R.R. Palmer), *The Coming of the French Revolution* (Princeton, NJ: Princeton University Press, 1967), 17.

[51] Fernand Braudel (trans. Siân Reynolds), *The Wheels of Commerce: Civilization and Capitalism, 15th–18th Century* (London, UK: Collins, 1982), 265–272.

The Premodern West: Individualism as Agent of Innovation—Bourgeois Individualism

In an overwhelmingly rural society, dominated by an entrenched aristocracy and an increasingly powerful state, the bourgeois individualism that emerged during the medieval and Renaissance periods was always a peculiar social phenomenon. Unlike both the aristocracy and the educated elite employed in the civil service, however, bourgeois individualism never primarily rested on state or military power. It was this that made it revolutionary. A peculiar outgrowth of the era of medieval serfdom, bourgeois individualism was also an urban phenomenon. It prospered, in part, because its serviced rural needs. Accordingly, just as scholarly individualism cannot be understood apart from the university and the absolutist state, bourgeois individualism cannot be understood apart from peasant individualism. They existed in a symbiotic relationship, both economically and, ultimately, politically. Primarily concerned with an increase in wealth, the underlying aspirations of the bourgeoisie and peasantry were always fundamentally different from those of the aristocracy and the scholarly elite, both of whom were *primarily* interested in prestige and power. In the eighteenth and nineteenth centuries, this focus on wealth rather than power was to bring bourgeois and peasant individualism into an epoch-defining conflict with state absolutism. In every generation, it made bourgeois and peasant individualism the primary drivers of western innovation.

The medieval merchant and trader were, in many ways, a social aberration. In a society where most were legally bound to the land, Henri Pirenne observed:

> ... they presented the strange picture of circulating everywhere without being claimed by anyone. They did not demand freedom; it was conceded to them because no one could prove that they did not already enjoy it.[52]

The medieval town where they lived was also a haven of freedom. It was, Cipolla concluded:

---

[52] Henri Pirenne (trans. Frank D. Halsey), *Medieval Cities: Their Origins and the Revival of Trade* (Princeton, NJ: Princeton University Press, 1952), 126.

... another world from a judicial view ... The merchants, the professionals, the craftsmen who lived in the towns did not recognize the control of the rural world or its values ... With the appearance of the medieval city and the emergence of the urban bourgeoisie, a new Europe was born.[53]

As an idealized *description*, Pirenne and Cipolla's depictions of bourgeois circumstance in the Middle Ages have merit. It does not get us very far, however, in terms of explanation. Towns were hardly a medieval invention. The city-states of ancient Phoenicia, Greece and Carthage all engaged in long-distance trade. Africa and Asia also long boasted complex systems of exchange. Between 1600 and 1800, India was home to a "sophisticated mercantile order organized [around] the manufacture and export of cotton textiles".[54] Given the near universality of urban centers and commercial exchanges across human history what, if anything, was unique about the medieval and Renaissance city? If there was a difference, when and why did the medieval city depart from the historic norm?

The classic answer to these questions is contained in the so-called "Pirenne Thesis", which argues that the medieval city and bourgeoisie were as much products of social destruction as of economic innovation. In Pirenne's estimation, the decisive factor in the collapse of Roman antiquity—and, hence, the opportunity for a fundamentally different civilization and economic order—was not the German invasions of the fifth century AD but rather the Arab conquests of the seventh century. As a result of the Arab conquests, Pirenne argued, the large-scale oceanic trade that (supposedly) survived the Germanic invasions was brought to end. The Mediterranean became "a Moslem lake".[55] This shattering of "the Mediterranean unity" that hitherto characterized western civilization was, Pirenne believed, "the most essential event of European history which had occurred since the Punic Wars. It was the end of the classical tradition".[56] As Western Europe slowly recovered after the demographic collapse of the late Carolingian era (c. 887), Pirenne also concluded that the medieval

---

[53] Carlo M. Cipolla, *Before the Industrial Revolution: European Society and Economy, 1000–1700*, second edition (London, UK: Routledge, 1981), 147, 149.

[54] Parthasarathi, *Why Europe Grew Rich*, 185.

[55] Pirenne, *Medieval Cities*, 25.

[56] Henri Pirenne (trans. Bernard Miall), *Mohammed and Charlemagne* (New York, NY: Barnes & Noble, 1939), 164.

city acted as an organizing force, first as "fortress", then as commercial center and, finally, as a source of independent political power.[57]

Many of the points of fact upon which Pirenne's thesis rested are highly dubious. The Mediterranean economy prior to the Arab conquests was not as healthy as Pirenne imagined. Nor were the Arab conquests as destructive as he depicted. His claim that the "Empire of Charlemagne" was "a State without foreign markets, living in a condition of almost complete isolation", is overstated.[58] Despite these factual shortcomings there is, nevertheless, conceptual merit in the Pirenne Thesis. The economic and political placement of the early medieval city *was* profoundly different from that found in other historic civilizations. Most feudal princes lacked both the inclination and capacity to exert effective day-to-day control over the cities within their realm. Unlike the imperial Caesars and governors of Rome, few feudal lords based themselves in a city. Instead, they lived in rural fortresses. In terms of an organized princely state with bureaucrats and civil government, there was little of note. To the extent that there was any system of monetary exchange, this was in the hands of urban burghers rather than the state. In short, the urban bourgeoisie was strong largely because the state was weak.

The key to the bourgeoisie's financial power, allowing them to engage in not only new forms of long-distance trade but also to act as paymasters to Europe's princely states, was the *instrumentum ex causa cambii*, or the "bill of exchange".

Like many revolutionary innovations, the "bill of exchange" was the product of necessity. In medieval Europe, the transport of merchandise was inherently risky. Even more hazardous was the prospect of returning home with a purse full of gold. To understand how the "bill of exchange" mitigated such perils, let us take the hypothetical example of a Venetian merchant engaged in trade along the Flanders–Italy corridor. If our hypothetical Venetian wished to purchase Flemish cloth from a Parisian merchant at the Champagne trade fair, he could deposit money (for example, 200 Venetian ducats) with a Venetian bank or finance house. In return, he would receive, having paid a commission, a "bill of exchange" or "draft" payable in Paris in French livres. On obtaining the cloth from

[57] Pirenne, *Medieval Cities*, 75, 93.

[58] Ibid., 29. For a critique of the "Pirenne Thesis", see Fernand Braudel (trans. Siân Reynolds), *The Identity of France: People and Production* (London, UK: Fontana Press, 1990), 99–120.

his Parisian counterpart, the Venetian would provide in exchange both his "draft" and a "duplicate receipt" which verified that the "draft" was backed by physical currency. On returning to Paris the French merchant could then exchange this draft for local currency. Now, let us assume that our Venetian has also sold another Parisian a shipment of spice for 200 Venetian ducats, and obtained in exchange a "draft" or "bill of exchange" payable in Venice. On returning to Venice our merchant then presents this "draft" to his banker, receiving in exchange his original 200 Venetian ducats, minus a commission.[59] Under this arrangement the need for physical currency is largely eliminated. The Venetian's original deposit provided, in effect, merely a surety. This could have been dispensed with if he had "credit" with his bank. All that needed to now occur was a resolution of accounts between bankers. Typically, settlement occurred at the trade "fairs" (for example at Champagne and Piacenza). Bankers invariably arrived at these events with "masses of bills of exchange" but little in the way of cash, the need for the latter negated by the fact that credits and debits almost always "cancelled each other out".[60]

The power that the "bill of exchange" vested in the medieval and Renaissance bourgeoisie can hardly be exaggerated. "Bills of exchange" acted as de facto currency, traded at a discount from one merchant to another. This allowed an exponential increase in "money supply". By the fifteenth century the issuance of "cheques" was also normalized, Pacioli advising his readers in 1494 that a cheque was a "legal document under federal law"—by which he meant that it enjoyed guaranteed acceptance by the banks "which are found today in Venice, in Bruges, in Antwerp, Barcelona, and other places familiar to the world of commerce".[61] Socially and culturally, the growth of finance houses bound by agreed norms—honoring distant "bills of exchange" and "cheques"—transformed the bourgeoisie from a localized phenomenon into a transnational force.

Militarily weak but financially strong, Europe's urban bourgeoisie had a complex relationship with princely authority. Perceiving urban burghers to be a lesser threat than their armed feudal vassals and rivals, medieval princes granted both the nascent bourgeoisie and the towns within which

---

[59] This example draws on that provided in, Pacioli, *Accounting Books and Records*, 56–58.

[60] Braudel, *Wheels of Commerce*, 90–91.

[61] Pacioli, *Accounting Books and Records*, 53.

they resided a series of "rights"—or, to be more exact, "privileges"—in return for loans and other forms of financial support.[62] In the era of the European absolutist state (c. 1550–1789) this princely dependency on the bourgeoisie became ever-more pronounced. The scale of this dependency is best demonstrated by the experiences of the kingdom that boasted Europe's largest bureaucracy and professionalized army, the Spanish Hapsburgs. In 1562, the Spanish crown—supported by the revenues of Castile, Aragon, Catalonia, southern Italy, Milan, the Low Countries and a vast influx of American silver—spent more than 25% of its annual budget on interest.[63] Every year the bullion of the Americas was pledged against new loans before it arrived. Largely obtained from Genovese finance houses, the interest burden from these loans forced Philip II into a series of defaults and loan consolidations. With every renegotiation the Spanish position deteriorated. For all their legal training, Spain's civil servants were "no match for the *hombres de negocios*" of Genoa, who proved to be "centuries ahead" of them "in the world of international finance".[64]

Politically, the democratic instincts of Europe's nascent bourgeoisie can be doubted. Burghers constantly negotiated privileges that favored themselves at the expense of their poorer neighbors. As employers, they were often worse than the aristocracy. The condition, for example, of Flemish cloth workers—one of the lynchpins of the medieval economy—was "very miserable", producing "a brutish lower class, uneducated and discontented".[65]

If the premodern bourgeoisie were often undemocratic, no one can doubt their individualistic ethos. In northern Europe the individualist ethos of the nascent bourgeoisie also found expression in new forms of religious organization, most notably Calvinism. According to Max Weber, Calvinists differed from others in both their "piety" and "extraordinary capitalistic business sense". Together, Weber argued in his *The Protestant Ethic and the Spirt of Capitalism*, these attributes made "the Calvinist

---

[62] Ibid., 213.

[63] North and Thomas, *Rise of the Western World*, 129.

[64] Braudel, *Wheels of Commerce*, 511.

[65] Pirenne, *Medieval Cities*, 154.

diaspora the seedbed of the capitalistic economy".[66] Such comments are overstated. As R.H. Tawney noted in his *Religion and the Rise of Capitalism*—published contemporarily with Weber's study in the early 1920s—in Renaissance Europe, "It was predominately Catholic cities which were the commercial capitals of Europe, and Catholic bankers who were its leading financiers".[67] A perusal of John Calvin's main work, *Institutes of the Christian Religion*, also suggests little that inherently favored capitalism or even the accumulation of wealth.[68] Rather than Calvinism being the *cause* of bourgeois individualism, it is more likely that bourgeois individualism found in Calvinism a spiritual soul-mate, transforming it into an image in its own liking. Nowhere was the Calvinist emphasis on self-reliance, thrift and spiritual equality before God more evident than in the New England provinces of North America. Visiting the region in 1830, Alexis de Tocqueville, a French Catholic, disdainfully referred to its founding fathers as "sectarian fanatics". At the same time, however, he expressed admiration for the ways in which a Puritan religious faith underpinned self-government and political liberty. In the Puritan communities, Tocqueville concluded, "Liberty looks upon religion as its companion … as the guardian of morality, morality as the guardian of law and the security that freedom will last".[69]

Despite its financial and cultural dynamism, the bourgeoisie's capacity to effect societal-wide changes outside England and the Netherlands—commercial nations *par excellence*—was strictly limited. Everywhere, the bourgeoisie suffered from numerical inferiority. In Venice in the late sixteenth century the mercantile elite who dominated economic and political life amounted to only 6% of the city's population.[70] Sociologically and culturally, the bourgeoisie that did exist was constantly threatened by atrophy, defections to the aristocracy, and economic suffocation at the hands of the absolutist state. Of all the threats it faced, the latter was

[66] Max Weber (trans. Talcott Parsons), *The Protestant Ethic and the Spirt of Capitalism* (New York, NY: Charles Scribner's Sons, 1958), 43.

[67] R.H. Tawney, *Religion and the Rise of Capitalism*, second edition (Harmondsworth, UK: Penguin, 1938), 93.

[68] John Calvin (trans. John Allen), *Institutes of the Christian Religion*, sixth American edition (Philadelphia, PA: Presbyterian Board of Publication, 1813), 2 vols.

[69] Alexis de Tocqueville (trans. Gerald E. Bevan), *Democracy in America, and Two Essays on America* (London, UK: Penguin, 2003), 55–56.

[70] Kamen, *Iron Century*, 168.

the most significant. Although individual bourgeoisie benefited from the purchase of Royal Charters and other monopoly rights, the overall effect of the absolutist state was deleterious. Internal taxes and levies on the transport of goods were typically onerous. In France on the eve of the Revolution, a load of wood transported from one side of the country to the other was subjected to thirty-five separate tariffs, levied at twenty-one locations.[71] Even more deleterious were the restrictions imposed by the various "guilds", each of whom typically purchased a state-enforced monopoly over a given aspect of production. Under an Edict of 1673, the French guild system was legally entrenched, the state enforcing work monopolies in return for revenue. In the case of the dying of cloth, state-imposed regulation ran to 317 separate articles.[72] There was, however, a mass social class that viewed state-imposed taxes and monopolies with even more disfavor than the urban bourgeoisie—the peasantry.

THE PREMODERN WEST: INDIVIDUALISM AS AGENT OF INNOVATION—PEASANT INDIVIDUALISM

It would be fair to say that the European peasantry has had a bad press in history, derided for being culturally backward and having a collectivist ethos hostile to innovation. Karl Marx had a particularly dim view of the peasant's economic capacity. Of the peasant of mid-nineteenth-century France, Marx wrote:

> Their field of production, the small holding, admits no division of labour … no application of science, and therefore … no variety of talent … A few score of these make up a village, and a few score of villages make up a Department. In this way … the French nation is formed … much as potatoes in a sack form a sack of potatoes.[73]

Views such as those articulated by Marx, which depict the European peasantry as a talentless "sack of potatoes", are misguided. A creation of serfdom, the medieval peasant little resembled the slave of Roman

---

[71] Braudel, *Identity of France*, 491.

[72] North and Thomas, *Rise of the Western World*, 63.

[73] Karl Marx, "The Eighteenth Brumaire of Louis Bonaparte", in Karl Marx and Frederick Engels, *Selected Works*, vol. 1 (Moscow, USSR: Foreign Languages Publishing House, 1951), 302–303.

antiquity. Legally, the serf—like their feudal lord—was a vassal, who was given occupation of a plot of land in return for a range of services (for example, working on their lord's land, payment of a share of their crop, and so on). As a vassal, the serf typically came under the "king's justice" in ways comparable to that of a "freedman". Serfs were, therefore, not "chattels" who could be bought and sold. Theoretically, they could not be mistreated with impunity.[74] Economically, the Western European serf, "owned the land to which he was bound … in most ways that mattered … Ownership stimulated him to work and to produce the surpluses without which the superstructure of society … would have been impossible".[75]

De facto ownership of the land forged a unique form of individualism that was different in fundamental ways from scholarly, aristocratic and bourgeois individualism, but was nevertheless seminal to the emergence of new iterations of western civilization.

Whereas both the educated elite in the civil service and the aristocratic elite were interested in prestige and power, peasant individualism—like bourgeois individualism—was directed toward the accumulation of wealth. By comparison to bourgeois individualism, however, the time frames within which peasant individualism operated were much longer. Sudden profit and loss were the bourgeois norm. In a peasant's life, by contrast, longer time horizons were demanded. Under the three-field system that was the norm in northwestern Europe—whereby a field went from fallow to wheat to secondary crops (such as oats and barley) over successive seasons—the peasant had to think in three-year cycles. Improvements in soil fertility, and in the size of one's stock of animals, were multi-generational endeavors. Both reward and risk crept forward almost imperceptibly, evident in slowly ripening crops or fields parched by unrelenting sun. Peasant prosperity was also constantly threatened by war, banditry, and other forms of violence. This made peasant individualism inherently conservative; they were supporters of law and order. On the other hand, the peasant's (supposed) protectors, the aristocracy and the monarchical state, imposed heavy burdens, albeit ones that varied markedly over time. As a rule of thumb, payments to the feudal lord for use of the land became progressively less onerous in Western

[74] Lefebvre, *French Revolution*, 131–132; North and Thomas, *Rise of the Western World*, 20, 63–64.

[75] Braudel, *Identity of France*, 136.

Europe (although not, as previously noted, in Eastern Europe and Iberia). Converted into monetarized quit-rents, the value of these payments was then eroded by inflation. Conversely, the growth of the absolutist state resulted in an increasingly heavy tax burden. In France, a direct tax, the *taille*, was imposed for the first time in 1370. Given the tax-exempt status of the nobility and the clergy, payment of the *taille* fell largely upon the peasantry.[76] In France's Beauvais region, the *taille* amounted to 20% of the peasant's income in the mid-1600s. Other taxes consumed a further 8%. Church tithes took 10%.[77] This tax burden grew markedly in the eighteenth century. In French-controlled Flanders, direct taxes grew by 28% during the reign of Louis XVI.[78] In the Limousine region, they consumed 50 to 60% of gross peasant production in 1766. Another 12 to 15% had to be set aside for seed.[79]

If the "Pirenne Thesis" argued that the urban bourgeoisie was central to a new form of western civilization during the Middle Ages, what can be called the "Bloch – Braudel thesis" makes similar claims on behalf of the peasantry.

Like Pirenne before them, Bloch and Braudel located the birth of a new iteration of western civilization in the social transformation of late Carolingian France (c.AD 800–880).[80] Like Pirenne, they identified in this new civilization a continental rather than a Mediterranean orientation.[81] Where they differed from Pirenne was in tracing the origins of this new iteration of western civilization to the countryside rather than the town. "Everything", Braudel argued, "began in the countryside ... The origins of the demographic explosion lay in the countryside". Every economic advance was "rooted in the peasantry".[82] To the peasantry,

---

[76] North and Thomas, *Rise of the Western World*, 82.

[77] Kamen, *The Iron Century*, 210.

[78] Lefebvre, *French Revolution*, 131–132.

[79] C.B.A. Behrens, *The Ancient Regime* (London, UK: Thames and Hudson, 1967), 32.

[80] Pirenne, *Mohammed and Charlemagne*, 234; Braudel, *Identity of France*, 136–140; Marc Bloch (trans. L.A. Manyon), *Feudal Society*, second edition (London, UK: Routledge, 1962), xxvi.

[81] Pirenne, *Medieval Cities*, 26–27; Bloch, *Feudal Society*, 40, 69; Braudel, *Identity of France*, 150.

[82] Braudel, *Identity of France*, 138.

192   B. BOWDEN

Bloch claimed in like fashion, fell the task of rebuilding and recolonizing an economically shattered Europe.[83]

As previously noted, the monasteries were the great innovators of the Middle Ages. The peasant, nevertheless, showed what Cipolla referred to "as a remarkable capacity for assimilation".[84] Across Western Europe, innovation and adaptation occurred in a series of waves. The most significant of these, which occurred between the end of the Carolingian era (c. 887) and the mid-fifteenth century, was also the first. The heavy wheeled plow allowed the cultivation of the river-valley soils that were beyond the capacity of the primitive swing plows of antiquity. Soft, horse neck-collars permitted the harnessing of horses in agriculture, an animal with four to five times the pulling power of oxen. In northern Europe, the adoption of the three-field system reduced dependency on a single crop. The arrival of the village blacksmith in the twelfth century facilitated a greater use of metal implements. Medieval farming also benefited from new crops, most notably rye and durum wheat. Oats also became commonplace for the first time. By 1500, pasture crops (lucerne, clover, sainfoin) were making an appearance and boosting livestock productivity.[85] After 1500, a second wave of innovation and adaptation benefited from the new crops obtained from the "Columbian exchange", including potatoes, maize and tomatoes. As a result of peasant ingenuity, agricultural yields soared. By the sixteenth century, Western European cereal yields were more than double those of the thirteenth century.[86] Without these gains any increase in population would have been impossible. By 1340, Europe's population (80 million) was more than three times that of its pre-Carolingian low-point (25 million).

While peasant individualism was the undoubted bedrock of medieval, Renaissance and early modern Europe's economic achievement, we should nevertheless not exaggerate the peasantry's successes. Improved agricultural yields resulted in more people, but not higher living standards. As noted in Part I, pre-industrial calorific consumption in Europe was barely sufficient for a subsistence existence. Often it was insufficient.

---

[83] Bloch, *Feudal Society*, 61–62.

[84] Cipolla, *Before the Industrial Revolution*, 169.

[85] Parain, "Evolution of Agricultural Production", 125–179.

[86] Fernand Braudel (trans. Siân Reynolds), *The Structures of Everyday Life: Civilization and Capitalism, 15th–18th Century* (London, UK: Collins, 1981), 123.

At a societal level, the result—as previously noted—was a series of devastating Malthusian traps. This agricultural deficiency was due as much to socio-political failings as to technological shortcomings. Throughout the late medieval and early modern periods, the countries with the best agricultural productivity were Belgium, England and the Netherlands. These countries were also Europe's freest.

The link between the peasants' performance and their socio-political environment was particularly evident in Holland in the fourteenth and fifteenth centuries. Unlike most of their European counterparts, the Dutch were also never afflicted by absolutist governments addicted by high taxes. Despite a series of environmental problems—flooding, soil subsidence, peat bogs—Holland, and the Netherlands more generally, continued to boast agricultural yields well above the European norm.[87] Between the early 1500s and 1730, English agricultural productivity also doubled, benefiting from similar socio-political factors. As Allen notes, "This was the era" when England's independent "yeomen farmers were at their apogee".[88] English peasants were also spared the heavy direct taxes that were the European norm. Most English tax revenues came from customs duties, most particularly on wool exports.[89] State absolutism also failed to permanently establish itself, the Stuart dynasty's efforts eventually ending in civil war and revolution.

In pointing to the achievements of Dutch and English agriculture, it should be noted, this is not arguing that favorable socio-political factors were *sufficient* to allow a *permanent* escape from the Malthusian trap that impacted all Europe. On the contrary, as noted in Chapter 5, the decisive improvements in agricultural productivity were a product of the mid-to-late nineteenth century, rather than the eighteenth—and certainly not the sixteenth and seventeenth centuries. It was only with mechanization and artificial fertilizers that agricultural production soared decisively upward. Even with these benefits, European farmers struggled to compete with New World imports. Amid rising global supply, the benchmark London wheat price lost 58.2% of its value between 1871 and 1901, falling

---

[87] Robert C. Allen, "Progress and Poverty in Early Modern Europe", *Economic History Review*, Vol. 56, No. 3 (2003), 409, Figure 2.

[88] Allen, *British Industrial Revolution*, 59.

[89] North and Thomas, *Rise of the Western World*, 83.

from $1.92 to $0.81 (historic US dollars).[90] A boon for consumers, this collapse in price spelled disaster for Europe's small-scale wheat farmers. While production in Central and Western Europe (including Italy, but excluding Iberia and Russia) went up by a third to 971 million bushels between 1875–1879 and 1910–1913, the great bulk of this increase was due to the introduction of American-style extensive farming on the Hungarian plains. In Belgium, the Netherlands and Denmark—historically the home of Europe's most productive farmers—output stagnated at low levels, their combined production rising by a mere 2 million bushels to 27 million bushels between 1875–1879 and 1910–1913. In Britain during the same period, production fell precipitously from 80 million bushels to 56 million bushels.[91] What we are thus dealing with in relation to the Western European peasantry and yeoman farmers of the eighteenth and nineteenth centuries is a population that was (outside England and the Low Countries) still an overwhelming majority, whose interests favored innovation and wealth creation, which was capable of decisively altering the balance of political power, but which was nevertheless doomed to perpetual decline outside a few, specialized sectors (for example, dairy and viniculture). In Britain and the Low Countries in the early modern era, the dynamism of the agricultural sector was seminal to the growing dynamism of these societies as a whole. Elsewhere, the peasantry not only sustained society (albeit not very well), they also held the fate of nations in their hoary hands.

REVOLUTION, FREEDOM AND THE STATE

Between the English Civil War (1642–1651) and 1848, the Year of Revolutions, the western world was reforged. In the Americas, democratic ideals overlapped with campaigns for national independence under George Washington, José de San Martin, Simón Bolivar and others. In Europe, revolutions destroyed many of the absolutist states. This transformation did not, however, occur in a vacuum. Instead, revolutionary

[90] Bradley Bowden, "Transformation: The First Global Economy", in Bradley Bowden, Jeffrey Muldoon, Anthony Gould and Adela McMurray (eds.), *Palgrave Handbook of Management History* (Cham, Switzerland: Palgrave Macmillan, 2021), 288.

[91] C. Knick Harley, "Western Settlement and the Price of Wheat 1872–1913", *Journal of Economic History*, Vol. 38, No. 4 (1978), 866.

movements were inspired and bound by the various forms of individualism upon which western civilization was recreated during the medieval, Renaissance and early modern periods.

Inevitably, Europe's aristocracy and the peculiar form of individualism associated with this class—an abiding concern with prestige, cultural superiority, affection for monarchical power—found themselves out of favor. In his highly influential *Common Sense*, published on the eve of the American Revolution, the English-born Thomas Paine lambasted the concept of a hereditary aristocracy. "Most wise men", Paine advised his fellow Americans:

> ... have ever treated hereditary rights with contempt ... For all men, being original equals, no one by birth could have a right to set up his own family in perpetual preference to all others.[92]

The resonance of these sentiments is indicated by the fact that hereditary aristocracy was never permanently established in any New World society. It even found itself on the defensive in Europe. In his *Reflections on the Revolution in France*, Edmund Burke waged a passionate defense of Britain's "mixed constitution", whereby power was distributed between the House of Commons, the House of Lords and a hereditary monarch. He could not bring himself, however, to defend the privileges of a hereditary aristocracy. Instead, Burke advocated a meritocracy, declaring:

> ... do not imagine that I wish to confined power, authority, and distinction to blood and names and titles. No, Sir. There is no qualification for government but virtue and wisdom.[93]

Hostility to hereditary titles created problems not only for the aristocracy. It also caused difficulties for those who feared unrestrained popular democracy. Politically, this necessitated a search for alternatives to not only state absolutism but also Britain's "mixed constitution" with its House of Lords. At both a theoretical and a practical level this search

---

[92] Thomas Paine, "Common Sense", in Moncure Daniel Conway (ed.), *The Writings of Thomas Paine*, vol. 1 (London, UK: G.P. Putnam's Sons, 1894), 79.

[93] Edmund Burke, *Reflections on the Revolution in France* (Hamilton, Canada: McMaster University, nd), 42, https://socialsciences.mcmaster.ca/econ/ugcm/3ll3/burke/revfrance.pdf.

for alternatives can be traced back to the English Civil War and the political writings of the poet John Milton, who was one of the most fervent supporters of Cromwell's Commonwealth.

In Milton's estimation, the most effective boundaries for any popular democracy were those rooted in the Protestant faith and an understanding that "libertie" entailed serving God according to his "reveal'd will".[94] As noted earlier, this intertwining of democracy with nonconformist religious belief subsequently became a defining characteristic of politics in America's New England region. As the English Civil War demonstrated, however, religious belief not only united, it also divided. In the immediate aftermath of Britain's "Glorious Revolution" of 1688, John Locke pursued a more secular line of reasoning. In Locke's opinion, oppressive power was best restrained through law rather than religion.[95] Locke also argued that laws should be made through common consent.

Such beliefs, however, left hanging questions as to the actual political structures that are best placed to determine a society's laws. In North America, amid the looming War of Independence, the publication of Paine's *Common Sense* brought these questions to the fore. *Common Sense* was, Bradley Thompson observes, "the first truly revolutionary pamphlet published before the Declaration of Independence", the first to look for solutions outside "the categories of eighteenth-century English jurisprudence".[96] Whereas other American leaders regarded Britain's system of checks and balances with favor, Paine condemned it as "a rotten constitution", arguing in favor of a popularly elected unicameral legislature with untrammeled authority.[97] This was not a solution that gained much support among other revolutionary leaders. As Bernard Bailyn noted in his classic study, *The Ideological Origins of the American Revolution,* not only did most believe "that a healthy society was a hierarchical society", they also feared the prospect of "democratic despotism".[98] Rather than

[94] John Milton, "The Ready and Easy Way to Establish a Free Commonwealth", in John Milton, *Areopagitica and Other Political Writings of John Milton* (Indianapolis, IND: Liberty Fund, 1999), 439.

[95] John Locke, *Two Treatises of Government* (London, UK: Thomas Tegg and Others, 1823), 193.

[96] C. Bradley Thompson, *America's Revolutionary Mind* (New York, NY: Encounter Books, 2019), 250.

[97] Paine, "Common Sense", 74–75.

[98] Bailyn, *American Revolution*, 283.

favoring the unicameral model advocated by Paine, most of America's founding fathers embraced instead an idealized image of republican Rome with its division of power between a popular assembly, an executive with limited tenure, and a supervisory senate.

On the eve of the Revolution, John Adams in his *Thoughts on Government* took this republican model and outlined how it could be applied to American circumstance. Declaring "good government" to be an "empire of laws", Adams advocated not only a dispersion of power between a directly elected assembly, an upper house and the executive branch, but also a supervisory judiciary. Distinct "from both the legislative and executive", this independent judiciary would, Adams believe, ensure that future governments would be restrained within a web of law.[99] In the wake of the revolutionary wars, it was this model that became the basis for the new republic.

The disastrous excesses of the French Revolution cemented the prestige of the American republican model. Over the ensuing 250 years it rivaled the British constitutional model in terms of global popularity. While the British parliamentary model was adopted by both European constitutional monarchies (such as Norway, Denmark, the Netherlands) and nations that fell under England's colonial umbrella (for example, Australia, New Zealand, Canada), the American constitutional system was embraced everywhere by republican regimes. Today, even communist regimes—China, Vietnam, North Korea—disguise centralized power behind the façade of elections and American-style constitutional guarantees.

The crisis of aristocratic governance was not only political. It was also cultural and economic. By comparison with other social classes the aristocracy had a greater propensity to spend money than to accumulate it. To "live nobly" meant not only luxurious homewares, it also entailed high levels of education and awareness of the latest artistic and literary trends.[100] Of Paris' aristocratic elite, the English agronomist Arthur Young observed on the eve of the French Revolution, "This society does like other societies – they meet, converse, offer premiums and publish

---

[99] John Adams, *Thoughts on Government* (Washington, DC: Heritage Foundation, n.d.), 4, 6.

[100] Kamen, *Iron Century*, 139–146.

nonsense. This is not of much consequence, for the people, instead of reading their memoirs, are not able to read at all."[101]

A product of this society, Tocqueville saw in American-style democracy the way of the future. He, nevertheless, despised its lack of intellectual obtainment. "There is no class, then, in America", Tocqueville sneered, "which passes to its descendants the love of intellectual pleasures along with its wealth".[102] Among economic and political historians, more than a few have shared Tocqueville's attitude. Like Tocqueville, the American economic historian John Nef viewed the advance of democracy and industrialization as unstoppable. But, like Tocqueville, he lamented the loss of the aristocratic "eighteenth-century civilization, with its ordered balance, its good taste, its restraint, and its sense of form".[103] Such arguments are not totally without merit. It was the era of aristocratic dominance that delivered Mozart, Shakespeare and much of our cultural heritage. To lament the passing of the age of aristocracy is, however, misguided. As Young observed of pre-revolutionary Paris, the aristocratic culture of eighteenth-century Europe was one of mass illiteracy. In 1800, the only European nations where most could read and write were the capitalistic-oriented Britain and the Netherlands.[104] The societies where the aristocracy maintained its sway into the early twentieth century—Spain, Russia, the Austro-Hungarian Empire—were not only economically backward, they were also prone to revolution and disintegration.

As the western societies of Europe, the Americas and Oceania moved inexorably toward democracy and industrialization, no issue was more divisive—and more important to individualism in all its manifestations—than the role of the state. Initiating a debate that still resonates, Thomas Hobbes held the state to be the key defender of private property and, hence, economic prosperity. Where, Hobbes observed in 1651:

> ... men live without security other than what their own strength and their own invention shall furnish them ... there is no place for industry, because

---

[101] Arthur Young, *Travels in France, 1787, 1788, and 1789* (London, UK: George Bell and Sons, 1909), 24.

[102] de Tocqueville. *Democracy in America*, 65.

[103] John U. Nef, "The Industrial Revolution Reconsidered", *Journal of Economic History*, Vol. 3, No. 1 (1943), 27.

[104] Allen, "Poverty and Progress", 415.

the fruit thereof is uncertain, and consequently no culture of the earth ... no arts; no letters.[105]

Writing more than a century later, John Locke held a very different view. Rather than regarding the state as the best protector, Locke perceived in its "arbitrary power" the greatest threat to liberty and property.[106] The great eighteenth-century British jurist Sir William Blackstone saw dangers even in a system of law. As Blackstone expressed it:

> ... even laws themselves, whether made with or without consent, if they regulate and constrain our conduct in matters of mere indifference ... are regulations destructive of liberty.[107]

In North America, a Lockean hostility to an obtrusive state was all-pervasive.[108] When, therefore, Paine proclaimed, "Government, even in its best state, is but a necessary evil", he expressed sentiments that were near universal among revolutionary leaders.[109] At the other end of the spectrum, Rousseau's political philosophy—with its emphasis on all-powerful "general will"—implied the existence of an all-powerful state. If the general will were to prevail, Rousseau wrote, it was "essential" that there "be no partial society within the State".[110] Among German philosophers, support for a strong state was even more evident. For Immanuel Kant, the "Enlightenment" implied "freedom of mind" rather than "civil freedom". Absolutist monarchies such as that of Frederick the Great, by "setting themselves up" as social "guardians", Kant wishfully concluded, actually facilitated rather than suppressed freedom by allowing

---

[105] Thomas Hobbes (ed. A.P. Martinich), *Leviathan* (Peterborough, CAN: Broadway Press, 2002), 62.

[106] Locke, *Two Treatises of Government*, 199.

[107] Sir William Blackstone, *Commentaries of the Laws of England in Four Books*, vol. 1 (Indianapolis, IND: Liberty Fund, 2010).

[108] Thompson, *America's Revolutionary Mind*, 32.

[109] Paine, "Common Sense", 69.

[110] Jean-Jacques Rousseau (trans. G.D.H. Cole), "The Social Contract", in Jean-Jacques Rousseau (ed. G.D.H. Cole), *The Social Contract and Discourses* (London, UK: J.M. Dent and Sons, 1950), 27.

more time for "self-incurred tutelage".[111] Hegel was even more enthusiastic in supporting a powerful state. Contradicting the ideals proclaimed in the American *Declaration of Independence* and the French *Declaration of the Rights of Man and the Citizen*, Hegel concluded "Freedom" does not exist as a "natural" condition. Rather, he argued, it is only through "the State" that the conditions of freedom "are realized".[112] Following in Hegel's footsteps, Marx and Engels also associated the "dictatorship of the proletariat" with state power. "The proletariat will", they advised in the *Communist Manifesto*, "centralize all instruments of production in the hands of the State".[113]

If the state was to profoundly influence the scope for individualism in the wake of the revolutionary struggles of the eighteenth and nineteenth centuries, it was also the case that earlier forms of individualism—and the social interests that underpinned them—determined the nature and extent of these revolutions.

Traditionally, the excesses of the French Revolution have been associated with "democratic despotism" and a surrender to populist demands. This is certainly how Burke perceived the Revolution, finding in it proof that, "in a democracy the majority of the citizens is capable of exercising the most-cruel oppression upon the minority".[114] Although there is truth in such observations, the Revolution's failings were in fact not primarily due to common folk. Instead, they were caused by an educated elite who seized power amid chaos and then sought to recreate society in line with their own imaginings. Among the 749 deputies elected to the National Convention in 1792, lawyers were most numerous. Danton, Robespierre, Saint-Just and Brissot all studied law. Marat and Desmoulins were journalists. None boasted pre-revolutionary wealth. Ideology and the pursuit of power were their guiding stars. The most murderous, Robespierre and Saint-Just, were those who prioritized ideology. Both dedicated their short lives to instigating a "Reign of Virtue". Of Robespierre, Stanley Lomis noted, "Neither money nor the things that money can buy were

---

[111] Immanuel Kant, "An Answer to the Question, What Is Enlightenment?", in Jostein Grupsrud, Hallvard Moe, Anders Molander and Graham Murdock (eds.), *The Idea of the Public Sphere: A Reader* (Lanham, ML: Lexington Books, 2010), 6–7, 3.

[112] George Hegel (trans. J. Sibree), *Philosophy of History* (New York, NY: Dover Books, 1956), 40–41.

[113] Marx and Engels, "Manifesto of the Communist Party", 50.

[114] Burke, *Revolution in France*, 103.

of the slightest interest to him".[115] Such people, Camus observed in reflecting upon all modern revolutionary movements, are proof of the maxim that "pure and unadulterated virtue is homicidal".[116] To this we can add another maxim: that the most despotic of regimes stem not from unrestrained democracy but rather from the seizure of power by an ideologically driven elite dedicated to a reconstruction of society, no matter what the cost.

In all the great revolutions up to, but excluding, the Russian Revolution of 1917, it was the individualism of the peasant and small-scale producer that delineated the limits of possibility. A numerical majority in every society other than England and the Low Countries, they had little to fear from democracy per se. Like the bourgeoisie, they favored markets and private property. They also favored virtually all the attributes historically associated with capitalism: education, equality of opportunity, appointment on the basis of merit, and low taxation. As small-scale producers, they feared not only an overly obtrusive government but also private-sector monopolies that underpaid primary producers and overcharged consumers. In the United States, these fears underpinned the farmer-inspired populist and anti-trust movements of the 1880s and 1890s. Nothing caused the peasant or small-scale producer greater fear, however, than chaos and political extremism that negatively impinged upon private property and the proper functioning of markets. Forced to choose between democracy and stability they invariably chose the latter.

Seminal to the success of any pre-industrial revolution, the peasant or farmer also tended to apply the handbrake that curtailed its progress. This had both positive and negative long-term consequences for western civilization. In the United States, where the War of Independence never degenerated into a social revolution, farmers and small-scale producers remained resolute in their support of both the Republic and limited government. By contrast, the extremism and chaos of the French Revolution caused that nation's peasantry to swing behind Napoleon and his bureaucratic Empire. In the wake of the 1848 Revolution, they swung behind Napoleon III. One of the consequences of this constant favoring of Bonapartist options was the entrenchment of new forms of state

---

[115] Stanley Lomis, *Paris in the Terror* (Harmondsworth, UK: Penguin, 1964), 263.

[116] Albert Camus, *The Rebel: An Essay on Man in Revolt* (New York, NY: Alfred A. Knopf, 1978), 207.

power in France in lieu of the old absolutist state. Even more perceptive as to the nature of French politics than American affairs, Tocqueville observed that the Bonapartist state was an inevitable result of the collapse of local government during the Revolution. Accordingly, he argued, "Napoleon should be neither praised nor blamed for having concentrated almost the whole administrative power in his hands for, after the sudden disappearance of the nobility ... these powers descended upon him automatically".[117] Sociologically, the inevitable beneficiaries of this were the many survivors of France's educated elite who found jobs in the new state bureaucracy, people who distinguished themselves from Robespierre and Saint-Just by preferring power over ideology. Despite the ascendancy of the Napoleonic state in France, however, the nation's peasants and small farmers retained a deep-seated suspicion of any manifestation of state power that threatened their private property rights.

It is thus evident that premodern western individualism manifested itself in different ways. Some favored capitalism and innovation. Others benefited from state absolutism. By shaping and delineating the revolutionary struggles that recreated western civilization, the clash of these different expressions of individualism ultimately produced societies characterized by not one but two tendencies. One, driven by bourgeois individualism, continued to favor markets, competition and innovation. The other, associated with an educated "Brahmin" elite, saw advantage in curtailing capitalistic tendencies and concentrating power in their own hands as they occupied the proliferating agencies of state power. Yes, it is true, that these tendencies manifested themselves differently in different nations. But they were present, nevertheless, in all.

---

[117] de Tocqueville, *Democracy in America*, 785.

CHAPTER 9

Slavery and Its Legacies

Writing in the aftermath of World War II, W.E.B. Du Bois—described as "the greatest black intellectual in the twentieth century"[1]—reflected bitterly on the relationship between Africa, slavery, and the West. In Du Bois's estimation, it was not only "the sugar empire and cotton kingdom" of the United States that rested upon Africa and slave labor. They were also "the foundation upon which the [whole] capitalist system" was "raised".[2] Where, however, Du Bois pointed to the ways in which African slave labor had enriched the Americas and the West more generally, others pointed to the ways in which slavery acted as a millstone around the neck of western progress. After touring the United States in the 1830s, Alexis de Tocqueville concluded that slavery was "not an institution which can last". Where it existed, it poisoned popular culture, introducing "idleness into society ... It weakens the powers of the mind and dampens

---

[1] Henry Louis Gates, Jr., "The Black Letters on the Sign: W.E.B. Du Bois and the Canon", in W.E.B. Du Bois (ed. Henry Louis Gates, Jr.), *The World and Africa: Color and Democracy* (Oxford, UK: Oxford University Press, 2006), xvi.

[2] W.E. Burghardt Du Bois, "The World and Africa", in W.E.B. Du Bois (ed. Henry Louis Gates, Jr.), *The World and Africa: Color and Democracy* (Oxford, UK: Oxford University Press, 2006), 144.

© The Author(s), under exclusive license to Springer Nature Switzerland AG 2022
B. Bowden, *Slavery, Freedom and Business Endeavor*,
Palgrave Debates in Business History,
https://doi.org/10.1007/978-3-030-97232-5_9

human society".[3] The contrast between the economic backwardness of the American South and North's prosperity was even more evident to the escaped slave and would-be abolitionist, Frederick Douglass. On settling in Massachusetts, Douglass was astonished to find a level "of wealth, comfort, taste, and refinement, such as I had never seen in any part of slaveholding Maryland". Even more "astonishing", he recorded:

> ... was the condition of the colored people ... I found many, who had not been seven years out of their chains, living in finer houses, and evidently enjoying more of the comforts of life, than the average of slaveholders in Maryland.[4]

Debates as to the importance of slavery and its legacies have arguably never been more significant than now. Intellectually, the argument that slavery was the central factor in western prosperity found cogent expression in the *New York Time Magazine*'s *1619 Project*. Across its articles, a bleak accusative message was articulated: that the arrival of African slaves in Virginia in 1619 defined America as a nation of "racism" and "inequality", that "a new economy that was global in scope" and "capitalist" in orientation was first forged among the South's plantations.[5] Politically, this message resonated among those who expressed support for Black Lives Matter, an organization whose founders contend that a legacy of "deadly oppression confronts African Americans everywhere".[6] Across academia, a host of studies have reinforced the message that the modern West was not only founded in slavery but bound by its legacies. Sven Beckert's *Empire of Cotton*, for example, argued that, "Slavery stood at the center of the most dynamic and far-reaching production complex

---

[3] Alexis de Tocqueville (trans. Gerald E. Bevan), *Democracy in America and Two Essays on America* (London, UK: Penguin Books, 2003), 426, 41.

[4] Frederick Douglass, *Narrative of the Life of Frederick Douglass as American Slave* (Boston, MA: Anti-slavery Office, 1846), 114.

[5] Jake Silverstein, "1619—Editor's Note", in Jake Silverstein (ed.), *1619 Project* (New York, NY: *New York Times Magazine*, 2019), 4; Mathew Desmond, "Capitalism", in Jake Silverstein (ed.), *1619 Project* (New York, NY: *New York Times Magazine*, 2019), 32.; Nikole Hannah-Jones, "The Idea of America", in Jake Silverstein (ed.), *1619 Project* (New York, NY: New York Times Magazine, 2019), 24.

[6] Black Lives Matter, *Celebrating Four Years of Organizing to Protect Black Lives* (Black Lives Matter, 2018), 5, https://blacklivesmatter.com/resources/.

in human history".[7] In Edward Baptist's estimation, the market value of the United States' 3.2 million slaves in 1850 was "almost equal to the entire gross national product".[8] According to James Walvin, "Legions of working people, on both sides of the Atlantic derived much of the energy they required ... from the [slave-grown] sugar they consumed".[9]

Invariably, these recent studies draw upon earlier debates as to the importance and efficiency of slavery. Initiating the so-called "Great Divergence Debate"—which posited that Western European living standards only diverged from those found elsewhere during the nineteenth century—Kenneth Pomeranz concluded that slavery provided Europe with vital flows "of needed resources".[10] Between 1971 and 1992, Robert Fogel and Stanley Engerman controversially argued that slavery was never the inefficient monster of popular imagination. So efficient was the slave system of the American South, Fogel and Engerman argued, that even slaves enjoyed an "average pecuniary income" that was 15% higher than that obtained by the typical "free agricultural worker" (in other words, the wealth that slaves consumed was greater than that obtained by free citizens).[11] Others have asserted, however, that the (supposed) efficiency of slavery vis-à-vis free labor was made possible not through a bounty of output but a surfeit of misery. In "The Denial of Slavery in Management Studies", Bill Cooke thus concluded that slavery in the

---

[7] Sven Beckert, *Empire of Cotton: A Global History* (New York: Knopf, 2014). 244. For similar arguments, see: Walter Johnson, *River of Dark Dreams: Slavery and Empire in the Cotton Kingdom* (Cambridge, MA: Harvard University Press, 2013).

[8] Edward E. Baptist, *The Half that has Never been Told: Slavery and the Making of American Capitalism* (New York, NY: Basic Books, 2014), 352.

[9] James Walvin, *Resistance, Rebellion & Revolt: How Slavery was Overthrown* (London, UK: Robinson, 2019), 36.

[10] Kenneth Pomeranz, *The Great Divergence: China, Europe, and the Making of the Modern World Economy* (Princeton University Press, 2000), 17.

[11] Robert William Fogel and Stanley L. Engerman, *Time on the Cross: The Economics of American Negro Slavery* (Boston, MA: Little Brown and Company, 1974), 239; Robert William Fogel and Stanley L. Engerman, *Time on the Cross: Evidence and Methods— A Supplement* (Boston, MA: Little Brown and Company, 1974), Appendix B. Also see, Robert W. Fogel and Stanley L. Engerman, "The Relative Efficiency of Slavery: A Comparison of Northern and Southern Agriculture in 1860", *Explorations in Economic History*, Vol. 8, No. 3 (1971), 353–367; Robert W. Fogel, *Without Consent or Contract: The Rise and Fall of American Slavery* (New York, NY: W.W. Norton, 1989); Robert W. Fogel and Stanley L. Engerman (eds.), *Without Consent or Contract: Conditions of Slave Life and the Transition to Freedom—Technical Papers* (New York, NY: W.W. Norton, 1992).

American South was far from being a primitive, pre-capitalist institution. Instead, it was the (supposed) proving ground for new exploitative techniques: division of labor, "Taylorist" control and a "managerial identity" rooted in racism.[12] The belief that western prosperity was founded in slavery and racism has also been seminal to the emergence of "Critical Race Theory and Whiteness Studies" programs. The "era of Western European expansion that began in the sixteenth century", Ruth Frankenberg observed in a discipline-defining study, saw the construction of the dual identities of "whiteness" and "westernness". In the process, she suggested, race became a justification for slavery even as slavery redefined western society in racial terms.[13]

The issue of slavery, it is clear, is one that is now central to our understandings of not only western civilization's past but also its present. We are thus confronted with a number of fundamental questions. Why have so many civilizations embraced slavery when, according to Adam Smith, "The experience of all ages and nations ... demonstrates that the work done by slaves, though it appears to cost only their maintenance, is in the end the dearest of any"?[14] Was slavery in the American South, if not elsewhere, as efficient as claimed by Fogel, Engerman, Cooke and others? Were the profits of slavery and the slave trade decisive factors in the rise of the modern West? What were slavery's long-term legacies?

The problematic nature of current debates can be ascertained through a consideration of the twenty or so slaves deposited in Virginia in 1619, an event that provided the starting point for the much-cited *1619 Project*. Anyone reading the *1619 Project* is led to the inescapable conclusion that the slaves of 1619 were subject to life-long bondage. One is also led to believe that their bondage initiated a slave-plantation system that continued in uninterrupted fashion from 1619 to emancipation in 1865.

---

[12] Bill Cooke, "The Denial of Slavery in Management Studies", *Journal of Management Studies*, Vol. 40, No. 8 (2003), 1895–1918. For similar arguments, see: William Dusinberre, *Them Dark Days: Slavery in the American Rice Swamps* (New York, NY: Oxford University Press, 1996); Mark M. Smith, *Mastered by the Clock: Time, Slavery and Freedom in the American South* (Chapel Hill, NC: University of North Carolina Press, 1997); J.P. Reidy, *From Slavery to Agrarian Capitalism in the Cotton Plantation South: Central Georgia 1800–1880* (Chapel Hill, NC: University of North Carolina Press, 1992).

[13] Ruth Frankenberg, *White Women, Race Matters: The Social Construction of Whiteness* (Minneapolis, MN: University of Minnesota Press, 1993), 16, 12.

[14] Adam Smith (ed. Andrew Skinner), *The Wealth of Nations: Books I-III* (London, UK: Penguin Classics, 1999), Book III, Chap. II, para. 9.

Such conclusions are inaccurate. Yes, it is true, the slaves of 1619 did find themselves part of an emerging plantation economy. This economy, however, was built upon white indentured servant labor—a system with which English employers were familiar—rather than slavery, an institution with which they were unfamiliar. Reflecting upon the experiences of all of Virginia's Africans before 1660, Edmund Morgan concluded:

> ... some were free or became free; some were servants or became servants. And all, servant, slave, or free, enjoyed rights that were later denied all Negroes in Virginia.[15]

Across the seventeenth century, indentured servants recruited from Britain and Ireland were responsible for 80% of the immigrants to the Chesapeake (Virginia, Maryland) district. As a result, African Americans comprised less than 15% of the population in 1700.[16] Only when the supply of servants petered out did plantations belatedly embrace slavery.

If the plantations of British North America were initially built upon white indentured labor rather than African slaves, it is also the case that barely 4% of those who made the infamous Middle Passage were destined for territories in what would become the United States.[17] Similarly, Fig. 9.1, which draws upon the Trans-Atlantic Slave Trade Database, indicates that the major slave traders were not from Britain and its North American colonies but rather Portugal and its principal colony, Brazil.[18] If slavery was the key to European wealth then we would expect that Portugal would have prospered to a greater extent than its European rivals. However, this is not what transpired. Instead, Portugal, along with Spain, proved an economic laggard. In the case of Britain—which was the dominant slave trader between 1751 and 1800—it is also hard to identify a link between involvement in the slave trade and domestic living standards. The period of peak British involvement (1751–1800) was one of

---

[15] Edmund S. Morgan, *American Slavery, American Freedom* (New York, NY: W.W. Norton & Co., 1975), 127.

[16] Christopher Tomlins, "Reconsidering Indentured Servitude: European Migration and the Early American Labor Force, 1600–1775", *Labor History*, Vol. 42, No. 1 (2001), 9–10, Table 1.

[17] Walvin, *Resistance, Rebellion & Revolt*, 8.

[18] Trans-Atlantic Slave Trade Database, *Flag of Carrier*, https://www.slavevoyages.org/voyage/database#tables [Accessed 23 August 2021].

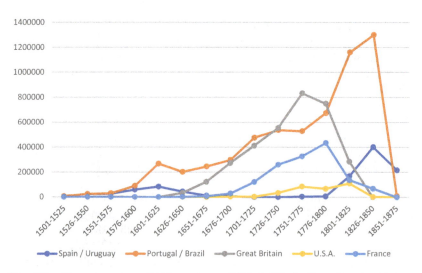

Fig. 9.1 Transportation of African slaves, 1501–1875, by flag of carrier (*Source* Trans-Atlantic Slave Trade Database, https://www.slavevoyages.org/voyage/database#tables)

declining rather than rising living standards. Conversely, Britain's disengagement with the slave trade was associated with rising rather than declining living standards.[19]

How then to explain the slave trade phenomenon and its relationship with the modern iteration of western civilization?

As noted in the introduction to Part 2, the key to understanding slavery in the Americas is to recognize the pre-industrial scale of slave-based production. In 1770, for example, the French colony of Saint-Domingue (modern-day Haiti) was the world's leading sugar producer with a slave population of 600,000. Saint-Domingue, however, only produced 60,000 tons (12 million lbs.) a year.[20] Even if we assume that only half of Saint-Domingue's slave population was engaged in sugar production, we are left with a per capita production of 400 lbs.

---

[19] E.H. Phelps Brown and Sheila V. Hopkins (1956) "Seven Centuries of the Prices of Consumables, Compared with Builders' Wage Rates", *Economica*, Vol. 23, No. 92 (1956), Appendix B.

[20] Walvin, *Resistance, Rebellion & Revolt*, 33. 74–75.

of raw sugar a year, or 1.1 lbs. a day. At most, the calorific value of this output was around 1,700–1,800 calories, whereas a field-hand was probably expending 4,000 calories per day. When, therefore, Pomeranz declares that plantation-grown sugar provided an important source of additional calories for European societies,[21] he fails to factor in the *costs* of maintaining such societies in terms of imported foodstuffs and manufactured goods. Also not factored in are the calories expended along pre-industrial logistics chains. In short, rather than adding to the West's calorific bounty, plantation economies such as Saint-Domingue were sinkholes for resources, both in terms of consumables and human lives. The plantations remained profitable only because—as in imperial Rome—slavery was directed toward high-priced goods (sugar, tobacco, coffee, cotton) that could bear the costs of inefficient production.

Inevitably, slavery's pre-industrial foundations restricted its possibilities. Compared to the waves of immigrants who flooded the Americas in the second half of the nineteenth century, African slaves were few. In 1830, the slave population of the entire Caribbean was 3.25 million, a total less than that found today in Santo Domingo, the capital of the Dominican Republic (3.7 million). While, as previously noted, African slaves made up the bulk of those who made the Atlantic crossing before 1820, their numbers were always constrained by the limited capacity and slow speed of pre-industrial shipping. Even at its height the slave trade bore no comparison to the scale of mid-to-late nineteenth-century immigration. In 1874, for example, some 818,839 immigrants disembarked in the United States in a single year. By comparison, only 748,612 slaves were transported in British ships to *all* the Americas in the entire 25-year period between 1776 and 1800; years that represent the peak of British involvement in the slave trade.[22] The legacy of this imbalance was incalculable. In mainland America—Brazil, Venezuela, the United States—peoples of African ancestry were swamped by new arrivals who had little knowledge of slavery and little interest in its legacies. Reflecting on the impact of mass immigration into Latin America, Braudel concluded, "They created modern Brazil, modern Argentina, modern

[21] Pomeranz, *The Great Divergence*, Appendix D.

[22] Trans-Atlantic Slave Trade Database, *Flag of Carrier*; United States Department of Commerce, *Historical Statistics of the United States: Colonial Times to 1970* (Washington, DC: Department of Commerce, 1975), Series C 89–119.

Chile".[23] Such comments, no doubt, understate the achievements of earlier, largely African immigrant generations. But they nevertheless point to the far-reaching transformation that swept over the New World in the nineteenth century.

As slavery was progressively abandoned across the Americas, both former slaves and slave owners typically found themselves stranded in an agricultural economy that boasted little in the way of either innovation or economic diversity. Touring the great Black Belt of the American South in 1890, Du Bois mournfully recorded how the great antebellum "Cotton Kingdom" had become a mere "shadow of a marvelous dream", a place where:

> The whole land seems forlorn and forsaken. Here are the remnants of the vast plantations of the Sheldons, the Pellots, and the Ransons ... The houses lie in half ruin, or have wholly disappeared ... now only the black tenant remains.[24]

THE NATURE OF SLAVERY

Western civilization—like most other civilizations—has had a troubled relationship with slavery, a practice constantly at odds with the value it placed on individual freedom.

This tension between slavery and freedom is evident in the opening pages of Homer's *Iliad*, the first and greatest literary work in the entire history of western civilization. As warriors who placed individual freedom and prestige above any other virtue, Agamemnon and Achilles quarreled over captive slave girls. Forced to surrender his captive, Chryseis, Agamemnon seizes Achilles's captive in recompense. In doing so, he humiliates Achilles by declaring, "mine own self will I go to thy hut and take Briseis of the fair cheeks ... that though mayest well know how far greater I am than thou".[25] Ill-advised, this humiliation caused Achilles

---

[23] Fernand Braudel (trans. Richard Mayne), *A History of Civilizations* (London, UK: Penguin, 1993), 440.

[24] W.E. Burghardt Du Bois, *The Souls of Black Folk* (Chicago, IL: A.C. McClurg & Co., 1903), 116–17.

[25] Homer (trans. Andrew Lang, Walter Leaf and Ernest Myers), *The Iliad* (London, UK: Macmillan Collector's Library, 2020), 9.

to withdraw from combat with almost fatal consequences for the Greek cause.

The fact that the source of the Homeric quarrel, Chryseis and Briseis, were both captives of war points to a fundamental truth: most slaves were obtained from peoples who were different. This targeting of the ethnic, linguistic or religious "other" was as evident among pre-contact Aztec society, the Ottoman Turks and countless other communities as it was in western antiquity. Sometimes, as with the Aztecs, the "other" were primarily targeted for religious sacrifice. Among the most valued possessions of a wealthy Aztec, so the survivors of the Aztec Empire recorded in their native Nahuatl, was "the sacred reed box" that contained the hair of sacrificed slaves.[26] Other societies, such as Ottoman Turkey, targeted the "other" as sex slaves for a military or social elite. As late as the 1850s, Georgian and Circassian females were still being shipped across the Black Sea in their thousands for the slave markets of Istanbul and the Balkans. Some were sold by financially desperate parents. Greater numbers came from raids along the Caucasian frontier with Russia.[27] On occasion, slaves were destined for positions of comparative privilege. In the Roman Republic, as noted in Chapter 7, the conquest of Greece brought a flood of educated Greeks on to the market: people who were acquired as tutors, secretaries, architects and financial managers. Such people, Plutarch observed, fundamentally altered household dynamics. "For", Plutarch recorded, while "the management of a household is a financial activity in so far as it deals with lifeless things ... it becomes a political activity when it deals with human beings".[28] On plantations in the Antebellum South, the slaves of the main household also boasted privileges and skills far removed from that of the field-hand. Recalling the Maryland plantation of his youth, Frederick Douglass noted that:

> ... the home plantation ... wore the appearance of a country village ... The shoemaking and mending, the blacksmithing, cartwrighting, coopering,

---

[26] Fray Bernardino de Sahagun (trans. Charles E. Dibbe and Arthur J.O. Anderson), *Florentine Codex: Book 9—The Merchants* (Salt Lake City, UT: University of Utah Press), 67.

[27] Ehud R. Toledano, *The Ottoman Slave Trade and Its Suppression 1840–1890* (Princeton, NJ: Princeton University Press, 1982), 7, 17, 115–23.

[28] Plutarch (trans. Rex Warner), *Fall of the Roman Republic* (London, UK: Penguin Classics, 2005), 112.

weaving, and grain-grinding were all performed by slaves on the home plantation ... Few privileges were esteemed higher ... than that of being selected to do errands at the Great House Farm.[29]

Although slaves occupied many positions, most were found in three industries: mining, large-scale construction (for example, building aqueducts, canals, and so on) and, more particularly, agriculture.

In antiquity, mining was brutally hard and dangerous work that few wished to undertake. Mining was, nevertheless, central to the success of the Athenian, Carthaginian and Roman empires. Boasting few agricultural advantages, Athenian fortunes were transformed when a rich seam of silver was discovered at Laurion in the fifth century BC. Worked on an industrial scale, the slave mines of Laurion provided one of the two planks upon which the flowering of Athenian democracy rested, the other being the enforced tribute of the Delian League.[30] The Laurion operation, however, paled into insignificance when compared to the gold and silver mines of Iberia that Rome inherited from the Carthaginians in the wake of the Punic Wars. These mines, it has been observed, "saw some of the most advanced and large-scale applications of technology to economically critical work ever to be practiced before the European industrial revolution".[31] The mineral wealth that underpinned the sinews of empire, however, came at horrific cost. Slaves were deliberately "worked to death", an outcome explicitly recognized in the Roman practice of sending condemned criminals to their deaths at the mines rather than on the cross.[32] Ravenous in their consumption of human life, Rome's mining operations proved unsustainable. With the stabilization of the frontiers, the supply of fresh slaves faltered. Then, between AD 165 and AD 180, the Antonine Plague dealt a devastating blow to the Empire's labor market. By the time the Antonine Plague had run its course the key Iberian mines were abandoned.[33]

---

[29] Frederick Douglass, *Narrative of the Life of Frederick Douglass: An American Slave* (Boston, MA: Anti-slavery Office, 1846), 12.

[30] Andrew Wilson, "Machines, Power and the Ancient Economy", *Journal of Roman Studies*, Vol. 92, No. 1 (2002), 17, 30.

[31] Ibid., 24, 17.

[32] Ibid., 27, 24.

[33] Christopher Howgego, "The Supply and Use of Money in the Roman World, 200BC to AD300", *Journal of Roman Studies*, Vol. 82, No. 1 (1992), 17, 30.

In the sixteenth century, the Athenian and Roman mining experience was replicated on an even grander scale at the great Andean silver mine at Potosi, an operation that flooded Europe with so much silver that it unhinged the value of physical currency. Discovered in 1545, and worked with the newly discovered (and deadly) mercury extraction method, Potosi featured a workforce of 13,500, of whom 4,500 worked underground for a week at a time before rotating to surface jobs. Thousands of others worked on the mine's artificial lakes and crushing plants. By the 1570s, Potosi had metamorphized from work camp into a city of 150,000, placing it behind only London, Paris and Seville in terms of "European" cities.[34] Attempts to draft African slaves into the mines failed because of the bitter cold and their susceptibility to altitude sickness. Instead, Native Americans were recruited in their tens of thousands. In describing their conditions, one observer recorded how Potosi resembled, "a mouth of hell, into which a great mass of people enter every year and are sacrificed by the greed of the Spaniards".[35]

Long after slavery was abolished in most other domains it continued to characterize the inhospitable mining camps of totalitarian regimes. In the 1930s, the Soviet Union's Dalstroi gold-mining complex in the remote Kolyma Peninsula dwarfed even Potosi in its voracious appetite for human life. Discovered in 1932, the gold from the Kolyma deposit—one of the richest in history—was key to Soviet survival. By 1939, Dalstroi featured a permanent population of more than 160,000, few of whom survived more than a few months. In describing the Kolyma experience, Tim Tzouliadis recorded in his *The Forsaken*:

> From breaking the ground with picks and pushing the endless wheelbarrows filled with frozen earth the prisoners' hands became grotesquely misshapen into blackened claws ... their labour stripped first the fat from their bodies and then burned up their muscles too, until nothing was left but their skin and bones.[36]

---

[34] John Hemming, *The Conquest of the Incas* (London, UK: Macmillan, 1970), 407–408.

[35] Cited, Ibid., 369–370.

[36] Tim Tzouliadis, *The Forsaken: Hope and Betrayal in Stalin's Russia* (London, UK: Little, Brown, 2008), 177.

214   B. BOWDEN

Similar scenes were witnessed on the great Soviet construction projects. On the Volga–Moscow canal project—which employed 200,000 at its peak—working conditions were almost unbearable for even the fittest. Work on the project, Karl Schlögel noted:

> ... halted only when the temperature reached −30C ... They stood in water and swampy ground and were unable to warm themselves ... In the winter the corpses were piled up in heaps.[37]

The historic use of slavery (or de facto slavery) in historic mining and construction projects is explicable in part by the fact that most pre-industrial societies comprised "one vast peasantry". There was little in the way of waged labor that could be attracted to distant projects for months or years at a time. Even in Rome, the most complex society of European antiquity, there was no large pool of waged labor. As Keith Hopkins noted in his study of Roman slavery: "The Romans had no tradition which legitimized the regular employment of free men".[38] In the 1930s, the absence of a large pool of waged labor was almost as apparent in the Soviet Union as it had been in imperial Rome. Even Moscow was a "peasant metropolis", full of new recruits from the countryside, many of whom lived in shanties with rabbits, pigs and chickens.[39] For the Soviets, there was little benefit in luring this nascent working class to an early grave on the Kolyma Peninsula when a potential slave labor force existed in its bursting prisons.

Two other factors explain why some pre-industrial societies used slaves in large-scale mining and construction projects, and others did not. First, such projects were capital-intensive endeavors that were beyond the means of the typical landowner or merchant. In antiquity, virtually all the great building projects—the pyramids, the Athenian Acropolis, the Roman roads and aqueducts—were state-sponsored. Similarly, the Laurion and Dalstroi mining operations were state-run affairs. Although the vast Potosi silver mine that underpinned the finances of Hapsburg Spain was operated by private concerns, every part of the production and

---

[37] Karl Schlögel (trans. Rodney Livingstone), *Moscow 1937* (Cambridge, UK: Polity, 2012), 283–286.

[38] Keith Hopkins, *Conquerors and Slaves* (Cambridge, UK: Cambridge University Press, 1978), 109.

[39] Schlögel, *Moscow 1937*, 49.

transport process was state supervised. As Mark Greengrass observes, the Hapsburgs treated the silver production of the Americas "like a crop from a domain, one which could be harvested as and when it required. In times of difficulty, it seized privately owned silver on its arrival in Seville, compelling the owners to accept interest-bearing bonds in return".[40] Invariably, such slave-staffed endeavors required more than an ability to assemble armies of forced laborers. One also had to command a logistics chain capable of sustaining slave-labor projects over a considerable time period. Where political power was fragmentary, as in feudal Europe, the only large-scale projects that were possible were ones that drew on localized resources, typically over a very long time period. Feudal Europe was thus dotted with cathedrals inspired by local need and primarily built with local labor. It was incapable, however, of replicating imperial Rome's slave-based building record in terms of aqueducts and roads.

If slavery in mining and construction was associated with a powerful state, its use in agriculture reflected more prosaic factors, albeit ones that only existed within a system of state-imposed security that protected property owners and restrained would-be runaways.

In the Mediterranean basin during antiquity, as in most other agrarian societies, peasant proprietorship was the overwhelming norm. Typically, the peasant calendar was organized around the grain crop. Other work demands—a vegetable garden, a few vines, some olives and perhaps a cow or two—were modest. The strength and weakness of this system was that it never fully taxed the peasant's time. In republican Rome, Hopkins observed, "Most Romans were under-employed. Even independent yeoman living just above the level of subsistence had plenty of time with nothing to do".[41] Often, this peasant "leisure" was marshaled for war and military campaigns. The problem with this "solution" is that wars tended to go on interminably, undermining the viability of not only the peasant's holding but also agricultural production more generally. This is what happened in republican Rome, the historian, Appian, recording how "the Italian people dwindled in numbers and strength, being oppressed by penury, taxes, and military service".[42]

---

[40] Mark Greengrass, *Christendom Destroyed: Europe 1517–1648* (London, UK: Penguin Books, 2015), 109.

[41] Hopkins, *Conquerors and Slaves*, 24.

[42] Appian (trans. Horace White), *Roman History: The Civil Wars—Book 1* (Cambridge, MA: Loeb Classical Library, 1913), 7.

The Roman solution to this agrarian problem was, as noted in Part 1, the *latifundia*, the vast slave estate created by buying up the farms of penurious peasants and staffing them with captured prisoners of war and their descendants.

The dynamics of the slave plantation, both in the Roman era and all subsequent epochs, are well captured in the study to which we have made frequent earlier references—Cato the Elder's *De Agricultura*. The key to an efficient estate, Cato indicated, revolved around the full—if not, over-full—utilization of labor. By growing multiple crops—wheat, vines, olives, fruit—labor could be switched from one crop to another as the season demanded. The slave estate should, Cato advised, be as self-sufficient as possible. Labor requirements also needed to be carefully calculated so as to avoid excessive labor costs. On a 160-acre mixed-farm specializing in olives, Cato calculated that an overseer, a housekeeper and eleven field-hands would suffice. The "old and sick" should be sold off along with "old cattle" and "worn-out oxen".[43] When inclement weather made work impossible, "the slaves' rations should be cut down as compared with what is allowed when they are working". Cato also advised that a well-run estate kept clothing to a minimum. "Allow each hand a smock and a cloak every other year", Cato recommended, along with a bi-annual issuance of "heavy wooden shoes".[44]

Parallels between Cato's advice and the circumstances described in the recollections of Frederick Douglass and Booker T. Washington—the preeminent African American intellectuals of nineteenth-century America—are striking. Of his life on a Maryland tobacco-plantation, Douglass remembered that field-hands, male and female alike, received an annual clothing issuance "of two coarse linen shirts, one pair of linen trousers … one jacket, one pair of trousers for winter". Children under working age obtained two "coarse linen shirts per year. When these failed them, they went naked until the next allowance-day".[45] Booker Washington remembered similar circumstances on his Virginian plantation. As on the *latifundia* of Cato's era, clothes were issued only once a year. Washington's shoes were, like those of Roman times, rough "wooden"

---

[43] Cato the Elder, "De Agricultura", in A Virginian Farmer, *Roman Farm Management: The Treatises of Cato and Varro* (New York, NY: Macmillan, 1913), 27–28, 22, 31–32.

[44] Ibid., 25, 37.

[45] Douglass, *Life of Frederick Douglass*, 9–10.

affairs. There was little in the way of bedding, Washington recalling how he used to sleep with his siblings "on a bundle of filthy rags laid upon the dirt floor".[46] Douglass recalled families sleeping "on one common bed – the cold damp floor".[47] In terms of food, consumables and machinery, the plantations of Douglass's and Washington's youth were as self-sufficient as Cato's ideal *latifundia*. The diet on Douglass's plantation revolved around boiled corn "mush", eaten with "oyster shells" and "bare hands".[48] Work was unrelenting. A lack of rest, Douglass ruefully recorded, owed less to "the want of beds, than the want of time to sleep".[49]

In comparison to Cato's *latifundia*, the slave plantations of Douglass's and Washington's remembrance differed in only one fundamental way: they did not sell off the "old and sick" alongside the "worn-out oxen". Instead, as Douglass recorded, those "too old for field-labor" were entrusted with the raising of children.[50] A practice that Cato would have condemned as superfluous expenditure, this benign attitude toward child rearing nevertheless boosted the supply of a vital commodity: the slaves themselves. As a result, the United States proved "more successful in producing slaves by natural increase than any other slave-employing society in the Americas".[51] Even though the importation of new slaves was outlawed in 1808, slave numbers grew at an exponential rate. Between 1800 and 1810 the US slave population rose by a third. In the ensuing decade, it again rose by a third. In consequence, by 1825 a third of all slaves in the Americas resided in the United States. On the eve of the Civil War, it was home to 4 million slaves. By contrast, in 1790 the slave population had numbered but 694,280.[52]

Inevitably, the relationship between master and slave was conflicted at every level. At one level, slaves were simply chattels, property that

---

[46] Booker T. Washington, *Up from Slavery: An Autobiography* (Tuskegee, AL: Tuskegee Institute, 1901), 8–9, 6.

[47] Douglass, *Life of Frederick Douglass*, 10.

[48] Ibid., 27.

[49] Douglass, *Life of Frederick Douglass*, 10.

[50] Ibid., 2.

[51] Hugh Thomas, *The Slave Trade: The History of the Atlantic Slave Trade 1440–1870* (London, UK: Picador, 1997), 568.

[52] Ibid., 570; Joseph J. Ellis, *Founding Brothers: The Revolutionary Generation* (New York, NY: Vintage Books, 2000), 102.

could be disposed of as if they were "worn-out oxen". Yet, even the most cold-hearted could hardly have avoided noticing that their slave was a human being, sharing characteristics common to all people. Everywhere, slavery introduced a dangerous dynamic into the household or plantation. Across history, slave rebellion—both at an individual and collective level— was commonplace. In his initial biography, Douglass located "the turning point" in his "career as a slave" in a successful brawl with a particularly vicious white overseer, a victory that dispelled forever "the dark night of slavery" that had bowed his spirit.[53]

The slave's dual nature—part chattel, part human—was reflected in their legal treatment. Devoid of any protection for most of Roman history, slaves were, however, explicitly recognized as more than mere chattels under the reforms of Antoninus Pius (AD 138–161), which outlawed the killing of slaves "without good grounds".[54] Of dubious practical benefit, these safeguards were nevertheless strengthened in AD 319 by the Christian sympathizer, Constantine the Great, who criminalized intentional slave homicide. In the post-Roman world, the Germanic Visigoth kingdom in Spain (c. 462–711), in reviving slavery, also revived the protections afforded slaves. Subsequently, in relocating slavery to the Americas, the Portuguese and Spanish brought with them this inherited tradition, a legal system that permitted floggings but which (theoretically) outlawed maiming or killing without due legal process. By contrast, would-be New World slave owners who hailed from Northwest Europe, a region where slavery was long extinct, acquired African slaves in the absence of any system of legal regulation. Among British colonies, the underlying common law assumption was that the deliberate killing of a slave could only be justified if the plaintiff was acting in self-defense. Most colonial authorities, however, either ignored such niceties or drafted provisions that overrode them. Ambivalence as to the status of slaves also characterized US circumstances after independence. North Carolina showed the least sympathy for slave killers, executing two masters between 1840 and 1856. In 1853, South Carolina also sent a slave killer to the

---

[53] Douglass, *Life of Frederick Douglass*, 72, 63.

[54] Andrew T. Fede, *Homicide Justified: The Legality of Killing Slaves in the United States and the Atlantic World* (Athens, GA: University of Georgia Press, 2017), 17.

gallows.[55] Even where the law offered protection, however, its application depended on white witnesses coming forward. This rarely happened. As Douglass noted when reflecting upon a beating that he received while working on the Baltimore waterfront, "If I had been killed in the presence of a thousand colored people, their testimony combined would have been insufficient to have arrested one of the murderers".[56]

As a system of production, rural slavery in the western tradition was premised on three factors without which it could not survive: commercial markets for plantation produce; a comparatively cheap slave reservoir; and a system of law and order that deterred runaways. In the late Roman Empire, as the frontier defenses collapsed, all these factors disappeared. Many slaves abandoned the *latifundia* to which they were tied, often congregating in vast rebel formations. Everywhere, slave-purchase prices rose to unprecedented levels. In Greece in the sixth century AD, slaves were four times dearer than they were during the classical era.[57]

Amid the decline of empire, Western Europe progressively abandoned slavery in favor of a novel social formation—serfdom. To the extent that slavery survived on a large scale it did so only in Visigoth and, subsequently, Moorish Iberia.

In normal parlance, the terms "slave" and "serf" are often used interchangeably. The implication is that there was not much difference between slave and serf circumstance. Any such conclusion is, however, unwarranted. For, with serfdom, the landlord effectively surrendered hereditary control of the land in return for pre-determined services and a share of the crop. Unlike the free peasantry of Greek and Roman antiquity, who were continually dragged away from their farms for interminable military campaigns, the serf was also a full-time farmer. Military defense was the preserve of a new knightly class. The product of dire necessity, serfdom represented a fortuitous historical turning point that led to the permanent extinction of slavery in the European hinterland.

[55] Ibid., 22–28, 41–42, 10.

[56] Douglass, *Life of Frederick Douglass*, 97.

[57] R.P. Duncan-Jones, "Two Possible Indices of the Purchasing Power of Money in Greek and Roman Antiquity", *Publications de l'Ecole Francaise de Rome*, Vol. 37, No. 1 (1978), 163–164.

The Economics of Slavery

It has become increasingly fashionable to argue that slavery, as practiced in the American South, was capitalism personified. It was, Cooke argues, seminal to "the development of capitalism". To ignore this reality, Cooke suggests, is to engage in a "logic of denial".[58] For Dusinberre, as for Cooke, antebellum slavery "is what capitalist development is all about – the increase of labor productivity by combining an ever-increasing proportion of capital with the labor of an individual worker".[59] In contributing to the "New History of Capitalism" literature, Beckert, in his *Empire of Cotton*, similarly argues that antebellum slavery provided the "beating heart" of nineteenth-century capitalism.[60]

The view that slavery was an extreme form of capitalism is not one that Marx would have endorsed. Indeed, in Volume 3 of *Capital* he specifically rejected the idea. A slave workforce, Marx sensibly argued, bore no resemblance to waged labor. It was, instead, part of the slave owner's stock of capital. Nor, he suggested, could the money spent on a slave be considered part of the stock of capital that aided the extraction of "surplus labor" from one's captive workforce. "On the contrary", Marx concluded:

> It is capital which the slave owner has parted with, it is a deduction from the capital which he has available for actual production. It has ceased to exist for him.[61]

In other words, by investing "capital" on slave purchases a plantation owner is foregoing investments in machinery or transport equipment. Similarly, a slave's death diminishes the slave owner's stock of capital. In this a slave owner's circumstance bears no resemblance to that of the feudal lord who suffers the death of a serf. It is the land that the feudal lord "owns", not the serf. As long as another serf inherits the plot, no loss is incurred. Even further removed from the slave owner's situation is

---

[58] Cooke, "Denial of Slavery in Management Studies", 1900–1901.

[59] Dusinberre, *Them Dark Days*, 404–405.

[60] Beckert, *Empire of Cotton*, xvi, 37.

[61] Karl Marx (ed. F. Engels), *Capital: A Critique of Political Economy*, Vol. 3 (Moscow, USSR: Foreign Languages Publishing House, 1959), 788–789.

the employer of waged labor. If a worker suddenly dies there is no direct loss given that the employee is typically paid only for completed services.

Among Marxists, it should be noted, there are many who have rejected assertions that pre-Civil War slavery represents simply an extreme form of capitalism. Where such thinking errs, the Marxist accounting historian Rob Bryer observed, was in reducing capitalism to a single dynamic: exploitation. In truth, Bryer argued, slavery was only interested in output-maximization. By contrast, modern capitalism primarily seeks marketplace advantage by lowering "the cost of production".[62] The non-Marxist accounting historians, Thomas Tyson and David Oldroyd, came to similar conclusions after a detailed study of Southern plantation records. Most plantation accounts, they concluded, "were noteworthy for their lack of focus on maximizing productivity and minimizing costs".[63] This focus on output rather than costs was hardly accidental. On a slave plantation, slaves were a "sunk cost". There was little they could do to reduce this capital cost other than cut "maintenance" to the bare bones.

If we are to regard slavery in the Americas to be a manifestation of modern capitalism than we must logically consider the *latifundia* of Cato's time in the same light. For, as the preceding section indicated, there were no significant differences between the practices outlined in Cato's ideal *latifundia* and those experienced by Douglass and Washington in the plantations of Maryland and Virginia. Yes, it is true, that slave plantations sold into what were undeniably capitalist production systems in Europe and the American Northeast. There were equally, however, many non-capitalist producers from Asia and Africa who sold into the same markets (for example, home-made Indian cotton textiles). Accordingly, to equate "capitalism" simply with commercial exchange and labor exploitation is to reduce the concept to meaninglessness. Far from being an extreme manifestation of capitalism, slavery is its polar opposite. As the Marxist theorist, Perry Anderson reflected, slavery converts living

---

[62] Rob Bryer, "Americanism and Financial Accounting Theory—Part 1: Was America Born Capitalist?", *Critical Perspectives in Accounting*, Vol. 23, No. 7–8 (2012), 528, 542.

[63] Thomas N. Tyson and David Oldroyd, "Accounting for Slavery During the Enlightenment: Contradictions and Interpretations", *Accounting History*, Vol. 24, No. 2 (2019), 221.

beings "into inert means of production", quashing the "social rationale for invention" that lies at capitalism's heart.[64]

In comparison to waged labor, slavery entailed high up-front capital costs. In Athens in the fifth century BC, a skilled laborer had to expend half their gross annual earnings to buy a slave. In Egypt in the first century AD, the price of a slave was equivalent to almost three years' earnings for a skilled worker.[65] In Virginia in the seventeenth century a slave cost between £25 and £30. By contrast, a white indentured laborer in the 1650s could be engaged on a five- to seven-year contract for £10 to £12. Given that the five-year mortality rate for new arrivals in mid-seventeenth century Virginia was "better than fifty-fifty", few plantation owners initially risked the higher cost of a slave, fearing their investment would end up in an early grave.[66] Even where slave owners appeared to avoid the "up-front" purchase price by relying on "natural increase", there was still a significant (if disguised) capital cost. For, by raising slave children, plantation owners were effectively internalizing the purchase price, paying for the upkeep of not only children but their aged minders.

The persistence of slavery, despite the substantial costs that it entailed, both in the post-Columbian Americas and elsewhere, suggests that it offered advantages that waged labor did not. In *The Wealth of Nations*, Smith attributed the survival of slavery in British America and the Caribbean simply to the "much greater" profits that plantation produce received compared to those of grain growing.[67] Such an explanation, however, still leaves hanging an essential question: why not use waged labor? Four explanations suggest themselves: a surfeit of potential slaves (prisoners of war, prison population or a pre-existing slave trade), an endemic shortage of waged labor, a demand for high-value commodities associated with high labor-utilization levels and previous historical preferences.

In ancient Rome the first three of these factors combined to entrench the *latifundia* as the principal supplier of grain, olive oil and wine to commercial markets. Slavery in the Americas, however, presents us

[64] Perry Anderson, *Passages from Antiquity to Feudalism* (London, UK: NLB, 1974), 24, 26–27.

[65] Duncan-Jones, "Two Possible Indices", 162–163.

[66] Alan Taylor, *American Colonies: The Settling of North America* (London, UK: Penguin, 2001), 153–154.

[67] Smith, *The Wealth of Nations*, Book III, Chap. II, para. 10.

with more complex circumstances. Not all settler societies opted for slavery. French Canadians preferred fur trading and subsistence agriculture. Household agriculture, maritime commerce and manufacture was the norm in New England. Even where British colonists opted for a plantation economy, they initially preferred white indentured labor. In the British colonies that did eventually opt for large-scale slavery, a number of factors appear to have combined to push them in this direction: a declining supply of indentured labor, a pre-existing slave trade in neighboring Spanish and Portuguese colonies, and a ready supply of cheap land lacking a labor force. In contrast, Spanish and Portuguese colonists were familiar with slavery prior to their arrival in the Americas. In the post-Roman world, as noted previously, slavery persisted to a much greater degree south of the Pyrenees than it did north of the Pyrenees. At the peak of Visigoth prosperity perhaps a quarter of the population were slaves.[68] In Moorish Spain (711–1492), slavery remained an economic fact. Then, during the Christian Reconquest, southern Spain and Portugal became the preserve of large estates worked by Moorish peoples under conditions of actual or de facto slavery. As Portuguese ships advanced down Africa's coast, they also actively participated in the local slave trade. Increasingly, slaves were also exploited in Spain and Portugal's newly obtained colonies in the Atlantic islands: the Azores, the Canary Islands and Madeira. In 1550, even Lisbon "boasted 10,000 resident slaves in a population of 100,000".[69]

That Portugal introduced a slave-based plantation economy into the Americas is thus hardly surprising. One is, however, left with a counterfactual question: would slavery had become a factor in the Americas if it was settled solely from northwestern European societies where slavery had become extinct? One suspects it would have occurred in a more hesitant and muted fashion than that which transpired.

If historical experiences were as important as economic factors in causing New World societies to embrace slavery, we are nevertheless left with another key question: why did societies such as the Antebellum South continue to embrace slavery even after waged labor was readily available?

[68] Fede, *Homicide Justified*, 23.
[69] Thomas, *The Slave Trade*, 119.

After touring the American South during the early 1830s, Tocqueville attributed the persistence of slavery to racial divisions and fears. "The threat of a struggle ... between the whites and the blacks", Tocqueville reflected, "constantly haunts the imaginations of Americans like a nightmare". For a majority of white Southerners, he believed, slavery was supported more as a form of social control rather than as economic benefit.[70] There was, however, an economic imperative that was arguably even more important. The bulk of Southern agricultural investment was tied up in the value of their slaves. In this, Southern plantation owners fundamentally differed from their farming counterparts in New England and the Midwest where rural wealth was concentrated in land values. For the Southern plantation owner, therefore, abandonment of slavery entailed the surrender of most of their "capital".

By sinking so much of their capital in an "asset" that could not be easily diverted into other productive uses, slave owners also denied themselves the flexibility that capitalism demands. As Schumpeter noted, "The fundamental impulse that ... keeps the capitalist engine in motion comes from ... new methods of production or transportation ... new forms of industrialization".[71] By the mid-nineteenth century, antebellum slavery was already an economic as well as a social dinosaur, wedded to a production system whose broad features had remained unchanged since Cato's time. Bound within an antiquated economic system, the Antebellum South was incapable of replicating the patterns of industrialization in the North. On the eve of the Civil War, the South provided jobs for only 29,626 urban factory workers. By comparison, the Midwest and Northeast employed 126,767 and 826,130, respectively.[72] Largely devoid of factories, the South had effectively lost the Civil War before the first bullet was fired.

[70] De Tocqueville, *Democracy in America*, 420, 423.

[71] Joseph Schumpeter, *Capitalism, Socialism and Democracy*, 3rd edition (New York, NY: HarperPerennial, 1950), 83.

[72] David B. Meyer, "The Industrial Retardation of Southern Cities", *Explorations in Economic History*, Vol. 25, No. 4 (1988), 374.

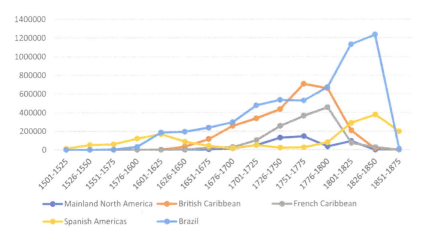

Fig. 9.2 Transportation of African slaves, 1501–1875, place landed (*Source* Trans-Atlantic Slave Trade Database)

SLAVERY IN THE AMERICAS: THE SOURCE OF WESTERN WEALTH?

Slavery washed over the Americas in four advancing and receding waves. In the first period (c. 1440–1500), which can be regarded as the prehistory of American and Caribbean slavery, Portuguese and Spanish colonizers perfected new forms of plantation slavery in the Atlantic islands: the Azores, Cape Verde, Madeira (Portugal) and the Canaries (Spain). By 1550, Madeira was the world's largest sugar exporter, giving Portugal a supremacy which it cemented with its colonization of Brazil. Under Spanish suzerainty, the slave estates of the Canaries rivaled those of Madeira in terms of sugar production. In the closing years of the fifteenth century, the Portuguese also converted the West African island of São Tomé into a slave-based sugar exporter.[73]

The second period of Atlantic slavery (c. 1501–1675), as Fig. 9.2 indicates, involved the migration of the Spanish and Portuguese slave economies to the Americas. Throughout this entire period, slavery largely remained the preserve of Spanish and Portuguese colonies. According to the Trans-Atlantic Slave Trade Database, 537,873 African slaves were

[73] Ibid., 70–77.

landed in Spanish colonies during this period. Another 650,195 arrived in Portuguese holdings. By comparison, only 5,649 slaves were landed in British North America. The French Caribbean saw the arrival of but 21,777. In the British Caribbean, large-scale slave-landings characterized only the final twenty-five years of this period, a time when 114,378 were transported. Prior to this only 37,426 were landed. In the ensuing period (c. 1676–1800), when the slave trade reached its peak, British and French colonies rivaled those of Spain and Portugal as destinations for the first—and last—time. Even during this period, however, it was only in the years between 1776 and 1800 that the number of slaves landed in the British Caribbean (706,518) exceeded those deposited in Brazil (528,156). Across this entire third period, 2.4 million slaves were landed in the British Caribbean. Another 373,151 were transported to British North America. In the French Caribbean islands, 1.2 million slaves were landed. By contrast, Brazil and Spanish America saw the arrival of 2.5 million and 192,783, respectively.[74]

The final period of the Atlantic slave trade (1801–1875), like the first, was dominated by Spain, Portugal and their colonial offshoots. In this closing era of American slavery, 2.38 million slaves were landed in Brazil. Another 860,589 arrived in Spanish America, most of whom were landed in Cuba. Slave arrivals in the British Caribbean (218,475)—virtually all of whom would have been landed prior to Britain's outlawing of the slave trade in 1807—were less than 10% of the Brazilian figure. Even fewer (99,549) arrived in the French Caribbean. Slave arrivals in the United States (93,581) were fewer again.[75]

From start to finish, Atlantic slavery was predominately an Iberian affair. Across the 375 years of Atlantic slavery the combined number landed in the British Caribbean and in North America (3.24 million) was only 45.4% of that deposited in Brazil and Spanish America (7.12 million). If it is true, as Hannah-Jones, Desmond and many others have argued, that Europe owed its "wealth" and "renown" primarily to slavery, then it would logically follow that Spain and, more particularly, Portugal would have been the wealthiest European societies. As noted in Chapter 5, however, this was not the case. If we turn to Figs. 9.3 and 9.4, which compare changes in Dutch, British and Portuguese per

---

[74] Trans-Atlantic Slave Trade Database, *Place Landed*, https://www.slavevoyages.org/voyage/database#tables [Accessed 23 August 2021].

[75] Ibid.

9 SLAVERY AND ITS LEGACIES 227

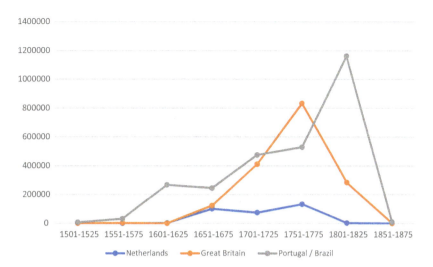

Fig. 9.3 Transportation of African slaves, 1501–1875, by flag of carrier: Netherlands, Great Britain and Portugal / Brazil (*Source* Trans-Atlantic Slave Trade Database)

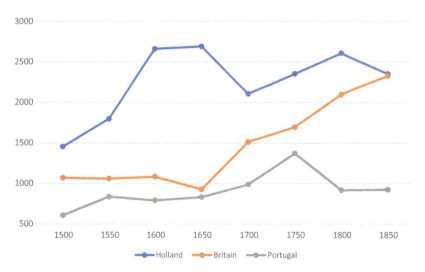

Fig. 9.4 Output per capita in constant US dollars, 1990 value (*Source* Palma and Reis, "From convergence to divergence", Table 4)

capita output with involvement in the slave trade, there are few evident correlations between national income and slavery. Dutch "economic take-off" occurred between 1500 and 1600, prior to its participation in the slave trade. Conversely, the period of its (modest) involvement—which peaked between 1650 and 1750—was associated with static or declining per capita wealth.[76] It is also difficult to draw correlations between Portuguese involvement and changes in per capita output. The marked expansion in Portuguese per capita output between 1500 and 1550 pre-dated its large-scale involvement in the Atlantic slave trade and was due to Portugal's opening up of new Asian trade routes. Palma and Reis similarly attribute the improvement in Portuguese circumstance between 1650 and 1750 to factors other than slavery, notably an expansion in maize (corn) agriculture and Port wine exports to Britain.[77] As was the case with the Netherlands, the peak period for Portuguese and Brazilian involvement in the slave trade (1750–1825) was associated with deteriorating rather than improving economic circumstance.

Only with Britain is there evidence of a correlation between engagement in the slave trade and rising per capita output, most particularly in the years between 1650 and 1750. By 1700, the re-export of colonial goods produced with slave labor—principally tobacco and sugar—was undoubtedly one of the most "dynamic" elements in the British economy.[78] There were, however, many other dynamic elements in British society at this time. Robert Allen, for example, primarily attributes the expansion of both the Dutch and English economies between 1500 and 1700 to the success of the so-called "new draperies", that is the cheap woolen textiles that drove Italian exporters out of the market.[79] We also need to remind ourselves that, as discussed in Part 1, Britain in the mid-eighteenth century was still a pre-industrial society where most lived

[76] Nuno Palma and Jaime Reis, "From Convergence to Divergence: Portuguese Economic Growth 1527–1850", *Journal of Economic History*, Vol. 79, No. 2 (2019), 500, Table 4; Bas J.P. van Bavel and Jan Luiten van Zanden, "The Jump-Start of the Holland Economy During the late-Medieval Crisis", *Economy History Review*, Vol. 58, No. 3 (2004), 503–532.

[77] Palma and Reis, *Portuguese Economic Growth 1527–1850*, 498–499.

[78] Ralph Davis, "English Foreign Trade, 1770–1774", *Economic History Review*, Vol. 15, No. 2 (1962), 291.

[79] Robert C. Allen, *The British Industrial Revolution in Global Perspective* (Cambridge, UK: Cambridge University Press, 2009), 19, 157.

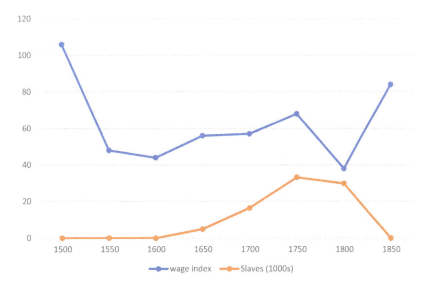

Fig. 9.5 British transportation of African slaves, 1501–1850, in thousands/real wage of skilled building workers in southern England, 1264–1597 (1447 = 100) (*Note* see footnote[81]. *Sources* Brown and Hopkins, "Seven centuries of ... builders' wage rates", Appendix B; Trans-Atlantic Slave Trade Database)

an existence close to bare subsistence. The produce obtained from the plantation economies of the America—coffee, tobacco and sugar—were luxuries beyond the reach of most. If we, therefore, turn our attention from per capita output to living standards or real consumption wage—as we do in Fig. 9.5, which compares the number of slaves carried by Britain on an annualized basis (measured in thousands) with the real-wage index for a skilled building worker in southern England—it is evident that Britain's involvement in the slave trade provided little benefit to most.[80] Instead, the peak years for British participation in the Atlantic slave trade were associated with static or declining real wages.

---

[80] Phelps Brown and Hopkins, "Seven Centuries of ... Builders' Wage Rates", Appendix B.

[81] Slave figures are 25-year averages. Those for 1800 are for the preceding 25-year period given abolition in 1808; other figures are ensuing 25-year average.

Abolition

In many recent accounts it is not slavery that is depicted as the outlier in western history but rather its abolition. In his article in the *1619 Project*, Desmond, for example, declared that "the British abolition of the slave trade was a turning point in modernity". Yet, having made this declaration, he immediately suggests that abolition was nothing but a financial ploy, that "avenues to profit indirectly from slavery grew in popularity as the institution of slavery grew more unpopular".[82] Hannah-Jones's comments on the slave trade's abolition were even more fleeting. By 1776, she suggests, "Britain had grown deeply conflicted over its role in the barbaric institution".[83] What caused it to be "deeply conflicted" is never explained. According to Leon Phipps and Simone Phipps in a separate study, "slavery was abolished only when it was no longer [economically] feasible".[84] Again, no explanation as to the factors that made it no longer feasible is forthcoming.

As Allen Guelzo notes, there is also an increasing penchant to explain abolitionism in terms of "self-emancipation" and "black agency".[85] To the extent to which people of European ancestry opposed slavery they did so, it is argued, only at the prodding of the enslaved and recently freed. In Hannah-Jones's account, emancipation only occurred when runaway slaves "began taking up arms for his [Lincoln's] cause as well as their own".[86] Similarly, in Walvin's opinion it was the "defiance" of "the enslaved themselves" that proved "the crucial final factor in bringing down slavery". In Britain, he suggests, it was "the local black community" that "came to form a critical mass that swung opinion against the slave trade".[87]

There is, undeniably, an essential truth to the argument that slaves and their freed compatriots were campaigners in their own freedom. The

---

[82] Desmond, "Capitalism", 38.

[83] Hannah-Jones, "Idea of America", 18.

[84] Leon C. Prieto and Simone T.A. Phipps, *Why Business Schools Need to Address Black History: It's Time to Decolonize the Business Curriculum* (Cambridge, MA: Harvard Business Publishing—Education, 18 February 2021), 2.

[85] Allen C. Guelzo, *Redeeming the Great Emancipator* (Cambridge, MA: Harvard University Press, 2016), 137–138.

[86] Hannah-Jones, "Idea of America", 24, 20.

[87] Walvin, *Resistance, Rebellion & Revolt*, 55, 109, 123.

Northern Star, established by Frederick Douglass in 1847 and sold from 1851 as *Frederick Douglass' Paper*, was not only the first African American abolitionist newspaper, it was the first African American newspaper of any description.[88] As such, it gave African Americans their own authentic voice within the abolitionist campaign. During the Civil War, African Americans fought under Union banners in their tens of thousands. In Britain, African slaves and their free cousins *were* plaintiffs and witnesses in judgments that caused a definitive rejection of slavery. Such efforts were, however, but one current in a tide of opinion whose key motive forces were located deep within British and American society. Yes, Douglass was an important abolitionist. He was, however, plucked from obscurity by William Lloyd Garrison and the Massachusetts Anti-Slavery Society. Douglass never forgot the sacrifices that they made on his behalf. Pausing to pay thanks at the end of his long life, he declared:

> To these friends, earnest, courageous, inflexible, ready to own me as a man and brother, against all the scorn, contempt, and derision of a slavery-polluted atmosphere, I owe all my success in life.[89]

Massachusetts abolitionists were not the only people to whom Douglass owed a debt. English benefactors, fearing that Douglass would be arrested as a fugitive slave, purchased his freedom so that he could campaign unhindered. When Douglass started his own newspaper, its operation was underwritten by another wealthy benefactor, Julia Crofts. For his part, Douglass always appreciated that he played but a bit part in the story of American emancipation, heaping praise instead on Abraham Lincoln. Lincoln was, he recorded, "a man who in the order of events was destined to do a greater service for his country, and to mankind, than any man who had gone before him in the presidential office".[90] In Britain, the local African community certainly played a role as plaintiffs and witnesses in court cases. As a political force, however, they were inconsequential.

How then to understand abolition? If we perceive abolitionism as, primarily, an *organized* political movement, then we are forced to

---

[88] Frederick Douglass, *The Life and Times of Frederick Douglass from 1817 to 1882* (London, UK: Christian Age Office, 1882), 228, 223.

[89] Ibid., 428.

[90] Ibid., 304, 282.

conclude that it had its roots in the moral outrage shared by Quakers and other nonconformist believers.

In reflecting upon the origins of the British Institution for the Abolition of the Slave trade (Abolition Society), Thomas Clarkson—described by Douglass as the man "who inaugurated the antislavery movement for England and the civilized world"[91]—was certain that Christianity was abolitionism's guiding star.[92] When the Abolition Society was established in 1787, Quakers provided most of its foot soldiers. Every Quaker, on both sides of the Atlantic, Clarkson recorded, "was nourished ... in a fixed hatred against it [slavery]".[93] In North America, the Quakers of Pennsylvania passed a motion condemning the slave trade as early as 1696. Nineteenth-century American abolitionism was likewise underpinned by religious fervor. The movement's "most prominent voice" was undoubtedly William Lloyd Garrison. Deeply religious, Garrison founded the preeminent abolitionist newspaper, the *Liberator*, in 1831 and the New England Anti-Slavery Society a year later. By 1838, a national organization with Garrison at its head, the American Anti-Slavery Society, claimed 1,350 branches and 250,000 members.[94] In Britain, Clarkson played a similar role. Part-publicist, part-organizer, Clarkson was a former Cambridge University divinity student who forsook a religious career for a life as a professional abolitionist. Inside parliament, Clarkson's closest collaborator was another deeply religious figure, William Wilberforce. Among the wider community, few were more vocal in support than John Wesley, the founder of the Methodist Church.

If abolitionists such as Garrison and Clarkson were politically vocal, we should nevertheless not exaggerate their significance. Most Americans and Britons were not Quakers. In 1787, Clarkson was a 27-year-old whose only claim to fame was a prize for a Latin language student essay on slavery. In the United States, Garrison-style abolitionists were, as Guelzo observes, "never a political constituency large enough to be

---

[91] Ibid., 209.

[92] Thomas Clarkson, *The History of the Abolition of the African Slave-trade by the British Parliament*, vol. 1 (London, UK: Longman, Hurst, Rees and Orme, 1808), 5.

[93] Ibid., 128.

[94] David Walker Howe, *What Hath God Wrought: The Transformation of America 1815–1848* (Oxford, UK: Oxford University Press, 2007), 425–426.

worth factoring with".[95] The core argument of Garrison and like-minded abolitionists—that the Northeastern states should secede from the United States so as to free themselves from the taint of slavery—was a view that most rejected. Even Frederick Douglass eventually disassociated himself from it, arguing instead that, "the Constitution of our country is our warrant for the abolition of slavery in every state of the Union".[96]

To comprehend the power that abolitionism eventually exerted we need to turn our attention to the ideas and interests predominant in the wider society. Arguably the best place to begin such a consideration is with a work that did more than any other to transform legal and social attitudes: Sir William Blackstone's *Commentaries on the Laws of England*, the first volume of which was published in 1753.

As holder of Oxford University's newly created Vinerian professorship of common law, Blackstone redefined British law. Building upon what he referred to as common law's "ancient collection of unwritten maxims and customs", Blackstone wove into this venerable fabric a new, largely Lockean understanding of "natural" law. According to Blackstone, "natural liberty" was something every Briton enjoyed "as a free agent".As previously noted, Blackstone also argued that so "deeply implanted" was Britain's "spirit of liberty" that even:

> ... a slave or a negro, the moment he lands in England, falls under the protection of the laws, and so for becomes a freeman.[97]

Blackstone's understandings were not ones that sprang idly into his mind. Instead, they were central to a society that placed a growing emphasis on capitalist virtues of property ownership and economic liberty. As slavery grew in significance in Britain's colonial empire it thus found itself at odds with the society's cultural ethos, threatening many while providing benefit to comparatively few. For one did not need to be a legal theorist to realize that slavery could leak out of slave ships and plantations into the very fabric of British (and American) society, threatening the livelihoods of artisans, agriculturalists and factory operatives alike.

---

[95] Guelzo, *Redeeming the Great Emancipator*, 139.

[96] Douglass, *Douglass from 1817 to 1882*, 227.

[97] Sir William Blackstone, *Commentaries on the Laws of England in Four Books*, vol. 1 (Indianapolis, IN: Liberty Fund, 2010), 34, 96.

234   B. BOWDEN

In the wake of the publication of Blackstone's *Commentaries* one witnesses in the English-speaking world a progressive drawing of lines around slavery in all its manifestations. The first such "line in the sand" came in 1772 with Lord Mansfield's ruling in *Somerset v Stewart*. In this case, James Somerset, a Jamaican slave brought to England by one Charles Stewart, claimed his freedom on the basis that English law did not recognize slavery. Guided by Blackstone's *Commentaries*, Lord Mansfield granted Somerset his freedom, ruling that:

> The state of slavery is of such a nature, that it is incapable of being introduced on any reasons, moral or political ... it's so odious, that nothing can be suffered to support it, but positive law.[98]

Effectively, Lord Mansfield held that any slave who touched British soil was instantly free.

Handed down four years before the American Declaration of Independence, the Mansfield judgment moved abolitionism to center stage. For, if slavery was "odious" to British society, how could the slave trade be justified? What about slavery in the Caribbean and North America? These are questions that few literate Britons or Americans were able to avoid. In North America more than twenty newspapers discussed Lord Mansfield's judgment.[99] In 1788, even the City of London lent its support to the slave trade's abolition. Although an initial House of Commons vote was lost by 88–163, parliament's leading politicians—Charles Fox, William Pitt and Edmund Burke—voted in favor.[100] Subsequently, in 1804, the House of Commons voted to end the slave trade by a two-thirds majority. Three years later the House of Lords also voted in favor.[101]

Why, having outlawed the slave trade, did Britain not move against slavery in its Caribbean colonies for a further 26 years? Reason is found in the semi-autonomous status of the various colonies, each of which boasted elected assemblies. For, while Britain lacked any "positive law"

[98] Lord Mansfield, "Somerset v Stewart". In: Capel Loftt, *English Reports*, vol. 92 (London, UK: Capel Loftt, 1772), 510.

[99] Kenneth Morgan, "Review: A Slaveholders' Constitution", *Reviews in American History*, Vol. 39, No. 2 (2011), 255.

[100] Thomas Clarkson, *The Abolition of the African Slave-trade by the British Parliament*, vol. 2 (London, UK: Longman, Hurst, Rees and Orme, 1808), 337.

[101] Ibid., 494, 575–78.

that allowed slavery, the West Indian and North American colonies did, most adopting a variant of the "Act for the Better Organizing and Governing of Negros" legislated in Barbados in 1661.[102] In the wake of the American War of Independence, and confronted with a series of grueling conflicts with France in the Revolutionary and Napoleonic Wars, Britain also had little appetite for further colonial rebellions. It was to thus avoid conflict with these colonial legislatures that the British Abolition Society opted to focus on the slave trade, rather than slavery per se.[103] Among abolitionists there was also an expectation that the ending of the slave trade would choke slavery to death. Such expectations, however, were unfulfilled. Accordingly, it took further popular campaigns and further parliamentary legislation in 1833 to end British colonial slavery, West Indian slaves becoming fully free from 1 August 1838.

Britain's rejection of slavery left the United States as the English-speaking world's great oddity. In the 1830s, Tocqueville detected what he described as almost two distinct civilizations within America's borders. Slavery, Tocqueville concluded, not only meant that "the southern states" had different "interests" to those found among "the English in the North". It also gave "them different customs".[104] The cultural differences between North and South were ones that became more pronounced over time. Between the War of 1812 and the Civil War in 1861 more than 1 million left Virginia—the most populous state at the time of independence—for new homes in both the Midwest and Deep South. As "Yankees" from New England also moved westward, the result was not a mingling of cultures but rather the emergence of "distinct cultural zones". "Yankees and Butternuts", Daniel Howe observed, "spoke with different accents, ate different foods, and practiced agriculture differently".[105]

The lasting divisions that slavery introduced into American society has generated an enduring debate as to why the nation's founding fathers left the matter largely to one side in their final Constitution. One school of thought finds in this evidence of moral cowardice and deep-seated racism. America's "founding ideals of liberty and equality were",

---

[102] Fede, Homicide Justified, 44.

[103] Clarkson, *Abolition of the African Slave-trade*, vol. 1, 286.

[104] De Tocqueville, *Democracy in America*, 453, 440.

[105] Howe, *What Hath God Wrought*, 138.

Hannah-Jones asserts, "false when they were written", the whole independence struggle having been concocted "to ensure that slavery would continue" free of looming British restrictions.[106] Others hold that most of the founding fathers, abhorring slavery, believed it would die a natural death.[107] Neither of these arguments are convincing.

A problem that was insoluble short of Civil War in the mid-nineteenth century, it is hard to see how the founding fathers could have resolved their differences in 1787. The provisions of the first American Constitution, the *Articles of Confederation*, had provided merely for "mutual friendship", an alliance in which, "Each State retains its sovereignty, freedom, and independence".[108] The fact that a very different union emerged from the Constitutional Convention of 1787 was never preordained. Indeed, on the eve of the Convention (May–September 1787) it looked decidedly unlikely. Accordingly, as Joseph Ellis concluded, although slavery "was clearly incompatible with the principles of the American Revolution", to extinguish it in 1787 would have risked "extinguishing the nation itself".[109] If, however, the Constitution failed to extend the promise of freedom contained within the Declaration of Independence to the nation's slaves, it was equally true that it provided no explicit guarantee of slavery's future. As Sean Wilentz recently noted, "the framers left room for political efforts aimed at slavery's restriction and, eventually, its destruction".[110] Every effort was made to avoid even mentioning the term "slavery". Even the infamous "three-fifths"

---

[106] Hannah-Jones, "Idea of America", 14, 18. For similar views, see: Juan Williams, "The Survival of Racism Under the Constitution", *William and Mary Review*, Vol. 34, No. 1 (1992), *10–11*; David Waldstreicher, *Slavery's Constitution: From Revolution to Ratification* (New York, NY: Hill and Wang, 2009), 17; Alfred W. Blumrosen and Ruth G. Blumrosen, *Slave Nation: How Slavery United the Colonies & Sparked the American Revolution*, argues that Lord Mansfield's judgment precipitated the Revolution as a means of avoiding the judgement's effects; a position echoes in the *1619 Project*.

[107] Eric Foner, *Free Soil, Free Labor, Free Men: The Ideology of the Republican Party before the Civil War* (Oxford, UK: Oxford University Press, 1995), 85; Bernard Bailyn, *The Ideological Origins of the American Revolution*, 50th anniversary edition (Cambridge, MA: Belknap Press, 2017), 232–46; C. Bradley Thompson, *America's Revolutionary Mind* (New York, NY: Encounter Books, 2019), 359–386.

[108] United States Second Continental Congress, *Articles of Confederation and Perpetual Union between the States* (Williamsburg, VA: Alexander Purdue, 1777), Art. II, III.

[109] Ellis, *Founding Brothers*, 17.

[110] Sean Wilentz, *No Property in Man: Slavery and Antislavery at the Nation's Founding* (Cambridge, MA: Harvard University Press, 2018), 3.

contained in Article 1, Section 2, Clause 3 of the Constitution—which had the *practical* effect of boosting Southern representation—avoided reference to "slavery". Instead, it apportioned representation according to the "number of free Persons" and "three-fifths of all other persons ... excluding Indians not taxed". The clause that effectively prohibited the abolition of America's slave *trade* until 1808—when it was abolished—also avoided mention of slavery, stating instead: "The Migration or Importation of such Persons as any of the States now existing shall think proper to admit, shall not be prohibited by the Congress prior to the Year one thousand eight hundred and eight" (Article 1, Section 9, Clause 1).

With the future status of slavery left hanging, the cultural zones of the South and the North were never destined for mutual cohabitation. When the inevitable rupture came the flashpoint was not, however, at the competing societies' historic meeting points along the rivers that flowed into the Chesapeake. Rather, it occurred in the new territories of the American West.

At independence, Virginia provided the new nation with its center of gravity. Outwardly, this dominance continued after independence. In the first thirty-six years under the new Constitution, a Virginian served as the US president in thirty-two of these. Beneath the surface, however, a host of changes eroded Virginian and Southern preeminence. One was immigration. From 1840, a virtual tsunami of people descended on America's ports as a revolution in shipping lowered costs and transit times. Between 1850 and 1855, 2.12 million were landed, a total that equated to half of America's enslaved population.[111] Many found work in the North's expanding industrial sector. As a wave of humanity descended upon Northern cities, another moved westward. In 1800, barely 300,000 lived west of the Appalachians. By 1820, more than 2 million did so. Many settled in the Northwest Territory (the future states of Ohio, Indiana, Michigan, Illinois, Wisconsin), where slavery was outlawed under the Northwest Ordinance of 1787. By 1820, Ohio, admitted to statehood in 1803, was the fourth most populous state in the Union. The Old South (Maryland, Virginia, the Carolinas) also witnessed westward emigration that affected the free and slaves alike. Between 1810 and 1820, 100,000 slaves were force-marched from the Chesapeake region

[111] Department of Commerce, *Historical Statistics*, 97, General Note; 106, Series C 89–119.

to the new cotton and sugar districts of the Mississippi Valley and the Deep South (Alabama, Mississippi, Louisiana).[112] By 1860, more slaves resided in the Deep South and Mississippi Valley than in the old Southern heartlands.

Collectively, the transformations of the Antebellum Period posed a fundamental question: were the new western territories to be slave or free? Superficially, divisions were mollified by the "Missouri Compromise" of 1820, which allowed for a future balance of free and slave states while restricting slavery to the south of the $30°\ 30'$ parallel. Continual westward migration, however, placed a constant question mark over this settlement. "What it all came down to", Eric Foner observed:

> ... was whether the western social order would resemble that of the South or the North ... slavery in the territories struck millions of Northerners in a way in which abstract discussions of slavery could not.[113]

In the decades before the Civil War this issue polarized America. In the North, it produced new political parties: the Liberal Party (1840–1860), the Free-Soil Party (1848–1854) and, eventually, the Republican Party. Established in 1854, the Republican Party, in particular, represented a broadening of the anti-slavery movement to include a diverse, if unstable, coalition. Some favored immediate abolition. More conservative elements representing the "border states", most notably the Blair family (Francis Preston Blair, Sr., Francis Present Blair, Jr., and Montgomery Blair), only wished to restrict slavery in the new territories. Even these more conservative elements, however, assumed an increasingly activist role. When the escaped slave, Dred Scott, sued for his slavery, Montgomery Blair acted as his attorney.

Yes, it is true, that the Republican Party initially sought to restrict rather than abolish slavery. When the Civil War commenced, this remained its objective. It is also true, however, that restriction led inexorably in the direction of abolition. In part, the Republican Party's transformation simply reflected the pressure of circumstance. With Congress' passage of the *Kansas-Nebraska Act 1854*—which overturned the "Missouri compromise" by opening up both Kansas and Nebraska to

---

[112] Howe, *What Hath God Wrought*, 140, 130.

[113] Foner, *Free Soil*, 56–57.

slavery—a policy of simple restriction was made problematic. To an even-greater degree, as Frederick Douglass recognized, the Republican Party's transformation was a product of Lincoln's genius in holding together a coalition of forces, and steering them toward not only battlefield victory but also the Thirteenth Amendment and emancipation. Ratified in December 1865, ten months after Lincoln's assassination, the Thirteenth Amendment brought a definitive end to North American slavery, declaring:

> Neither slavery nor involuntary servitude, except as a punishment for crime whereof the party shall have been duly convicted, shall exist within the United States, or any place subject to their jurisdiction.

LEGACIES

The most significant legacy of slavery in the Atlantic basin was its abolition, a rejection that spilled over into a crusade against slavery in every corner of the globe. In the regions where it had long held sway, however, it also left behind a suite of bitter legacies: poverty, racial division and stunted economic opportunities. Nowhere were these bitter legacies more significant than in the American South.

Even before the Civil War it was the South's poverty that struck visitors, not its wealth. In the wake of the Civil War, much of the South was in ruins. Twenty-seven percent of the white male population aged between 17 and 45 was lost.[114] Tramping through the South's famed "Black Belt", named for its black earth, in 1890, Du Bois found nothing but poverty. "The key note of the Black Belt", Du Bois recorded, "is debt … the merchants are in debt to the wholesalers, the planters are in debt to the merchants, the tenants owe the planters".[115] Farm statistics support this observation. As Fig. 9.6 indicates, the average farm in the South in 1890 was worth only 38.1% of the typical Midwest farm. Even the typical farm in the recently settled Northern Plains was worth more than twice as much. By 1910, a farm in the South was, on average, worth only a quarter of the value of a Midwest homestead.[116] Industrially, as well,

[114] Guelzo, *Redeeming the Great Emancipator*, 1110.

[115] Du Bois, *Souls of Black Folk*, 137, 126.

[116] Department of Commerce, *Historical Statistics*, Series K17–81.

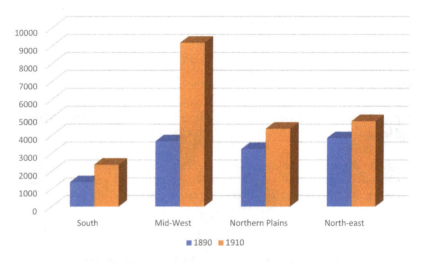

Fig. 9.6 Average US farm values, 1890 and 1910 (historic dollars) (*Source* US Department of Commerce, *Historical Statistics: Immigration,* Series K17–81)

the South remained a laggard. In 1880, despite a significant expansion of tobacco processing and textile manufacture, the South provided jobs to only 67,737 urban factory workers, compared to 29,626 in 1860. By comparison, Midwestern urban factory employment grew from 126,767 to 485,973 between 1860 and 1890.[117]

In the wake of the Civil War a new generation of African American intellectual leaders offered their compatriots two competing visions. One, associated with Booker Washington, emphasized political quiescence, racial reconciliation, entrepreneurship, and wealth creation. The other, advocated by W.E. Burghardt Du Bois, was more assertive, favoring the formation of a highly educated African American elite. Increasingly, Du Bois linked this goal to a Pan-African union, arguing in favor of an African identity that transcended space and time.[118]

Intellectually, Washington and Du Bois were both products of the African American universities that emerged in the wake of the Civil War. Du Bois was a graduate of Tennessee's Fisk University. In 1897,

---

[117] Meyer, "Industrial Retardation of Southern Cities", 374, 377.

[118] Gates, Jr., "Black Letters on the Sign", xv, xviii.

having studied at the University of Berlin and obtained a PhD from Harvard, he assumed a position of intellectual leadership as Professor of History and Economics at another black institution, the University of Atlanta. Washington, born into slavery, worked his way through Virginia's Hampton Normal and Agricultural Institute before setting up his own college, the Tuskegee Institute. As African American intellectuals, both Du Bois and Washington were beneficiaries of selfless Reconstruction-era endeavors by Northern educationalists. Fisk University owed its origins to General Clinton Fisk, who provided the college's first buildings. Virginia's Hampton Institute owed its existence to another veteran, General Samuel Armstrong, a person described by Washington as, "The noblest, rarest human being that it has ever been my privilege to meet".[119]

An educationalist first and foremost, Washington placed little value on political agitation, perceiving in it "a false foundation" for African American progress. Invariably, he lamented, it distracted from the most "fundamental matters", which pertained to "securing property" through economic success.[120] African American people, he argued, were thus ill-served by slavishly following the curriculum of "New England education as it then existed". Instead, African American college education had to be constructed upon principles that were in "sympathy with agricultural life".[121] At the forefront of Washington's thinking was the circumstances of the African American tenant farmers whom he saw all around him, an agricultural society where "the whole family lived in one room" and planted "nothing but cotton".[122] Such families, he passionately argued, *should* be granted their political rights. But to succeed, they also needed "property" and economic respect. For, he proclaimed in his "Atlanta Declaration" of September 1895, "No race that has anything to contribute to the markets of the world is long in any degree ostracized".[123] Accordingly, an education at the Tuskegee Institute placed as much emphasis on inculcating a respect of thrift and manual labor as it did on traditional academic skills. "No student", Washington recorded, "no matter how much money he [or she] may be able to command,

---

[119] Washington, *Up from Slavery*, 30.

[120] Ibid., 44.

[121] Ibid., 61, 65.

[122] Ibid., 57–58.

[123] Ibid., 106, 114.

is permitted to go through [the] school without manual labor". As the African American community slowly prospered, he optimistically forecast, there would come an inevitable point "when the South will encourage all of its citizens to vote", black and white alike.[124]

Du Bois had a very different understanding of both education and of the place of African Americans in the world. Elitist by temperament and training, Du Bois reveled in the great works of western civilization. When Du Bois sat in the hallowed halls of the university, he recorded in *The Souls of Black Folk*:

> I sit with Shakespeare and he winces not. Across the color line I move arm and arm with Balzac and Dumas ... I summon Aristotle and Aurelius ... and they come all graciously.[125]

Famously identifying "the color line" as *the* "problem of the twentieth century", Du Bois saw African American salvation not in a class of yeoman farmers but rather in a highly educated elite.[126] Declaring Booker Washington to be "the most distinguished Southerner since Jefferson Davis"—a very backhanded compliment—Du Bois was dismissive of the Tuskegee Institute's favoring of "triumphant commercialism" over "French grammar". Instead, he believed, African American colleges had to offer a curriculum founded upon that "taught in the groves by Plato".[127] Looking around him in 1900, Du Bois saw progress on every front. More than 400 African Americans had graduated from Harvard, Yale and the other top Northern universities. Thousands more were graduating from Southern colleges. Comparatively few were what Du Bois referred to as "vulgar money-getters". Only 6% of graduates were found among the ranks of "merchants, farmers and artisans". Instead, a majority (53%) were educators. Another 17% worked in the professions. A similar percentage were employed as preachers.[128] As time went on, Du Bois saw this African American elite assuming leadership of the broader Pan-African

---

[124] Ibid., 102, 120.

[125] Du Bois, *Souls of Black Folk*, 109.

[126] Ibid., vii.

[127] Ibid., 43, 82.

[128] Ibid., 100–105, 79.

world. At the Versailles Peace Conference in 1919, where a Du Bois-organized Pan-African Congress was run in parallel, Du Bois proposed placing Germany's former African colonies under the oversight of "educated Blacks" drawn from "the civilized Negro world".[129] As Du Bois grew older his contempt for "money-getters" became more manifest. By the 1950s, Du Bois favored a fusion of Marxism and Pan-Africanism, advocating "socialism founded on old African communal life".[130] Du Bois had, in short, abandoned the idealized image of Platonic learning that characterized his youth in favor of an idealized African village.

For a business historian there is something inherently appealing about Washington's vision that is absent in Du Bois: a concern for ordinary people, thrift, hard work and wealth creation. Unfortunately for Washington, it was Du Bois's vision that best aligned with the future course of events.

The problem with Booker Washington's vision was not just Southern racial hostility. Its hopes for a prosperous class of African American yeoman farmers were also doomed from the start. The agricultural legacy of slavery ran deep: debt, poverty, chronic under-investment. Figure 9.7—which traces patterns of Southern farm ownership among whites and African Americans between 1910 and 1969—indicates comparatively few prospered under the Southern sun, whether white or black. At every point, it should be noted, there were more white tenant farmers and sharecroppers than there were African Americas. While more whites progressed to full ownership than African Americans, most did not. Even where they did, few managed farms large enough to ensure long-term viability. African Americans, however, fared even worse. By 1969, most African American farms lay abandoned.[131]

If Washington's vision for the African American peoples of the South turned to dust, what of Du Bois's hopes for an educated African American elite? What does the fate of this vision tell us of competing legacies of freedom and racism, of inequality and opportunity?

---

[129] W.E. Burghardt Du Bois, "The Collapse of Empire", in W.E.B. Du Bois (ed. Henry Louis Gates, Jr.), *The World and Africa: Color and Democracy* (Oxford, UK: Oxford University Press, 2006), 6–7.

[130] W.E. Burghardt Du Bois, "A Future for Pan-Africa: Freedom, Peace and Socialism", in W.E.B. Du Bois (ed. Henry Louis Gates, Jr.), *The World and Africa: Color and Democracy* (Oxford, UK: Oxford University Press, 2006), 189.

[131] Department of Commerce, *Historical Statistics*, Series K 109-153.

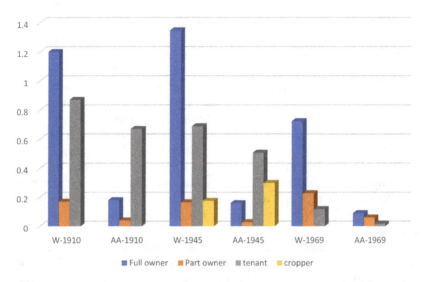

Fig. 9.7 US South, farm ownership by race, 1910–1969, in millions (*Note* Key, W = white, AA = African American. *Source* US Department of Commerce, *Historical Statistics: Commerce,* Series K109–153)

By the end of the twentieth century, Du Bois's dream of a dynamic, college-educated African American population was largely fulfilled. In 2000, 20.5% of African American labor force participants aged over 25 years were college educated. Although, proportionately, both the college-educated African American and Hispanic were still a significantly smaller cohort than the college-educated white, they were expanding at a faster rate. Between 2000 and 2019, the share of the African American and Hispanic populations with a college education aged 25 or older grew by 56.1 and 62.8%, respectively. As a result, almost a third of African Americans have a degree. In contrast, the percentage with a degree among whites and Hispanics was 41.3 and 21.8%, respectively. African Americans were also far more likely to have a trade qualification or some other form of non-college qualification than either a white or Hispanic. Thirty-one percent held such a qualification. By comparison, only 27.5% of whites and 20.6% of Hispanics, respectively, boasted such qualifications. As Figs. 9.8 and 9.9 indicate, college-educated white males and white females were also far *less* likely to be employed and active in the labor market than

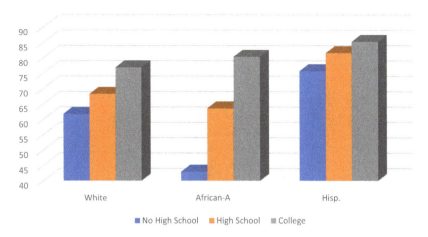

Fig. 9.8 Male labor force participation, 25 years and over, by educational qualification and race, 2019 (*Source* US Bureau of Labor Statistics, *Labor force ... by race and ethnicity*, 2019)

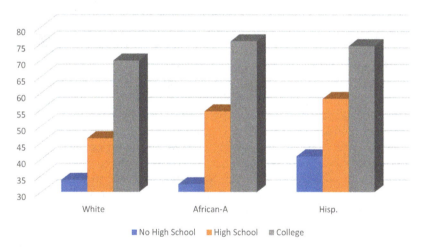

Fig. 9.9 Female labor force participation, 25 years and over, by educational qualification and race, 2019 (*Source* US Bureau of Labor Statistics, *Labor force ... by race and ethnicity*, 2019)

246   B. BOWDEN

either their African American or Hispanic job rivals. In 2019, only 76.7% of college-educated white males were in the labor force. The employment ratio (the percentage with an actual job) for this cohort was 75.2%. By comparison, the labor force participation rate for male college-educated African Americans and Hispanics was 80.3 and 85.2%, respectively—with corresponding employment ratios of 78 and 83%, respectively. Among the college educated, a white female was also *less* likely to be employed and in the labor force than their African American and Hispanic counterparts. In 2019, 69.5% of college-educated white females were in the labor force (employment ratio of 68.2%). The figures for their African American and Hispanic counterparts were 75.7 and 74.2%, respectively—with employment ratios of 73.6 and 72.3%, respectively.[132]

With regard to the college educated it is thus difficult to detect a pattern of systematic racism. While Hispanics and African Americans are less likely to have a college education than whites, if they do have a degree then they are *more* likely to be employed.

When we turn our attention to those without post-school qualifications a more complex picture emerges. African American males without a high school qualification have a much lower labor force participation rate (42.9%) and employment ratio (39%) than either whites (61.7% participation; 59% employment ratio) or, more particularly, Hispanics (75.6% participation, 72.8% employment ratio). A similar, if less pronounced, pattern is found among those with only a high school qualification. Among this cohort, 63.5% of African American males are in the labor force (59.3% employment ratio), compared to 68.2% of whites (employment ratio, 66%) and 81.5% of Hispanics (79.2% employment ratio), respectively. Among females, however, an African American with only a high school education (54.5% participation, 51.4% employment ratio) is *more* likely to be active in the labor force and employed than their white counterpart (46.3% participation, 44.8% employment ratio). Even more favorably placed were their Hispanic colleagues (58.3% participation, 56% employment ratio).[133]

---

[132] United States Census Bureau, *Statistical Abstract of the United States 2010* (Washington, DC: Census Bureau, 2011), Table 579; United States Bureau of Labor Statistics, *Labor Force Characteristics by Race and Ethnicity, 2019—Report 1088* (Washington, DC: Bureau of Labor Statistics, 2020).

[133] Ibid.

If racial discrimination is the determinant factor in US employment, then we have to conclude that employers discriminate in favor of African American and Hispanic college graduates over their white counterparts, and that they also favor African American females and Hispanics with only a high school education over similarly qualified white females. In relation to males, we would similarly have to conclude that systematic racism manifests itself in a universal preference for Hispanics. In *no* educational category, whether male or female, do whites boast a labor force participation rate (or employment ratio) that is higher than that for *both* their African American *and* Hispanic counterparts.

To what, other than hyperbole, can we attribute the vast contemporary literature on systemic racial discrimination when there is so little evidence of it in employment rates?

One evident problem relates to African Americans, both male and female, without a high school education. In this educational category, labor force participation is low in absolute terms and, in the case of males (but not females), significantly lower than that for whites and Hispanics. This points, however, not so much to systematic racism as to an eternal truth espoused by Booker Washington, that there is no substitute for an education that trains one for gainful employment.[134] If we look beyond this specific problem to the wider labor market, we can detect trends that are evident in virtually every advanced economy, namely a decline in participation rates driven by a hollowing out of manufacturing and other high-wage industries. In the United States, as Fig. 9.10 indicates, this trend has impacted those boasting only a high school education most severely, whatever their race. It has, however, impacted whites and African Americans more severely than Hispanics. On a lesser scale, a similar problem is even found among the college educated. Between 2000 and 2019, labor force participation fell from 79 to 73% among whites. Among African Americans it declined from 84.4 to 77.7%. Even Hispanics witnessed a decline.[135] There has, in short, been a tightening of the labor market for every gender and race, an outcome ill-suited to social harmony. While this may manifest itself in racial tensions, however, it is primarily a problem of economic policy, rather than race.

---

[134] Washington, *Up from Slavery*, 65.

[135] US Census Bureau, *Statistical Abstract, 2010*, Table 579; US Bureau of Labor Statistics, *Labor Force, 2019*, Table 6.

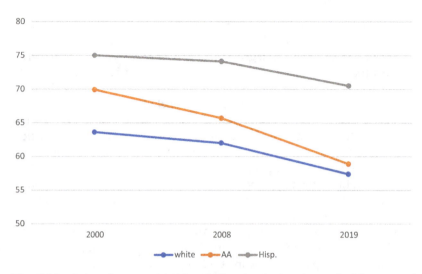

Fig. 9.10 Labor force participation, high school education only 25 years and over, by race, 2000, 2008, 2019 (*Sources* US Census Bureau, Statistical Abstract, 2010; US Bureau of Labor Statistics, *Labor force … by race and ethnicity*, 2019)

PART III

Global Transformation: The Embrace and Rejection of an Industrialized Western Civilization

In the decades after 1850 a profound transformation occurred in the human condition as a revolution in transport and production created a globally integrated market economy. Initially, the primary beneficiaries of this transformation were Japan and the societies of European ancestry in the Old and New World. From the 1920s, however, the populace of Africa, the Middle East and Asia also experienced improved material circumstances even as they languished under colonial control.

Everywhere, societies were confronted with profound and often difficult choices. Constantly, the principles of economic and political liberalism—which prioritized business endeavor, individualism and market solutions—rubbed up against both the growing authority of the modern state and collectivist ideologies opposed to the individualistic ethos of capitalism. In this tenson between individualism and collectivism, the growing footprint of the state favored the latter, just as market solutions benefited the former. Part 3 addresses these enduring tensions.

CHAPTER 10

Global Transformation

Writing amid the horrors of World War I, Oswald Spengler concluded in his *Decline of the West* that the "unshakeable truths and eternal values" of western civilization meant little to other cultures. Nor, he argued, did other cultures "orbit round" the West as if it were the center of the universe. Instead, they followed their own orbits, frequently surpassing the West in "spiritual greatness and soaring power".[1]

Of undoubted truth for most of human history, Spengler's conclusions were nevertheless an inaccurate summation of post-1850 global circumstance. For better or for worse, every society—whether located on the High Plains of the American West, the semi-arid landscapes of the Australian interior, or the agricultural regions of Africa or Asia—found itself drawn within the orbit of the newly industrialized West. Prior to this transformation, however, many societies were still virtually untouched by the West. Touring the High Plains of the American West in the 1830s, George Catlin, for example, recorded how he:

> ... gazed over the interminable and boundless ocean of grass-covered hills and valleys ... a vast country ... where the buffaloes range, the

[1] Oswald Spengler (trans. Charles Francis Atkinson), *The Decline of the West*, revised edition (New York: Alfred A. Knopf, 1927), 12, 8.

© The Author(s), under exclusive license to Springer Nature   251
Switzerland AG 2022
B. Bowden, *Slavery, Freedom and Business Endeavor*,
Palgrave Debates in Business History,
https://doi.org/10.1007/978-3-030-97232-5_10

elk, mountain-sheep, and the fleet-bounding antelope ... [where Native Americans live in a] state of original nature, beyond the reach of civilized contamination.[2]

On the eve of the Civil War, the United States boasted only 330 miles of railroad west of the Mississippi. By 1890, however, almost 50,000 miles of track crisscrossed the region, turning it into the world's preeminent granary. In the vast continental spaces of Australia, a similar transformation was evident. In 1830, only 30,000 Europeans called Australia home. As late as 1860, the entire continent possessed only 243 miles of railroad track. By 1890, however, more than 10,000 miles of road had been laid down. In the wake of the railroads came a new generation of pastoralists who turned much of eastern Australia into a vast sheep paddock. Between the 1870s and 1890s, New South Wales alone laid out more than 1.6 million miles (2.6 million km) of fencing. Nationally, sheep numbers soared from less than 16 million in 1862 to almost 90 million in 1892, providing the woolen mills of Europe with an almost limitless supply of fleece.[3]

It was not only the settler societies of North America and Oceania that were transformed by the revolution in transport. Whereas railroads were a novelty in the 1830s, by 1914 more than 625,000 miles (1 million km) of road were in operation, linking even the remotest regions with global markets.[4] In few countries were the transformative effects of the railroad more evident than in India, where railroad mileage surged from 734 miles in 1860–1861 to 32,839 miles in 1914. As the cost of travel fell inexorably, passenger numbers soared. Whereas barely half a million traveled on India's railroads in 1854, by 1914, a record 438.4 million traveled the system.[5] In much of the vast literature on British rule in India the impact of this transformation—which allowed for the cheap

[2] George Catlin, *Letters and Notes on the Manner, Customs and Condition of North American Indians*, vol. 1 (New York, NY: Dover Publications, 1973), 59–60.

[3] Ian Glover, "Fence Me in", *Outback*, no. 62 (2008), 32; N.G. Butlin, *Investment in Australian Economic Development 1861–1900* (Canberra, AUS: Australian National University Press, 1972), 67.

[4] E.J. Hobsbawm, *The Age of Empire 1873–1914* (London, UK: Guild Publishing, 1987), 62.

[5] United Kingdom Parliament, *Statistical Abstract Relating to British India, 1840–1865* (London, UK: Her Majesty's Printing Office, 1865), *Figure 38*; United Kingdom Parliament, *Statistical Abstract Relating to British India, 1885–86 – 1894–95* (London, UK:

10 GLOBAL TRANSFORMATION 253

transport of goods as well as people—is perceived as wholly destructive. Writing in 1929, Mahatma Gandhi saw in British investment and imports nothing but "ruin to the peasantry of India".[6] In his study of British rule, Parthasarathi also associated this period of Indian subordination with "economic decline", "backward conditions" and the orientation of agricultural production away from vital food production toward export staples.[7] There is some truth in these allegations. The arrival of steam-powered British boats effectively destroyed Indian shipping, the number of Indian craft falling from more than 46,000 in 1853 to fewer than 1,000 in 1901.[8] The extension of the railroads also contributed to the destruction of the homespun cotton textile industry. By the 1880s, British cotton imports controlled almost two-thirds of the Indian market.[9] Despite such effects it is nevertheless a fallacy to perceive the (forced) Indian integration into the new global economy in wholly negative terms. In the last quarter of the nineteenth century an increasing share of British India's budget was devoted to developmental projects: railroads, roads, construction and irrigation works. By 1901, Britain was spending as much money on these sorts of projects as it was on its Indian army, civil service and general administration. Improved irrigation resulted, in turn, in a massive increase in the acreage given over to agriculture. As Fig. 10.1 highlights, almost all this increase was associated with food crops rather than export-oriented staples. Whereas the acreage given over to non-food crops remained static at around 24 million acres between 1885–1886 and 1912–1913, the cultivated area devoted to grains, pulses and other food

Her Majesty's Printing Office, 1895), *Figure* 80; United Kingdom Parliament, *Statistical Abstract Relating to British India, 1910–11 – 1919–20* (London, UK: Her Majesty's Printing Office, 1920), Figure 124.

[6] Mahatma Gandhi, *Collected Works of Mahatma Gandhi*, vol. 46 (New Delhi, India: Government of India Publications Division, 1999), 92.

[7] Prasannan Parthasarathi, *Why Europe Grew Rich and Asia Did Not: Global Economic Divergence 1600–1850* (Cambridge, UK: Cambridge University Press, 2011), 261, 2020, 185, 258, 4–6.

[8] United Kingdom Parliament, *Statistical Abstract Relating to British India, 1894–95–1903–04* (London, UK: Her Majesty's Printing Office, 1904), Figure 172.

[9] Stephen Broadberry and Bishnupriya Gupta: "Lancashire, India, and Shifting Competitive Advantage in Cotton Textiles, 1740–1850", *Economic History Review*, Vol. 62, No. 2 (2009), 285, Table 3.

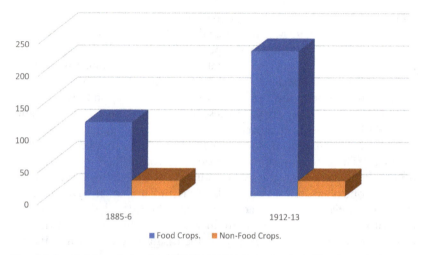

Fig. 10.1 Cultivated acreage, British India—non-food and food (excluding oil seeds and sugar) (*Sources* Calculated from UK Parliament, *Statistical Abstract ... British India*, 1876–1877 to 1885–1886, 1903–1904 to 1911–1912)

crops (excluding oil seeds and sugar) grew from 114 million acres to 225 million acres.[10]

Almost everywhere, the post-1850 revolution in transport made the global market the prime determinant of price. Reflecting on the compression of global wheat prices in the second half of the nineteenth century, the American sociologist, Thorstein Veblen, identified 1882 as the "turning point" after which date prices were determined by "the aggregate volume of the world's crops".[11] As Fig. 10.2 indicates, in 1871 there was a substantial price difference between the wholesale price of wheat in London compared to the price paid in the grain-exporting cities of Chicago (United States) and Melbourne (Australia). This made the growing of wheat a highly profitable endeavor. As increased production flooded global markets, however, this price differential disappeared. By

---

[10] United Kingdom Parliament, *Statistical Abstract Relating to British India, 1876–77–1885–86* (London, UK: Her Majesty's Printing Office, 1886), *Figure* 25; UK Parliament, *Statistical Abstract ... British India, 1894–95–1903–04*, Figure 120.

[11] Thorstein Veblen: "The Price of Wheat Since 1867", *Journal of Political Economy*, Vol. 1, No. 1 (1892), 82.

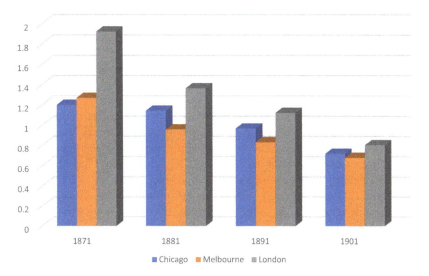

Fig. 10.2 Benchmark wheat prices: Chicago, Melbourne and London, 1871–1901 (US dollars) (*Source* Bowden, *Transformation: The First Global Economy*, 288, Figure 6)

1901, even the London benchmark price had lost 58.2% of its 1871 value in the face of abundant supply, an outcome that cut both bread prices and farm profits.[12] Increasingly, only the largest and most efficient farmers survived. Fewer and fewer people worked on the land.

Outside the rural sector a series of technological and managerial innovations transformed the nature of work and everyday life. Across the globe, as noted in Part 1, society after society broke through the Malthusian ceiling that had curtailed living standards, population growth and life expectancy from time immemorial. Initially, as noted in this book's introduction, the principal beneficiaries of this surge in global production were Japan and the European societies of the Old World, North America and Australasia. Increasingly, however, other societies shared the benefits

---

[12] Bradley Bowden, "Transformation: The First Global Economy, 1750–1914", in Bradley Bowden, Jeffrey Muldoon, Anthony Gould and Adela McMurray (eds.), *The Palgrave Handbook of Management History* (Cham, Switzerland: Palgrave Macmillan, 2020), 288.

of this global bounty. Between 1913 and 1950, India's Human Development Index—a measure of life expectancy, education and per capita wealth—almost doubled. Between 1950 and 2000, it doubled again. Similar trends were found across Latin America, the Middle East and Asia.[13]

At the heart of this new global production system, as noted in Chapter 5, was a process of mechanization centered around the displacement of natural sources of energy by carbon-based reserves (peat, coal, oil, gas). While, it is true, that steam power provided the decisive technological breakthrough during the Industrial Revolution (c. 1760–c. 1830), the voracious coal appetite of the early machines made them a comparative rarity. By 1860, however, a new generation of compound-condensing engines only needed 2 lbs. of coal to produce each hp·h; an outcome far removed from the 44 lbs. consumed by early Newcomen steam engines.[14] This allowed not only a proliferation of steam engines among the world's factories it also facilitated the extension of mechanization to shipping, the railroads, construction and agriculture.

Within this new mechanized world, three wonder products initially stood out from the rest: oil, steel and electricity.

In the oil industry it was John D. Rockefeller's Standard Oil Trust that was the great pioneer, exercising control over every aspect of production and distribution. Initially, Standard Oil's efforts were directed toward lighting rather than heating or power generation. As a result, the retail price of kerosene plunged from 21.5 cents to 7.7 cents per gallon (3.8 l), making kerosene lighting an affordable option for the first time.[15] Previously, night-time life had been characterized by either perpetual darkness, smelly tallow candles or dirty wood fireplaces—or, if one was wealthy, whale-oil lamps. Increasingly displaced by electric power after 1882 (when Edison first demonstrated the potential of this alternative

---

[13] Nicholas Crafts, "The Human Development Index 1870–1999: Some Research Estimates", *European Review of Economic History*, Vol. 6, No. 2 (2002), 395–405; United Nations Development Programme, *Human Development Report, 2019* (New York: New York Development Programme, 2019), Table 2.

[14] R.C. Allen: "Why the Industrial Revolution Was British: Commerce, Induced Invention, and the Scientific Revolution", *Economic History Review*, Vol. 64, No. 2 (2011), 373.

[15] Ron Chernow, *Titan: The Life of John D. Rockefeller*, second edition (New York, NY: Vintage Books, 2004), 258.

energy source), oil famously found an even more important niche for itself in the automobile industry—a sector that transformed the lifestyles of countless millions, allowing them to live at considerable distance from their place of work.

In many ways, steel's global impact was even more revolutionary. Whereas a revolution in iron production had underpinned industrialization between 1780 and 1850, steel—which was far lighter, stronger, and more flexible than iron—was the key to subsequent successes. In 1850, the entire global output probably amounted to no more than 70,000 tons. Following the invention of the Bessemer process in 1850, however, production soared, Britain's output growing from 40,000 tons in 1850 to 1.44 million tons in 1880.[16] As steel became more plentiful so too did a host of applications that transformed everyday life: wide-span bridges, high-rise buildings, automobiles, fridges, high-precision tools, and much more.

It was, however, electrification that most clearly differentiated the new industrial era from pre-industrial life. As an industry, the Russian revolutionary, Vladimir Lenin, observed at the dawn of the twentieth century, electrification typified "the modern technical achievements of capitalism".[17] Whereas earlier inventions were often the result of artisanal efforts and happenstance, electrification rested on scientific research and high levels of capital investment. Outside the home, electrification allowed for electrified subways and tramways, well-lit streets and the pumping of reticulated water and sewerage. Inside the home, it was associated with not only lighting but also telephones, radios, televisions and a host of labor-saving devices (including washing machines and vacuum cleaners, for example).

POLITICAL AND SOCIAL CHOICES IN A MULTIFACETED CIVILIZATION

As has been argued throughout this book, the new iteration of western civilization always entailed more than mechanization and material plenty. Rather, it involved three other attributes: economic liberalism (secure

[16] E.J. Hobsbawm, *Industry and Empire* (Harmondsworth, UK: Penguin Books, 1969), 116.

[17] V.I. Lenin, "Imperialism, the Highest Stage of Capitalism", in V.I. Lenin, *Selected Works*, vol. 2 (Moscow, USSR: Foreign Languages Publishing House, 1946), 692.

258   B. BOWDEN

private property rights, freedom of choice, a preference for market solutions), political liberalism (democracy, the protection of individual rights), and an increasingly powerful state capable of marshaling the resources of the society for both good and evil. Always in tension, these multifaceted attributes continually tugged western societies in different directions, confronting them with difficult and sometimes dangerous choices. For non-western societies drawn into the orbit of the industrialized West the choices were even more difficult. Many believed that they could pick one attribute while ignoring the rest. Whereas the populace typically found the West's material plenty and its transformation of everyday life most attractive, social elites were more often than not entranced by the prospect of indigenizing western bureaucratic and military power. By picking and choosing from the western smorgasbord, each society thus had the potential to turn itself into one that resembled either nineteenth-century Britain with its emphasis on individualism and free markets, or Nazi Germany with its preference for state domination.

Economically, the new iteration of western civilization entailed individualism rather than collectivism, and risk rather than security. Across the mid-nineteenth century Anglo Saxon world, there was little in the way of state intervention, whether for the purposes of economic coordination or social security. On the eve of World War I, however, only Britain remained loyal to the principle of free trade. In most other nations, restrictive tariffs directed toward the protection of local manufacturing were the norm. Typically, it was private-sector firms of unprecedented size that posed the greatest threat to free markets prior to World War I. Among the defenders of the traditional principles of economic liberalism—John Stuart Mill, Alfred Marshall, Friedrich Hayek—this development was never welcomed as a "natural" market outcome. Instead, it was perceived as a threat to both liberty and prosperity.

"It has never been supposed", Marshall observed, "that the monopolist in seeking his own advantage is naturally guided ... [by] the well-being of society regarded as a whole".[18] There was one thing, however, that free-market liberals feared even more than encroaching private-sector monopolies, namely public-sector monopolies. Hayek recorded in *The Road to Serfdom*, "Even if the railways, roads and air transport, or the supply of gas and electricity, were all inevitably monopolies, the consumer

---

[18] Alfred Marshall, *Principles of Economics*, eighth edition (London, UK: Macmillan, 1949), 395.

is unquestionably in a much stronger position than when they [the economic services] are 'coordinated' by a central control".[19] Mill viewed state-controlled monopolies with even-greater hostility. If key services (such as rail, roads and finance) were allowed to fall into government hands, he argued in his study *On Liberty*, it would result in a society that was free only "in name".[20]

Arguably, the biggest threat to economic liberalism that was *intrinsic to the very structure* of the new iteration of western civilization was neither private-sector nor public-sector monopolies. Rather, it was the potential for an alliance between the bureaucratic state on the one side and corporate monopolies on the other, a threat that has manifested itself in a more pronounced form in some western societies than in others.

If we look across the liberal-democratic societies of Western Europe and North America, we can observe not one but three markedly different experiences in relation to the corporate power of business. At one pole sits pre-1945 Germany, a society where industrialization was built on the deliberate fostering of business cartels by a powerful, often militaristic state. In every regard, Trebilcock reflected, "the [German] cartel was a deeply conservative organization aiming at the orderly exploitation of consumers and markets, the elimination of competition, and the pooling of profits".[21] Constantly, this German model veered in authoritarian directions. At the other pole sits France, a society characterized since Napoleonic times by a centralized state but a dispersal of economic power among a plethora of small-scale enterprises. In this "diversity", Fernand Braudel located both the "tragedy" of France's historic economic performance and "the secret of its charm".[22] Fiercely protective of both their properties and political liberties, the French have, like their British rivals, remained implacable foes of totalitarianism. In between these two poles sits the United States, a nation where the steady growth of corporate giants in every facet of life has constantly faced opposition from a society

[19] F.A. Hayek, *The Road to Serfdom* (London, UK: George Routledge & Sons, 1944), 146.

[20] J.S. Mill (ed. John Gray and G.W. Smith), *On Liberty* (London, UK: Routledge, 1991), 124.

[21] Clive Trebilcock, *The Industrialization of the Continental Powers, 1780–1914* (London, UK and New York: Longman, 1981), 65.

[22] Fernand Braudel (trans. Siân Reynolds), *The Identity of France: People and Production* (London, UK: Fontana Press, 1990), 669, 666.

wedded to the principles of small government and economic liberalism. Even here, however, there is growing evidence of an erosion of the principles of economic liberalism. Writing in 2020, Joel Kotkin, worried about an alliance between a new corporate "oligarchy", largely based in the tech sector, and what he referred to as the "clerisy", a university-educated elite that favors a monopolization of decision making by properly informed "experts".[23]

The tension between collectivism and individualism is as pronounced in the political and social spheres as it is in economics. As Hayek accurately observed, in every aspect of life the difference between collectivism and individualism ultimately comes down to risk.[24] For the individual, freedom necessarily entails risk in terms of the choices one makes, whether they relate to job selection, purchases or provision for one's ultimate retirement. Conversely, collectivism frees the individual from not only the risk involved in their choice but also choice itself. Collectivism, however, does not negate the need for choice. Rather, it transfers decision making to a collective entity, which in modern societies is typically the state. In the COVID-19 pandemic of the 2020s, for example, governments around the globe often denied their citizens the ability to choose between normalcy and the risk of disease. Instead, the latter was given primacy at the expense of not only normalcy but also individual choice.

Across the western world, state intervention in the "common good" has long been promoted not only in the name of equality but also as a superior value system to capitalist-aligned individualism. Delivering a series of lectures in the early 1880s, Arnold Toynbee declared that the evils of modern capitalism stem from "the substitution of competition for the medieval regulations which had previously controlled the production and distribution of wealth". In doing so, he argued, society had turned its back on "the whole meaning of civilization", which was premised on "human interference ... to prevent the weak from being trampled underfoot".[25] Across the generations, socialists and supporters of the political Left more generally, have been equally vocal in advocating state "interference" in the pursuit of socially admirable objects. In their *Communist*

---

[23] Joel Kotkin, *The Coming of Neo-Feudalism: A Warning to the Global Middle Class* (New York, NY: Encounter Books, 2020), 7, 1–2.

[24] Hayek, *Road to Serfdom*, 94.

[25] Arnold Toynbee, *Lectures on the Industrial Revolution of the 18th Century in England* (London, UK: Longmans, 1894), 84–86.

Manifesto of 1848, Marx and Engels famously declared that with the victory of socialism the "proletariat will use its political supremacy to ... centralise all instruments of production in the hands of the State".[26] Admittedly, in Western Europe, North America and Australasia this form of socialism remained a distinctly minority opinion. Far more common is the "Fabian" or "Social-Democratic" variety in which state interference is directed toward what the Australian political theorist, Bede Nairn, referred to as "civilizing capitalism": a process associated with alleviating capitalism's "excesses" through a mixture of state-imposed regulatory controls and social security benefits.[27]

The great strength of Fabian-type state interference was that each proposal—state-funded welfare, minimum wages, child-care subsidies and so on—was readily defensible. Even Hayek, the most vocal defender of free markets, supported state intervention that facilitated a "comprehensive system of social insurance".[28] Once one concedes the need for state interference in one domain, however, as one invariably must, one is confronted with the problem of where to draw the line. One consequence of this has been the progressive expansion of the state's economic footprint. As noted previously, the US government spending in 2019, prior to the COVID-19 pandemic and associated "stimulus" expenditure, amounted to 38.1% of GDP. French government spending was equivalent to 55.2% of GDP. Such levels of state spending necessarily entail a reprioritizing of economic goals according to politically determined choices.

More fundamentally, government spending also entails the assertion of one set of moral values at the expense of others. For in any society, there is typically little unanimity as to either moral values or personal objectives. Most, one suspects, place the economic well-being of immediate family at the center of their moral universe. Others are guided primarily by religious belief, a hankering for social equality, climate change fears, or a myriad of other concerns. Many share the sentiments of the ex-Australian prime minister Kevin Rudd, who declared climate change to

---

[26] Karl Marx and Frederick Engels, "Manifesto of the Communist Party", in Karl Marx and Frederick Engels, *Selected Works*, vol. 1 (Moscow, USSR: Foreign Languages Publishing House, 1951), 50–51.

[27] Bede Nairn, *Civilising Capitalism: The Beginning of the Australian Labor Party*, second edition (Melbourne, AUS: Melbourne University Press, 1989), 1–8.

[28] Hayek, *Road to Serfdom*, 90.

be "the great moral challenge of our generation". Others regard climate change fears as nothing more than hot air. When, therefore, a government makes one set of concerns and moral values the guiding light for government interference in the economy—such as we currently witness in the global embrace of a "net zero" increase in carbon dioxide omissions—it does so at the expense of others. By prioritizing "renewable energy", for example, governments foster jobs in one sector (solar panels, wind-turbine manufacture, and other renewables) at the expense of jobs and livelihoods in another (coal mining, oil exploration). In the process, one set of moral values is legitimized, while others are delegitimized.

At the most essential level, the growing economic footprint of the modern state represents a societal preferencing of collectivism over individualism. Now a near universal feature of western societies, this preferencing of collectivism has also oft characterized the ways in which other societies have both embraced and rejected the new iteration of western civilization. The Soviet Union, China, Vietnam, Cuba, Laos and North Korea all sought to build an alternative social order on a hardline Marxist model. In calling for a boycott of British goods in the 1920s, Mahatma Gandhi proclaimed a message of rural self-sufficiency within the collectivist framework of traditional village life—a message that profoundly shaped economic policy in post-independence India.[29] In the 1960s, the West Indian-born Algerian revolutionary, Franz Fanon, urged African independence movements to support both socialism and the (supposed) collectivist values of traditional African societies.[30] Embracing a Pan-African identity, the African American theorist, W. E. B. Du Bois also called for a rebuilding of African society on the basis of "a socialism founded on old African communal life"[31].

If, in the 1960s and 1970s, rejection of the principles of economic and political liberalism was most evident in the so-called "Third World", we can today detect similar tendencies in the very heartlands of western civilization. As Kotkin recently observed, there is an evident "loss of faith in the basic values of our society", a crisis of confidence that has seen "key

---

[29] Gandhi, *Collected Works*, vol. 46, 161.

[30] Franz Fanon, *The Wretched of the Earth* (Harmondsworth, UK: Penguin Books, 1967), 140, 37–39.

[31] W.E. Burghardt Du Bois, "A Future for Pan-Africa – Freedom, Peace, Socialism", in W.E.B. Du Bois (ed. Henry Louis Gates, Jr.), *The World and Africa: Color and Democracy*, (Oxford, UK: Oxford University Press, 2006), 189.

institutions – the academy, the media, the corporate hierarchy, and even some churches – reject many of the fundamental ideals that have long defined western culture".[32]

Writing in 1917, Spengler detected a similar existentialist crisis in western civilization: a crisis of beliefs and values that left each individual as if they were "standing before an exhausted quarry".[33]

That Kotkin and Spengler could express similar fears almost a century apart easily leads to the conclusion that there is nothing much to fear, that western civilization will survive this crisis of confidence just as it survived the wars and revolutions of the early twentieth century. Any such conclusions are, however, misguided. As we shall observe in this book's final two chapters, the modern iteration of western civilization always contained within it the seeds of its own destruction. Economic and political liberalism never reigned supreme and unchallenged. Instead, collectivist models that directed society toward one state-endorsed objective or another constantly threatened the primacy of individual choice and freedom. Now, as in 1917, the fate of western civilization hangs in the balance.

[32] Kotkin, *Coming of Neo-Feudalism*, 171.
[33] Spengler, *Decline of the West*, 40.

CHAPTER 11

A Globalized Civilization: Ascendancy, Contradictions and Interdependence

At the nineteenth century's mid-point there were few who could not sense a profound change in the human condition. The Year of Revolutions, 1848, was a year when an upswelling of democratic fervor brought a definitive end to the absolutist order that had reestablished itself in continental Europe in the wake of the Napoleonic Wars. Issuing their *Communist Manifesto* amid the revolutionary turmoil, Karl Marx and Frederick Engels, observed how:

> In place of old wants, satisfied by the productions of the country, we find new wants, satisfied by the products of distant lands and climes. In place of the local and national seclusion and self-sufficiency, we have intercourse in every direction, universal inter-dependence of nations.[1]

According to Marx and Engels, the revolutions of 1848 heralded far more than mere economic and political change. They also announced a revolutionary new social class, the proletariat, a class of factory workers who

---

[1] Karl Marx and Frederick Engels, "Manifesto of the Communist Party", in Karl Marx and Frederick Engels, *Selected Works*, vol. 1 (Moscow, USSR: Foreign Languages Publishing House, 1951), 36.

© The Author(s), under exclusive license to Springer Nature Switzerland AG 2022
B. Bowden, *Slavery, Freedom and Business Endeavor*,
Palgrave Debates in Business History,
https://doi.org/10.1007/978-3-030-97232-5_11

265

would be the flagbearers of socialism; a class that would grow in importance even as "other classes decay and finally disappear in the face of modern industry".[2]

If the *Communist Manifesto* heralded the birth of a political movement that would in the decades ahead result in socialist regimes in much of Eastern Europe and Asia, the Year of Revolutions also witnessed a reassertion of the promise of free-market capitalism in John Stuart Mill's greatest work, his *Principles of Political Economy*. Like Marx and Engels, Mill detected a profound alteration in economic circumstances associated with the "most marvelous inventions".[3] Like Marx and Engels, Mill also detected in the new industrial working class a powerful economic and political force. "The working classes", Mill observed, "have taken their interests into their own hands, and are perpetually showing that they think the interests of the employers not identical with their own, but opposite to them".[4] If Mill was in agreement with Marx and Engels as to the proletariat's significance, he differed from them in terms of his vision for the future. The socialist call to substitute state direction for free-market competition, he advised, was the "greatest" of "errors". For, Mill noted, "wherever competition is not, monopoly is". And no form of monopoly was worse than one under state direction.[5]

In the competing visions of Marx and Mill the new industrial iteration of western civilization was thus offered at its inception two different futures, one centered around markets and competition and the other built upon state direction and control.

Across the latter half of the nineteenth century, Mills' free-market vision enjoyed a clear ascendancy. During this half century, the dynamic potential that both Marx and Mill identified in the new industrial capitalism was evident on almost every front. After stagnating for millennia, life expectancy experienced a dramatic improvement. As Fig. 11.1 indicates, in 1900 the average Briton boasted a life expectancy eleven years longer than that enjoyed by their predecessors in 1800. In France, the

[2] Ibid., 42.

[3] John Stuart Mill, *Principles of Political Economy* (Amhurst, NY: Prometheus Books, 2004), 644.

[4] Ibid., 696.

[5] Ibid., 725.

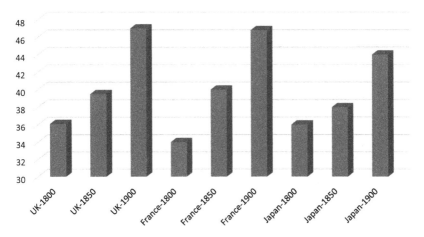

Fig. 11.1 Life expectancy, 1800–1900: UK, France and Japan (*Source* Steckel and Floud, "Conclusions", p. 424, Table 11.1)

average citizen lived twelve years longer. In Japan, where western technology and economic models were grasped with unusual enthusiasm, life expectancy also rose by twelve years. In every case, most particularly in Britain and Japan, the greatest improvements occurred in the second half of the nineteenth century rather than the first. As Fig. 11.2 highlights, improvements in literacy paralleled gains in life expectancy. In 1800, barely half the adult British population was literate. By 1900, literacy was almost universal. In France, literacy rose from 40% in 1800 to 95% in 1900. Japanese literacy grew from 20 to 54.5%. Once more, gains were concentrated in the second half of the nineteenth century.[6]

Significantly, the benefits of improved life expectancy and literacy were not confined to a handful of "imperial" nations. In the Maya regions of Central America, as noted in Chapter 4, integration into the global market brought to a conclusion the devastating cycle of growth, famine and depopulation that had bedeviled its people from time immemorial. In India, British rule brought in its wake a system of government-supported English-language schools. As Fig. 11.3 indicates, attendance

---

[6] Richard H. Steckel and Richard Floud, "Conclusions", in Richard H. Steckel and Roderick Floyd (eds.), *Health and Welfare During Industrialization* (Chicago, IL: University of Chicago Press, 1997), Table 11.1.

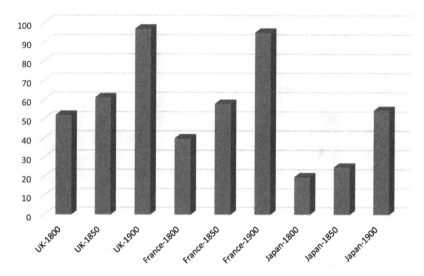

Fig. 11.2 Literacy, 1800–1900: UK, France and Japan (*Source* Steckel and Floud, "Conclusions", p. 424, Table 11.1)

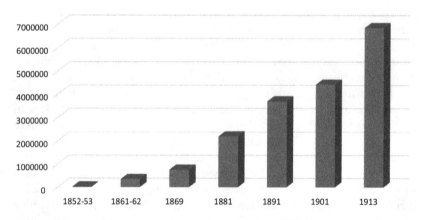

Fig. 11.3 Attendance, Indian government-supported schools, 1852–1853 to 1913 (*Source* UK Parliament, *Statistical Abstract ... British India*, 1840–1865, 1884–1885 to 1894–1895, 1903–1904 to 1912–1913)

at these scholarly institutions grew exponentially. By 1913, more than 6.8 million were in attendance.[7] While this total represented barely 4% of the eligible population, this education system nevertheless bequeathed India an English-speaking intellectual elite that remains one of its great strengths.

At the heart of the new global economy, as noted in the introduction to Part 3, was a revolution in steam-powered railroads and shipping. In shipping, a new era was heralded when the Isambard Kingdom Brunel-designed *SS Great Britain* in 1845 became the first iron-hulled, screw-propellor-driven ship to cross the Atlantic. More efficient than earlier paddle wheels, screw propellors were also virtually immune to storm damage, allowing steamers to compete with sail on the wild Southern Ocean voyages to Australasia for the first time. Effectively, the world became a much smaller place. Whereas in the 1830s it had often taken six weeks or more to make the Atlantic crossing, by the 1880s it took but ten days. Another technological marvel, the telegraph, allowed almost instantaneous communication between far-distant regions. In 1851, the world's first underwater cable linked Britain with the continent. By 1880, there was 97,568 miles of oceanic cable, linking Europe, North America, Africa, the Middle East, India and Australasia.[8] Personal communication became even easier after Alexander Bell's patenting of the telephone in 1876. By 1911, 2.8% of London households boasted a telephone. In New York, 8.3% of homes were connected. In Los Angeles, an extraordinary 24% of homes bore witness to the technology.[9] Reflecting on the integrated global economy created through this communications revolution, the English economist, John Maynard Keynes, recalled how on the eve of World War I, a person:

---

[7] United Kingdom Parliament, *Statistical Abstract Relating to British India, 1840–1865* (London, UK: Her Majesty's Printing Office, 1865), Figure 47; United Kingdom Parliament, *Statistical Abstract Relating to British India, 1885–86–1894–5* (London, UK: Her Majesty's Printing Office, 1895), Figure 105; United Kingdom Parliament, *Statistical Abstract Relating to British India, 1903–04–1912–13* (London, UK: Her Majesty's Printing Office, 1913), Figure 111.

[8] Niall Ferguson, *Empire: How Britain Made the Modern World* (Melbourne, AUS: Penguin Books, 2008), 166–168.

[9] E.J. Hobsbawm, *The Age of Empire 1873–1914* (London, UK: Guild Publishing, 1987), 347, Table 6.

... could order by telephone, sipping his morning tea in bed, the various products of the whole earth, in such quantity as he might see fit, and reasonably expect their early delivery upon his doorstep; he could at the same moment and by the same means adventure his wealth in the natural resources and new enterprises of any quarter of the world.[10]

If technology and economic prowess were key to the forging of an industrial civilization with a global reach, so too was western expertise in organized violence. As Samuel Huntington observed in his *The Clash of Civilizations and the Remaking of World Order*:

The West won the world not by the superiority of its ideas or values or religion ... but rather by its superiority in applying organized violence. Westerners often forget this fact; non-Westerners never do.[11]

In his *Decline of the West*, Oswald Spengler identified Cecil Rhodes as the embodiment of this "new age" of western expansion: a person who created a vast personal empire in southern Africa, dominating the region's gold and diamond fields, and massacring the Matabele warriors of what is now Zimbabwe with machine-guns wielded by his own personal army. Like many others, Spengler was unimpressed by this imperial adventurism, seeing in it a cultural over-reach, "a doom, something daemonic".[12]

Behind the West's imperial success in the late nineteenth century stood an increasingly powerful bureaucratic state. For Max Weber, the administrative bureaucracy that emerged in the West during the latter half of the nineteenth century was profoundly different from earlier expressions of state power, finding expression "only in the most advanced institutions of capitalism"—most particularly "the modern state". Operating "in a precisely regulated manner", the new western bureaucracies, Weber argued, little resembled the "large political structures" found in most premodern societies, where "the ruler" typically exercised power "through personal trustees, table-companions, or court-servants". By comparison, he concluded, the interests of western rulers and business

[10] John Maynard Keynes, *The Economic Consequences of the Peace* (London, UK: Macmillan and Co., 1920), 9.

[11] Samuel Huntington, *The Clash of Civilizations and the Remaking of World Order* (New York, NY: Simon & Schuster, 2003), 51.

[12] Oswald Spengler (trans. Charles Francis Atkinson), *The Decline of the West*, revised edition (New York: Alfred A. Knopf, 1927), 38–39.

leaders were, within a modern bureaucracy, totally separate from the objectives of the organizations over which they presided. Accordingly, Weber believed, the monarch or president of a modern state was nothing more than its "first official", just as the "modern entrepreneur" in a large firm was nothing but its "first officer".[13] In this, modern bureaucracies differed markedly, Weber argued, from even the sophisticated systems that characterized Confucian China. Where modern bureaucracies have an identity and purpose separate from those who administer it, China's Confucian system was, Weber concluded, of a "semi-patrimonial" type, premised on:

> ... the subordination of the officials to the ruler, of the lower to the higher-ranking officials, and particularly of the subjects to the officials and the ruler, on the cardinal virtue of filial piety.[14]

There is both truth and exaggeration in Weber's analysis. As observed in Chapter 6, the bureaucratic state was in truth an original creation of the Age of Absolutism (c. 1550–1789), a time when state machines harnessed for the first time the capabilities of a new "Brahmin elite" graduating in ever-greater numbers from Europe's universities. The capabilities of the post-1850 bureaucratic state, however, far exceeded that of its absolutist predecessor; a power that in the twentieth century was to be unleashed with destructive force against both foreign foes and—in the case of Nazi Germany, Fascist Italy, Francoist Spain and the Soviet Union—domestic enemies. As Weber accurately observed, at the heart of this power was the "social prestige" of the "patent of education". Everywhere, the growing number of university graduates were drawn toward the power, prestige and security of bureaucratic positions like bees to a honey pot.[15]

The French existentialist philosopher Albert Camus was one of many who perceived the growth of the modern state in far less benign terms than Weber, lamenting what he called, "the terrifying growth of the modern State". Everywhere, Camus recorded, humanity increasingly

---

[13] Max Weber (ed. Guenther Roth and Claus Wittich), *Economy and Society* (Berkely, CA: University of California Press, 1978), 956–957.

[14] Ibid., 999, 1050.

[15] Ibid., 1000.

found itself under the control of either "a rational or irrational State".[16] Writing during World War II, Friedrich Hayek came to similar conclusions. The rise of totalitarianism, he concluded, was not an aberrant outcome, a matter of historical misfortune. Rather, it was a near inevitable result of an enthusiasm for state direction and control at the expense of economic liberalism and individualism. Amid the carnage of World War II, Hayek also noticed with regret that across the ranks of modern society there were few who were more enthusiastic in their support of state control than the university-educated intelligentsia. Indeed, he observed, among the "progressive" intelligentsia, socialism had "displaced liberalism as the doctrine held by the great majority".[17]

There is, no doubt, an element of undue pessimism to Camus and, more particularly, Hayek's observations. Across the decades, totalitarian regimes have been resisted as well as embraced. Nazi Germany and the Soviet Union are now a dusty memory. Enthusiasm for socialism among the university educated has waxed and waned. Certainly, there is no reason to conclude that the university educated, who are typically individualistic by both inclination and training, are destined to be enthusiasts for state regulation simply because of their education. Where they enter into the service of a business in a competitive area of the economy, as a countless number have done, they typically embrace the free-market ethic of business. If we should treat the fears of Camus and Hayek with caution, we should nevertheless not reject them as baseless. Certainly, the competition between collectivism and individualism, and between economic liberalism and state control, has turned out to be a far more complex matter than Mill envisaged it to be in 1848. Typically, the state's economic footprint has advanced by creep rather than by revolution. In 2019, as noted in the introduction to Part 3, government spending across the OECD was typically in the range of 40–50% of GDP. Where services are "outsourced", the private-sector firms that are the beneficiaries of this process become de facto clients of the state, depending on government contracts for their survival.

If the growth of the modern state belied Mill's expectation that markets would prevail over systems of state direction, it was also the case

---

[16] Albert Camus (trans. Anthony Bower), *The Rebel: An Essay on Man in Revolt* (New York, NY: Alfred A. Knopf, 1978), 177, 250.

[17] F.A. Hayek, *The Road to Serfdom* (London, UK: George Routledge & Sons, 1944), 10, 18.

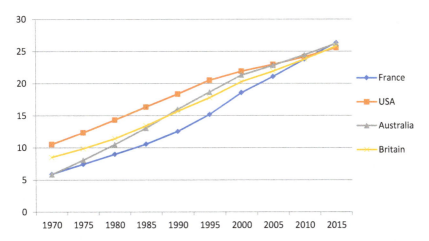

Fig. 11.4 Percentage of adult population with university degree, 1970–2015: France, the United States, Australia and Britain (*Source* Bowden, *Work, Wealth and Postmodernism*, Figure 8.12)

that Marx's belief that the industrial proletariat would sweep all before it was similarly contradicted by the course of events. In every western society, the old blue-collar working class appears to be in near-terminal decline. Conversely, as Fig. 11.4 indicates, the university educated have grown in number and importance.[18] Collectively, these two developments—the growth of the state's economic footprint and the growing social dominance of the university educated—bring the fears of Camus and Hayek once more to the fore. Across the sweep of the modern iteration of western civilization we can certainly detect, as Hayek did in 1944, a progressive "moving away from the basic ideas" upon which the entire culture "has been built": individualism, economic liberalism and a commitment to free markets.[19] Ever-greater numbers identify their own personal interests with an expansion of the state sector and its many agencies. Increasingly, we can also detect across broad swathes of academia and in our cultural institutions a hostility to the very concept

[18] Bradley Bowden, *Work, Wealth and Postmodernism: The Intellectual Conflict at the Heart of Business Endeavour* (Cham, Switzerland: Palgrave Macmillan, 2018), 282, Figure 8.12.

[19] Hayek, *Road to Serfdom*, 10.

of western civilization. We are thus informed that western civilization is founded upon racism and "whiteness", that "whiteness ... is structural privilege", that "modern management procedures" are an outgrowth of slavery and a continuing drive for "unremitting workplace supervision".[20] Given such trends, it is evident that we cannot understand the global transformation that occurred after 1850 by simply focusing on private-sector trends and the transformation of everyday life. We also need to pay heed to the growth of the state and its ever-increasing association with a growing university-educated professional class. We need, in short, to understand the modern iteration of western civilization as a contradictory phenomenon, a social order whose stability is far more fragile than it superficially appears.

THE TRANSFORMATION OF EVERYDAY LIFE: THE RISE AND DECLINE OF THE INDUSTRIAL WORKING CLASS

A civilization embodies far more than the "high culture" (music, literature, architecture and so on) that is typically its most lauded expression. Instead, at its core, a civilization finds expression in personal experiences and the shared bonds of family and community; bonds underpinned by accepted-as-fact rituals, values and social norms. Inevitably, within any civilization, its everyday expressions are not uniform, either for individuals or the communities and social classes to which they belong. At any given point in time, some individuals and communities prosper while others suffer social and economic regression. Some communities and social groups benefit from changes in technology and trade. Others find that the tides of change no longer run in their favor. To understand any civilization, therefore, we need to look beneath the surface and explore the diversity and contradictions that lay at its core.

If every historic civilization found its most glittering expression in the urban centers that were the abodes of monarchs, priests and merchants, the experiences that city life afforded were nevertheless atypical. Most

---

[20] Birgit Brander Rassmussen, Eric Klinenberg, Irene J. Nexica and Matt Wray, "Introduction", in Birgit Brander Rassmussen, Eric Klinenberg, Irene J. Nexica and Matt Wray (eds.), *The Making and Unmaking of Whiteness* (Durham, NC: Duke University Press, 2001), 11, 13; Mathew Desmond, "Capitalism", in Jake Silverstein (ed.), *1619 Project* (New York, NY: *New York Times Magazine*, 2019), 32.

remained trapped in a peasant subsistence economy. The new industrialized iteration of western civilization that emerged around 1850—as mechanization spread from textiles to engineering, transport, construction and agriculture—broke with this historic pattern. For the first time, an urban life as a waged worker, rather than as a self-employed agriculturalist or artisan, became the common fate.

In its industrial heyday, between 1850 and the 1960s, the beating economic heart of this new expression of western civilization was located in factory towns dominated by blue-collar workers and their families. And among these factory towns, none were more important to a society's success than those located in the great coal and steel regions of north England, the Ruhr, Pennsylvania and the like. In Australia, this iconic expression of the new civilization manifested itself to the full in the great mining and industrial center of Newcastle, a town whose fortunes—like that of its English namesake—long rested on its coalfields. In 1900, the local newspaper recorded, "The city of Newcastle is practically kept alive by the great coaling industry". So dense was the smoke from the coking ovens and factories that the "whole city" was "practically hidden from view", leaving the "small houses" of the town's working population with a "smoke-begrimed and dirty appearance".[21] At the core of this industrial township was Carrington, a city within a city, bound by the Hunter River and its harbor extensions on three sides and, from 1915, the furnaces and mills of BHP's steelworks on the fourth. Within its humble weatherboard worker's cottages, four generations of Carrington residents carved out a lifestyle that was quintessentially working class, one that differed only in degree from that found in places like Sheffield (England) or Pittsburg (United States).

Collectivist in ethos, the residents of Carrington were fiercely loyal to their trade unions, their class and, above all, to each other. Politically, they tended to vote for "renegade" Labor Party politicians who put their loyalties to their constituents ahead of their commitments to their party.[22] While life in Carrington was hard, it was also secure. Periods of unemployment, even during the Great Depression of the 1930s, were relatively rare as son followed father into the steelworks. As Australian living standards

---

[21] *Newcastle Morning Herald*, 2 May 1900.

[22] Bradley Bowden, "The Hunter", in: Jim Hagan (ed.), *People & Politics in Regional New South Wales, 1856 to the 1950s* (Sydney, AUS: Federation Press, 2006), 60–63.

rose, so too did those in Carrington, offering many a life outside not only the steelworks but also Newcastle. From the 1970s onward, however, the dreams and aspirations of Carrington's residents slowly evaporated as the aging steelworks lost its capacity to compete with imported steel. After a series of ever-more devastating job layoffs, the furnaces fell permanently silent in 1999. By this stage, few Newcastle workers labored in manufacturing. As I walked the streets of Carrington in 2002, I witnessed nothing but despair, poverty, violence, drug abuse and social dysfunction. Fourteen years later, the streets of Carrington and Newcastle were very different. In 2016, the number of Newcastle workers engaged as managers and professionals (25,135) was almost equal to the combined population of tradespeople (12,273), machine operators (5,986) and laborers (8,519).[23] By 2021, the old Carrington working class had long gone, driven out by rising rents and house prices. Now renovated, a typical Carrington "worker's cottage" today leaves the purchaser little change from a million dollars. Amid a gentrified professional population that votes in increasing numbers for Green Party candidates, only the nearby coal loaders that make Newcastle the world's largest coal port hark back to its once dominant industrial culture.

The story of Carrington is one that is replicated, in one form or another, in virtually every nation on the planet.

In the twenty-first century, steel is in higher demand than ever. Today's Carrington, however, is far more likely to be found in China or India than in the old western heartlands. In 2021, both these societies produced a staggering 1.4 billion tons of steel, totals that far exceeded the production of the third-placed United States (333 million tons). By comparison, Britain, in 1850 when it was the "workshop of the world", produced but 47,000 tons. Thirty years later, when steel was seminal to not only the railroads but also a new generation of steam-powered ships, Britain's output was still only 1.4 million tons—one-thousandth of that forged today by China and India.[24] The decline of steel production in places like Carrington and Sheffield is thus not a reflection of falling demand. Rather, it reflects Asian competitive advantage built around lower labor costs and modernized mills, and a western policy proclivity to outsource

---

[23] Australian Bureau of Statistics, *2016 Census Community Profiles: Newcastle* (Canberra, AUS: Australian Bureau of Statistics, 2019), Code 1103 (SA3).

[24] E.J. Hobsbawm, *Industry and Empire* (Harmondsworth, UK: Penguin Books, 1969), 116, 134.

manufacturing more generally. There is a growing hostility to the very concept of an energy-intensive economy in the old western heartlands, which is pushing industry "offshore".

Although modern-day steelworkers engage in work processes that differ little from those once witnessed in Carrington, the political and social context in which they live their lives is often fundamentally different. In Carrington, it was not only shared experiences at work that gave people a sense of common identity. As citizens of a democratic society, they also joined trade unions and political parties and voted in ways that were often different to fellow workers who resided in adjacent communities. This is a situation that little resembles the experiences of industrial workers in today's China. As Elly Leung's powerful recent study, *The (Re-)Making of the Chinese Working Class* reveals, the Chinese regime has created a vast underclass of people who are referred to— both by the society at large and the workers themselves—as low *suzhi* or, literally, people of "low personal quality". Representing a majority of China's industrial workforce, low *suzhi* workers are described by Leung as people existing in a netherworld of "semi-citizenship". According to the Communist Party's mouthpiece, the *China Daily*, this teeming mass are "barbarians", people who need to "improve" themselves by following the directions of their "high quality superiors at work in the cities".[25] Vast numbers of Chinese workers also live not in residential communities bound by a sense of common identity, but rather in huge company dormitories or in nearby temporary lodgings. Of the accommodation enjoyed by workers adjacent to the vast Foxconn factory in Shenzhen—that she herself lived in as part of her research—Leung records:

> The rooms of the lodging were small; old; filthy; smelly, dark and filled with mosquitos and cockroaches ... walls were broken or sagging; the bed frames were snapped or cracked ... there were no flush toilets in the stinky washrooms ... Externally, it was surrounded by the murky and smelly rivers of sewage; the streets were filled with piles of garbage alongside cockroaches and rats ... The streets were always crowded with workers ... They all looked angry; they never smiled.[26]

---

[25] Elly Leung, *The (Re-)Making of the Chinese Working Class: Labor Activism and Passivity in China* (Cham, Switzerland: Palgrave Macmillan, 2021), 87–90.

[26] Ibid., 105.

In writing of the work practices created by modern factories and their associated systems of management there is a tendency to perceive it as nothing more than a process for de-skilling and degradation. This is certainly how Harry Braverman famously saw it in his 1974 study, *Labor and Monopoly Capital*. "The transformation of working humanity ... into an instrument of capital", Braverman declared, "is repugnant ... whether their pay is high or low ... since the workers ... are simply utilized in inhuman ways".[27] Among the industrializing societies of Africa, Asia and the Middle East, many perceived industrialization in like fashion. In Iran, the dissident intellectual, Jalal Al-i Ahmad associated the advance of "the machine" with social disorientation. By embracing "the machine", Al-i Ahmad lamented, Iran witnessed more than the destruction "of the pastoral and rural economy". It also witnessed intellectual "occidentosis", in which people abandoned their religious "faith" in favor of western norms and modes of existence. Women, rather than being "the preservers of tradition", were drawn "into the street", becoming wearers "of powder and lipstick".[28]

The advance of industrialization was, no doubt, even more destructive of cultural norms in Iran or India than it was in England or France. To perceive industrial work and the social relationships that it engenders in totally negative terms, however, is an error. By its very nature, industrial work—unlike the labor of the individualistic peasant farmer or university-trained professional—builds cohesion. Either everyone works together on the assembly line or no one works. In the years after 1850, the growth of an industrial working class was also inseparable from the advance of democracy across Europe and much of the New World. As noted in the introduction to this chapter, this was something that was appreciated as much by Mill as by Marx.

In Britain, as late as 1867, only 8% of the male population were able to vote. After the Reform Acts of 1867 and 1882, 29% of males were franchised. In 1918, universal male franchise became a fact with the vote also extended to females aged over 30. In Belgium, a general strike in 1894 resulted in the percentage of the male population enjoying the

---

[27] Harry Braverman, *Labor and Monopoly Capital: The Degradation of Work in the Twentieth Century*, 25th anniversary edition (New York, NY: Monthly Review Press, 1998), 96.

[28] Jalal Al-i Ahmad (trans. R. Campbell), *Occidentosis: A Plague from the West* (Berkeley, CA: Mizan Press, 1984), 69, 94, 70.

vote growing from 3.9 to 37.3%. In France, Germany, Denmark and Switzerland, universal male suffrage was also the norm by the 1880s.[29]

The numerical expansion of an industrial working class also underpinned the rise of new social-democratic and labor parties. Only in the United States, where Samuel Gompers directed the American Federation of Labor away from political entanglements—and where an aspiration to owning one's own business or farm was all-pervasive—did these new socialist-oriented parties fail to assume political significance. Elsewhere, they became de facto states within states. As Robert Michels observed in 1911, the "gigantic" new working-class parties required "a no less gigantic apparatus of editors, secretaries, bookkeepers, and numerous other employees".[30] If the rise of an industrial working class was associated with an expansion of democracy and new forms of political representation, we should nevertheless be wary of assuming that this was an *inevitable* effect of industrialization. Many societies (China, Iran, the Soviet Union) have, after all, industrialized without granting their workers much in the way of either freedom or workplace rights. Rather it was the case that workers in the classic West (Europe, North America, Australasia), experienced industrialization in fortuitous circumstances, in societies where a democratic ethos enjoyed deep roots within the civilization. The great democratic revolutions that provided the basis for everything that followed—Britain's "Glorious Revolution" of 1688, the American Revolution (1776) and the French Revolution (1789)—all *preceded* industrialization. They were not a consequence of it.

As a class, industrial workers were, like farmers, people who were primarily concerned with material artefacts rather than theoretical abstractions. In forming trade unions, they were mainly interested in sharing the wealth of capitalism rather than in destroying it. Yes, intense class conflict remained a feature of the industrial age, just as it had characterized the pre-industrial era. The great difference, however, is that conflict took place—for the first time in human history—in an economy that had broken through the "Malthusian ceiling" that had previously restricted most to a life of misery. In Britain, as observed in the introduction to this book, the real wage of a skilled building worker rose six-fold between

---

[29] Hobsbawm, *Age of Empire*, 65.

[30] Robert Michels, *Political Parties: A Sociological Study of the Oligarchic Tendencies of Modern Democracy* (Kitchener, CAD: Batouche Books, 2001), 165.

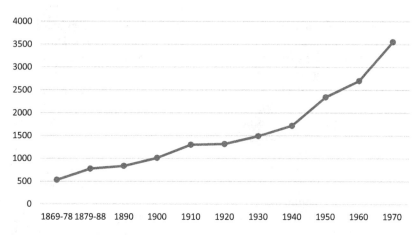

Fig. 11.5 Growth in real per capita GNP, the United States 1869–1878 to 1970 (constant 1958 prices) (*Source* US Department of Commerce, *Historical Statistics*, Series F-1-5)

1800 and 1930. In the United States, as Fig. 11.5 indicates, real per capita gross national product (GNP) grew almost 2.5-fold between the 1870s and 1910. Then, after the disappointment of the years between 1910 and 1940, when real per capita GNP still rose by 32.4%, American workers enjoyed unprecedented prosperity between 1940 and 1970 amid a further doubling of real per capita GNP.[31] Similar trends were apparent in every other liberal democracy.

Industrialization and rising per capita wealth were also associated with something else that was entirely historically novel—mass consumerism.

In what the German neo-Marxist, Herbert Marcuse, referred to as the "affluent society",[32] production increasingly shifted from capital goods to consumer items: pre-made boots and clothing, pre-packaged food and beverages and, above all, electrical goods (vacuum cleaners, radios, fridges) and motor vehicles. In each of these domains the United States was long the undoubted leader. By 1939, the United States was

---

[31] United States Department of Commerce, *Historical Statistics of the United States: Colonial Times to 1970—Bicentennial Edition* (Washington, DC: United States Department of Commerce, 1975), Series F-1-5.

[32] Herbert Marcuse, *One Dimensional Man* (Boston, MA: Beacon Press, 1964), 247–257.

producing 150 new fridges each year for every 10,000 people. Canada, by comparison, produced only 50 per 10,000, and Britain but eight. Even in Britain, however, consumer goods were responsible for 20% of industrial output by 1935 as radios, electric lighting, vacuum cleaners and electric irons became ubiquitous features of urban life.[33] Everywhere, the consumer revolution resulted in a reorientation of production toward goods associated with private use. In the second half of the nineteenth century, for example, the railroads were the principal customers for the iron, steel and engineering industries. In the United States in 1881, rails alone absorbed 34% of national pig iron output and 76% of steel production. By 1938, however, the automobile industry was the key driver of US manufacturing, absorbing 51% of its strip steel, 54% of its alloy steel, 53% of its malleable iron, 69% of its plate glass and 90% of its gasoline.[34]

It was not only consumer goods that were "democratized" in the "affluent society". So too was entertainment. Across the globe, cinema became the "palace of dreams", making Los Angeles the cultural capital of the world. Having fled Nazi Germany for California, the "Frankfurt School" Marxists, Max Horkheimer and Theodor Adorno, identified the new "film factories" as a more decisive guarantee of the future of capitalism than any advance in material living standards. Holding the enthusiasm for cinema and television in contempt, Horkheimer and Adorno also claimed that these new technologies tended to "make the people smarter and more stupid at once".[35] Across the Middle East and Asia, defenders of traditional values expressed similar sentiments, Al-i Ahmad locating in the urban addiction to western cinema the worst expression of "occidentosis". Among the Iranian population, he lamented in the 1960s, many refused to return to the village of their birth because "there is no cinema there".[36] Cinema and television were, however, not simply agents of cultural destruction. There were also weapons in a cultural "cold war" that threatened totalitarian regimes everywhere.

---

[33] Hobsbawm, *Industry and Empire*, 220, 223.

[34] W.W. Rostow, "Leading Sectors and the Take-off", in W.W. Rostow (ed.), *The Economics of Take-off into Sustained Growth: Proceedings of a Conference Held by the International Economic Association* (London: Macmillan/St Martin's Press, 1963), 5, Footnote 3.

[35] Max Horkheimer and Theodor W. Adorno (trans. Edmund Jephcott), *Dialectic of Enlightenment* (Stanford, CA: Stanford University Pres, 2002), xi, xv, xvii, xvii.

[36] Al-i Ahmad, *Occidentosis*, 57.

In Stephen Kotkin's opinion, the uptake of television within the Soviet Union—where it was found in 93% of homes by the 1980s—was decisive in corroding support for Russian communism. For, once the last Soviet leader, Mikhail Gorbachev, allowed western television programs, citizens gained a portal into an alternative world, in the process developing an "infatuation with the western consumer culture".[37]

If the old industrial working class was a beneficiary of the "affluent society", it was also its victim. As noted in the introduction to this chapter, the core assumption of Marxism was the belief that the industrial working class would grow in importance even as the "other classes decay and finally disappear". In truth, it was the industrial working class that withered away in every western society. Across the historic West, manufacturing employment fell not only in relative terms but also absolutely. In the United States, factory employment fell from a peak of 17.2 million in 1953 to 14.7 million in 2017 before rebounding to 14.9 million in 2018 under Trump's protectionist policies. In Australia, manufacturing employment also peaked in the 1950s. In 1954, Australia's factories provided jobs for 1.2 million workers. By 2019, however, they employed just 886,100. In Canada, one in seven factory jobs were lost between 2004 and 2008 alone, leaving the country with fewer than 2 million manufacturing workers. By 2018, only 1.65 million remained.[38] In Britain, evidence of decay was evident as early as the 1920s. In part, problems stemmed from the continued preeminence of the family firm in manufacturing and retail. Even more significant was the British propensity to invest overseas. Of the £350 million that British society committed annually to net investment prior to 1914, £200 million typically "went abroad". Of the money that was invested at home, little found its way from London's financial markets to the factories in Britain's north.[39] Failing to modernize, Britain's once world-leading textile and engineering sectors went into a death spiral. Production of woven cloth fell from 8,050 million square yards to 2,100

---

[37] Stephen Kotkin, *Armageddon Averted: The Soviet Collapse, 1970–2000* (Cambridge, UK: Cambridge University Press, 2001), 43.

[38] Bradley Bowden, "Trade Union Decline and Transformation: Where to for Employment Relations?" in Bradley Bowden, Jeffrey Muldoon, Anthony Gould and Adela McMurray (eds.), *The Palgrave Handbook of Management History* (Cham, Switzerland: Palgrave Macmillan, 2020), 963, 997.

[39] Sidney Pollard, *Britain's Prime and Britain's Decline: The British Economy 1870–1914* (London, UK: Edward Arnold, 1989), 92.

million square yards between 1913 and the 1950s.[40] As British industry lost its competitive advantage, so the Marxist historian, Eric Hobsbawm noted, it retreated "into trade and finance".[41] The result was Britain's transformation into what were almost two countries, a declining industrial economy in the north and west and a prosperous south-east built around London's finance sector. By 2020, Joel Kotkin observed, London had become a place that:

> ... now exists mainly for investors, their student offspring, and highly-educated professionals ... Today only three of the city's thirty-two boroughs are affordable for people of median income.[42]

THE TRANSFORMATION OF EVERYDAY LIFE: THE RISE AND RISE OF THE SALARIED PROFESSIONAL CLASS

The decline of the old industrial working class is not just a sociological phenomenon. Rather, it profoundly alters the orientation of the entire civilization. For it is not only the old industrial working class that has suffered decay and diminishment. So too have the institutions, most notably trade unions, that were its creation. As blue-collar employment in not only manufacturing but also mining, transport and agriculture fell away, union membership went into steep decline almost everywhere. Or, to the more exact, unions both declined and were transformed into something which they previously were not: instruments of power for a rising professional middle class who benefited from an expansion of state-subsidized employment.

In Australia, where union density stood at an incredible 64.9% in 1948, the correlation between the disintegration of the blue-collar working class and union decline is striking. Between 1947–1948 and 2016 Australian union density fell from 64.9 to 14.6%. During the same period, the percentage of workers engaged in blue-collar pursuits declined from 60.7 to 21.9%.[43] Increasingly, moreover, unionism was associated with neither

---

[40] Hobsbawm, *Industry and Empire*, 189, 252.

[41] Ibid., 191.

[42] Joel Kotkin, *The Coming of Neo-Feudalism: A Warning to the Global Middle Class* (New York, NY: Encounter Books, 2020), 133.

[43] Bowden, "Trade union decline", 980, Figure 5.

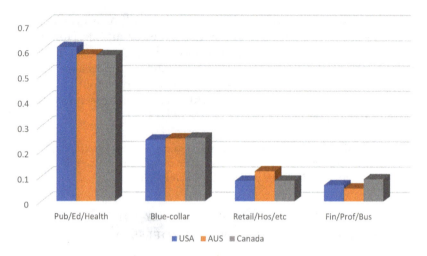

Fig. 11.6 Union membership by occupational categories, 2017–2018: the United States, Australia and Canada (in percent) (*Note* Canadian and US figure for 2017. Australian figures for 2018. *Source* Bowden, "Trade Union Decline and Transformation", Figure 4)

industrial workers nor low-wage service employees, but rather with comparatively well-paid professionals employed in a handful of industries. By 2018, as Fig. 11.6 suggests, workers from just three industries, each associated with professional employment—public administration, health, education—accounted for 58% of unionists. Less than a quarter were from blue-collar industries. Fewer came from private-sector service industries, be they ones associated with low wages or high pay. Near identical circumstances prevailed in Canada and the United States and, indeed, most other OECD economies.[44]

The ascendency of salaried professionals within the ranks of organized labor points to the growing dominance of the professional middle class in western society more generally. In 2019, for example, there were 14.7 million US workers engaged in "managerial occupations". Another 7.2 million were listed as business and finance professionals. The health and education sectors employed 18.5 million professionals. A further

[44] Ibid., 978, Figure 4.

16.1 million professionals were engaged in computing, architecture, engineering, the physical and social sciences and in legal services. Collectively, these sectors boasted 56.5 million workers. By comparison, the combined number of workers in manufacturing (15.1 million), construction (8.4 million) and transport (6.7 million) totaled but 30.2 million.[45]

In his recent study, *The Coming of Neo-Feudalism*, Joel Kotkin argues that the emergence of this salaried middle class is a fundamentally new phenomenon, heralding what he refers to as the "clerisy", a "new form of aristocracy".[46] Similarly, Christopher Lasch, in his *The Revolt of the Elites and the Betrayal of Democracy*, also saw in the "new professional and managerial elites" a "new class", whose "livelihoods rest not so much on the ownership of property as on the manipulation of information and professional expertise".[47] While the social weight of this class is, no doubt, greater than ever, the idea that its ascent is a recent phenomenon is nevertheless erroneous. In country after country, salaried professionals were key to the emergence of the modern bureaucratic state during the European Age of Absolutism. In the post-1850 world, they were also key to the growth of the private sector as the combination of a consumer revolution and a revolution in transported demanded a corresponding revolution in business organization. The result, Alfred Chandler famously observed, was the "multiunit enterprise" that internalized a host of functions: purchasing, production, human relations, industrial research, marketing and so on.[48]

Typically, late nineteenth- and early twentieth-century multiunit enterprises expanded both horizontally (merging with or taking over rivals in the same product line) and vertically (in mergers and takeovers that delivered control of their entire logistics chain). As a result, Chandler observed in what is arguably the most-cited sentence in business history:

---

[45] United States Bureau of Labor Statistics, *Economic News Release: Table 3—Union Affiliation of Employed Wage and Salary Workers by Occupation and Industry, 2019–2020* (Washington, DC: Bureau of Labor Statistics, 2020), https://www.bls.gov/news.release/union2.t03.htm.

[46] Kotkin, *Coming of Neo-Feudalism*, 1, 7.

[47] Christopher Lasch, *The Revolt of the Elites and the Betrayal of Democracy* (New York and London: W.W. Norton & Co., 1995), 33–34.

[48] Alfred D. Chandler, J., *The Visible Hand: The Managerial Revolution in America Business* (Cambridge, MA: Belknap Press, 1977), 7–8.

... the visible hand of management replaced the invisible hand of market forces in coordinating the flow [of goods] from the suppliers of raw materials to the ultimate consumer.[49]

Chandler also observed that to achieve this coordinating feat each enterprise was required to employ a vast "hierarchy of middle and top salaried managers".[50] By 1860, Chandler estimated, America's railroads "probably employed more accountants and auditors than the federal or any state government".[51] In Britain, this new class of private-sector managers, administrators, typists and the like, grew almost ten-fold between 1851 and 1911, its numbers rising from 91,000 to 900,000. Of the latter cohort, 17% were female.[52] On the eve of World War I, Hobsbawm estimates, this salaried middle class was already more numerically significant than Britain's old economically independent middle class of shopkeepers, small-business owners and self-employed professionals (barristers, doctors, and so on).[53]

As salaried professionals grew in number and importance, their life experiences—built around education, social mobility and suburban living away from the old inner-city factory belt—came to redefine western civilization to an even-greater degree than the circumstances of the proletariat.

Whereas it had been wealth that had primarily demarked the older, economically independent middle class, the hallmark of the growing class of salaried professionals was educational attainment. In both the historic West and the societies drawn into its orbit, the advance of secondary and, more particularly, university education went hand in hand with its ascendancy. In Britain the number of so-called "public schools" (that is, the elite private schools) grew from nine in the 1840s to 160 in the early 1900s. Typically, not only in Britain but also in France and Germany, the expansion of secondary education was associated with a focus on cultural attributes that distinguished one from the "lower classes". In 1890, French *lycées*, for example, spent 77% of their time instilling the

---

[49] Ibid., 315.

[50] Ibid., 3.

[51] Ibid., 110.

[52] Hobsbawm, *Age of Empire*, 52.

[53] Hobsbawm, *Industry and Empire*, 167–169.

virtues of a "classic" education (philosophy, languages, history, geography). Even in Prussia, with its supposed militarist and business focus, three times as many students were enrolled in classic *gymnasiums* in 1885 as in technical-oriented colleges. Western-style universities also became a global phenomenon. By 1920, Asian societies boasted twenty universities, compared to only five in 1875. In Latin America, the number of universities grew from thirty to forty between 1875 and 1913. In Europe, there were 150 universities by 1913. It was, however, the society that came to be most associated with a middle-class existence, the United States, which boasted the largest number of universities. On the eve of World War I, a college education was offered at some 500 institutions.[54]

One of the attributes that defined the new professional middle class was found in the ways it treated its female members. While working-class females participated in the new industrial economy in ever-greater numbers—with Britain's female textile workers outnumbering males by 272,000–250,000 in 1851—few worked after marriage. Nor did most boast anything more than an elementary education. In contrast, middle-class families increasingly sent their daughters not only to secondary school but also to university. In France, the number of female *lycées* went from zero to 138 between 1880 and 1913. In Britain, the number of publicly funded female secondary schools rose from ninety-nine in 1904–1905 to almost 400 on the eve of World War I. In terms of university education, the United States was, once more, the undoubted leader. By 1910, there were 56,000 females enjoying a college education. In contrast, female enrolments at French, German and Italian universities at this time ranged between 4,500 and 5,000.[55] Initially, no doubt, most middle-class parents would have seen the education of their daughters as an end in itself, rather than as a gateway to a career. Across all classes, only 10% of married British women worked in 1914. Nevertheless, the combination of female education and the expansion of white-collar employment—as teachers, nurses, typists and so on—*did* open up the prospect of a long-term career.

The new professional middle class was demarked by lifestyle as well as education. Traditionally, society's economically independent middle class of shop-owners, merchants and the like, lived in the inner city, either

[54] Hobsbawm, *Industry and Empire*, 178, 174, 345, Table 5.

[55] Hobsbawm, *Age of Empire*, 203–204.

above or adjacent to their work premises. In doing so, they constantly rubbed shoulders with laborers and other urban workers. It was this familiarity that made the bourgeoisie the natural leader of the democratic revolutions that swept Europe between 1789 and 1848. The salaried middle class who grew in number after 1850 lived differently. Taking advantage of new suburban railroads and tramways, they created something entirely novel: the satellite residential suburb that existed only to provide homes for people of like circumstances. By the 1870s, Hobsbawm observed:

> The ideal middle-class house was no longer ... an apartment [but] ... rather a suburbanized country house ... in a miniature park or garden ... It was designed for the convenience of private living rather than social status-striving and role-playing.[56]

Boasting separate bedrooms, kitchens and living areas, the typical suburban house nevertheless lacked something that had been a ubiquitous feature of earlier middle-class homes—servant quarters. Whereas domestic service was still the most common area of female employment in the late nineteenth century, giving jobs to 1.4 million in Britain in 1871, the spread of suburban living made them an increasing rarity. By 1951, only 1% of British families had servants.[57]

Everywhere, the growth of suburban living and the disappearance of servants was associated with another profound alteration in family circumstance: the so-called "demographic transition". Historically, in virtually every pre-industrial society—where Malthusian mechanics exerted an iron grip—a high birth rate had to compensate for a high death rate. Even in (largely Protestant) Northwest Europe, where delayed marriage produced an unusually low birth rate, a woman who survived to fifty in the late eighteenth century gave birth to 4.9 children on average.[58] As industrialization took hold and material circumstances improved, however, the death rate fell. Initially, it was young adults rather than the very young who benefited. In England and Wales, for example, the mortality rate for males aged between 15 and 19 fell by a third between 1838–1942 and

[56] Ibid., 166.

[57] Hobsbawm, *Industry and Empire*, 156–157, 278.

[58] Gregory Clark, *A Farewell to Alms: A Brief Economic History of the World* (Princeton, NJ: Princeton University Press, 2007), 75.

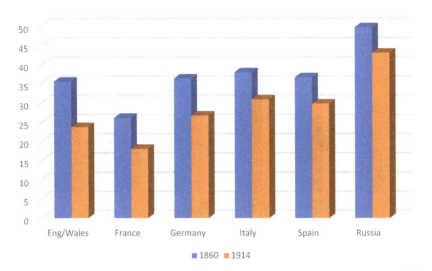

Fig. 11.7 European birth rates, 1860–1913 (births per thousand) (*Source* Trebilcock, *Industrialization of the Continental Powers*, Table 7.12b)

1878–1882, whereas the death rate for those aged under four declined by only 9%.[59] Improvements in material circumstances also caused a spike in the birth rate. People could afford more children. Together, these two factors fueled a dramatic expansion in European population, which almost doubled to 266 million between 1750 and 1850. Then, as people became accustomed to the changed demographic circumstances, the birth rate also began to collapse.

This change, it should be noted, *preceded* any significant advance in contraceptive methods. Instead, as Figs. 11.7 and 11.8 indicate, the more industrialized the society, the more marked was the fall in both the birth rate and the death rate.[60] The partial exception to this rule was France, a society where the birth rate began falling earlier and faster than in other industrializing societies. As the "demographic transition" took hold,

---

[59] Richard Floyd and Bernard Harris, "Health, Height, and Welfare: Britain, 1700–1980", in Richard H. Steckel and Roderick Floud (eds.), *Health and Welfare During Industrialization* (Chicago, IL: University of Chicago Press, 1997), 98, Table 3.1.

[60] Clive Trebilcock, *The Industrialization of the Continental Powers, 1780–1914* (London, UK and New York: Longman, 1981), 451–452, Tables 7.21b, 7.21c.

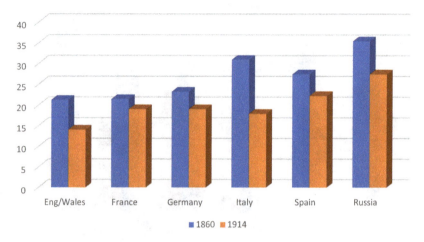

Fig. 11.8 European death rates, 1860–1913 (births per thousand) (*Source* Trebilcock, *Industrialization of the Continental Powers*, Table 7.12c)

wealthy societies were increasingly associated with low rather than high birth rates. The same rule came to apply to families. Previously, large families were typically associated with wealth. In late Tudor to early Stuart England, a rich man fathered 9.2 children on average, while his economically deprived neighbor could lay claim to only 6.4. In late Victorian and Edwardian England, however, the reverse applied. In 1891, professional families had 4.9 children on average, a total that fell to 3.8 in 1911. By contrast, laboring families averaged 6.4 children in 1891 and 4.9 in 1911. In explaining the more rapid decline in the birth rate among the professional middle class, Gregory Clark attributes it to a preference for quality over quantity. Fewer children allowed each child a "better" education.[61]

As a social class, salaried professionals always sought to distinguish themselves politically as well as economically from the farming and working-class populations from which they had ascended at some point in their family past. Between 1850 and the 1960s, the professional middle class were almost always conservative in their political inclinations. Indeed, the predilection of the middle class to vote for the Right and the working class to vote for the Left seemed an iron-law of politics. Since

---

[61] Clark, *Farewell to Alms*, 87, 291–292.

the 1960s, however, the reverse has increasingly applied. It was an alliance of the blue-collar working class, farmers and small-business owners that propelled Donald Trump to the American presidency in 2016 and almost sustained him in office in 2020. In Britain, a similar coalition was behind the Brexit referendum of 2016. Conversely, university-educated professionals are today bastions of the Left. They also tend to be enthusiasts for a range of "woke" political causes: climate change abatement, gender diversity, racial and gender "equity" targets, open immigration and others.

Is the professional middle class's tendency to vote in opposite ways to the working class just a "form of snobbery", as Hobsbawm suggested in the 1980s?[62] Or does it reflect something more fundamental, a tendency to be "naturally attracted to the idea of a society ruled by professional experts … that is, by people like themselves" as Kotkin suggests?[63]

In large part, it would appear, the shifting attitudes of the professional middle class reflects changes in its numerical and social fortunes. As noted in Fig. 11.4, in 1970 those educated to university level amounted to only 10.5% of the adult population even in the United States. In Australia, Britain and France they represented between 5.5 and 8.5% of the total. Yes, it is true, that salaried professionals as a class was much larger. Without a university degree, however, any claim to intellectual and social leadership was threadbare. Instead, salaried professionals typically assumed subaltern positions within the corporate sector. As the university educated grew exponentially in number after 1970, however, this changed. Reflecting on the predilection of France's university educated for postmodernist ideas—a tendency that has since become pronounced in other western societies—Michele Lamont argued that "consumption" of such philosophies represented a "cultural *produit de luxe*". Barely "accessible even for the highly-educated", the capacity to discuss such ideas with any degree of competence, Lamont argued, set one off from the less well educated.[64] At the same time, employment opportunities for the university educated were increasingly found in the public sector or quasi-public sector (for example, education, health, and cultural institutions). Not only did this development link the immediate self-interest of the

---

[62] Hobsbawm, *Age of Empire*, 181.

[63] Kotkin, *Coming of Neo-Feudalism*, 92.

[64] Michael Lamont: "How to Become a Dominant French Philosopher: The Case of Jacques Derrida", *American Journal of Sociology*, Vol. 93, No. 3 (1987), 595.

university educated with an expansion of state funding, it also increased the intellectual distance between work undertaken and the mechanics of production. A salaried professional working for the Pennsylvania Railroad or Standard Oil in the nineteenth century, for example, could hardly have escaped some awareness of market forces and the complexities of industrial processes. By contrast, awareness of the mechanics of capitalist production is hardly a necessary attribute for the typical professional employed today in education or health care.

One consequence of this distance between the life experiences of the university educated and the mechanics of production is the growing tendency to offer simple theoretical solutions to complex practical issues. Nowhere is this more evident than in discussions of climate change, where solutions (for example, achieving "net zero by 2050") are demanded with little appreciation of the devastating consequences that this will entail for the world's energy-intensive economies. Evidence of this was readily available in Britain in 2020–2021, where, after decades of heavy investment in "renewables", solar and wind still made little contribution to electricity generation—and almost nothing to its transport requirements. While "renewables" were responsible for 43% of Britain's power generation, wind and solar only contributed 28.5% of the renewable total. Instead, the greatest contributor to the renewable total (33%) was "solid biomass", a category that largely involved the burning of imported wood chips.[65] Other forms of biomass and biofuels (such as ethanol obtained from corn crops) represented 31.3% of the renewable total. Having cut its coal-fired power generation to near zero, Britain found itself instead increasingly dependent on oil and gas for its power generation. The risks that this entailed were brutally exposed in the autumn of 2021, when the global energy market suffered severe shortages of coal, oil and gas in the aftermath of the bitter Northern Hemisphere winter of 2020–2021. Forced to restart mothballed coal-fired power stations, Britain witnessed power shortages and price spikes that made many areas of production uneconomic. As a spokesperson for British Steel lamented, "The colossal [energy] costs we now face make it impossible to profitably make steel at certain times of the day".[66] The situation became even more dire with the Russian invasion of Ukraine in February 2022; an invasion that saw oil,

[65] United Kingdom Department for Business, Energy and Industrial Strategy, *Digest of UK Energy Statistics: Annual Data for UK, 2020* (London, UK: Government Publishing Service, 2021), Chart 6.1.

[66] Joe Wallace and Collin Eaton, "Scramble for Gas as Northern Winter Looms", *Weekend Australian*, 9–10 October 2021, 26.

gas and energy prices more generally spike to the near-record territory. Amid a European-wide energy crisis, the Boris Johnson-led Conservative government committed to a massive expansion of nuclear power to ally rising public concerns as to the inflationary costs of rising energy bills. It also abandoned its previous opposition to an expansion of North Sea oil and gas production, promising instead to fast-track new petroleum projects.

DIFFERENT MODELS

The idea of a single, monochrome "West" disappears the moment one moves from civilization-wide generalities to national specifics. Instead, what we witness is a variety of national models that have, as often as not, varied markedly over time.

Between 1846, when it abolished the Corn Laws that had restricted agricultural imports, and World War I, Britain resembled the perfect *laissez-faire* state with little by way of either taxation or government spending. Even its vast overseas empire was maintained with surprisingly little expense. By 1950, however, the British economy was characterized by nationalization, regulation and an extensive welfare state. It was, Hobsbawm approvingly declared, "the most state-planned and state-managed economy ever introduced outside a frankly socialist economy".[67] Then, under the direction of Margaret Thatcher (prime minister, 1979–1990), Britain rolled back much of the state's economic footprint. By 2000, government spending represented "only" 36.3% of GDP, compared to 53.5% in 1980.[68]

Across the Channel, France was the original home of the "Bonapartist state", a highly centralized bureaucratic machine that allowed a directing will to control much of French life. The Third (1870–1940) and Fourth (1946–1958) Republics were, however, characterized by weak rather than strong states. In 1960, government spending represented only 23.2% of French GDP, a total that was lower than not only Britain (36.8%) but also

---

[67] Hobsbawm, *Industry and Empire*, 245.

[68] Organisation for Economic Co-operation and Development, *OECD Data: General Government Spending 1970–2019*, https://data.oecd.org/gga/general-government-spe nding.htm. Note: all subsequent post-1970 figures on government spending are drawn from this source unless indicated.

the United States (29.8%).[69] Then, under the Fifth Republic, the state's footprint expanded enormously. By 2008, French government spending represented 53.3% of GDP, a total almost identical to that witnessed in Britain when Thatcher assumed office.

In Germany, following unification in 1871, economic progress was built upon the collaboration of business cartels and a militaristic state. Pre-1914 Germany was, Clive Trebilcock observed, a society dominated by "a collectivist" form of industry that led in the direction of "gigantism", whereby larger cartel members bought out "smaller ones in order to acquire their production quotas".[70] The dangers of this alliance of big business and the state were tragically exposed by Germany's slide into totalitarianism in the early 1930s. Since 1917, Russia, Italy, Spain, Portugal, Greece and the entirety of Eastern Europe have also experienced decades of totalitarian rule. While the United States has been a haven for democracy, by the late nineteenth century it was also the abode of many of the world's corporate giants. If the passage of the Sherman Antitrust Act of 1890 curtailed the growth of German-style cartels, it also, paradoxically, hastened further consolidation. As Chandler noted, the Sherman Act "provided a powerful pressure that did not exist elsewhere to force family firms to consolidate their operations into a single, centrally operated enterprise".[71] For while the Sherman Act restricted cartels and trusts, it had little authority over firms acting singularly.

Although there is considerable national variation among societies of European ancestry, there are also common themes. If we look across all modern societies, one obvious characteristic is the tendency of the state to increase its economic and social footprint. Even here, however, there are major differences.

Figures 11.9 and 11.10—which trace historic patterns of taxation and government spending in the United Kingdom, the United States, France and Sweden—indicate that low levels of taxation and spending were the

---

[69] Esteban Ortiz-Ospina and Max Roser, "Government Spending", *Our World in Data*, https://ourworldindata.org/government-spending. Note: all subsequent pre-1970 figures on government spending are drawn from this source unless indicated.

[70] Trebilcock, *Industrialization of the Continental Powers*, 68.

[71] Chandler, *The Visible Hand*, 499.

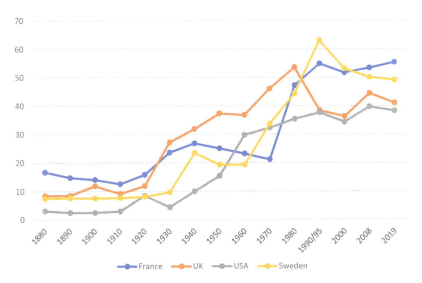

Fig. 11.9 Government spending as share of GDP, 1880–2019: United Kingdom, United States, France and Sweden (*Sources* Ortiz-Ospina and Roser, "Government Spending"; OECD, *General Government Spending 1970–2019*)

norm prior to World War I.[72] In Sweden and the United States, a low-tax, low-spend model was maintained until the 1930s and 1940s, respectively. In the United States, government spending still represented only 9.97% of GDP in 1940. The vast literature that suggests that Franklin Roosevelt's New Deal represented a gigantic Keynesian "stimulus spending" program is, it is evident, one founded in myth. Yes, it is true, that the Roosevelt New Deal administration doubled federal spending when compared to the previous Hoover government, which had in turn doubled its spending in response to the Wall Street crash and subsequent Depression. Such increases, however, occurred from a low base. Both the Hoover and, more particularly, the Roosevelt administrations also offset increased spending

---

[72] Pre-1990 taxation figures are drawn from Esteban Ortiz-Ospina and Max Roser, "Taxation", *Our World in Data*, https://ourworldindata.org/taxation. Post-1990 figures are from, Organisation for Economic Co-operation and Development, *Global Revenue Statistics Database, 1990–2019*—https://stats.oecd.org/Index.aspx?DataSetCode=RS_GBL. Note: all subsequent taxation figures are drawn from these sources unless otherwise indicated.

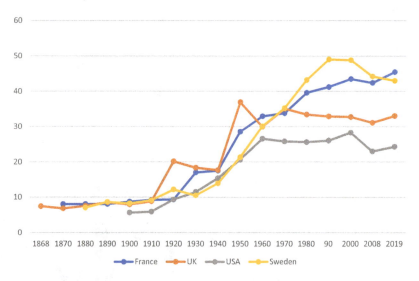

Fig. 11.10 Taxation as share of GDP, 1868–2019: United Kingdom, United States, France and Sweden (*Note* UK figures from 1868; French figures from 1870; Swedish figures from 1880; US figures from 1900. *Sources* Ortiz-Ospina and Roser, "Taxation"; OECD, *Global Revenue Statistics Database*)

with increased taxation. As Price Fishback notes, the resultant deficits "were miniscule".[73] By 1938, the federal deficit had virtually disappeared. State governments also expanded their range of taxes, even as many cut back spending. In consequence, by the late 1930s the state-government sector was running surpluses.[74] Not until 1960 did government spending assume significant peace-time proportions. Even then, the United States still boasted a smaller state sector than the European norm. Since the Thatcherite reforms of the 1980s, British tax and, to a lesser degree, spending patterns have also drawn closer to those of the United States.

In the popular mind, it is Sweden that embodies the modern welfare state with its patterns of high taxation and spending. Until 1930, however, Sweden stood out for its low-tax, low-spend form of government. When it did embrace the welfare state, with government spending

[73] Price Fishback: "US Monetary and Fiscal Policy in the 1930s", *Oxford Review of Economic Policy*, Vol. 26, No. 3 (2010), 386.

[74] Ibid., 386, 402–403.

representing 63% of GDP in 1995, it was also eventually forced into retreat in the face of growing deficits. By 2019, Swedish government spending represented "only" 49% of GDP, a 14% point fall from the peak of 1995. In the wake of the student and worker protests of May 1968, France also became an enthusiast for high-taxing and even higher-spending government. By 2019, government spending represented 53.3% of French GDP, a total matched only by Finland.

A perusal in the differences in scale in Fig. 11.9 (spending) and Fig. 11.10 (taxation) highlight the fact that the modern state has shown a propensity to increase spending at a much faster rate than revenue would allow. In France, for example, government spending represented 54.8% of GDP in 1995, whereas taxation amounted to only 41.2%. In 2019, not that much had changed. While taxation was the equivalent to 45.4% of GDP, government spending represented 55.3%. In the United States, where government spending ranged between 32.2% (1970) and 39.7% (2008) between 1970 and 2019, taxation revenue has seldom budged higher than a quarter of GDP. In the wake of the Thatcherite reforms, British governments have also been more successful in restricting taxation than it has in spending. In 2019, British government spending (41% of GDP) was also significantly higher than taxation revenues (33% of GDP). One consequence of this proclivity to spend at a faster rate than tax receipts would allow is found in an ever-growing debt. As Fig. 11.11 highlights, by 2019 government debt as a percentage of GDP in Britain and the United States was little different to that obtained in France. For while governments in the latter two societies have spent less than France, they have also raised less in taxation. Among the four nations we have been considering, only Sweden has sought to close the gap between government income and expenditure over the last quarter century.[75]

At the core of rising government debt is a relentless growth in "social expenditures" (for example, education, health, subsidized child care) that belies the popular narrative on "neo-liberalism" and the supposed retreat of the "social-democratic" state. As Fig. 11.12 highlights, such expenditures, measured as a share of GDP, have also been consistently higher in the supposed "neo-liberal" societies of Britain and the United States than

---

[75] Organisation for Economic Co-operation and Development, *OECD Data: General Government Debt 1995–2019*, https://data.oecd.org/gga/general-government-debt.htm# indicator-chart.

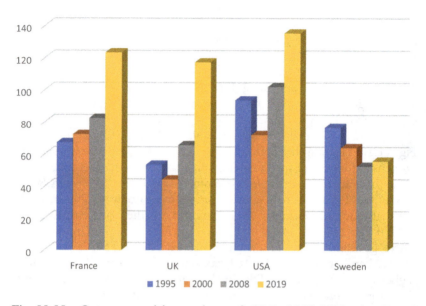

Fig. 11.11 Government debt as share of GDP, 1995–2019: the United Kingdom, the United States, France and Sweden (*Source* OECD, *OECD-Data: General Government Debt*, 1995–2019)

they have been in historically "social-democratic" Canada and Australia.[76] In the United Kingdom this outcome reflects, in part, the continued nationalization of the fast-growing health sector, whereas in the United States it points to the high-tax, high-spend policies of many Democrat-run states (such as California) vis-à-vis Republican-administered states (such as Texas).

The political-economic models that have emerged within western societies since 1850—even among those that have avoided a descent into complete totalitarianism—is thus one marked by considerable variation. This variation can be best understood, as indicated in Table 11.1, by considering each society against a vertical axis that measures state power and a horizontal axis that assesses a society's level of economic concentration, whether associated with private or state ownership. In the late

---

[76] Organisation for Economic Co-operation and Development, *Social Expenditure—Aggregated Data, 1980–2019*, https://stats.oecd.org/index.aspx?datasetcode=socx_agg.

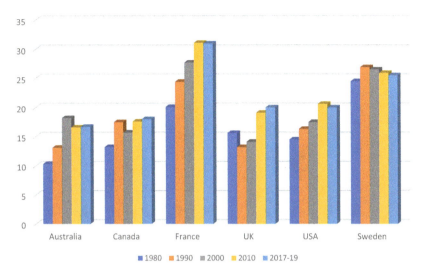

Fig. 11.12 Government social expenditure as share of GDP, 1980 to 2017–2019: the United Kingdom, the United States, France, Sweden, Canada and Australia (*Source* OECD, *Social Expenditure—Aggregated Data*, 1980–2019)

nineteenth century, both Britain and the United States, for example, were characterized by low levels of taxation and state intervention. In the United States, only a favoring of high protective tariffs directed toward the fostering of local manufacturing represented a significant betrayal of the principles of classic liberalism. Whereas, however, much of the American economy was dominated by a handful of corporate giants—for example, Standard Oil, Carnegie Steel, J. P. Morgan—Britain continued to be characterized by small family firms that lacked both "financial power" and "political punch".[77] But by the early 1950s, Britain boasted not only a larger number of corporate giants—Unilever, BP, Anglo-Dutch Shell—but also, more significantly, an array of nationalized industries: coal mining, road transport, health care, power generation and the railways. Most homes constructed in the post-1945 decade were built by the public sector. By the early 1950s, 22% of English and Welsh homes were

---

[77] Pollard, *Britain's Prime and Britain's Decline*, 230.

Table 11.1 Different political-economic models, 1850–2021

Interventionist state					*High industry concentration*
	Peronist Argentina Second Empire France				Britain—1950s Germany—1890–1914
			French 5th Republic 1970–2019		
		French Third and Fourth Republics		USA—2020–2021	
				USA—1870–1914	
Laissez-faire state	Britain—1846–1914				*Low industry concentration*

publicly owned.[78] By comparison with late nineteenth-century Britain, France under the Second Empire of Napoleon III (1852–1870), was a society characterized by a much more powerful state. Economically, however, France remained a society dominated by small family-owned enterprises.[79]

Given the temporal and spatial variation in patterns of state intervention, is it even possible to speak of a "western" economic and social model that has had enduring force? If so, does the growing economic footprint of the modern state represent a fundamental threat to the model of civilization that emerged around 1850? The short answer to these questions is, yes and yes.

At its outset, the reforged western civilization was defined by three features, each of which was integral to its success: democracy, liberalism (such as individual rights, protection of property, a preference for market solutions) and an energy-intensive economy. Significantly, the connection between these three elements has been inherently unstable. As a political system, democracy is, at least in the short term, compatible with a powerful bureaucratic state, most particularly when the extension of state power adds to the majority's material benefit. An energy-intensive economy is, in the modern world, a characteristic feature of authoritarian regimes as well as liberal democracies. Of the three characteristic features of modern western civilization, it is thus, as argued in Part 2, liberalism that is most decisive and also the most elusive element. It is liberalism, not democracy, that underpins individualism and entrepreneurship. Without liberalism, a society seeking to replicate western success finds itself lumbered with an outwardly healthy corpse.

As the state's footprint grew in significance in the latter half of the twentieth century, old debates as to the appropriate role of the state once more moved to center stage.

Significantly, in articulating what has come to be referred to as the "neo-liberal" critique of the modern state, the Chicago-based economist, Milton Friedman placed his primary emphasis on freedom rather than economic performance—even while believing that possession of the

---

[78] Hobsbawm, *Industry and Empire*, 266–267.

[79] See, for example, the commentary in, Karl Marx, "The Eighteenth Brumaire of Louis Bonaparte", in Karl Marx and Frederick Engels, *Selected Works*, vol. 1 (Moscow, USSR: Foreign Languages Publishing House, 1951), 303.

former was key to the latter. "As liberals", Friedman recorded in *Capitalism and Freedom*, "we take freedom of the individual, or perhaps the family, as our ultimate goal in judging social arrangements".[80] And the "fundamental threat to freedom", Friedman argued—as had Mill, Bentham and Hayek before him—was:

> ... power to coerce, be it in the hands of a monarch, a dictator, an oligarchy, or a momentary majority. The preservation of freedom requires the elimination of such concentration of power to the fullest extent.[81]

What gave the modern bureaucratic state its popular appeal, Friedman argued, was its association with an ever-increasing array of benefits and services. "Welfare rather than freedom", Friedman concluded, "became the dominant note in democratic countries".[82]

In contrast to this neo-liberal critique, which places matters relating to freedom and power at center stage, supporters of state interference rarely, if ever, worry themselves about such matters. Instead, matters relating to inequality and wealth redistribution are typically given pride of place. In his *Capital in the Twenty-First Century*, Thomas Piketty, for example, argues that the concentration of a disproportionate share of private wealth in the hands of a few "rests on public poverty", that is, the wealthy are not contributing enough to the state with its redistributive capacities.[83] This redistributive focus also characterizes the so-called New Green Deal, a US legislative proposal brought before Congress by Alexandria Ocasio-Cortez in February 2019 that subsequently became the basis for the Biden administration's "Build Back Better" program. Calling for a government-led "national, social, industrial and economic mobilization on a scale not seen since World War II", the New Green Deal pointed to "the greatest income inequality since the 1920s" as proof of the need for action, alongside "climate change, pollution, and environmental destruction [that] have exacerbated racial, regional, social, environmental and

---

[80] Milton Friedman (in association with Rose Friedman), *Capitalism and Freedom*, fortieth anniversary edition (Chicago and London: Chicago University Press, 2002), 12.

[81] Ibid., 15.

[82] Ibid., 10–11.

[83] Thomas Piketty, *Capital in the Twenty-First Century* (Cambridge, MA: Cambridge University Press, 2014), 566.

economic injustices".[84] To the extent that the state is seen as a source of oppression in such redistributive narratives, it is found in the association of the state with capitalism, colonialism and racism. As Joe Feagin expresses it in his highly influential study, *The White Racial Frame*:

> The European theft of land and super-exploitation of enslaved labor were presided over by ever-growing and bureaucratized nation-states, the latter usually described by Western social scientists as signs of the modernization process. From its beginnings, European colonialism relied not only on a growing entrepreneurial bourgeoisie but also on these nation-state governments.[85]

Seen from this latter perspective, the problems associated with the bureaucratic state relate not to its power per se, but rather its historic linkages with capitalism, colonialism and racism. Accordingly, what is sought is not the diminishment of the state's power but rather its redirection toward a "liberty-and-justice frame" undertaken as part of a "deframing and reframing" of society's "dominant racial frame".[86]

Despite the supposed ascendancy of "neo-liberalism" that has become a ubiquitous feature of academic discourse, a perusal of Figs. 11.9, 11.10, 11.11 and 11.12 suggests a reverse conclusion: that "neo-liberals" in the post-Thatcher (1979–1990) and Reagan (1981–1989) era have lost the intellectual and policy debate. If, to date, the principles of democracy and freedom have survived this shift, the economic consequences have nevertheless been disastrous, manifest in anemic (and often negative) growth in productivity and per capita GDP. To the extent that the world has witnessed technological innovation in the last twenty years it has been largely confined to information technology, a sector where the flow-on effects to the world of material production are typically modest. As Fig. 11.13 indicates, the result has been two decades of declining multifactor productivity. In the thirteen years between 2007 and 2019, France, Canada and Australia experienced negative productivity growth in five of

---

[84] United States House of Representatives, *Resolution Recognizing the Duty of the Federal Government to Create a New Green Deal* (Washington, DC: House of Representatives, 5 February 2019), https://s3.documentcloud.org/documents/5729033/Green-New-Deal-FINAL.pdf [accessed 28 December 2021].

[85] Joe R. Feagin, *The White Racial Frame: Centuries of Racial Framing and Counter-framing*, third edition (New York and London: Routledge, 2020), 37.

[86] Ibid., 246.

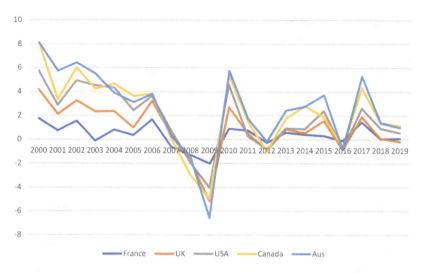

Fig. 11.13 Annual changes in multifactor productivity, 2000–2019: France, the United Kingdom, the United States, Canada and Australia (*Source* OECD, *OECD-Data: Multifactor Productivity*, 1985–2019)

them. In Britain, productivity went backward in six. Even in the United States, a society where the state's economic footprint is less than elsewhere, productivity went backward twice (2008, 2011) and was close to zero on two other occasions (2013, 2016).[87]

Paradoxically, the growth in the state's economic footprint amid an expansion of "social expenditures" (see Fig. 11.12), has been associated with increased inequality. As Thomas Piketty noted in his *Capital in the Twenty-First Century*, the bottom 50% of Western Europe's population own "less than 10% of national wealth".[88] Similar circumstances were identified in virtually every other modern society. Logically, such outcomes should not come as a surprise. A job is typically a better guarantee of economic security than a welfare cheque. As Piketty himself conceded, the main *causal* factor behind increased inequality "over the

---

[87] Organisation for Economic Co-operation and Development, *OECD Data: Multifactor Productivity 1985–2019*, https://data.oecd.org/lprdty/multifactor-productivity.htm#indicator-chart.

[88] Piketty, *Capital in the Twenty-First Century*, 257.

past few decades" is a "return to a regime of relatively slow growth". Under this "regime", Piketty accurately observed, economic mobility is inevitably curtailed. In consequence, wealth concentrates in two groups, whom Piketty describes as a new class of "supermanagers" and those benefiting from "hyperpatrionial" outcomes, such as inherited wealth.[89]

In pursuing a political-economic model that emphasizes public-sector expenditure and employment over private-sector prosperity and productivity, and redistribution over wealth creation, it is evident that the societies of the twenty-first century West are obtaining neither greater income inequality nor productivity-based prosperity.

GLOBAL INTERDEPENDENCE

The post-1850 "West" appeared to the Indigenous peoples of the Americas, Africa, Asia and Oceania in many guises: destroyer, customer, supplier, educator, modernizer. How one perceived the new industrialized civilization depended in large part on where one stood. For the Native American peoples of the American and Canadian West—a people whom George Catlin described in the 1830s as living "entirely in a state of primitive wilderness"[90]—the advance of the industrialized civilization spelled the irretrievable destruction of their way of life. In the vast stretches of northern Australia, the new civilization's advance also entailed destruction of the Indigenous population's traditional way of life. At the same time, however, it involved new working experiences as fencers, station-hands and, above all, as mounted stockmen in the export-oriented cattle industry. Until the advent of helicopter mustering in the 1960s the Aboriginal stockman was an iconic figure in the Outback. As workers, one official observed in the early 1930s, Aboriginal stockmen were far superior to the "often useless" whites who offered themselves.[91]

For the Egyptian family of Sayyid Qutb, the future leader of the Muslim Brotherhood, the new civilization presented itself in the early twentieth century as an avenue for social mobility, Qutb's mother telling him:

[89] Ibid., 25, 264–265.

[90] George Catlin, *Letters and Notes on the Manner, Customs and Conditions of North American Indians*, vol. 1 (New York: Dover Publications, 1973), 23.

[91] Cited, Ros Kidd, "Missing in Action: Industrial Relations and Aboriginal Labour", in Bradley Bowden, Simon Blackwood, Cath Rafferty and Cameron Allan (eds.), *Work & Strife in Paradise: The History of Labour Relations in Queensland 1859–2009* (Sydney, AUS: Federation Press, 2009), 134–135.

When you get older you will go to Cairo and stay with your uncle and you will get an education there and become an effendi [official] and receive a salary ... Then you will have lots of money in your pocket.[92]

In the wake of a successful bureaucratic career, however, Qutb came to perceive the world that the West had reforged in a different light. The global order created by "capitalism", Qutb advised the faithful, was centered around a spiritual void and "greed for wealth".[93]

Among the Indigenous peoples of Africa, Asia and Oceania, the "West" loomed large after 1850 in ways that were both destructive and transformative. Seen from this perspective, it was easy to conclude that "western" success was built on the transferred riches of the non-western world. As previously noted, this is certainly how the West Indies-born, French-educated, Algerian revolutionary, Franz Fanon perceived it. This is also certainly how the Russian Marxist, Vladimir Lenin, saw it in his highly influential *Imperialism, the Highest Stage of Capitalism*. Imperialism was, Lenin declared:

> ... capitalism in that stage of development in which the dominance of monopolies and finance capitalism has established itself ... in which the division of the world among the international trusts has begun.[94]

For an Indian dockhand standing on the waterfront of Bombay or Madras in 1910, and witnessing the seemingly endless supplies of cotton, jute and tea being loaded for export, the words of Lenin would have appeared as self-evident truths. Similarly, for Jawaharlal Nehru, India's post-independence prime minister, such trends were proof of an entirely exploitative relationship. It was, Nehru recorded in 1936, the "exploitation of India that gave England the needed capital to develop her great industries".[95] Even the published Indian customs receipts, a summary of which appears in Fig. 11.14, provided apparent confirmation. In every

---

[92] Sayyid Qutb (trans. John Calvert and William Shepherd), *Child from the Village* (Cairo, Egypt: American University in Cairo Press, 2005), 129.

[93] Sayyid Qutb, *Milestones*, https://cryptome.org/2017/10/Milestones-Qutb.pdf, 26.

[94] V.I. Lenin, "Imperialism, the Highest Stage of Capitalism", in V.I. Lenin, *Selected Works* (Moscow, USSR: Foreign Languages Publishing House, 1946), 709.

[95] Jawaharlal Nehru, "India and the world, 6 January 1936), in Jawaharlal Nehru, *Selected Works of Jawaharlal Nehru* (Delhi, India: Jawaharlal Nehru Memorial Fund, 1988), 53.

11 A GLOBALIZED CIVILIZATION: ASCENDANCY, CONTRADICTIONS ... 307

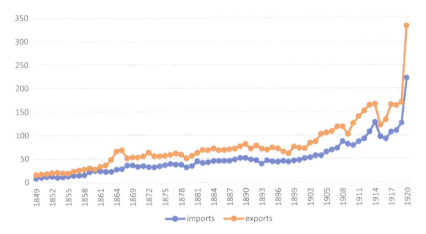

Fig. 11.14 Merchandise imports and exports, British India, 1849–1920 (British pounds sterling, millions) (*Sources* UK Parliament, *Statistical Abstract ... British India*, 1840–1865, 1885–1886 to 1894–1895, 1894–1895 to 1903–1904)

year between 1849 and 1920, India's merchandise exports exceeded its imports.[96] Prior to 1860, as Fig. 11.15 highlights, opium was the lead export, a narcotic that was shipped to China by British traders in exchange for tea. During the American Civil War, cotton assumed pride of place. Between 1890 and 1920, jute, cotton and cereals competed for first place.[97]

If a dockhand or customs clerk in Bombay had reason to conclude that India's exports were central to Britain's success, a dockhand located in London or Liverpool would have garnered a different view. As Fig. 11.16, which draws upon British customs' records, indicates, India's contribution to British merchandise imports was modest in the extreme, typically representing between 7 to 8% of the total. By the 1890s, Australia made a larger contribution. West Indian, Chinese and Egyptian imports were

---

[96] UK Parliament, *Statistical Abstract ... British India, 1840–1865*, Figure 29; UK Parliament, *Statistical Abstract ... British India, 1885–86–1894–95*, Figures 108, 109; UK Parliament, *Statistical Abstract ... British India, 1910–11–1919–20*, Figure 133.

[97] UK Parliament, *Statistical Abstract ... British India 1840–1865*, Figure 33; UK Parliament, *Statistical Abstract ... British India 1885–86–1894–95*, Figure 117; UK Parliament, *Statistical Abstract ... British India 1910–11–1919–20*, Figure 138.

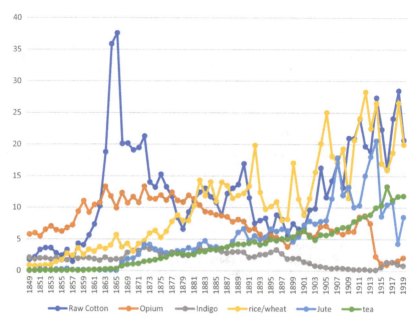

Fig. 11.15 Principal merchandise exports, British India, 1849–1919 (British pounds sterling, millions) (*Sources* UK Parliament, *Statistical Abstract … British India*, 1840–1865, 1885–1886 to 1894–1895, 1894–1895 to 1903–1904)

even more inconsequential. By 1900, Argentinian imports were more significant than all three, considered individually. After 1870, French imports overshadowed the *combined* imports from the West Indies, China and Egypt. As is self-evident, it was the United States that was Britain's most important source of imports, a nation over which Britain had long lost any colonial claim. In 1880, the United States provided almost a quarter of British imports. By 1900, it was providing well over a third. As Fig. 11.17 indicates, India was more significant as an export destination. Even here, however, we should not overstate the case. Between 1855 and 1900, India typically took only 8–11% of Britain's exports. By 1900, Australia was taking more. China, Egypt and the West Indies were

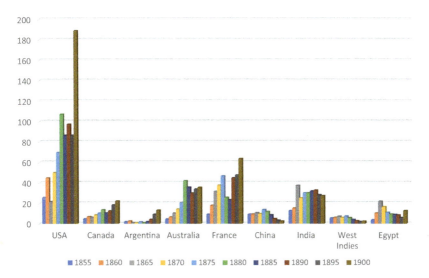

Fig. 11.16 British merchandise imports by nation of origin, 1855–1900 (British pounds sterling, millions) (*Sources* UK Parliament, *Statistical Abstract … United Kingdom*, 1853–1867, 1871–1885, 1886–1900)

of little consequence. In 1900, Canada imported more British goods than China and the West Indies combined, and Argentina almost as much.[98]

In explaining Britain's relationship with its key suppliers around 1900, Hobsbawm recorded:

> Argentine and Uruguayan *estancieros*, Australian wool-growers and Danish farmers had no interest in encouraging national manufacturers, for they did very well out of being economic planets in the British solar system.[99]

---

[98] United Kingdom Parliament, *Statistical Abstract of the United Kingdom 1853–1867* (London, UK: George R. Eyre and William Spottiswoode, 1868), 14–15, Table; United Kingdom Parliament, *Statistical Abstract of the United Kingdom 1871–1885* (London, UK: Eyre and Spottiswoode, 1886), 41–47, Table 22; United Kingdom Parliament, *Statistical Abstract of the United Kingdom 1886–1900* (London, UK: Eyre and Spottiswoode, 1901), 50–57, Table 26.

[99] Hobsbawm, *Industry and Empire*, 40.

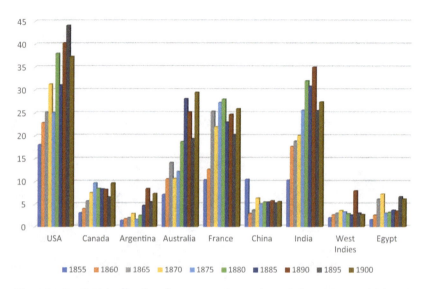

Fig. 11.17 British merchandise exports by nation of destination, 1855–1900 (British pounds sterling, millions) (*Sources* UK Parliament, *Statistical Abstract ... United Kingdom*, 1853–1867, 1871–1885, 1886–1900)

Seen from this perspective, the peoples of the New World existed in a relationship of dependency with the societies of the Old World. As a resident of Victoria's Western Districts, long regarded as the nation's preeminent wool country, I doubt, however, that too many Australian sheep-lords ever saw themselves as mere "planets in the British solar system".

Interdependency, rather than dependency, best sums post-1850 global relationships. Between 1851 and 1892, for example, the US wheat exports rose from 1 million bushels (one bushel is 60 lbs.) to 152 million bushels as farmers benefited from the elimination of the effects of distance.[100] At the same time, Britain's reliance on imported wheat became almost total. Sociologically, this transformation proved the final nail in the coffin for Britain's aristocracy as the agricultural value of land in Essex and Kent was equalized with that of Iowa and Nebraska. Across England, the grand country estate became an economic millstone, falling into disrepair unless sustained by income from other pursuits.

[100] US Department of Commerce, *Historical Statistics*, Series U 274–294.

Across southern Europe, the effects of New World supply were even more destructive. As early as 1850, US wheat landed in Spain was cheaper than the local product. Similar circumstances prevailed in Italy. Although both Spain and Italy resorted to agricultural tariffs these merely entrenched increasingly backward rural sectors. In southern Italy, only 200,000 additional jobs were generated between 1861 and 1936, even though the population grew by 5.7 million.[101]

In a global economy where the tyranny of distance was largely abolished, market forces and monetarized relationships became the key drivers of economic decisions. Admittedly, there were exceptions to this rule. The consumption of opium was forced upon China in the so-called Opium Wars (1839–1842, 1856–1860) to offset the balance-of-payments deficits that western powers were incurring in their Chinese trade. Until exposed by the British public servant (and future Irish revolutionary), Roger Casement, the Belgium Congo under the personal rule of Leopold II (1885–1908) was a monstrous place, the population subject to effective slavery in the interests of a single individual. In adding to the land dedicated to cotton during the American Civil War, however, Indian farmers were not driven by British guns. Rather, they undertook the switch because higher prices made it highly profitable. In India, as elsewhere, farmers increasingly engaged in export-oriented agricultural for like reasons. In the case of India, the balance-of-trade merchandise surplus evident in Fig. 11.14 was offset by the inflow of British "treasure" (silver and gold currency), evident in Fig. 11.18. During the American Civil War, treasure imports grew from £10.7 million in 1861 to £23 million in 1864, offsetting the merchandise surplus that India incurred. When Britain drew on Indian resources during World War I, an even bigger transfer occurred, Indian treasure imports rising from £14.4 million in 1915 to £78.2 million in 1920.[102] If some Indians were disadvantaged by their society's incorporation into global markets, others grew rich.

British transfers of treasure entailed investment in Indian tea-plantations, jute mills and mines, as well as commodity purchases. For as wealth accumulated in Britain and other industrializing societies, a growing class of middle-class investors ventured their capital abroad,

---

[101] Trebilcock, *Industrialization of the Continental Powers*, 327.

[102] UK Parliament, *Statistical Abstract ... British India 1840–1865*, Figure 29; UK Parliament, *Statistical Abstract ... British India 1910–11–1919–20*, Figures 144, 145.

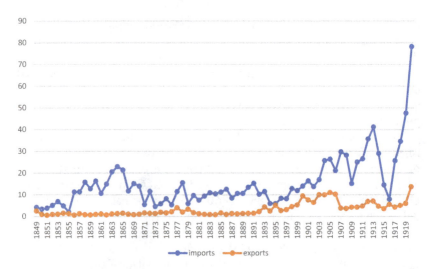

Fig. 11.18 Imports and exports of treasure, British India, 1849–1920 (British pounds sterling, millions) (*Sources* UK Parliament, *Statistical Abstract … British India*, 1840–1865, 1885–1886 to 1894–1895, 1894–1895 to 1903–1904)

seeking more remunerative returns than what they could obtain in home markets. Lenin, in his *Imperialism, the Highest Stage of Capitalism*, identified overseas investment as the modern world's defining characteristic, declaring:

> Under the old capitalism … the export of goods was the most typical feature. Under modern capitalism … the export of capital has become the typical feature.[103]

Despite their imperial conquests, however, comparatively little of this investment went into African or Asian societies, although what was invested often had an outsized effect. In the 1880s, British investment in India represented less than a fifth of its overseas total. Far more, some 30% of the total, went to Britain's white-settler colonies (Canada, Australia, South Africa, New Zealand). Similar totals went to South America, most

---

[103] Lenin, "Imperialism", 687.

particularly Chile, Uruguay and, above all, Argentina.[104] In Lenin's estimation, the purpose of such investments was purely exploitative. A similar Manichean perspective is evident in Parthasarthi's *Why Europe Grew Rich and Asia did Not*, where he concludes that "the British colonial state had little desire or interest in promoting industrial development".[105] What is overlooked in this black-and-white view of the world is the ways in which the pursuit of self-interested profits delivered the recipients of investment a legacy of enduring assets. It was, for example, the British railway system that forged a unified national market in India for the first time. Entirely new industries—coal mining, airlines, mechanized textile manufacture—were created. In the opinion of the British management historian, Sidney Pollard, this pattern of investment was entirely destructive of Britain's—not India's—long-term interests. By 1914, he observed, a third of Britain's wealth was located overseas, denying its own industries the funds desperately needed for modernization.[106]

If Britain's colonial investments disadvantaged rather than benefited its own narrow industrial interests, Britain's survival after 1851 was nevertheless totally reliant on the new global patterns of interdependence. Without the meat and cereal of the North American prairies and the South American pampas, its people would have starved. Without the cotton of India, Egypt and the United States, and the wool of Australia, its textile mills would have failed. Conversely, without export markets the farmers of Argentina, Canada, Australia and India, would have enjoyed less prosperous circumstances—if they survived at all. By the close of the nineteenth century, however, Britain had lost its central position in the world market to two rising powers: the United States and Germany. In reflecting upon the importance of German economic success to European and, indeed, world prosperity on the eve of World War I, John Maynard Keynes recorded:

> The statistics of the economic interdependence of Germany and her neighbours are overwhelming. Germany was the best customer of Russia, Norway, Holland, Belgium, Switzerland, Italy, and Austria-Hungary; she was the second-best customer of Great Britain, Sweden, and Denmark …

[104] Hobsbawm, *Industry and Empire*, 147–148.

[105] Prasanan Parthasarthi, *Why Europe Grew Rich and Asia Did Not: Global Economic Divergence 1600–1850*, (Cambridge, UK: Cambridge University Press, 2011), 259.

[106] Pollard, *Britain's Decline*, 61–62, 230.

She was the largest source of supply to Russia, Norway, Sweden, Denmark, Holland, Switzerland, Austria-Hungary, Romania, and Bulgaria; and the second largest source of supply to Great Britain, Belgium, and France.[107]

Without the integration of a prosperous, liberal-democratic Germany into the global economy, Keynes concluded in his *The Economic Consequences of the Peace*, nothing but disaster would result. The subsequent history of the twentieth century provided proof of this conclusion.

SAMENESS

Across the globe, we have witnessed in the post-1850 world a convergence in terms of life expectancy, nutritional standards, literacy, access to the internet, patterns of consumption and lived experiences more generally. At the same time, a combination of migration, travel and overseas study and work has collapsed the physical barriers between the old western heartlands and the rest of the world, creating cosmopolitan, multi-racial cities and societies that are nevertheless clearly western in economic and technological orientation. In London, 37% of the population are currently immigrants. In Brussels, 40% of the population are born elsewhere. In Australia, almost a third of the population was born overseas in 2020 with a third of these were born in Asia.[108] In Canada, where more than a fifth of the population is born overseas, two-thirds of the immigrants who arrived between the 2011 and 2016 census came from Asia. More disembarked from Africa than Europe.[109] For most immigrants, disembarkation seldom involves the cultural and economic wrench of yesteryear. Instead, most find the day-to-day attributes of life and work to be broadly similar to that which they left behind—a point of departure to which they will most likely return easily and often.

Sameness in terms of the *material* attributes of everyday life, however, has *never* entailed sameness in terms of economic outcome, either at an individual or a national level. Nor has it *ever* produced societies with

[107] Keynes, *Economic Consequences of the Peace*, 14–15.

[108] Kotkin, *Coming of Neo-Feudalism*, 124; Australian Bureau of Statistics, *Migration Australia, 2019–2020*, (Canberra; AUS: Australian Bureau of Statistics, 2021), Table 1.2.

[109] Statistics Canada, *Immigration and Ethnocultural Diversity: Results from the 2016 Census*, The Daily—Immigration and Ethnocultural Diversity: Key Results from the 2016 Census (statcan.gc.ca) [accessed 26 November 2021].

identical social structures. On the contrary, as noted in Table 11.1, even *within* the historic West there was *always* more than one model of the new industrialized iteration of western civilization. Outside the historic West, the process of global transformation has been even more complex. It was certainly *never* simply a process of imperial dictation, as Lenin would have us believe. Rather, it was the product of a process of acceptance and rejection that expressed itself in a myriad of ways. Even within the historic West itself, support for the three key attributes of the new iteration of western civilization—democracy, liberalism and an energy-intensive economy—has waxed and waned. Today, increasing numbers reject some or all of these characteristic features. It is thus evident that the modern version of western civilization—like every civilization before it—constantly confronts its members with fundamental choices. It is to the nature of these choices that we turn in our final chapter.

CHAPTER 12

Choices and the *Milletization* of Western Society

In most societies, across time and space, a person's identity has been inseparable from the collective entity to which they belong, be it a clan, tribe, religious or ethnic group. Describing the situation that prevailed among the peasantry of imperial Russia in the mid-nineteenth century, the Russian novelist, Alexander Herzen, observed:

> The Russian peasant has no real knowledge of any form of life but that of the village commune: he understands rights and duties only when these are tied to the commune and its members.[1]

Although most land in central Russia belonged to the aristocracy, it was the commune, the *mir*, that allocated labor, collected taxes and determined who would be selected for military service. At regular intervals, the *mir* also redistributed land between peasant households in a system that Herzen idealized as "rural communism".[2] Things were little different in pre-Columbian Inca society. The ordinary Inca, Hemming recorded,

---

[1] Alexander Herzen, "The Russian People and Socialism", in Alexander Herzen (ed. Richard Wolheim), *From the Other Side & The Russian People and Socialism* (London, UK: Weidenfeld and Nicholson, 1956), 183.

[2] Ibid., 189.

© The Author(s), under exclusive license to Springer Nature Switzerland AG 2022
B. Bowden, *Slavery, Freedom and Business Endeavor*,
Palgrave Debates in Business History,
https://doi.org/10.1007/978-3-030-97232-5_12

317

"farmed and lived collectively, with no private property, strongly bound to their families and clans, villages and fields".[3]

No task is more difficult for a culture that gives primacy to collective expressions of identity than that of balancing concerns of dissimilar groups. Superficially, none achieved this task more successfully than Ottoman Turkey. Whereas ancient Rome sought to overcome competing loyalties (between, for example, the Gauls, Germans, Greeks and so on) by extending Roman citizenship in ways that created linguistic and cultural homogeneity, Ottoman Turkey instituted what is known to history as the *millet* system. Under this system, each religious and ethnic *millet*—Armenian Christians, Greek Orthodox, Georgian Christians and others—had the legal right to use its own language, operate its own churches and schools, and even maintain its own judicial system. Except in matters pertaining to state security, members of each *millet* typically sought justice according to their own laws, rather than those that applied to Ottoman Muslims. In describing the *millet* system, Ebubekir Ceylan argues that Ottoman Turkey "was a classic example of a plural society", one that "was committed to the protection, promotion and maintenance of ethno-cultural diversities".[4] Similarly, for Barkey and Gavrilis the Ottoman system was proof of a society which "understood that ... diversity could not and should not be assimilated into an overarching principle of sameness".[5]

As with other systems of rigorously enforced collective identity, the Ottoman *millet* guaranteed group diversity at the expense of individual identity. Except through conversion to Islam, whereby one totally and utterly renounced one's original identity, it was impossible for an individual to have beliefs and behaviors that conflicted with the norms of the *millet* into which they were born. Individual conformity was the price of group diversity. As Christopher de Bellaigue notes, each *millet* was a mini empire within an empire, a theocracy in which ecclesiastics "judged their

---

[3] John Hemming, *The Conquest of the Inca* (London, UK: Macmillan, 1970), 58.

[4] Ebubekir Ceylan, "The *Millet* System in the Ottoman Empire", in Judi Upton-Ward (ed.), *New Millennium Perspectives in the Humanities* (Provo, UT: Brigham Young University Press, 2002), 245, 247.

[5] Karen Barkey and George Gavrilis, "The Ottoman *Millet* System: Non-territorial Autonomy and Its Contemporary Legacy", *Ethnopolitics*, Vol. 15, No. 1 (2016), 24.

own" in ways that reinforced group identity.[6] The inevitable result of this was the mind-numbing conservatism for which the Ottoman Empire was infamous. Neither the Empire nor the individual *millet* had any interest in promoting ideas and behaviors that challenged the *status quo*. Not until the mid-nineteenth century did Ottoman society witness books and newspapers produced with a movable-type printing press. In the absence of cheap books, literacy remained in the vicinity of 3%. A society composed largely of illiterates, Ottoman Turkey lagged its European neighbors in almost every field.[7]

If conformity was one cost of group diversity under the *millet* system, an even-greater danger lurked beneath the surface. Reinforcing rather than bridging group divides, the *millet* system only survived as long as the iron hand of the Ottoman state kept a firm lid on the bubbling ethnic pot. When the lid came off the pot as Ottoman Turkey "modernized" in the late nineteenth and early twentieth centuries, the result was communal strife: the forcible expulsion of ethnic Turks from the newly independent Balkan states; the Armenian Genocide (1915–1917); the vicious Greco-Turkish War of 1919–1922 and its associated population exchanges; and long-running Kurdish struggles for autonomy and independence.

The Turkish experience is hardly unique. Rather, the pattern that we witness in Turkey—whereby an attempted process of "modernization", "democratization" and "westernization" results in prolonged communal strife—is almost the norm. Nigeria, for example, has known virtually continuous communal and religious strife since independence, the worst divisions being associated with the catastrophic Biafran War (1967–1970). When South Sudan gained independence from Sudan in 2011 after decades of ethnic warfare, the result was not peace and progress but a renewed civil war as the dominant South Sudanese ethnic groups turned on each other.

In pre-1947 India, the preeminent political leader of the Congress Party, Jawaharlal Nehru, readily dismissed suggestions that India would descend into communal strife once British rule came to an end. Nehru informed a British official in 1936, "India has never known in the whole course of her long history the religious strife that has soaked

---

[6] Christopher de Bellaigue, *The Islamic Enlightenment: The Modern Struggle Between Faith and Reason* (London, UK: Vintage, 2017), 69.

[7] Ibid., xv, 62–65.

320   B. BOWDEN

Europe in blood". Instead, he declared, "Indian religion, culture and philosophy" was always rooted in principles of "tolerance".[8] When the British declared Indian independence, however, the result was a wave of communal violence that cost up to 1 million people their lives as India was sundered into two and, ultimately, three distinct nations: India, Pakistan and Bangladesh.

Why is it that so many societies that have embraced, or sought to embrace, western models of democracy, statehood and governance have descended into communal division and violence? The short answer is that western-style democracy with its associated system of individual rights is incompatible with deeply rooted collective-based systems of identity, be they ones associated with race, religion, ethnicity or class.

The reason for this incompatibility is found in the fact that, in a democracy, each communal group sees the modern state and its various agencies as a prize that is not only worth fighting for but also one that must be kept out of the hands of rival groups at all costs. In a democracy, in short, there is no iron lid on the pot as there was in Ottoman Turkey and British-ruled India. Instead, there is a competition for power, which, if pursued in ways that give primacy to group identity, is contrary to democratic norms and, indeed, the health and survival of the democracy itself. For if one identity group, or alliance of identity groups, consolidates its power at the expense of others, then democracy no longer exists as a mechanism for freedom. Rather, it becomes a device for the suppression of alternative identities (for example, Christian, social conservative and so on). Yes, it is true that in a democracy, various groups come together to pursue shared interests. In a liberal democracy, nevertheless, the constitutional assumption is that each person assumes rights and responsibilities as an individual, rather than as a member of this or that identity group. As Article VI of the French *Declaration of the Rights of Man and the Citizen* states, "All citizens being equal in its eyes are equally admissible to all public dignities, offices and employments, according to their capacity, and with no other distinction than that of their virtues and talents".

At its core, therefore, the modern iteration of western civilization represents the formal and informal supremacy of individual expressions of identity over collective manifestations. This outcome is something that

[8] Jawaharlal Nehru, "Letter to Lord Lothian, 17 January 1936", in Jawaharlal Nehru, *Selected Works of Jawaharlal Nehru*, series 1, vol. 7 (Delhi, India: Jawaharlal Nehru Memorial Fund, 1988), 68–69.

has been long recognized by both critics and supporters of the new industrialized and democratized western civilization that gained world dominance from the mid-nineteenth century onward. Everywhere, Marx and Engels observed in the *Communist Manifesto*, bourgeois-dominated societies entailed the displacement of other considerations by "egotistical calculation" and "naked self-interest".[9] Similarly, in his *Capitalism and Freedom*, Milton Friedman located "the dignity of the individual", and the "freedom to make the most" of one's capacities according to one's "own lights", at the very "heart of the liberal philosophy" that underpins western capitalism.[10]

The post-1850 global ascendancy of the new industrialized iteration of western civilization forced not only African, Asian and Middle Eastern societies to constantly choose between individualistic and group-based expressions of identity. A similar clash of cultural values has also characterized the West's European and American heartlands. In the first half of the twentieth century, this clash largely revolved around differences in social class. In the closing decades of the twentieth century and the opening ones of the twenty-first century, new forms of identity associated with gender, sexuality, religion and, above all, race have taken the form of de facto millets. Invariably, the spokespeople for these de facto millets argue that identity primarily stems from group rather than individual characteristics. In his highly cited *The White Racial Frame*, Joe Feagin, for example, argues that every aspect of western culture, most particularly in the United States, is "framed" in ways that privilege white racial interests. Whereas Ottoman Turkey enforced a system of *millets* that placed Muslims on top, Feagin detects "a hierarchical structure of racial classes with whites firmly at the top". So deeply entrenched is this "hierarchical structure", he argues, that other racial groups can only resist by articulating their own "counter-frames" in ways that reject "white norms and folkways".[11] As with the Ottoman *millets*, those who have views at odds with the supposed interests of their racial group are

[9] Karl Marx and Frederick Engels, "Manifesto of the Communist Party", in Karl Marx and Frederick Engels, *Selected Works*, vol. 1 (Moscow, USSR: Foreign Languages Publishing House, 1951), 35.

[10] Milton Friedman (in association with Rose Friedman), *Capitalism and Freedom*, fortieth anniversary Edition (Chicago and London: Chicago University Press, 2002), 195.

[11] Joe R. Feagin, *The White Racial Frame: Centuries of Racial Framing and Counter-Framing*, third edition (New York and London: Routledge, 2020), 206, 227.

regarded as misguided—if not dangerous heretics. According to Feagin, Latinos who identify themselves first and foremost as American citizens, sharing common interests and values with their white compatriots, "have intentionally suppressed the view of themselves as part of a racial group substantially subordinated by whites".[12] Increasingly, people in every western society obtain "offices and employments" not according to "their virtues and talents" but rather according to the "equity" targets set aside for the de facto millet to which they belong.

If the choice between individualism and collectivism remains central to the social and political norms and structures of *every* contemporary society, a similar set of choices are demanded in the economic sphere. As noted in the previous chapter, such choices are complicated by the fact that there was never a single monochromatic western economic model. Even among liberal democracies, some societies have, at various times, favored much higher levels of state intervention and corporatist forms of business organization than others. In the colonial world, moreover, western bureaucracies and military strength were more apparent than a *laissez-faire* economy. It was these features, not individualism and democracy, that attracted what de Bellaigue refers to as "coercive modernizers"; an extensive group that boasts among its members Kemal Ataturk, Saddam Hussein, Gamal Nasser and Juan Peron. Colonial education systems were also typically directed toward the needs of state administration rather than those of indigenous businesses. In colonial India, as Fig. 12.1 indicates, the university system produced many lawyers and humanities graduates—virtually all of whom were destined for colonial bureaucracies—but few doctors or engineers.[13] One enduring effect of this type of educational system, in India as elsewhere, was to link social prestige with state employment. As noted in the previous chapter, when Sayyid Qutb, the future leader of the Muslim Brotherhood, was dispatched to Cairo in search of an education, his family's great hope was that he would become an *effendi* (state official). Other leaders perceived colonial-era university education less benignly. In India, as prime minister, Nehru bemoaned the colonial education system of which he himself was

[12] Ibid., 227.

[13] United Kingdom Parliament, *Statistical Abstract Relating to British India, 1867–68–1876–77* (London, UK: Her Majesty's Printing Office, 1877), Figure 99; United Kingdom Parliament, *Statistical Abstract Relating to British India, 1903–04–1912–13* (London, UK: Her Majesty's Printing Office, 1913), Figure 103.

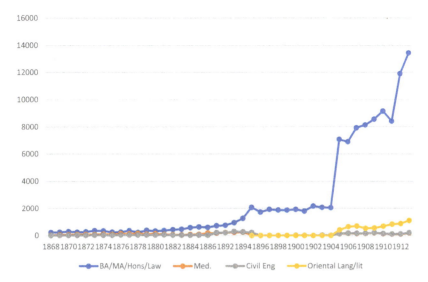

Fig. 12.1 University graduates per year by academic discipline, British India, 1868–1913 (*Sources* UK Parliament, *Statistical Abstract … British India*, 1867–1868 to 1876–1877, 1884–1885 to 1894–1895, 1903–1904 to 1912–1913)

a product, noting a graduate tendency to seek after "desk jobs" while regarding manual labor "as beneath their dignity".[14]

Given the power and prestige of colonial-era state machines it was hardly surprising that most post-independence regimes in Africa and Asia favored either high levels of state intervention in the economy or outright socialism. For their part, indigenous businesses of any scale were regarded with distrust, as actual or potential foreign collaborators. "In underdeveloped countries", Franz Fanon, the French-educated leader of the Algerian Revolution recorded, "the bourgeoisie should not be allowed to find the conditions necessary for its existence and growth". Instead, socialism should be embraced in the interests of the laboring poor.[15]

---

[14] Jawaharlal Nehru, "The Scope for Agricultural Growth: Speech 19 December 1951", in Jawaharlal Nehru, *Selected Works of Jawaharlal Nehru*, series 2, vol. 17 (New Delhi, India: Jawaharlal Nehru Memorial Fund, 1975), 71.

[15] Franz Fanon, *The Wretched of the Earth* (Harmondsworth, UK: Penguin, 1967), 140, 59.

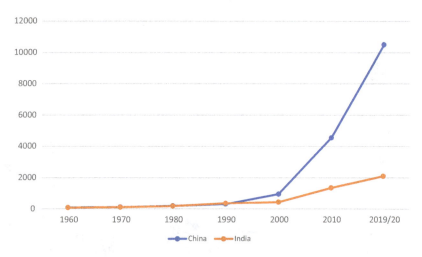

Fig. 12.2 Indian and Chinese per capita GDP (2020 US dollars), 1960 to 2019–2020 (*Source* World Bank, World Bank Data—Development Indicators)

Addressing India's Chamber of Commerce and Industry as prime minister in 1952, Nehru expressed similar sentiments, advising his audience that:

> We are not willing to give private enterprise the high place which some countries have given it. On the other hand, we are ready to view it with suspicion.[16]

There is no doubting the suffocating economic effects of this hostility to markets and free enterprise. In India and China—nations that encompass more than a third of the world's population—this suffocating effect was particularly marked as both embraced highly regulated, state-directed economic models. As Fig. 12.2 indicates, between 1960 and 1990 the per capita real GDP of both nations, measured in 2020 US dollars, advanced at a near identical anemic pace. Conversely, the partial deregulation of both economies since the early 1990s, and an associated embrace

---

[16] Jawaharlal Nehru, "Private Enterprise and Democracy: Speech to Indian Chamber of Commerce and Industry, 29 March 1952", in Jawaharlal Nehru, *Selected Works of Jawaharlal Nehru*, series 2, vol. 17 (New Delhi, India: Jawaharlal Nehru Memorial Fund, 1975), 279.

of markets and private enterprise, has underpinned a marked improvement in the economic circumstances of the typical Chinese and Indian citizen. Between 2000 and 2019, Indian per capita GDP rose 4.7-fold to US$2,101. Chinese gains were even more impressive, per capita GDP rising almost 11-fold to US$10,500 between 2000 and 2020.[17]

The post-2000 economic progress of India and, more particularly China, highlights the fact that although choices are shaped by past experiences, the past is not destiny. Instead, at both the individual and societal level, we are confronted with choices as important as any that have confronted earlier generations.

Industrialization and Societal Choices: The Experiences of Egypt, Iran and India

No culture or civilization readily abandons its past and the shared system of rituals and economic practices that have given it meaning. Even if a society is occupied militarily by a foreign power, it will typically cling to its traditional culture. Historically, most conquerors have been assimilated into the society that they have conquered, rather than the reverse. As a revolution in transportation occurred around 1850, however, no society was able to avoid interaction with the West in ways that permanently effected traditional modes of existence.

As markets brought both western goods and technologies to every corner of the globe, there were few issues as divisive in the colonial world as policies that either favored or hindered western-style mechanization. For mechanization entailed far more than new technologies. It also involved the loss of traditional jobs, the creation of entirely new occupations, and the large-scale movement of people from the land.

In the nineteenth and early twentieth centuries, mechanization in the colonial world typically appeared as an imposition.

Exposed to the virtues and vices of the West by Napoleon's famous victory at the Battle of the Nile in 1798, Egypt was the first non-European society outside the Americas and Oceania to pursue a policy of (forced) industrialization. Under a series of "modernizing" rulers—most notably Muhammed Ali (1805–1849) and Ismail I (1863–1879)—Egypt

---

[17] World Bank, *World Bank: Data—Development Indicators, GDP per Capita* (current US Dollars) (Washington, DC: World Bank, 2020), https://data.worldbank.org/indicator/NY.GDP.PCAP.CD?end=2018&locations.

witnessed mechanized textile mills, shipbuilding yards, telegraphs, railroads and, most spectacularly, the construction of the Suez Canal, which opened for business in 1869. In his account of the "Islamic Enlightenment", de Bellaigue described this Egyptian transformation as a process of "jolting disaggregation".[18] Some Egyptians, as noted in the references to Qutb's childhood account of life in early twentieth-century Egypt, experienced this as educational and social opportunity. Others experienced it as forced labor, crippling taxes and squandered resources. Driven by state decree, Egypt's nineteenth-century "modernization" campaign did as much to hinder as help private-sector growth.[19] Bankrupted by Ismail I's modernization campaign, Egypt fell under de facto or actual British control from 1882 to 1953 as France and Britain intervened militarily at the behest of distressed bond holders. Freed from western tutelage by Gamal Nasser, Egypt promptly returned to a policy of state-driven "modernization".

Unsurprisingly, Egypt's process of authoritarian modernization provoked an authoritarian response. In founding the Muslim Brotherhood in 1928—an organization that has since grown into one of the most significant mass movements in the Muslim world—Hasan al-Bana called upon his supporters to "dissociate" themselves "from organizations, newspapers, committees, schools, and institutions which oppose your Islamic ideology". Brotherhood supporters were also asked to boycott goods produced by non-Islamic societies.[20] Under al-Bana's successor, Sayyid Qutb, capitalism was associated with "a selfish and vengeful society", and the western "scientific method … with Godlessness".[21] Constantly torn between two authoritarian models—a conflict that during the Arab Spring saw both the election of a Muslim Brotherhood government (2012) and its military overthrow (2013)—Egypt has remained a society drawn toward western technologies and bureaucratic governance rather than economic or political liberalism. Economically, it has squandered the gains made in the nineteenth century when Egypt represented the Muslim world's most significant industrial pioneer. Although Egypt's

[18] de Bellaigue, *Islamic Enlightenment*, 25.

[19] Ibid., 22–23.

[20] Hasan al-Bana, "The Message of the Teaching", in Sayyid Qutb, *Milestones*, https://cryptome.org/2017/10/Milestones-Qutb.pdf, Appendix VIII, 256–59.

[21] Sayyid Qutb, *Milestones*, https://cryptome.org/2017/10/Milestones-Qutb.pdf, 61, 128.

per capita GDP grew 4.6-fold to US\$3,547 (2020 value) between 1990 and 2020, its performance was overshadowed by other developing societies. Whereas in 1965 Egypt's per capita GDP was 2.4 times larger than China's, by 2020 it was only a third of the size. Egypt's economic placement also declined markedly when compared to other "middle-income" societies (for example, Brazil, Mexico, Malaysia). Thus, whereas Egypt's per capita GDP was 92% of the "middle-income" average in 1990, by 2020 it represented only 68%.[22]

Hostility to western economic models built around markets and mechanization has been even more pronounced in the third-most populous Middle Eastern society, Iran.[23] Paradoxically, however, Iran was also the first Middle Eastern society to experience western-style constitutional government as a result of a popular uprising. Witnessing the Constitutional Revolution of 1906 at first hand, the British oriental scholar, Edward Browne, concluded that its most "remarkable feature" was the leadership role played by the Islamic "clergy".[24] Although this constitutional government was subsequently overthrown with the aid of Russian-trained Cossacks—a reactionary force which in 1921 installed one of its officers, Reza Pahlavi, as Shah—Browne was not the last to fancifully detect in the clergy a force for democratic change. Reporting on the Iranian Revolution of 1979 on behalf of the Italian newspaper *Corriere della Sera*, Michel Foucault identified a rare "beauty" that came from "living the Islamic religion as a revolutionary force".[25] Despite its dubious commitment to democratic norms, Iran's Islamic clergy has constantly reasserted its claim to be the great defender of traditional virtues. In the 1960s and 1970s such claims gained new credibility when articulated by Iran's most notable secular dissidents, Jalal Al-i Ahmad and Ali Shari'ati. Both gave voice to the unease created by the same

---

[22] World Bank, *Development Indicators, GDP per Capita*, https://data.worldbank.org/indicator/NY.GDP.PCAP.CD?end=2018&locations.

[23] In 2021, both Iran and Turkey had a population of 85 million. Egypt had 105 million.

[24] Edward G. Browne, *The Persian Revolution of 1905–1909* (Cambridge, UK: Cambridge University Press, 1910), 123.

[25] Michel Foucault, "Iran: The Spirit of a World Without Spirit", in Lawrence D. Kritzman (ed.) *Michel Foucault: Politics, Philosophy, Culture—Interviews and Other Writings, 1977–1984* (London and New York: Routledge, 1988), 216, 218.

process of "jolting disaggregation" that Egypt had previously witnessed—a process of top-down industrialization undertaken with unusual venality by Reza Shah and his son, Mohammad. In narrow economic terms, the dynasty's industrialization campaign was remarkably successful, the nation's per capita GDP rising 12.6-fold to US$2,427 (2020 value) between 1960 and 1979.[26] However, the very speed of this transformation, and its association with the Pahlavi family's unrestrained corruption, placed near-intolerable strains on Iranian life.

Published in edited form in 1964, Al-i Ahmad's *Gharbzadagi*, or *Occidentosis*, represents one of the most powerful denunciations of the western economic and social model ever published. In Al-i Ahmad's estimation, the mechanization of work traditionally done by village artisans spelled nothing but social disaster. For he observed, in reflecting upon Iranian circumstance:

> When the machine sets foot in the village ... it destroys all the accoutrements of the pastoral and rural economy ... It puts the worker in the local craft industries out of work. It closes the village mill. It renders the spinning wheel useless.[27]

Threatened with cultural "extinction", Al-i Ahmad believed that Iran had no option other than "to rise, dig in, and fight back" in defense of their traditional culture and Shiite faith.[28]

Where Al-i Ahmad drew inspiration from traditional society, the French-educated Ali Shari'ati crafted an even more uncompromising message from an unlikely basis: the "existentialist" philosophy of Jean-Paul Sartre. Using Sartre's philosophy as glue, Shari'ati pasted together a dissident analysis that appealed to both secular and religious audiences. So successful was Shari'ati in this endeavor that by the time of his death in 1978, he was, as Humid Algar noted, "the chief ideologue of the [looming] Iranian Islamic Revolution".[29] According to Shari'ati, Sartre's

---

[26] World Bank, *Development Indicators, GDP per Capita*, https://data.worldbank.org/indicator/NY.GDP.PCAP.CD?end=2018&locations.

[27] Jalal Al-i Ahmad (trans. R. Campbell), *Occidentosis: A Plague from the West* (Berkeley, CA: Mizan Press, 1984), 68–69.

[28] Ibid., 46.

[29] Ibid., 3.

existentialism represented the "metaphysical zenith" of western philosophy, exposing how an embrace of "science and technology" had caused the human spirit to be ground under the "pitiless wheels of mechanism".[30] If, however, existentialism revealed industrialization's destructive nature, Shari'ati advised his Tehrani audiences, it nevertheless failed to offer any solution to the spiritual void that was its inevitable consequence. Accordingly, Shari'ati', like Al-i Ahmad, argued that only Islam offered humanity a way out of the spiritual dead end that was the inevitable consequence of western-style industrialization. Islam was, he declared, "a philosophy of human liberation", one that "addresses economic welfare and social justice as principles of its social order".

As Shari'ati hoped, the Iranian Revolution that he advocated, but did not live to see, resulted in a near total rejection of all things western. This rejection, however, did not lead to the nirvana that he had predicted. Instead, it produced civil and international strife, political oppression and economic regression. As noted earlier, by the time the Shah was forced from power, Iran's per capita GDP had risen to US$2,427 (2020 value). In 2020, it stood at US$2,282—a 6% decline.[31] Clearly, it is not westernization that has driven Iran into an economic and social dead end over the last forty years. Rather, its woes are a consequence of its rejection of the West's economic and social promise, an outcome dictated in the final analysis by the powerful hold of traditional social and religious forces over Iranian culture.

If Iranian society chose to reject almost every aspect of the new, industrialized iteration of western civilization, India—perhaps more than any other society—has trod a complex path of acceptance, rejection and adaptation.

In part, India's reaction was one dictated not only by British military occupation but also by the destruction of much of its traditional economy. At the dawn of the nineteenth century, India was still the world's preeminent cotton textile producer and exporter. By the 1880s, however, British imports had captured almost two-thirds of the Indian market. Increasingly it was not only textiles that flooded Indian markets;

---

[30] Ali Shari'ati (trans. R. Campbell), *Marxism and Other Western Fallacies: An Islamic Critique* (Markfield, UK: Islamic Foundation Press, 1979), 28, 24.

[31] World Bank, *Development Indicators, GDP per Capita*, https://data.worldbank.org/indicator/NY.GDP.PCAP.CD?end=2018&locations.

330 B. BOWDEN

also arriving in ever-greater volumes were the building blocks of an industrialized economy: railway locomotives, communication equipment, iron and steel, and factory machinery. By 1920 the latter two categories, considered together, amounted to almost half the value of India's cotton textile imports.[32] As modern machinery became more readily available the traditional craft sector was also threatened by locally made "mill" goods as well as imports. In textiles, the mill sector's output grew 7.5-fold between 1900–1903 and 1936–1939 to 3,630 million square meters. Whereas output from the traditional craft sector was 63% larger than mill product in 1900–1903, by 1936–1939 the mill sector was manufacturing 2.6 times more cloth than home-based producers.[33]

The retreat of the traditional craft sector confronted Indian society with the same problems that had concerned Al-i Ahmad and Shari'ati. Whereas, however, Al-i Ahmad and Shari'ati were united in their rejection of "the machine", the two great leaders of the Indian independence movement, Mahatma Gandhi and Nehru, came to different conclusions. Gandhi, like Al-i Ahmad, found virtue in traditional village life, famously setting an example for his followers by spinning his own home-made "khadi" cloth. Associating "pure khadi" (that is, a total reliance on home-made product) with "pure swadeshi" (full independence), Gandhi also urged a life of simplicity, calling upon his supporters to give "up the use of those superfluous things that are not made here".[34] Gandhi also made it clear that he regarded factory-made cloth as inherently inferior to "khadi". Rather than increasing output, Gandhi declared in 1929, mill owners should "limit their profits" and "sell khadi".[35]

Drawn to a socialist model of industrialization after a visit to the Soviet Union in 1927, Nehru made no secret of his differences with Gandhi. Both before and after independence, Nehru identified poverty rather than

[32] United Kingdom Parliament, *Statistical Abstract Relating to British India, 1910–11–1919–20* (London, UK: Her Majesty's Printing Office, 1920), Figure 135.

[33] Gregory Clark, *A Farewell to Alms: A Brief Economic History of the World* (Princeton, NJ: Princeton University Press, 2007), 368, Table 17.3.

[34] Mahatma Gandhi, "What Comprises Foreign Goods", in Mahatma Gandhi, *Collected Works of Mahatma Gandhi*, vol. 46 (Ahmedabad, India: Gandhi Sevagram Ashram, n.d.), 12 May 1929, 3.

[35] Mahatma Gandhi, "Mill-Owners and Boycotts", in Mahatma Gandhi, *Collected Works of Mahatma Gandhi*, vol. 46 (Ahmedabad, India: Gandhi Sevagram Ashram, n.d.), 4 July 1929, 237.

the demise of the craft sector as India's central "economic problem". Nehru also argued that traditional craft activities could only function as "a small additional income" to that obtained from farming or factory work. In the agricultural sector, Nehru identified "the use of machinery, tractors, and the like" as the key to improved living standards, fancifully believing that India's peasants would join together in Soviet-style collectives so as to obtain the benefits of mechanization.[36] As prime minister, Nehru enthusiastically embraced rapid industrialization through a series of Five Year Plans.[37] Despite differing from Gandhi in his enthusiasm for industrialization, Nehru nevertheless shared with him a deep-seated belief that economic activity should be directed toward employment rather than profit maximization. In 1951, as prime minister, Nehru said:

> ... there should be no unemployment in the country ... We want obviously that production should increase ... But we wish to tie that up with providing work for the greatest number of people.[38]

In the wake of independence, Indian economic policy thus found itself torn between not two but rather three contradictory objectives: a spiritual attachment to "khadi" and home-based production; a desire to become a major industrial power with a world-class manufacturing sector; and the belief that economic activity should prioritize employment over profits. The negative consequences of these contradictory policies are most obvious in the textile sector, where governments of every ilk have consistently favored handloom weavers and small-scale producers over large modern mills. Since 1958, government support for the handloom sector has been coordinated through the activities of the Indian Handicrafts Development Corporation; an organization that the Ministry of Textiles reported in 2020 as having substantial "operating losses" due

---

[36] Jawaharlal Nehru, "Evolution of British Policy in India: September 1927", in Jawaharlal Nehru, *Selected Works of Jawaharlal Nehru*, series 1, vol. 2 (New Delhi, India: Orient Longman, 1975), 342; Jawaharlal Nehru, "The Peasant and the Land", in Jawaharlal Nehru, *Selected Works of Jawaharlal Nehru*, series 1, vol. 2 (New Delhi, India: Orient Longman, 1975), 439.

[37] Nehru, "Scope for Agricultural Growth", 227.

[38] Ibid., 226.

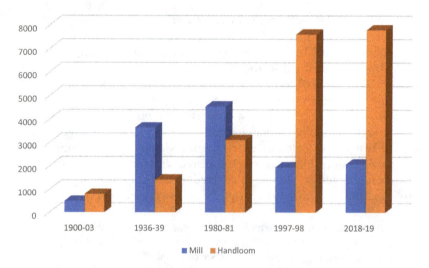

Fig. 12.3 Cotton textile output of the Indian mill and handloom sectors, 1900–1903 to 2018–2019 (in millions of square meters) (*Source* Clark, *Farewell to Alms*, Table 17.3; Indian Ministry of Textiles, *Report of the Office of the Textile Commissioner*, 2019–2020)

to "high overheads" and "underutilization of fixed assets".[39] Another government organization, the National Handloom Development Corporation, provides handloom operators with subsidized yarn and dyes. Exports are promoted by eleven separate marketing bodies. Handloom and small-scale power-loom producers are also supported by subsidies and concessional loans. As a result of these efforts the textile sector provided 45 million "direct" and 6 million "indirect" jobs in 2019–2020. Three-quarters of national production came from "handloom, handicrafts and small-scale loom units". The Ministry of Textiles also reported that India was responsible for "95% of the world's hand-woven fabric".[40] As Fig. 12.3 indicates, however, the fostering of the handloom and small-unit power-loom sectors has come at the expense of the mill sector. In 2018–2019, the output of the "mill sector" (2,078 million square

---

[39] Indian Ministry of Textiles, *Annual Report 2019–2020* (New Delhi, India: Ministry of Textiles, 2020), 19.

[40] Ibid., 20, 5–6, 3.

meters) was significantly less than that obtained in 1936–1939 (3,630 million square meters).[41] On three occasions (1974, 1986, 1995) the government has been forced to nationalize an ever-larger share of the "mill" sector for a range of reasons, including obsolete technology, excess manpower, and poor productivity. At the same time, the heavily subsidized "handicraft sector" suffers, according to the Ministry of Textiles, from "a lack of education, low capital, poor exposure to new technologies [and an] absence of market intelligence".[42]

Similar circumstances prevail in India's rural sector. In recommending a "fundamental shift" away from the pattern of regulation and subsidization that has characterized agriculture since independence, a government committee in 2018 painted a woeful picture of backwardness and under performance that acted as a millstone around the neck of the wider economy. In a sector dominated by "small and marginal farm holdings", the committee observed, mechanization was almost non-existent. In 2017–2018, mechanized farm power amounted to only 2 kilowatts per hectare, a result that compared "very poorly even with Asia–Pacific countries".[43] When, however, the Indian government acted on the committee's recommendations, passing legislation that exposed the agricultural sector to market forces, the result was a wave of national protests. In November 2021, the government capitulated, withdrawing its legislation, an outcome that guaranteed a continuation of rural backwardness.

THE MILLETIZATION OF THE MODERN WORLD

In 1994, Christopher Lasch, who was then terminally ill, lamented the ways in which the United States had become a nation of "homogenous enclaves" that acted as mini states within states. One of the "insidious" results of this, Lasch observed, was the "assumption that all members of a given group can be expected to think alike", an assumption that made one's beliefs "a function of racial and ethnic identity, of gender or

---

[41] Clark, *Farewell to Alms*, Table 17.3; Indian Ministry of Textiles, *Report of the Office of the Textile Commissioner, 2019–2020* (New Delhi, India: Ministry of Textiles, 2020), Figure 14.4.

[42] Ministry of Textiles, *Annual Report*, 12, 6.

[43] Committee on Doubling Farmers' Income, *Report of the Committee on Doubling Farmers' Income*, vol. 14 (New Delhi: India, Ministry of Agriculture and Farmers' Welfare, 2018), 18, 74.

sexual preference". Increasingly, he also noted, self-selected "spokespersons" enforced "conformity" by "ostracizing"—"cancelling" in modern terminology—"those who stray from the party line". At the same time, Lasch detected what he referred to as "the balkanization of opinion", in which "knowledge" came to be associated with "ideology" as each identity group constructed their own version of reality and truth.[44]

The trends that Lasch identified more than a quarter of a century ago have become ever-more evident. In the *Ethnic Studies Model Curriculum* adopted by the California Board of Education in March 2021, for example, we witness an explicit abjuring of "cliches about how we are all basically alike". Instead, Californian students are taught that they can only gain "knowledge of self" by locating "their own identities" in the "ancestral roots" of their ethnic group.[45] In virtually every domain—music, literature, sport—any sense of common identity as citizens has collapsed in the face of vigorously pursued "counter-frames". In an article published in the *Journal of the Society for Music Theory* in 2020, Philip Ewell lambasted the "deep-seated whiteness in music theory", and an associated preferencing of "the music of white persons" and "Austro-German composers" (for example, Mozart, Beethoven), "at the expense of other races, not to mention marginalized groups based on gender, LGBTQIA+, ethnic, religious, disablist, cultural, or other identities".[46] In other words, the music that we study and listen to should be determined not by the talent of the composer but rather according to a ratio that reflects the identities of potential audiences. Such demands inevitably entail the effective *milletization* of not only the society at large but also of every aspect of life. For whereas under the Ottoman Turks, each *millet* maintained a spatial as well as a cultural separateness, such a policy of physical segregation is impossible in modern interconnected societies. Instead, each identity group or *millet* demands a share of each pie (jobs, university places, and so on).

If the *milletization* of modern society is increasingly apparent, we are nevertheless left with a fundamental question: how did this state of

---

[44] Christopher Lasch, *The Revolt of the Elites and the Betrayal of Democracy* (New York, NY: W.W. Norton & Co., 1995), 17–18, 13.

[45] California State Board of Education, *Ethnic Studies Model Curriculum: Introduction and Overview* (Sacramento, CA: California State Board of Education, 2021), 3, 15.

[46] Philip A. Ewell, "Music Theory and the White Racial Frame", *Journal of the Society for Music Theory*, Vol. 26, No. 2 (2020), 1.1, 3.2, 1.4.

affairs come about? Explanation can be found in large part in the shifting dynamics of western societies since the Industrial Revolution.

One consequence of industrialization, improved transport and greater physical mobility was a more cosmopolitan workforce, drawn from far and near. This resulted in not only greater levels of ethnic and racial interaction but also ethnic pecking orders in the new industrialized workplaces. In Britain by the 1830s, E.P. Thompson recorded, "whole classes of work had passed almost entirely into the hands of Irishmen since the English either refused the menial, unpleasant tasks or could not keep up with the pace". In the industries where there was direct competition—construction, the waterfront, railroad building—"pitched battles" occurred, often with "mortal casualties".[47] In the New World the ethnic competition for jobs was even more pronounced. Australian trade unions campaigned against Asian workers. In the United States, members of recently arrived ethnic groups often served as strike breakers, seeking to drag themselves out of the bottom-order jobs to which they were assigned. White workers of all descriptions made common cause against African Americans. Recalling his experiences as an escaped slave on the New Bedford waterfront in the 1840s, Frederick Douglass wrote that, "such was the strength of prejudice ... that they refused to work with me".[48]

There are three things to note about this industrial-era competition for jobs. First, in a society where an overwhelming majority worked with their hands, job conflicts typically entailed fights over blue-collar jobs located at the bottom of the employment pecking-order. The second thing to note, as discussed in the previous chapter, is that pre-1914 state machines were typically small-scale affairs, taxing lightly and spending little. Most had neither the inclination nor the resources to engage in large-scale employment regulation. Where significant regulation was attempted—as occurred in Germany, Australia and New Zealand—it typically entailed generic laws relating to minimum wages, workers compensation and trade union regulation. If matters relating to race were addressed, they were directed against minority groups rather than in their favor. In Australia, this infamously entailed the introduction of a "White Australia" policy in 1901. In the United States it involved the even more infamous "Jim

[47] E.P. Thompson, *The Making of the English Working Class*, second edition (Harmondsworth, UK: Penguin Books, 1968), 475, 480.

[48] Frederick Douglass, *Narrative of the Life of Frederick Douglass as American Slave* (Boston, MA: Anti-slavery Office, 1846), 116.

Crow" laws that imposed a policy of racial segregation across most of the South. In terms of gender, regulation reinforced a subservient position for females even as new opportunities opened up for women in education, health care and clerical work.

While there were factors that hindered the economic advancement of women and ethnic minorities there was also a third, even more powerful factor at work that favored social progress, integration and cohesion. The collective nature of work in factories, construction and on the waterfront, and a comparative abundance of work both at home and abroad, produced new shared identities and solidarity. Individuals of diverse origins were eventually welcomed as workmates and equals. Of the circumstances of the Irish in industrializing Britain, E.P. Thompson observed it was "not the friction" which was "remarkable" but rather "the relative ease" with which they "were absorbed into working-class communities".[49] Similar comments could be made about Irish, Jewish, Italian and Hungarian immigrants in any New World society. Over time, rising living standards allayed even class division. Acknowledging that his predictions of catastrophic declines in British living standards had not transpired, Marx's co-author, Frederick Engels observed of Britain's growing class of mechanics and tradespeople in 1892 that, "they have succeeded in enforcing for themselves a relatively comfortable position, and they accept it as final".[50] Where oppression persisted, people could and did leave with comparative ease. In the United States the rolling-back of Reconstruction-era civil rights was associated in the 1870s and 1880s with an exodus of African Americans to the North's industrial cities. In recording the experiences of those who moved to the North, one African American journalist observed, "They sleep in peace at night; what they earn is paid to them, if not, they can appeal to the courts. They vote without fear of the shot-gun".[51] Even-greater numbers left in the "Great Migration" between 1916 and 1970. Of African Americans born between 1916 and 1932 in Georgia, 35% left for the North. In Alabama, 45% migrated. In Mississippi, at least half left. Most found a better life than

[49] Thompson, *Making of the English Working Class*, 480.

[50] Frederick Engels, "Preface to the 1892 Edition of the Condition of the Working-Class in England in 1844", Karl Marx, *Capital*, vol. 1 (Moscow, USSR: Foreign Languages Publishing House, 1954), 376.

[51] Cited, Page Smith, *The Rise of Industrial America: A People's History of the Post-Reconstruction Era* (Harmondsworth, UK: Penguin Books, 1984), 642.

the one that they left behind. Both wages and "total personal income" of those who partook in the Great Migration were "much higher" than those who did not.[52]

In the decades after 1960 all the earlier employment dynamics were upended. Employment in manufacturing declined, not only relatively but also absolutely. At the same time, job opportunities—and an associated competition for work—flourished in the professions, most notably education, health, business and finance, and general management. As noted in our previous chapter, the number of American adults who boasted a university degree rose from 10.5% in 1970 to 25.6% in 2015. During the same period, the number of British adults with a degree rose from 8.5% to 25.8%. At the same time, the economic footprint of the state—and job opportunities within state agencies—grew exponentially. In the United States, as noted previously, government spending as a share of GDP more than doubled between 1950 and 1980, rising from 15.4% to 35.4%. In France by 1980, government spending amounted to almost half the nation's GDP. In Britain, it was more than half. As the state grew, more and more people identified their own personal interest with its continued expansion. In the United States, a nation where the state's footprint is significantly smaller than in other western societies, almost one in five were *directly* employed in the public sector in 2020.[53]

The dynamics and opportunities for financial advancement in professional jobs are vastly different to those associated with both industrial and service work. Industrial and service workers are typically paid a "wage", accruing extra pay for longer hours. As wage-earners, most industrial and service workers do similar work for which they obtain similar pay. If one is an assembly-line worker or cleaner, there are typically limited opportunities for securing a higher wage once one completes an apprenticeship, other than progressing to a "management" job—where one becomes a salaried employee. By contrast, professionals are typically

---

[52] Dan A. Black, Seth G. Sanders, Evan J. Taylor, and Lowell J. Taylor, "The Impact of the Great Migration on Mortality of African Americans: Evidence from the Deep South", *American Economic Review*, Vol. 105, No. 2 (2015), 485, 489.

[53] United States Bureau of Labor Statistics, *Economic News Release:Table 3—Union Affiliation of Employed Wage and Salary Workers by Occupation and Industry, 2019–2020* (Washington, DC: Bureau of Labor Statistics, 2020), https://www.bls.gov/news.release/union2.t03.htm.

salaried employees. As such, they normally do not get paid extra for "overtime". Opportunities for promotion, however, are more readily available. Judging whether the work of a professional is deserving of promotion—or even of hiring in the first place—is, however, an inherently subjective exercise. It is certainly, for example, far easier to objectively assess the work of a carpenter than the teaching and research of a university lecturer or professor.

In professional employment, experience and accumulated expertise is also typically more important than it is in blue-collar work. Career "interruptions", most particularly for child care, will thus generally have a far more significant effect in professional jobs than in blue-collar work. Accordingly, one also witnesses far greater wage disparities in professional employment than in blue-collar or low-wage service jobs. In Australia in August 2020, for example, as Fig. 12.4 indicates, the median hourly wage of a female employed in the male-dominated construction industry was 3.8% *higher* than that obtained by the typical male; an outcome that reflects the greater concentration of female construction workers in professional employment (for example in accounting, human resources

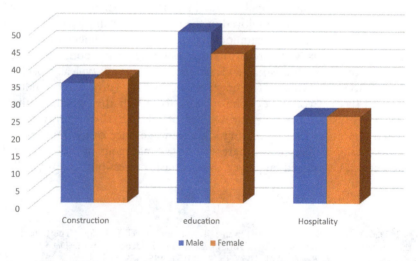

Fig. 12.4 Median hourly earnings, Australia, 2020 (Australian dollars) (*Source* Australia Bureau Statistics, *Characteristics of Employment, August 2020*, Table 3.2)

and so on) than in trade jobs. In female-dominated (and highly unionized) education, however, it was 16.7% *lower*.[54] This wage disparity—which sees a female in the education sector earn much more than her sister in construction but much less than her male co-worker—is *objectively* difficult to explain in terms of pervasive gender discrimination. If this were the case then we would expect that the female construction worker would suffer a greater disadvantage. A female schoolteacher or university lecturer, however, has greater grounds for arguing discrimination given the inherently *subjective* assessments that accompany promotion. She also has a greater incentive for arguing discrimination given the wage disparities within the industry. By comparison, as Fig. 12.4 indicates, there is little incentive to do this either in construction or hospitality with wages for males and females in the latter industry being an identical AUD\$25.00 in August 2020.

Politically, as noted in our previous chapter, the decline of the industrial working class in most advanced economies—and the associated rise of a tertiary-educated middle class—has also manifested itself in a profound shift in the concerns of the political Left. Until the 1960s the Left was guided in large part by Marxist ideology in ways that prioritized class, economics, and the creation and distribution of wealth. Since the 1960s, however, the Left has increasingly placed ideology and personal identity at center stage. In part this shift was guided by two sub-strands of Marxism. In France, Louis Althusser placed ideology rather than economics at the core of his analysis, calling for the Marxist capture of what he referred to as the "educational ideological apparatus", that is, schools and universities.[55] The so-called Frankfurt School (Herbert Marcuse, Max Horkheimer, Theodor Adorno, Jürgen Habermas), also argued that in the modern "affluent society" the overthrow of capitalism would primarily entail a "cultural" rather than a proletarian revolution. Far more significant than these two Marxist schools of thought, however, were the "postmodernist" critiques that emerged from France's preeminent educational institute, the *L'École Normale Supérieure*; an institution that included Michel Foucault and Jacques Derrida among its

---

[54] Australia Bureau of Statistics (ABS), *Characteristics of Employment, August 2020: Cat. No. 6333.0* (Canberra, AUS: Australian Bureau of Statistics, 2021), Table 3.2.

[55] Louis Althusser (trans. Ben Brewster), "Ideology and Ideological State Apparatus", in Louis Althusser, *Lenin and Philosophy and Other Essays* (New York, NY: Monthly Review Press, 1971), 103–104.

340   B. BOWDEN

students. For Derrida, the West's entire "logico-philosophical heritage" was constructed around "ethnocentrism" and the suppression of difference. If there was any hope for human emancipation, Derrida proclaimed in *Of Grammatology*, more was needed than a "Nietzschean demolition" of the whole western "metaphysical edifice" (which is the accepted principles of knowledge and understanding). One also needed to "deconstruct" language, seeking out "traces" of suppressed existence (such as minority groups being "written out" of history).[56] Taking inspiration from the German idealist philosopher, Fredrich Nietzsche, Foucault also associated the whole structure of western society with "violent and unfinalized" rules that enforced conformity. For Foucault, as with Nietzsche, the purpose of historical scholarship—and, indeed, all scholarship—was not the discovery of "truth" but rather the "decisive cutting of the roots" that caused one "to accept the world as it is".[57] Across his career, Foucault focused on an ever-expanding source of power, which he identified with individual oppression: "language" and "discourse",[58] the "disciplinary" society with its "infinitesimal surveillances",[59] the enforcement of a "unitary" sexual code that oppressed those that did not share society's heterosexual norms.[60]

In the confluence of factors that accompanied the rise of professional employment—a massive increase in the number of those educated at university, competition for professional employment, the inherently subjective nature of performance assessment in the professions, new "critical" theories that concern themselves with ideology and identity rather than economics—we can detect the changes that have *contributed* to the growing *milletization* of western societies, even if they do not *in themselves* explain it. Unlike industrial work, which tends to generate feelings of solidarity through collective work processes, professional work is also more individualistic and more prone to subjective work assessments. As

[56] Jacques Derrida (trans. Gayatri Spivak), *Of Grammatology* (Baltimore, ML: John Hopkins Press, 1976), 19, 10–11.

[57] Michel Foucault, "Nietzsche, Genealogy, History", in Paul Rabinow, *The Foucault Reader* (Harmondsworth, UK: Penguin, 1984), 85–86, 96.

[58] Michel Foucault (trans. Robert Hurley), *The History of Sexuality—An Introduction* (New York, NY: Pantheon Books, 1978), 94.

[59] Michel Foucault (trans. Alan Sheridan), *Discipline and Punish: The Birth of the Prison* (New York, NY: Vintage Books, 1991), 308.

[60] Foucault, *History of Sexuality*, 121.

the number of university educated reaches unprecedented peaks, intellectual debates in the university sector as to the nature of knowledge and identity also assume heightened importance. For not only is a person with a university degree more likely to read about "sexual identity" and "racial framing" than a plumber or a carpenter, they are also more likely to apply it to their own personal circumstances. This is *not* to argue that those who believe that our workplaces are sites of systematic discrimination do so simply out of opportunism. A university-educated member of a "minority" group, however, would have to be a naïve fool if they did not recognize that their own personal interest is served by the implementation of a largish employment target for their group. And most university-educated professionals are not naïve fools. Despite such factors, however, the *milletization* of society is not foreordained destiny. Rather, it is a matter of individual and societal choice.

To what extent, then, is the growing *milletization* of society a response to systematic discrimination? No doubt much of the population genuinely believes that modern societies are built on discrimination. In teaching employment relations at a major Australian university, I found that the great majority of my students sincerely held the view that female workers in Australia were paid less for the same work than male workers. This is hardly surprising. They are told this at every turn. In August 2021, an Australian government agency, the Workplace Gender Equality Agency, reported a 14.2% "gender pay gap" in terms of "full-time average weekly earnings"—a figure that was recited endlessly by politicians and the press.[61] In fact, however, equal pay for equal work has been enforced in Australia since 1972. The "gender pay gap" referred to relates to *aggregate* wage data. Some male-dominated industries, such as construction, pay more than female-dominated industries, such as retail. Conversely, some female-dominated industries, like education and health, pay better. Men are more likely to work longer hours, and to work in high-paid jobs in remote locations than women. Women are also more likely to take time off for child rearing, an absence that can delay their advancement through the professional job hierarchy. Australian women are today, however, also far more likely to boast a university degree and a professional job than a male—despite having a lower labor force participation

---

[61] Workplace Gender Equality Agency, *Australia's Gender Pay Gap Statistics: 21 August 2021*, https://www.wgea.gov.au/publications/australias-gender-pay-gap-statistics.

rate. Whereas more than 1.6 million females enjoyed professional employment in August 2020, less than 1.2 million men did so.[62] The so-called
"gender pay gap" is thus *not* evidence of discrimination. Rather, it is a
product of the freely made choices of men and women as to where, when
and how long they work.

The gap between popular perception and lived experience is also
evident in what is one of the most fraught issues in the modern world: the
circumstances of African Americans. Perhaps the best gauge of changing
attitudes, at both a personal and societal level, is found in the *Gallup
Race Relations Survey*, which has long taken the national pulse. When we
look at reported personal experiences, we witness a steady improvement
in circumstances. In mid-2020, only 17% of African Americans reported
that they were "treated unfairly" at work. This was the second-best score
obtained for this question since it was first reported in 1997. Only 18%
reported unfair treatment at a restaurant, bar, theater or other entertainment venue. Again, this was one of the best scores obtained in the last
twenty-three years. A similar percentage (19%) reported unfair treatment
in dealing with the police; a result that was a considerable improvement
on the 25% reported in 2004. When we look from personal experiences to
perceptions as to how African Americans are treated as a group, however,
a far bleaker picture emerges. In mid-2020, 66% of African American
adults were "very dissatisfied" with the way that "blacks" were treated as
a "group"—the worst result in the last 20 years and more than double
the figure recorded in 2001 (32%). Among "whites", the percentage
"very dissatisfied" with the treatment of African Americans was also at an
historic high at 39%; a dissatisfaction level more than four times higher
than that recorded in 2001 (9%). In terms of race relations between
"whites" and "blacks", 63% of African Americans declared them to be
"very bad" or "somewhat bad" in 2020. In 2001, only 28% of African
Americans shared this opinion. Among "whites", the percentage who
regarded "black–white" relations negatively rose from 36 to 54% between
2001 and 2020. Disturbingly, 21% of African American respondents to
the Gallup survey indicated support for violent protests as a means of
improving their racial circumstances, a figure that was more than double
that recorded in 1988 (10%). Only 38% of African American respondents
declared themselves unsympathetic to "looting" and "property crimes"

---

[62] ABS, Characteristics of Employment, Table 4.1.

carried out in conjunction with race protests. Even 38% of whites were sympathetic.[63]

The growing willingness to support or at least condone violent racial protests in the United States is hardly surprising. As the experiences of the Ottoman Empire demonstrated, the *milletization* of society and the belief that one's whole identity is subsumed within an ethnic or racial group, never leads to pluralism and harmony. Rather, it leads in the direction of social fragmentation, racial and ethnic insularity, and communal violence. If, in short, we cause people to believe that their whole identity is located within a particular ethnic, racial or sexual preference group, then we can hardly be stupefied when those same people fight for that identity group with all the energy that they possess. Certainly, if we look to Delgado and Stefancic's foundational study, *Critical Race Theory: An Introduction*, there is *expectation* that a greater awareness of one's ethnicity and racial circumstance will *inevitably* lead to a bare-knuckled struggle for power. Looking forward to the day when "minorities of color" became a numerical majority in the United States, Delgado and Stefancic suggest a "convulsive and cataclysmic" race war is as likely as a "peaceful" shift in power. If, or when, such a "cataclysmic" struggle occurs, they advise, then it will fall to "critical theorists and activists … to provide criminal defense for resistance movements and figures and to articulate theories and strategies for that resistance".[64] Such conclusions are not mere hyperbole. Rather, they are a logical and clear-sighted estimation as to where the deliberately fostered *milletization* of society is headed.

Economic and Social Choices

The existence of factors that favor the expansion of culturally distinct identity groups does not, however, mean the growing "milletization" of western society was preordained. As individuals and societies, we always have choices: whether to embrace individualism or collectivism; whether to pursue policies that favor industrialization or craft production; whether to support market competition or state-imposed regulation.

---

[63] Gallup, *Gallup Race Relations / Gallup Historical Trends*, https://news.gallup.com/poll/1687/race-relations.aspx [accessed 28 November 2021].

[64] Richard Delgado and Jean Stefancic, *Critical Race Theory: An Introduction* (New York and London: New York University Press, 2001), 130–131.

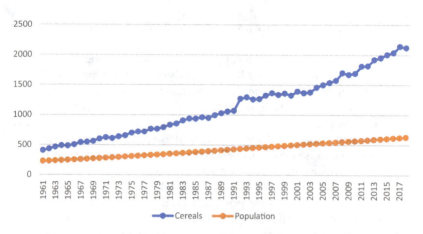

Fig. 12.5 Population and cereal production, low-income nations, 1961–2018 (population in tens of millions, cereals in million metric tons) (*Source* Calculated from World Bank, *Online Database—Indicators—Agricultural and Rural Development*)

In confronting these existentialist choices, ones that profoundly shape the nature of everyday life as well as the direction of entire societies, the entire history of western civilization has unfortunately become wrapped in misunderstanding. From every quarter, people are advised that our modern world is based on inequality, discrimination and misery. In summing up these sentiments in his *Specters of Marx*, Jacques Derrida recorded that, "never have violence, inequality, famine, and thus economic oppression affected so many human beings in the history of earth and humanity".[65] Widely believed, such comments are disconnected from reality. Everywhere, the application of science and technology has allowed escape from the Malthusian economy and its associated food shortages. On this front, achievements over the last two generations have been extraordinary. As Fig. 12.5 indicates, between 1961 and 2018 the World Bank estimates that the population of "low-income countries"— a statistical category largely made up of South Asian and Sub-Saharan African nations—rose 2.8-fold to 628 million. During the same period,

---

[65] Jacques Derrida (trans. Peggy Kamuf), *Specters of Marx* (New York and London: Routledge Classics, 2006), 106.

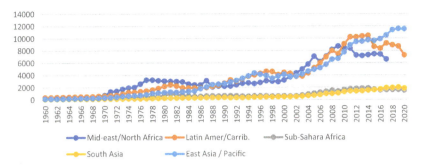

Fig. 12.6 Growth in GDP per capita, by region, 1960–2020 (in 2020 US dollars) (*Note* Middle East/North Africa Figures 1965–2017 only. *Source* Calculated from World Bank, *Online Database—Indicators—Economy & Growth*)

cereal output—the main proxy for food production—rose more than 5.2-fold to 2.2 billion metric tons.[66]

Nowhere, however, has economic advancement been automatic. Rather, it has entailed transformative and often disruptive change. It has always involved choices.

Writing of the choices before nations, Joseph Ellis in 2002 expressed the view that "some form of representative government based on the principle of popular sovereignty and some form of market economy" were the key "ingredients for national success".[67] While such association of progress with "western" norms are now suspect in many quarters, Ellis's opinion has nonetheless found confirmation in the varied progress of national and regional economies since 1960.

As Fig. 12.6 indicates, in the 1960s there was little difference in the per capita GDP of the Middle East and North Africa, Latin America, Sub-Saharan Africa, East Asia and South Asia. Sub-Sahara's GDP per capita ($128.83), expressed in 2020 US dollars, was not too different from that of East Asia ($147.17). Since 1960, however, those societies—most particularly in East Asia—that have embraced market-based policies have

---

[66] World Bank, *Online Database: Indicators—Agricultural and Rural Development*, https://data.worldbank.org/indicator/AG.PRD.CREL.MT?view=chart [accessed 13 November 2021].

[67] Joseph J. Ellis, *Founding Brothers: The Revolutionary Generation* (New York, NY: Vintage Books, 2002), 4.

fared better than those who remained wedded to policies of state direction, as has unfortunately too often been the norm in the Middle East and Sub-Saharan Africa. Between 1960 and 2019, East Asia's per capita GDP grew 78.5-fold to $11,533. Per capita GDP in Latin America and the Caribbean grew 28.2-fold to $10,432 between 1960 and 2014. By contrast, per capita GDP in Sub-Saharan Africa grew only 12.5-fold to $1,601 between 1960 and 2019. South Asia's per capita GDP growth during the same period, which witnessed a 23.8-fold expansion, was also less than Latin America and, more particularly, East Asia. Although per capita GDP in the Middle East and North Africa rose 27.3-fold to $8,719 between 1965 and 2009, these gains owed much to the bounty of oil and gas reserves. Largely devoid of institutions supportive of economic and political liberalism, many Middle Eastern/North African societies imploded in the Arab Spring of 2011. By 2017, per capita GDP in the region ($6,536) was a quarter less than it had been nine years before. Beset by internal divisions and a re-embrace of socialist-type models in many jurisdictions (for example in Bolivia and Venezuela) Latin America and the Caribbean have also witnessed declining economic fortunes since the Global Financial Crisis (2008–2009).[68]

The subdued economic circumstances that have characterized regional economies in Latin America, the Middle East and Sub-Saharan Africa since 2008 are hardly unique. As Fig. 12.7 indicates, the same phenomenon has characterized all the economies associated with the OECD.[69]

The stagnant rates of economic growth and labor force participation that currently blight most economies have many causes: a large-scale growth in the state's economic footprint, falling productivity, higher regulatory costs. They also reflect, however, a decreased commitment to the very concept of economic growth. In the past, societies have often been more willing to accept western technology and its energy-intensive production systems than economic or political liberalism. Among Asian and African societies, this remains the case. Electricity consumption remains, arguably, the best proxy for western-style modernity, bringing with it lighting, heating, cooling and a host of lifestyle accessories: fridges,

---

[68] World Bank, *Online Database: Indicators—Economy & Growth: GDP per Capita (current US dollars)*, https://data.worldbank.org/indicator/NY.GDP.PCAP.CD?view=chart [Accessed 14 November 2021].

[69] Ibid.

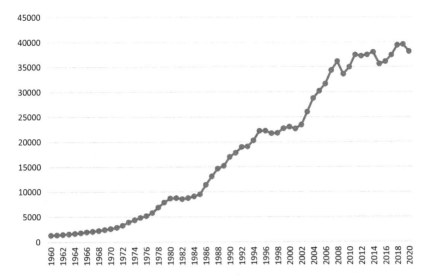

Fig. 12.7 Growth in GDP per capita, OECD average, 1960–2020 (in 2020 US dollars) (*Source* Calculated from World Bank, *Online Database—Indicators—Economy & Growth*)

stoves, washing machines, televisions, internet access. Accordingly, since 1960, electricity consumption has grown at an extraordinary rate. In South Asia, the percentage of the population with access to electricity rose from 46.9% to 94.4% between 1993 and 2019. Globally, per capita electricity consumption rose 2.6-fold to 3,131 kWh between 1960 and 2015.[70] Established technologies remain key to this achievement. Despite a vast expenditure on "renewables" (including solar, wind, solid waste, biofuels and so on), less than 10% of global power comes from non-hydro renewables. Conversely, two-thirds comes from fossil fuels.[71]

Long the least controversial aspect of modern western civilization, energy-intensive production systems and lifestyles have now arguably

---

[70] World Bank, Online Database: Indicators—Energy: Electric Power Consumption per Capita, https://data.worldbank.org/indicator/EG.USE.ELEC.KH.PC?view=chart [accessed 14 November 2021].

[71] World Bank, Online Database: Indicators—Energy: Electricity Production from Renewable Sources (excluding Hydroelectricity), https://data.worldbank.org/indicator/EG.ELC.RNWX.ZS?view=chart [accessed 14 November 2021].

become its most controversial feature. Among the advanced economies of the West, much of the population believe that our energy-intensive economy is now an existentialist threat to planetary survival.

Whether or not the increased temperatures that have characterized the industrial era are primarily due to industrialization is, however, a moot issue. As discussed in Chapter 4, however, fluctuations in climate are hardly new. The rising temperatures of the industrial era have also corresponded with a solar maximum associated with increased solar activity. As Valentina Zharkova's recent article in the journal, *Temperature*, indicates, this period of increased solar intensity now appears behind us as we enter into what Zharkova refers to as the "Modern Grand Solar Minimum" that she expects to last from 2020 to 2053. In her estimation, "this modern grand minimum" shares many features with the Maunder Minimum (1645–1710), a time during which "solar irradiance" fell by 0.22% and global temperatures by 1.0 to 1.5%. Accordingly, she believes that the new solar minimum will result in an "average terrestrial temperature" decline of "up to 1.0 °C", with adverse consequences for "agriculture, food supplies, and heating needs".[72] Perhaps, as with so many other climate predictions, Zharkova's analysis will prove to be misplaced. One needs to think very carefully, however, before one abandons the energy-intensive economy upon which our modern world is built. Without it the Malthusian economy once more beckons, and with it a return to poverty, misery and premature death.

What, then, of the future of the modern iteration of western civilization?

Writing amid the carnage of World War I, Oswald Spengler concluded that not only was our modern western civilization a recent phenomenon, it was also one with a "strictly limited" future. Everywhere, Spengler saw evidence of social division, economic stagnation and a spiritual crisis that presaged a catastrophic conclusion to the civilization's grand ambitions.[73] During World War II, the survival of the West and its values often hung by a thread. Reflecting on the growth of "racially homogenous enclaves" and the "balkanization of opinion" that accompanied the growth of "identity politics", Christopher Lasch was also pessimistic as

[72] Valentina Zharkova, "Editorial: Modern Grand Solar Minimum Will Lead to Terrestrial Cooling", *Temperature*, Vol. 7, No. 3 (2020), 221.

[73] Oswald Spengler (trans. Charles Francis Atkinson), *The Decline of the West*, second edition (New York, NY: Alfred A. Knopf, 1927), 39–40.

to the West's survival on the eve of his impending death in 1995. The "whole world", he lamented, "now seems to be going through a dark night of the soul".[74] In a similar personal situation to that experienced by Lasch in 1994, I cannot help but share his concerns. No civilization is guaranteed survival. Although our modern iteration of western civilization has delivered great benefits on many fronts—individualism, democracy, longer life expectancy, universal education, gender and racial equality—it has always emphasized values that entailed not only choice but also its universal twin—risk. As such it was always threatened by those for whom the perceived haven of collectivism offered greater enticements, namely security and a group-endowed sense of personal identity. Whether our civilization survives, therefore, comes down in the final analysis to choices. What do we prefer: individualism or collectivism? Choice or security? Freedom or collectivist control? An energy-intensive economy or another Malthusian catastrophe?

[74] Lasch, *The Revolt of the Elites*, 17–18, 246.

INDEX

0–9

1619 Project, xiii, 6, 17, 142, 143, 152, 204, 206, 230

3-Cs, the, 53, 136

A

Abbott, Elizabeth, 161

Abolition Society, 232, 235

absolutist state, 179–183, 187–189, 191, 194, 202

Achilles, 210

Adams, John, 197

Adorno, Theodor, 281, 339

A.E.G. (German electrical company), 109

Agamemnon, 210

Age of Absolutism

creation of the bureaucratic state, 271

emergence of salaried professionals, 285

Agrippa, Marcus, x

Algar, Humid, 328

Algeria

Algerian "Arab Spring" (2010–2012), 12

Arabo-Muslim, culture of, 3

Algerian War of Independence

expelling of its European population, 4

Front de Libération Nationale, 3

Al-i Ahmad, Jalal, 278, 281, 327–330

Allen, Robert, 12–14, 33, 49, 60, 69, 96, 97, 101, 104, 105, 116, 119, 120, 128, 132, 133, 168, 193, 198, 228, 256

Althusser, Louis, 339

American Anti-Slavery Society, 232

American Civil War. *See* Civil War (US); United States, the

American Federation of Labor, 279

American Fur Company, 16

American Revolution, 21, 27, 174, 195, 236, 279. *See also* United States, the

© The Editor(s) (if applicable) and The Author(s), under exclusive license to Springer Nature Switzerland AG 2022

B. Bowden, *Slavery, Freedom and Business Endeavor*, Palgrave Debates in Business History, https://doi.org/10.1007/978-3-030-97232-5

351

352 INDEX

ancient Athens
  Delian League, 172, 212
  democracy in, 23
  high capital costs of slavery, 222
  Laurion silver mine, 113
  legacies of, 21
  Peloponnesian War, 164, 171, 173
ancient Greece, vii, 171. *See also*
  ancient Athens
ancient Rome, vii. *See also* Republican
  Rome
  Antonine Plague, 175, 212
  citizenship and homogeneity, 318
  decline of, 174
  Mediterranean plundering, 164,
    174, 176, 215
  mining activities, 175
  Punic Wars, 174, 184, 212
  slave reforms, 112, 159, 173
  slavery in, 156, 222
Anderson, Perry, 221
Anglo-Dutch Shell, 299
Annales School (France), viii
Appian (Roman historian), 174, 215
Aquinas, St Thomas, 178
Arab Spring, 12, 326, 346
Argentina, 6, 63, 141, 169, 209, 300,
  309, 313
Armenian Genocide, xviii, 319
Armstrong, General Samuel, 241
Asia
  monsoon failure, effects of, 79, 80
  weather patterns, 79
Ataturk, Kemal, 322
Atlantic slavery, 225, 226. *See also*
  slavery
Auschwitz, 29
Australia
  Aboriginal, 40. *See also* Indigenous
    Australians
  Carrington, 275, 276
  convict and indentured labor, 162

El Niño and La Niña weather
  patterns, 79
Indigenous Australians, 40, 103
Indigenous school attendance, 39
Melanesian labor in Queensland,
  162, 163
Modern Slavery Act 2018, 155
population, 162, 314
road and rail development, 252,
  335
sheep industry, 252, 310
as source of British exports, 141
trade unions
  union membership, 283, 284
White Australia policy, 335
wool exports, 193, 313
Workplace Gender Equality Agency,
  341
Aztecs, 39, 51, 68, 211
  effects of cold climate on, 76
  slavery and ritual sacrifices, 159

B
Bailyn, Bernard, 21, 174, 196, 236
Baltic grain and timber trade, 123
Baptist, Edward, 205
Barbados, 235
Barkey, Karen, 318
Beckert, Sven, xii, 14, 17, 18, 204,
  205, 220
Bedeian, Art, 23
Belgium, 13, 22, 34, 116, 129, 193,
  194, 278, 313, 314
Belgium Congo, 311
Bell, Alexander, 269
Benedictine monasteries, 176
Berglund, Bjorn E., 75
Bermuda-Azores High, 79, 85
Bessemer process, 257
BHP, 275
Biden Administration

"Build Back Better" program, 302
New Green Deal, 302
bills of exchange, 186
biomass and biofuels, 292
"Black Death", 31, 92
Black Lives Matter, 204
Black Panthers, 3
Blackstone, Sir William, 22, 151, 152, 199, 233, 234
Blainey, Geoffrey, 103, 134
Blake McKay sole-sewing machine, 108
Bloch, Marc, viii, 48, 191, 192
Bolivar, Simón, 194
Bonaparte, Napoleon
Battle of the Nile, 325
Bonnet de Condillac, Etienne, 73
Boulton, Matthew, 132
bourgeois individualism, 183, 190, 202. *See also* individualism
Calvinism, 188
bourgeois society
and self-interest, 26
BP, 299
Braudel, Fernand, viii, xv, 16, 26, 31–34, 56–61, 63, 65, 68, 69, 76, 89–92, 100, 101, 103, 104, 111, 115, 118, 121, 123, 124, 126, 127, 131, 181, 182, 185–187, 189–192, 209, 210, 259
Braverman, Harry, 278
Brazil, 6, 141, 157, 173, 225, 226, 327
and slave trading, 207
slavery in, 209
transportation of African slaves, 32
Brexit referendum, 291
Bridgewater Canal, 123
Britain
abolition of the Corn Laws, 293
abolition of the slave trade, 38, 230

Bill of Rights, 22–24
birth rates, 288
"Black Death", 31, 92
Brexit referendum, 291
Bridgewater Canal, 123
building workers, real wages growth, 13, 229, 279
calorie intake, 32
Cambridge University, 232
Civil War (1642–1651), 23, 194
Coalbrookdale ironworks, 128
coal production, 128–130
cotton imports, 253
cotton textile production, 18
curtailment of slavery, 151
decline in factory employment, 282
deforestation in, 126
"enclosure movement", 59, 60
energy shortages, 2021, 292
female education and white-collar employment, 287
free trade, 258
George III, 174
"Glorious Revolution", 1688, 23, 196, 279
immigration to Chesapeake, 207
Industrial Revolution, xii, 13, 14, 17, 18, 47, 59, 97, 101, 104, 127, 139, 144, 147
coal production, 129
investment in India, 312
investment in white-settler colonies, 312
iron production, 127, 129
on the killing of slaves in colonies, 218
life expectancy in England, 267
Little Ice Age, 97
and the Malthusian trap, 82, 97, 104, 116, 193
and mass consumerism, 280
Modern Slavery Act 2015, 155

354 INDEX

nationalization, 293, 298
Oxford University, 233
population, 6, 18, 25, 33, 39, 47, 152, 194, 207, 267, 278, 291
real wages, 13, 37, 229
Reform Acts, 278
rise of salaried professionals, 283, 286, 291
slaves transported, xii
stagnation in food consumption, 116
steam power in, 14, 101
taxation, 293, 297, 299
trade in slavery, 96, 208, 226, 229, 234
transportation of African slaves, 208, 227
transportation of convicts, 162
urbanization, 116, 117
use of watermills, 101, 103
use of water power, 101
and woolen textile exports, 141, 228
British House of Commons, 195
British India. *See also* India
education, growth in attendance, 7
food crop cultivation, 253, 254
imports and exports of treasure, 1849–1920, 312
infrastructure expenditure, 297
merchandise imports and exports, 1849–1920, 307
principal merchandise exports and exports, 1849–1919, 308
university graduates by academic discipline, 323
British Steel, 292
Browne, Edward, 327
Brunel, Isambard Kingdom, 133
Bryer, Rob, 221
Buchenwald, 29

Burckhardt, Jacob, 22, 23, 93, 180, 181
bureaucratic state
compatibility with democracy, 301
emergence of salaried professionals, 285
rise of, 271
and university graduates, 27
Burke, Edmund, 27, 150, 153, 195, 200, 234

C
Caesar, Octavian, x
California Board of Education, 334
calorific energy, 53, 103, 131, 136
Calvinism, 187, 188
Camus, Albert, 2, 7, 201, 271–273
The Myth of Sisyphus, 7
Canada
fall in factory employment, 282
as source of British exports, 309, 313
union membership, 284
canal systems
advantages of, 123
Cantillon, Richard, 73
capitalism, vii, ix, x, xii–xiv, 19, 23, 25, 27, 54, 169, 179, 188, 201, 202, 220, 221, 224, 257, 260, 261, 266, 279, 281, 303, 306, 312, 321, 326, 339
as polar opposite of slavery, 221
Caribbean
collapse of the native population on European impact, 113
slave population, 157, 209
Carnegie Steel, 299
Carolingian era, 184, 192
Carolingian Period, xv
Carthage, 174, 184
Casement, Roger, 311

INDEX 355

Catholic Church, 89, 177
Catlin, George, 15, 16, 70, 251, 252, 305
 on Indigenous diet deficiencies, 305
Cato the Elder, 109, 156–158, 216
Ceylan, Ebubekir, 318
Chandler, Alfred, 107, 119, 120, 129, 133, 285, 286, 294
Charlemagne, 185
cheques, issuance of, 186
Chile, 79, 210, 313
 guano production, 62
China
 agriculture and rising productivity, 64
 Confucianism, 176
 Foxconn factory, Shenzhen, 277
 iron production, 127
 Opium Wars, 66, 311
 per capita GDP, post-1960, 324, 327
 proto-industrialization in Yangtze Delta, 118, 119
 Qing state, 66
 suzhi workers, 277
China Daily, 277
cinema and television, 281
Cipolla, Carlo, 12, 34, 89, 94, 95, 101, 103, 110, 111, 122, 125, 139, 140, 183, 184, 192
Cistercian monasteries, 178
civilization. *See also* western civilization
 characteristics of, 6, 30, 301, 315
 decline of, 45
Civil War (US), 28, 107, 141, 144–146, 152, 173, 224, 231, 235, 236, 238–240, 252, 307, 311
 and African American soldiers, xiii
Clark, Gregory, 50, 60, 97, 290

Clarkson, Thomas, 151, 232, 234, 235
Claudius (Emperor), 159
Clay, Henry (Senator), 121
Cleaver, Eldridge, 3
climate change, 82, 261, 291, 292, 302. *See also* Dark Ages Cooling Period; global warming; Little Ice Age; Maunder Minimum (1645–1710); Medieval Warming Period; Roman Warming Period
coal
 consumption of, 125, 131, 134
 expansion of production, 123
 trade in, 123
Coalbrookdale ironworks, 128
collective-based identity, 10
collectivism, x, xiv, xvii, 258, 260, 262, 272, 322, 343, 349
colonial education systems, 322
common law, 22, 151, 180, 218, 233. *See also* Britain
Confederate States (US), 17, 145
Constantine the Great, 218
Cooke, Bill, xii, xiii, 205, 206, 220
Copernicus, Nicholas, 94, 178
corn
 advantages of cultivation, 68
 Aztec cultivation of, 67, 68
 as central to pre-Columbian America, 68, 69
 establishment in Africa, 68
 nutritional problems, 69
 spread to Asia, 53, 69
Corriere della Sera (Italian newspaper), 327
Cort, Henry, 128
COVID-19, x, 10, 43, 170, 260, 261
Crafts, Nicholas, 37
Crassus (ancient Roman citizen), 159, 160
Cromwell, Oliver, 196

356 INDEX

Crumley, Carole, 75
Cuba, 173, 226, 262
 slavery in, 39

D
Darby family, 128, 129
Dark Ages Cooling Period, 74, 75, 88, 90
Davis, Jefferson, 242
Deane, Phyllis, 12, 124, 147
de Bellaigue, Christopher, 4, 11, 159, 160, 318, 319, 326
 "coercive modernizers", 11, 322
Deering Harvester Machine Company, 108
Defoe, Daniel, 120
Delgado, Richard, 41–43, 343
Delian League, 172, 212
democracy, xi, xiv, xvii, 6, 8–11, 21–25, 54, 135, 136, 152, 153, 155, 167–169, 171–173, 177, 195, 196, 198, 200, 201, 212, 258, 278–280, 294, 301, 303, 315, 320, 322, 349. *See also* individualism; liberalism
Denmark, 194, 197, 279, 313
Derrida, Jacques, 2, 3, 339, 340, 344
de Saint-Just, Louis Antoine, 200, 202
de San Martin, José, 194
Desmond, Matthew, 17, 142, 144, 204, 226, 230, 274
de Tocqueville, Alexis, 23
 on slavery, 203
 tyranny of the majority, 188
Domesday Book (England), 100
Douglass, Frederick, xi, 157–159, 204, 211, 212, 216–219, 221, 231–233, 239, 335
 Frederick Douglass' Paper, 231
 Northern Star, 231

Du Bois, W.E.B., 17, 203, 210, 239, 240, 242–244, 262
Du Pont, 109

E
Eastern Europe, 114, 182, 266, 294. *See also* Europe
 commercialization of agriculture, 114
 economic growth and labor force participation, 346
 recent stagnation of, 94
Egypt. *See also* Roman Egypt
 high capital costs of slavery in ancient times, 222
 Mamluks, 160
 modernization of, 326
 Muslim Brotherhood, 305, 326
 as supplier of Britain's cotton needs, 145
 western technologies and bureaucratic governance, 326
Ellis, Joseph, 236, 345
El Niño, 71, 80, 81
El Niño–Southern Oscillation, 53, 79–82
"enclosure movement", 59, 60
encomienda plantation system, 32, 114
energy
 increase in demand for coal, 132
 in iron production, 129
 nineteenth-century production revolution, 119, 130, 141
 steam-powered ships, 8, 140
 use in production, 99
Engels, Frederick, 22, 179, 189, 200, 261, 265, 266, 301, 321, 336
Engerman, Stanley, 205, 206
England. *See* Britain
Enlightenment, the, 199
Errazzouki, Samia, 165

INDEX 357

Europe. *See also* Eastern Europe
absolutist states, 179, 181, 182,
  187, 194
agricultural innovations, 49, 58,
  106, 113, 114, 116, 192, 193
birthrates, 288, 289
"Black Death", 92
calorific intakes, 57
cereal yields, 192
climate variation, 78
crop cultivation, 91, 190
Dark Ages Cooling Period, 75, 88,
  90
death rates, 288–290
emergence of modern Europe, 88
and feudalism, 90
growth of merchant marine, 101
iron production, 127
literacy rates, 33
Little Ice Age, 75, 88, 91
low alcohol beer production, 57
malnourishment, 60
and the Malthusian trap, 31, 53,
  88, 91, 92, 94, 193
medieval technological
  advancement, 22, 31, 48, 58,
  88, 90–92, 111, 126, 179, 185
Medieval Warming Period, 90, 91
merchant fleet carrying capacities,
  33
New World "grain invasion", 106
political economies of, 31, 34, 90
population decline in, 289
population growth in, 255, 304
real-wage fluctuations, 35, 92
rise of early modernity, 94
serfdom, 114, 219
slavery in, 19, 20, 164, 205, 207,
  219, 226
three-field cultivation system, 58,
  190, 192
urbanization, 116, 119

use of watermills, 101
wheat production, 57–59, 64, 190,
  194
Ewell, Philip, 334
existentialism, 329. *See also* Sartre,
  Jean-Paul

F
Fabian socialism, 261
Fagan, Brian, 71
Fanon, Franz, 3, 4, 6, 17, 169, 262,
  306, 323
Faustian pact, xvi
Feagin, Joe R., 42, 43, 303, 321
Febvre, Lucien, viii
Ferrel cell, 78
feudalism, 22, 26, 90
Fishback, Price, 296
Fisk, General Clinton, 241
Fisk University, 240, 241
Florence, 35, 51
  cloth trade, 118
Florentine Codex, 67
Fogel, Robert, 32, 205, 206
Foner, Eric, 238
food intake
  daily calorie requirements, 99
  and human survival, 99
Foucault, Michel, xiv, 154, 327, 339,
  340
Fox, Charles, 234
Foxconn factory, Shenzhen, 277
France
  aristocracy, 181, 182, 190
  COVID-19, associated stimulus
    expenditure, 170
  *Declaration of the Rights of Man
    and the Citizen*, 149, 200, 320
  decline in farm employment, 116,
    118
  deforestation, 90

358 INDEX

falling birthrate during
industrialization, 289
famines in, 60
female *lycées*, 287
government debt as share of GDP,
298
government social expenditure, 299
guild system, 189
L'École Normale Supérieure, 339
literacy, rises in, 267
National Convention, 1792, 200
peasantry's support of Napoleon,
202
population growth, 191, 303
road maintenance by the peasantry,
121, 299
slave and sugar economy in Haiti,
56
small family-owned enterprises, 301
state centralization, 259
taille, imposition of, 191
taxation, 294, 296, 297
universal male suffrage, 279
University of Paris, 178
urbanization, 117
use of canals, 124
Frankenberg, Ruth, 206
Frankfurt School, ix, 281, 339
Franklin Roosevelt's New Deal, 295
Frederick the Great, 199
freedom. *See* Foucault, Michel;
Nietzsche, Friedrich; Schelling,
Friedrich
characteristics of, 21
civil and natural, 150, 151
French Revolution, 24, 25, 32, 153,
182, 197, 200, 201, 279
Friedman, Milton, 301, 321
Friedman, Thomas, xiv
Front de Libération Nationale, 3. *See
also* Algeria
Fulton, Robert, 125

G

Gagarin, Yuri, 47
Galileo, Galilei, x
Gandhi, Mahatma, 253, 262, 330,
331
Gavrilis, George, 318
General Electric, 109
George III, 174
Germany
agricultural productivity, 109
cartels, 108, 259, 294
emigration, 16
fertilizer rates, 109
iron production, 129
Nazism
race-based identity under
Nazism, 41
rise as industrial superpower, 108,
118, 259
universal male suffrage, 279
urbanization, 117
as a wool exporter, 141, 313
Glasgow COP26 Climate Change
Conference, 131
global electricity consumption
rise in, 346
global warming. *See also* climate
change
atmospheric cells, 78
dangers of cold climate, 76
drought and cooling periods, 74
six European climatic periods, 74
Gompers, Samuel, 279
Gorbachev, Mikhail, 282
Great Britain. *See* Britain
Great Divergence Debate, 49, 168,
205. *See also* Pomeranz, Kenneth
Gross Domestic Product (GDP), 10,
18, 37, 48, 170, 261, 272,
293–297, 299, 303, 324, 325,
327–329, 337, 345–347
Guelzo, Allen, 230, 232, 233, 239

Gulf states
maritime craft, 102
Gutenberg printing press, 94

H
Habakkuk, H.J., 12, 124, 147
Habermas, Jürgen, 339
Hadley cell, 78
Haiti
slave population of, 143, 208
Hannah-Jones, Nikole, xiii, 6, 144, 152, 204, 226, 230, 236
Hargreaves, James, 97, 167
Harvard University, 241, 242
Hayek, Friedrich, 258–261, 272, 273, 302
Hegel, Georg, 28, 200
Herzen, Alexander, 317
High Middle Ages, the, 177
Hinton, Elias, 161
Hobbes, Thomas, 27, 198, 199
Hobsbawm, Eric, 144, 252, 257, 269, 276, 279, 281, 283, 286–288, 291, 293, 301, 309, 313
Holland. *See* Netherlands
Homer, 210
Hopkins, Keith, 112, 113, 164, 173, 214, 215
Horkheimer, Max, 281, 339
Howe sewing machine, 107
Hume, David, 27, 28
hunter-gatherer societies, 55
Huntington, Samuel
on rival civilizations to the West, 1, 2, 6, 270
Hussein, Saddam, 322

I
"identity politics", 348
rise of, xi
Iliad, The, 77

indentured servants, 49, 160–162, 207
India. *See also* British India; Nehru, Jawaharlal
communal violence on independence, 320
Congress Party, 319
cotton textiles, 96, 184, 221, 330, 332
effects of weather on agriculture, 79
Handicrafts Development Corporation, 331
Human Development Index, 256
infrastructure projects, British expenditure, 297
maritime craft, 102
mercantile class, 184
monsoon failure, 79
National Handloom Development Corporation, 332
per capita GDP, 324, 325
railroad expansion, 252, 253
as source of British exports, 313
as supplier of Britain's cotton needs, 145
urbanization, 116
Indian Ocean Dipole, 80, 81
individual identity, x, xvii, 10, 22, 40, 153, 318
individualism. *See also* democracy; liberalism
aristocratic individualism, 176
bourgeois individualism, 183, 188, 190, 202
peasant individualism, 183, 189, 190, 192
personal choice, 24
role of universities, 178–180, 183
scholarly individualism, 176, 178–180, 183
industrialization
ethnic and racial interaction, 335

360 INDEX

ethnic pecking orders in, 335
fights over blue-collar jobs, 335
improved material circumstances,
  288
and mass consumerism, 280
Industrial Revolution
  coal production, 129
  growth in industrial output, 14
  improvements in transportation,
    viii, 15
  as a managerial revolution, 148
  population mobility, 17
  real wages in Britain during, 13, 97
Intergovernmental Panel on Climate
  Change (IPCC), 74
International Scientific Committee on
  Price History, 48
internet, 8, 314, 347
  users of, 4
Intertropical Convergence Zone, 78,
  79, 82, 85
Iran
  Constitutional Revolution, 1906,
    327
  hostility to western economic
    models, 4, 327
  Iranian Revolution, 327, 329
Ireland, 56
  immigration to Chesapeake, 207
  transportation of convicts, 162
Islam, 1, 318, 329
  slavery in the Middle East and
    North Africa, 2
Islamic Brotherhood, 1, 5
Islamic Enlightenment, 4, 326
Islamic North Africa, 2
Ismail I (Egyptian ruler, 1863–1879),
  325
Italy
  merchant cities during the
    Renaissance, 22
  output per capita, 1500–1850, 20

Padua University, 180
peasant conditions, 32
post–sixteenth century decline, 19,
  32
University of Perugia, 178
urbanization, 116

J
Japan
  life expectancy, rises in, 9, 267
  literacy, rises in, 33, 268
  proto-industrialization in, 119
Jefferson, Thomas, xi
Journal of Management History, vii,
  xii, xix, xxvii, 19
Journal of the Society for Music Theory,
  334

K
Kant, Emmanuel, 199
Karmen, Henry, 179
Kolyma goldfield, eastern Siberia, 113
Komlos, John, 49, 98
Kotkin, Joel, 260, 263, 283, 285,
  291, 314
Kotkin, Stephen, 113, 170, 282

L
Lakota (Sioux), 16, 40, 70
Lamont, Michele, 291
La Niña, 79
Laos, 262
Lasch, Christopher, 41, 285, 333,
  334, 348, 349
latifundia (slave estate), 109, 112,
  174, 175, 216, 217, 219, 221,
  222. *See also* ancient Rome
Latinos
  as American citizens, 322
Leary, Timothy, 3

Lefebvre, Georges, 182
Left, the, 290, 291
    ideology and identity politics, 339
Lenin, Vladimir, 127, 169, 257
    on imperialism, 109, 169, 257,
        306, 312, 315
Leopold II, 311. *See also* Belgium
    Congo
Leung, Elly, xiv, 11, 277
Lewis, Thomas, 151
liberalism. *See also* democracy;
        individualism
    economic liberalism, 8, 22–24,
        257–260, 272, 273
    individualism and entrepreneurship,
        301
    political liberalism, xvii, 8–11, 24,
        25, 152, 258, 262, 263, 326,
        346
life expectancy, 34, 37, 49, 51, 52,
    57, 111, 255, 256, 266, 267,
    314, 349
Lincoln, Abraham, xi, xiii, 158, 159,
    231
Little Ice Age, 75, 88, 91, 97
Lloyd Garrison, William, 231. *See also*
    American Anti-Slavery Society
    Liberator, 232
Locke, John, 23, 27, 28, 149, 170,
    196, 199
    suspicion of state power, 27
Lomis, Stanley, 200
Louis XIV ("Sun King", 1643–1715),
    91
Luther, Martin, x

M
Madison, James, xi
Maghreb, 3
"Malthusian ceiling", 31, 33, 34, 36,
    50, 52, 279
"Malthusian trap"

demographic collapse and new
    social possibilities, 88
hypothesis of, 29
technologically-induced traps, 104
Malthus, Thomas, 29, 50, 52, 73, 97.
    See also "Malthusian trap"
Manichaeism, 3
Mansfield, Lord, 151, 234, 236
Marcuse, Herbert, ix, 280, 339
Marlowe, Christopher, x
Marshall, Alfred, 258
Marx, Karl, 22, 28, 179, 189, 200,
    220, 261, 265, 266, 273, 278,
    301, 321, 336
    Das Kapital, xiii
    on slavery, xiii, 220
Matabele warrior massacre, 270
Mayan civilization
    classical period, 82, 83
    and climatic variation, 53
    embrace of human sacrifice and
        slavery, 86
    four collapses of, 84, 86
    and the Intertropical Convergence
        Zone, 82, 85
    and land clearing, 84
    and the Malthusian trap, 30, 82
    "Three Rivers Region", 30
Maynard Keynes, John, 269, 313
McCloskey, Deidre, 24
McCormick Harvesting Machine
    Company, 108
Medieval Warming Period, 90, 91
medieval world
    demise of serfdom, 183
    political economies of, 26
    religious life, 176
    village blacksmiths, arrival of, 192
Meikle, Scott, 172
Mexico, 68, 327
    dry-land corn yields in colonial
        times, 68

362 INDEX

Michels, Robert, 279
Middle East, 2, 4, 55, 57, 58, 164,
176, 256, 269, 278, 281, 346
Middles Ages. *See* medieval world
milletization, x, xviii, 42, 43, 334,
340, 341, 343
millet system, 42, 318, 319. *See also*
Ottoman Empire
and conformism, xi, 42, 318, 319
in modern society and life, 334,
341
Mill, John Stuart, 27, 65, 66, 170,
258, 266, 272, 278, 302
on competition and monopolies,
259, 266
free market, visions of, 258, 273
Milton, John, 196
Mintz, Sidney, 56
Moche civilization (Peru), 51, 71
modern state, the, xvii, 27, 270, 301,
320
growth of, 271, 272
spending at higher levels than
revenue intake, 297
Montesquieu, 23
Morgan, Edmund, 161, 207
Morgan, J.P., 299
Morgan, Lewis, 125, 126
Morse, Samuel, viii
Mozart, Wolfgang, 198
Muhammad, Khalil, 143
Muhammed Ali (Egyptian ruler,
1805–1849), 325
multiculturalism, 42

N
Nairn, Bede, 261
Napoleon III, 201, 301
Nasser, Gamal, 322, 326
Nature (journal), 81
Nazi regime (Germany), 41. *See also*
Germany

Nef, John, 34, 57, 104, 105, 123,
127, 198
Nehru, Jawaharlal, 306, 319, 320,
322–324, 330, 331
enthusiasm for industrialization,
331
hostility to private enterprise, 324
"neo-liberal" critique. *See* Friedman,
Milton
Netherlands, the
feudal lords offering peasants their
freedom, 115
fluyt ships, 122
"Golden Age" (1570–1870), 34,
95, 122
Leiden University, 180
peasant innovations, 32, 64, 193
real wages in, 49
trade with the Dutch East Indies
(Indonesia), 95
transportation of African slaves, 227
wind power production, 100
"new capitalism", 148
Newcomen's steam engine, 125
New Mexico, 77
droughts in, 77
New South Wales, 252
self-government, 25
Newton, Isaac, 94
New World, xvi, 9, 16, 19–23, 32,
39, 62, 94, 114, 140, 141, 160,
193, 195, 210, 218, 223, 278,
310, 311, 335. *See also* Canada,
Caribbean, Maya, Mexico, United
States
crops, 56
grain invasion of Europe, 106
immigration, 16, 336
Potosi silver mine, 214
protein deficiencies in diet, 56
New Zealand, 103, 136, 141, 197,
312, 335

INDEX   363

wool exports, 193, 313
Nietzsche, Friedrich, 153–155, 340
Nigeria, 319
  Biafran War, 319
North Africa, 3, 53, 55, 57, 79, 160, 164, 165, 176, 345, 346
  slavery in, 165
North Atlantic Oscillation, 53, 79, 80, 82, 85
North Korea, 4, 197, 262

O
Ocasio-Cortez, Alexandria, 302
Oldroyd, David, 221
Old Testament, 77, 176
Olmstead, Alan L., 144
O'Rourke, Kevin, 106
Orwell, George, xiv
  1984, xiv
Ottoman Empire. *See* Ottoman Turkey
Ottoman Turkey
  Armenian Genocide, xviii, 42, 319
  communal strife in, 319
  Greco-Turkish War, 319
  janissary corps, 160
  Kurdish struggles in, 319
  literacy in, 319
  millet system, x, xviii, 42, 211, 318, 321
  slavery in, 160

P
Pacioli, Luca, 178, 186
Pahlavi, Reza (Shah of Iran), 327
Paine, Thomas, 195–197, 199
Pan-African Congress, 243
Parthasarathi, Prasannan, 81, 253
peasant individualism, 183, 189, 190.
  See also individualism
Peloponnesian War, 164, 171, 172

Pennsylvania Railroad, 292
Pericles, 171, 172
Peron, Juan, 322
Peru, 51, 78. *See also* Moche civilization (Peru)
  guano production, 62
Phipps, Simone, xii, 19, 230
Piketty, Thomas, 302, 304, 305
Pirenne, Henri, 22, 26, 88, 93, 122, 183–185, 191
  "Pirenne Thesis", 184, 185, 191
Pitt, William, 234
Pius, Antoninus, 218
Plutarch, 113, 156, 159, 174, 211
Poland, xii, 19, 32, 122, 182
Polar cell, 78
political–economic models, 1850–2021, 300
political liberalism, xvii, 8–11, 24, 25, 152, 258, 262, 263, 326, 346
Pollard, Sidney, 38, 130, 147, 148, 313
Polybius, 173, 174
Pomeranz, Kenneth, 49, 56, 205, 209
  Great Divergence Debate, 49, 168, 205
Portugal
  capture of Ceuta, 165
  colonization of Brazil, 225
  plantation slavery, 225
  and the slave trade, xii
  transportation of African slaves, 227
pre-industrial energy sources
  heating and smelting, 103
  shipping fleets, 101
  use of horses in agriculture, 100
  water and wind, 101
  wood, 103
pre-industrial society
  advantages of human labor over animal power, 111
  high value of livestock, 111

364 INDEX

labor-intensive work practices and
slavery, 111
labor shortages, 112
tyranny of distance, 120
use of slavery, 111
Price, Jacinta, 39, 40
Prieto, Leon, xii, 19

Q

Quakers, xiii, 232
Quesnay, Francois, 73
Qutb, Sayyid, 1, 2, 5, 305, 306, 322,
326. *See also* Islamic Brotherhood

R

racism, 36, 204, 206, 243, 274, 303
and slavery, 206
Rand, Ayn, xiv
Anthem, xiv
real wages, 35, 37, 43, 48–50, 92,
97, 229
Reconquista, 32, 114, 164
Reformation, xv
Renaissance, xv, 22, 23, 33, 93, 183,
186, 192, 195
representative democracy, 25, 54. *See
also* democracy
Republican Rome. *See also* ancient
Rome
demands of urban growth, 113
Italian people, decline of, 215
legacies of, 176
slavery in, 174
Return of the Jedi, 29
Rhode, Paul W., 144
Rhodes, Cecil, 270
rice
advantages over wheat, 64
difficulties in cultivating, 64
population increases, 64
production yields, 64

Robespierre, Maximilien, 200, 202
Rockefeller, John D., 48, 256
Standard Oil Trust, 256
Roman Egypt, 51, 112
cost of unskilled waged labor, 112
Rousseau, Jean-Jacques, 23, 149, 150,
153, 199
Rudd, Kevin, 261
Russell, J.C., 88, 89
Russia
1917 revolution, 201
Cossack presence in Iran, 327
iron production, 127
Muscovite and *boyar* pact, 115
rural communism, 317
urbanization, 116

S

Said, Edward, 2
Saint-Domingue. *See* Haiti
Sartre, Jean-Paul, 328
Schelling, F.W.J., 153, 154
Schlögel, Karl, 214
scholarly individualism, 176,
178–180. *See also* individualism
Schumpeter, Joseph, 167, 179, 181,
224
Scott, Dred, 238
serfdom, 112, 114, 189, 219. *See also*
peasant individualism
contrast with slavery, 112
decline of, 219
Europe's "second serfdom", 114
Shakespeare, William, 31, 198, 242
Shari'ati, Ali, 327–330
shipping, 8, 15, 54, 123, 124, 132,
133, 140, 209, 237, 256, 269
materials and powering of, 129
transformation into a mechanized
industry, 134
Silverstein, Jake, 6

INDEX 365

Singer sewing machine, 107
slavery. *See also* serfdom
  abolition of, xiii, 39, 230, 233
  African transportation to the
    Americas, 19, 224
  in the Americas, 225
  in ancient Greece, 171
  in ancient Rome, 156, 209, 222
  conflicts between masters and
    slaves, 217
  contrasts with serfdom, 114, 219
  cotton production, 17, 39, 142
  definition of, 155, 156
  disadvantages of, 165
  division of labor, 206
  economics of, 220
  legacies of, xiii, 204, 239
  natural increase in the United
    States, 157, 222
  occupations and industries, 163
  plantation economies, 21, 207,
    209, 223
  Potosi silver mine, 214
  and racism, 206
  reasons for, 234
  societies involved in, xii
  targeting of the "other", 211
  Trans-Atlantic Slave Trade
    Database, xii, 207, 225
  transportation of African slaves,
    208, 209, 225, 227
  in the United States, 152, 209, 235
Smith, Adam, 27, 73, 119, 122, 123,
    168, 170, 206
  on slavery, 65
Soho foundry, 132
Somerset, James, 151, 234
Southern Oscillation, 79
Soviet Union, 10, 113, 213, 214,
    262, 271, 272, 279, 282, 330
Spain
  independence struggles against, 16

  large estates worked by serf-like
    workforces, 32
  plantation slavery, 225
  pledging New World bullion against
    loans, 187
  population decline, 289
  Reconquista, the, 32
  slavery during Moorish period, 223
  and the slave trade, xii
  University of Salamanca, 179
  urbanization, 117
  Visigoth Kingdom, 218
  as a wool exporter, 141
Sparta, 164
Spengler, Oswald, xv, xvii, 36, 44,
    251, 263, 270, 348
Spotify, ix
Springfield Armory, 133
SS Great Britain, 269
SS Great Western, 133
Stalin, Joseph, 114
Standard Oil. *See* Rockefeller, John D.
State Board of Education (California),
    41
state control, x, 272
state intervention, 170, 258, 260,
    261, 299, 301, 322, 323
steam-powered ships, 15, 134, 135,
    276
  benefits of, 8
Steckel, Richard H., 69, 70, 267, 268
steel production, 140, 276. *See also*
    Australia
  innovations in production, 106
Stefancic, Jean, 41–43, 343
Students for Fair Admissions, 43
Sub-Saharan Africa, 5, 165, 345, 346
Sudan, 319
  South Sudanese independenc, 319
Supreme Court (United States), 43
Sweden, 127, 294–299, 313
Switzerland, 279, 313, 314

366 INDEX

T

Taney, Roger (US Supreme Court Chief Justice), 158
Tawney, R.H., 188
Taylor, Alan, 77, 143, 160–162, 222
"Taylorist" control, 206
telegraphs, viii, 135, 326
underwater cable links, 269
Thatcher, Margaret, 293, 294
the Algerian Revolution, 169, 323
the state, x, xvii, xviii, 10, 25–28, 50, 73, 87, 125, 155, 169–171, 179, 181, 185, 189, 199, 200, 234, 237, 260, 261, 272–274, 293, 294, 296, 302–304, 337, 346
role of, 23, 198, 301
Thomas, Sir Hugh, 19, 20, 32, 39, 69, 96, 113, 164, 217, 223
Thompson, Bradley, 27, 28, 196, 199, 236
Thompson, E.P., 335, 336
totalitarian rule
examples of, 294
Toynbee, Arnold, 260
trade unions, 275, 277, 279, 283, 335
transport revolution
effects on markets and competition, 8, 120
emergence of new industries, 9, 21, 299
railroads and iron, 106
reduction in travel times, 121
sea-borne transport, 122, 125
use of canals, 124
Trebilcock, Clive, 17, 32, 108, 109, 115, 117–119, 259, 289, 294, 311
Troy, 164
Trump, Donald, 282, 291
Tuchman, Barbara W., 90
Tyson, Thomas, 221

Tzouliadis, Tim, 114, 213

U

Uluru, 39
Unilever, 299
United Nations
Human Development Index (HDI), 37
measure of extreme poverty, 66
United States, the. *See also* American Revolution, the; Biden Administration; Civil War (US); Confederate States (US)
abandonment of African American farms, 243
abolitionism in, 152, 232
African American colleges, 241, 242
agricultural societies, Mississippi Valley, 51
American Revolution, 279
anti-trust movements, 1880s–1890s, 201
Blair family, 238
as Britain's most important source of imports, 308
Calvinism, 188
Chesapeake colony indentured servants, 207
Civil War, xiii, 107, 140, 144, 146, 217, 252
coal production, 129, 130
Constitutional Convention, 1787, 236
costs of slaves in Virginia, 237
cotton production, xii, 18, 21, 144, 145, 313
COVID-19, associated stimulus expenditure, x, 170
Declaration of Independence, xi
democratic ideals and independence, 194
erosion of economic liberalism, 260

ethnic groups, use of as strike breakers, 335
fall of factory employment, 282
farm mechanization, 108
farm ownership by race, 244
Federal Constitution, 1789, 151
female participation in education, 247, 287
first American Constitution, 236
Franklin Roosevelt's New Deal, 295
Free Soil Party, the, 238
Gallup Race Relations Survey, 342
government debt as share of GDP, 297, 298
government social expenditure, share of GDP, 299
government spending as share of GDP, 170, 261, 294, 295, 297, 337
Great Migration, 336
Gross Domestic Product (GDP) in, 18, 170, 294–297, 299, 304, 337
Gross National Product (GNP) in, 205, 280
health of Native American populations, 70
Hoover government, 295
immigration, 140
indentured servants, 160, 207
iron production, 129
Jim Crow laws, 28, 336
Kansas-Nebraska Act 1854, 238
labor force participation, 247
Liberal Party, 238
and mass consumerism, 280
Massachusetts abolitionists, 204, 231
mechanization of production, 15
multiunit corporations, 108
natural increase in slave populations, 217

paddle-steamers, 134
plantation economies, 21
poverty in the south, 239
Puritan communities, 188
race, education and labor participation, 41, 244, 247
racial privileges, 321
railroad development, 15, 107, 124, 140, 276, 281, 335
Reconstruction-era civil rights, 336
Republican Party, 238, 239
Sherman Antitrust Act 1890, 294
taxation, 294, 296, 297, 299
Thirteenth Amendment, 152, 239
union membership according to profession, 284
urbanization, 117
use of canals for transport, 124
voting rights in states of, 151
Wall Street crash, 295
universities
    attendance, 39, 267
    graduate employment opportunities, 291
    as a world phenomenon, 183, 287
University of Atlanta, 241
University of Berlin, 241
University of Geneva, 181

V
Veblen, Thorstein, 63, 108, 182, 254
Venice, 93, 121, 178, 186, 188
    Versailles Peace Conference, 1919, 243
Vietnam, 64, 197, 262
Visigoth Kingdom (Spain) incidence of slavery, 218
Voltaire, 23
Vries, Peter, 18

368 INDEX

W
Wage and gender discrimination, 339
Walker, Gilbert, 79
Walvin, James, 143–145, 157, 205, 207, 208, 230
Ward, Russel, 162
Washington, Booker T., 216, 217, 221, 240–243, 247
Washington, George, 194
water-borne transport. *See* shipping
Watt, James, 132
wealth concentration, 305
Weber, Max, 25, 187, 188, 270, 271
  on modern bureaucracies, 270, 271
western civilization. *See also*
    bureaucratic state, the;
    democracy; individualism;
    industrialization
  abolishment of the slave trade, 39
  and bureaucratic states, x, 10, 25
  choice between collectivism and
    individualism, x
  clash of cultural values, 321
  communal division and violence, 320
  decline of, 348
  democracy, xi, 10, 23, 301, 315, 349
  destruction of Indigenous
    traditional ways of life, 305
  economic and political liberalism,
    xvii, 10, 24, 263
  emergence of salaried middle class, 286
  energy-intensive production systems
    and lifestyles, 347
  features of, xvii, 6, 7, 10, 13, 24, 94, 301
  foundation of universities, 177, 179, 273
  and the Industrial Revolution, xv, 13, 38, 141, 148

  life expectancy, 349
  and the Malthusian ceiling, 31, 54
  medieval transformation, xvii, 9, 147, 315
  milletization of, x, xviii
  principles of inquiry, 94
  relationship to slavery, 208, 210
  religious life, 176
  representative democracy, 54
  role of the state, 23
  rural slavery and production, 219
  the state and university-educated
    professionals, 274
  technological and economic
    prowess, 270
Western Roman Empire. *See also*
    ancient Rome
  abandonment of slavery for
    serfdom, 114
  collapse of slave-operated
    latifundia, 112
wheat
  characteristics of, 58
  disadvantages in cultivation of, 62
  prices, 60
  production across continents, 61
  yields per acre, 62
Whitney, Eli, 133
Wilentz, Sean, 236
working class
  decline of, 273
  and democracy, 278
  expansion of, 279
  female participation in workforce, 278
World Bank, 37, 344
World War I, 63, 108, 251, 258, 269, 286, 287, 293, 295, 311, 313, 348
World War II, 17, 203, 272, 302, 348
Wren, Dan, 23

Y

Yale University, 133
Year of Revolutions (1848), 23, 25, 194, 265, 266
Young, Arthur, 197, 198
Yucatan
    arrival of steam-powered shipping and railroads, 87
    drought-induced famines, 86
    henequen production in, 87
    the Maya. *See* Maya

Z

Zharkova, Valentina, 348
Zoroastrian Persia, 176

CPSIA information can be obtained
at www.ICGtesting.com
Printed in the USA
LVHW082055070522
718180LV00004B/134